Experiential Activities
for Enhancing
Emotional Intelligence

A GROUP COUNSELING GUIDE TO THE KEYS TO SUCCESS

Scott I. Goldsmith

RESEARCH PRESS
PUBLISHERS

2612 North Mattis Avenue, Champaign, Illinois 61822
800.519.2707 / researchpress.com

6   5   4   3   2   15   16   17   18   19

Printed in the United States of America.

Photographs of activities and PDF versions of forms and checklists included in this book are available at www.researchpress.com/downloads.

The 5 Question Processing Model appears with permission of publisher. © 2004, *Open to Outcome: A Practical Guide for Facilitating & Teaching Experiential Reflection,* p. 42, Wood 'n' Barnes Publishing.

Challenge by Choice, Adventure Wave, and the Full Value Contract, also known as the Full Value Commitment, are concepts originated by Project Adventure. Challenge by Choice is a registered trademark of Project Adventure.

The activities Get 20 and Group Blackjack were created by Michelle Cummings of Training Wheels and appear in a different format in her book *Playing with a Full Deck* (2007).

GivaGeta Character Cards part of The World's Kindest Playing Cards are trademarks of GivaGeta, Inc.

ICE BREAKERS® mints is a registered trademark of The Hershey Company.

Jenga is a registered trademark of Hasbro, Inc. JENGA® & © 2013 Hasbro, Inc. Used with permission.

Teamwork & Teamplay cards and activities appear with permission of Dr. Jim Cain of Teamwork & Teamplay (www.teamworkandteamplay.com).

Copies of this book may be ordered from Research Press at the address given on the title page.

Composition by Jeff Helgesen
All photographs by the author © Scott I. Goldsmith
Diagrams by Jeff Helgesen, © Research Press
Illustrations by Chris Martin, © Research Press
Cover design by McKenzie Wagner, Inc.
Printed by Seaway Printing

ISBN 978-0-87822-686-3
Library of Congress Catalog Number 2014941319

This book honors the memory of my father and first experiential teacher, Ted Goldsmith. He taught me that just because we get older, doesn't mean we have to grow up.

In memory of La'Andrew, whose spirit and smile live on.

Table of Contents

IV. Appendices

Acknowledgments

It truly does take a village to write a book! My deepest, heartfelt thank-yous go to the following people:

- Kevin Brophy, for the early facilitation tutoring and opportunities. You helped set the foundation for all that followed!
- Laurie Roulier and Lilliana Cuevas, for helping me create and develop the Keys to Success idea through our early workshops
- Heather Wlochowski, for introducing me to a wider reality and being a fantastic training partner
- Chris Cavert, for always believing in my ideas, being honest with me, and providing the gentle nudges
- Tom and Jennifer Leahy, for providing so many of us with the blessing that is NCCPS
- Jim Cain and Michelle Cummings, for their leadership and willingness to share all they are with us each year. You have both been such inspiring role models and great friends throughout the process!
- My colleagues at Manchester Regional Academy, particularly Bruce Thorndike for all his support and for trusting that what I do makes a difference
- Mike Kakalow, for being such a great partner in adventure
- Leigh Ann Young and Cindy Henderson, for partnering up with me to play with their groups for all these years
- All of the students at MRA and New Horizons, for being such willing participants in all my experiments. You make great guinea pigs!
- All of my experiential teachers and colleagues at Project Adventure, especially Bart Crawford and Bryan McCormick and Sully through Northeast Adventures and Riverfront Recapture
- Rufus Collinson at Project Adventure, for all of her help with this project
- Even though I only had the pleasure of meeting him once, Karl Rohnke, for starting us all on this great path
- Jim Cantoni, for his support and willingness to share
- My late-date reviewers: Jodi Angus, Liza Bocchicho, Lisa Cheney, Nate Folan, "Montana" Jane Nelson Krizek, Chris Ortiz, Joe Peters, and Lindsey Shepherd. Your input was huge!

- All my colleagues at the Connecticut Experiential Education Association (CEEA), NCCPS and ropes courses, and other experiential educational programs across Connecticut and the rest of the U.S.A. You have all taught me so much.

- Judy Parkinson, for believing in me and supporting this project beginning to end. It's been a great ride!

- My editor, Kitty Creswell, for helping sculpt my manuscript into the book you hold now. If it weren't for her, this would not have happened!

- Chris Martin, for his great artwork

Of course, thank you to my family: my mom, Ellen, and my sister and brothers and the whole crew of great in-laws for all their support.

Last but far from least, I thank my wife, Deirdre, for the first three edits and her unconditional, ongoing love and support when I need it most and for being my copilot in everything I do! I also want to thank my daughters, Devin, Mallory, and Naomi, for helping me stay a kid! Grandpa Teddy would be so proud of you!

Introduction

Several years ago, two colleagues and I first presented a workshop entitled "The Keys to Success in Facilitating Groups with Adolescents" at the Connecticut School Counselor Association Annual Conference. The workshop included the rationale of the Keys to Success and its origins in theories on emotional intelligence. For two hours, participants were fully immersed in experiential activities as they learned how to use the Keys to Success to promote emotional intelligence through adventure-based counseling. In this program, through carefully developed and strategically sequenced activities, we brought the concepts of emotional intelligence and experiential learning (learning by doing) together. Conference attendees and participants responded. Our session became one of the best-attended and highly rated workshops at the conference. Follow-up presentations at other conferences achieved similar results and feedback.

While I was thrilled that we had identified an issue that obviously needed to be addressed and that our program was apparently answering a need, I kept feeling that there was something missing. Despite the participants' positive response at the end of the workshops, I still felt that we hadn't yet equipped them with everything they'd need to start implementing the model on their very next workday. The participants left the conferences with our printouts and a listing of resources about adventure-based and experiential activities. From the two hours of workshop instruction we'd offered, it was now up to them to select and purchase what they needed and piece it together on their own.

Around the same time, I found myself increasingly disenchanted with the different group counseling curriculum materials I had been using over the years. The catalogues would flow into my office. I would pour through them to find just the right activities and methods to address the needs of this or that group. Somehow, despite the attractive packaging and enticing descriptions, I found that the books and programs never fulfilled my expectations. They were either too prescriptive, too open-ended with no underlying theory, or the activities didn't draw the students in the way I felt they should.

After presenting our workshop several times, I realized what needed to be done. I needed to develop a book that would incorporate and expand upon the key elements from our workshop. I wanted it to contain a firm theoretical foundation while including activities that upper-elementary through high-school-age participants would find exciting. The activities had to be applicable and require minimal props and equipment. The activities also had to be useable for counselors, teachers, and other professionals working with groups of kids and adolescents. Lastly, the activities needed to be adaptable to a variety of groups and settings.

That is how this book was born.

The first section of the book provides the theoretical basis informing and underpinning all the activities. Section two provides facilitators with useful information that will help them prepare for their groups, plan for sessions, and adapt to the group's changing needs. The third section presents group activities and provides descriptions and practical guidance on props and settings. These pages also feature tips on how to introduce and run the games, modify them for different age groups or member needs, and debrief the sessions. The activities section also explains each activity's connection to program goals and member commitments. This book draws on the research and program elements developed by Project Adventure. Yet even so, there is plenty of room for any facilitator to mold the activities any way he or she sees fit, even if it leads to creating new activities. (And if you do...please pass along the ideas; I would love to hear about them!)

So, thank you for your interest in this book. Whether you're a counselor, teacher, youth services worker, or a group-home staff member, if you work with groups of middle- and high-school-age kids and are looking for fun, active ways to help them experience greater success in their lives, I'm confident you'll find in this book the strategies and activities you need. If you try them out, you will have taken a first step towards enjoying your groups more than ever and helping them meet with the personal success they seek.

How To Use This Book

A truly good book . . . . teaches me better than to read it. I must soon lay it down and commence living on its hint. . . . What I began by reading, I must finish by acting.

—*Henry David Thoreau*

This book is meant to move you, the facilitator, and your clients to action. How you choose to digest it will depend on what you hope to accomplish. This chapter provides some suggestions as to how to make the most of the book you're holding.

The first several chapters of this book provide the theoretical basis for using activity-based groups to help clients develop their emotional intelligence and social and behavioral skills. The chapters before the activity sections present a general discussion of emotional intelligence and the development of experiential learning. They introduce experiential counseling and include information on the Full Value Contract and the Adventure Wave, concepts developed by Project Adventure that are the cornerstones of experiential counseling. The chapters also present what I call the Keys to Success. The Keys serve as the blueprint for connecting experiential learning to the development of emotional intelligence.

The second section, Practical Considerations before You Begin, is aimed at helping facilitators prepare for their groups. It includes suggestions for choosing and screening potential group members, sequencing activities, and assessing and monitoring the group as it progresses. This section will help facilitators adapt to the changing needs of their participants. The first two sections are useful for those new to experiential counseling as well as those with group facilitation experience who want to expand their skill set and use experiential counseling methods to help clients develop emotional awareness and behavioral control and build and maintain positive relationships with others.

The final section of the book presents descriptions of activities that form the core of experiential counseling groups, from introductory activities (as found in the chapters "Name Games" and "Get to Know You") to more challenging, skill-building exercises (which appear in the chapters "Higher-Level Initiatives" and "Trust Activities"). In addition to instructions on facilitating the sessions, each activity includes information on how it relates to the Full Value Commitment (my take on Project Adventure's Full Value Contract) and the three Keys to Success. Each activity also includes suggestions for debriefing sessions. These questions will assist you in helping participants develop their emotional, behavioral, and social skills.

The activities are divided into several chapters, organized according to their general purpose and the level of cognitive or emotional challenge they present. Activities in earlier chapters are designed to be used primarily early on in a group's time together. These include activities found in "Beginning Group Activities," "Name Games," and "Tag

Games." The next three chapters—"Icebreakers," "Get To Know You," and "Low-Level Initiatives"—offer activities that require somewhat more cognitive and emotional investment from participants. Depending on your group, many of these activities can be used early in a group's development as well. The final chapters in this section, "Higher-Level Initiatives" and "Trust Activities," are significantly more cognitively and emotionally demanding. These activities are meant to be used with groups that have developed a firm basis of trust and connectedness.

At the end of the book in the appendices are numerous exercises and supports meant to be used as a supplement to activities. Several are designed to guide facilitators in helping their participants draw connections between their experience in the group activities and their real lives. (Worksheets from the appendices can be downloaded at www.researchpress.com/downloads.)

Three session outlines for facilitating eight-week Keys to Success groups on anger management, depression support, and leadership development also appear in the appendices. If you are planning to facilitate such a group, these sections of the book will give you solid insights for planning and monitoring your group and its progress. These session outlines provide guidance as to activity sequencing, types of introductions that best meet the needs of these types of groups, and suggestions for helping participants use their group experience to move toward desired outcomes.

The session outlines present advice on avoiding typical obstacles that group counselors may encounter and ideas on how to overcome these challenges. While these outlines present a specific format, facilitators should not limit their activity selection to only the ones described. The outlines can be modified to better fit a specific group's needs. It should be noted, too, that these outlines address only a few of the diverse types of groups that experiential counseling may benefit.

Activity Page Format

The Activity pages are designed to help facilitators find information that will help them decide when and with whom to use the activity, how to facilitate it, and how to help clients draw connections between the activity and their emotional and behavioral functioning. Each activity includes the following information:

Activity Overview

Some of the activities in this book I have created. Others are evolved versions of activities I learned from other practitioners or discovered in a book or on a website. The activities in this book represent my own version. Whenever possible, I have given credit to the person or publication as the source of the activity. Sometimes it is difficult to identify sources because the same activity may have several different names. Some variations simply stem from different people learning activities in different places. Sometimes names have been varied to help set the stage for how facilitators wanted their group to perceive the activity. For example, the activity Path to Success (p. 321) fits well with experiential counseling groups aimed at helping teens become successful, whereas when it is renamed Corporate Maze, it may also work well with corporate clients. Tracing the roots of an activity can be like tracing a family history. Sometimes, it's easy to find an activity's origin, other times, not so much. I have worked with so many great facilitators and trainers over the years, and each has my highest gratitude, even if not acknowledged directly by name.

Guidance on Matching Activities to Participants

Each activity provides information on the age range and number of participants best suited for the activity. This information is intended only as a guideline. With slight modifications, most activities can be adapted for groups made up of participants who are either younger or older than the target audience. For activities aimed at smaller groups, multiple small groups often work well.

Information on Props Needed

Experiential education and counseling makes use of materials, or "props," in group activities. In this book, I attempt to keep the number of props needed per activity to a minimum. Most of the props in the book can be created by the facilitator or purchased fairly inexpensively.

Activity Objectives

Facilitators will find the goals for each activity and information on how the activity connects to the Full Value Commitment and the Keys to Success. The identified connections to the Full Value Commitment and Keys to Success provide facilitators with guidelines on what to watch for as the activity unfolds and possible discussion topics during the debriefing.

Facilitator Guidelines

Each activity provides step-by-step guidelines on preparing for, introducing, facilitating, and debriefing the activity. The Facilitator Guidelines section organizes activities into the main elements of the Adventure Wave: the introduction, the action, and the debriefing. The Introduction/Metaphor provides facilitators with suggestions for the "artistic" portion of the activity introduction. How an activity is introduced influences how the group will perceive it and helps facilitators tie the activity to the Keys to Success during the debriefing.

The action of each activity is described in detail and presents facilitators with guidance on running activities successfully. The rules, suggestions for beginning and ending the action, and guidance on what to expect as the activity unfolds are included. Some activities feature one or more variations. These alternative versions are designed to either make an activity easier or more difficult for the group to carry out or to simply shift the focus of the activity.

The final section of the Facilitator Guidelines contains general suggestions and questions for use in debriefing the action. The suggested debriefing questions are intended to help clients connect their experience with the activity to one or more of the Keys to Success. In addition to these questions, facilitators can make use of additional debriefing questions offered in the appendices.

Using This Book

At the most basic level, counselors and group leaders can use this book to find activities that meet their goals in experiential counseling. Counselors can browse the activities until they find one that suits their purposes. As a facilitator, the more activities you know, the more prepared and the better able to adapt to different situations you will be. The activities in this book include many variations and can always be modified for younger or older participants and smaller or larger groups. Most require a minimal number of props. Additional photos of participants demonstrating the activities can be found at www.researchpress.com/downloads.

Read through the activities. Try some out with trusted colleagues or even trusted students! I have one group of students at the school where I work that I refer to as the "Guinea Pig Group." Because they are such a great bunch of kids, I can try my new activities with them and get honest, helpful feedback about the activities and my facilitation style.

This book can be a helpful reference and refresher throughout your journey to becoming the best experiential-counseling group facilitator you can be. However you choose to use this book, my hope is that it becomes as comfortable as a well-worn pair of jeans, as reliable as your dearest friend, and most importantly, as a useful guide that pushes you to action!

1 Experiential Learning, Teaching, and Counseling

Tell me and I'll forget; show me and I may remember; involve me and I'll understand.

—*Chinese proverb*

When we think of education, most of us picture a "traditional" school classroom with a lecturer dispensing knowledge to his or her students. This is often called the "didactic model of teaching." In the traditional classroom, the teacher is the expert and the student only a passive recipient of received wisdom. Experiential teaching methods foster learning through encouraging students to engage with their environment and reflect on what they observe. It involves students in the process of learning.

Experiential teaching provides for students' direct experience of phenomena, which, through their questioning and reflection on the experience, results in their learning. It's the science teacher who asks the kids what they think will happen when mixing cornstarch and water and has them try it and see. It's the math teacher that has students predict how many times a coin will land on heads when flipped then allows them to conduct the probability experiment to test their theories. In both cases, you can "tell" kids what will happen, but they most likely will understand the concept better if they experience it. This approach to learning allows students' understanding or orientation to the world to be challenged by what they observe and experience.

Formal theories on experiential learning may have found their basis in the writings of education theorist John Dewey (1938), who believed that learning is best accomplished when humans interact with their environment, encounter obstacles and manipulate their environment to overcome those obstacles. Learning occurs when our current mind set (schema) is challenged by an environmental factor (the experience). This creates an internal state of conflict between what we "know" and what we are "observing." The new information modifies our cognitive schema, resulting in learning. How did Columbus determine that the world was round? He set sail and had an experience that didn't match the cognitive schema of his day: that the world was flat.

Unlike the didactic model, experiential education lets students draw on all their senses when learning. While we all have different learning styles, many of us, particularly those with learning disabilities, may learn best kinesthetically (Mitchell, 2002). In an informal survey I conducted of my students at an alternative high school, 88% of them identified their predominant learning style as "kinesthetic" as opposed to visual or auditory. These students understand that they learn best by doing.

It's been said that we learn more through our experiences during the first five years of life than we do in a school-based didactic learning environment. Many of today's schools and teachers are striving to become more experiential in their approaches to teaching and learning. For example, 2013's National Teacher of the Year, Jeff Charbonneau, of Zillah High School in Washington State, gets his students interested in difficult subjects through interactive learning (www.UsNews.NBCNews.com, April 23, 2013). The 2012 National Teacher of the Year, Rebecca Mieliwocki, emphasizes the use of the Socratic method of questioning to stimulate students' critical thinking and create dynamic lessons (www.HuffingtonPost.com, April 24, 2012). To create interactive lessons, educators often employ a multimodal approach to teaching.

Multimodal approaches to learning are those that make use of more than one sense. By engaging various senses, educators are more likely to gain and hold the attention of their students. These approaches may be the most effective for learning (Lazear, 1991; Armstrong, 1994) as they make use of different learning styles. This is a central point in the multiple intelligences concepts so popular today (Gardner, 1983).

The Keys to Success approach applies the principles of experiential teaching and learning to group counseling. In carrying out the activities, participants learn key behavioral and emotional skills through their interactions with their environment and their fellow group members.

What Is the Connection between Experiential Teaching and Counseling?

Like teaching, some counseling can be viewed as didactic. A person with problems draws upon the expertise of a counselor to find solutions to the problems. This approach works well when the client is aware of his or her problems and conceptualizes them in a manner similar to the counselor's interpretation. The client must be motivated, insightful, and open to change, and the counselor must be skilled in the area of concern. Of course, as you may have discovered, many children and teens (and adults) don't fit this mold. Often, they are in denial that there is a problem or conceptualize it differently than do the adults in their lives. They often lack insight and motivation, making traditional counseling practices more difficult.

As is the case with experiential teaching, experientially based counselors rely on their client's direct experience and reflection on that experience to provide a platform for learning. A scenario is created in which there may be many possible outcomes. The client's curiosity is ignited, and there is motivation to engage in the activity. During the activity, the facilitator is free to observe how the client functions in real time rather than relying on secondhand verbal accounts of behavior.

Many of the activities may evoke emotions such as anger, frustration, confusion, and feelings of low self-efficacy. These emotions often trigger negative behaviors in the session that mirror the client's responses to situations outside the sessions. This has two distinct benefits. First, the counselor gains firsthand experience of the client's behavioral responses to negative emotions. Second, the facilitator is given a unique opportunity to intervene while the problem behavior is happening rather than simply processing it after the behavior has occurred. If you have ever had the experience of working with a teenager on anger management issues in individual counseling sessions, you may conclude, as I have, that it is often an exercise in futility. Many teens with anger management problems don't believe they have a problem. Difficulties in their lives are often viewed as someone else's fault. If they do recognize their problem, they can probably rattle off all the best ways to cope with their anger. Often, they possess knowledge of basic anger-management skills but don't use these skills when they become angry. At the end of an experiential activity, through questioning of one kind or another, the counselor guides the clients to find connections and meaning in the experience, thus fostering the client's learning about themselves and how they interact with the world around them.

Why Experiential Groups?

As an experiential counselor, you are provided with the unique opportunity of observing your clients' maladaptive emotional and behavioral responses and their difficulties with interpersonal skills. This allows you to intervene and help your clients reflect on these issues and change their behaviors. Experiential groups are designed around activities and explore the interactions between participants and their environments. These interactions are real experiences and create real emotions. If someone has an anger-management problem, it will most likely surface during an experiential group activity. When this occurs, the facilitator has an opportunity to observe and address the problem as it happens. In addition to the facilitator experiencing the client's maladaptive responses to anger firsthand, other group members become involved in this experience as well. They observe what happens and provide feedback to that client. This experience benefits both the struggling client as well as other group members, as they can reflect upon their own experiences and draw connections to the experiences of their peers.

Additionally, related to anger management is conflict resolution. Successful conflict resolution requires the ability to inhibit maladaptive behaviors when angry or upset while interacting with others in a way that leads to a positive outcome. This involves positive social-communication abilities. These skills are best learned and practiced within a safe group environment.

The group experience has several benefits that are not available through individual counseling. It provides social support, which is particularly beneficial for many participants. First, those with depression need the support of others but often lack the skills or motivation to reach out. Experiential groups allow them to learn and try out new skills. Additionally, by being around others, they realize that they are not alone in their suffering and are given the opportunity to build a supportive network amongst their peers. Experiential groups can also be considered an excellent choice for topics such as leadership development. To be an effective leader, you need to have highly developed social, communication, and problem-solving skills, the skills often focused on in experiential groups. Participants developing their leadership skills are also given the opportunity to try these skills in an experientially based group.

While depression support and leadership development may seem unrelated, participants in both types of groups need to focus on the three Keys to Success. Individuals who are depressed often have great difficulties regulating emotions and behavioral responses. This interferes with relationship development. Learning skills to manage emotions and behaviors will result in improved relationships, which, in turn, can help alleviate depressive symptoms. While developing leaders may or may not have significant difficulties in these areas, developing emotional and behavioral coping skills as well as interpersonal skills is essential to leadership success. In both cases, focusing on the three Keys to Success will help you foster positive outcomes for your participants.

Chapter Summary

While so-called traditional teaching methods portray the teacher as the expert and the student or client as a somewhat passive recipient of knowledge (the didactic approach), experiential teaching methods foster learning through creating interactions between the person and his or her environment. This approach can be powerfully effective. Through the students' reflection on these interactions, experiential counseling activities can lead to changes in the way the student thinks.

Experiential group counseling has several distinct advantages over other types of counseling. The activities used in experiential counseling can produce strong emotions, which often lead to the maladaptive behaviors the clients are working to address. Facilitators and group members can observe these behaviors firsthand. This allows the facilitator to intervene while a targeted behavior is occurring, as opposed to being able only to discuss it in the abstract with the client. Additionally, the participants receive valuable feedback from each other while the behavior is occurring. Experiential groups are also very conducive to leadership development.

2 Emotional Intelligence and the Three Keys to Success

In 1994, the concept of emotional intelligence gained national prominence following the publication of the best-selling book *Emotional Intelligence* by Daniel Goleman. The enticing subtitle, *Why It Can Matter More Than IQ*, may have been the general public's first introduction to the concept that success may be based as much on our emotional and social abilities as on our intellectual abilities. The idea that intellectual abilities may not be the main component in determining one's success in life, however, goes back much farther than the release of Goleman's book. To support his views, Goleman references the work of many researchers from varied backgrounds who indicate that how we deal with our own emotions has a great impact upon our day-to-day functioning.

One of the earliest incarnations of the concept of emotional intelligence came in the form of the 1920 *Harper's* magazine article "Intelligence and Its Use." The author, E. L. Thorndike, defined "social intelligence" as "the ability to understand and manage men and women, boys and girls, to act wisely in human relations" (Thorndike, p. 228). In 1943, the American psychologist David Wechsler recognized that intellectual abilities were not the only factor in predicting one's success in life. Wechsler is well known for the development of the Wechsler Intelligence Scale for Children (WISC) and Wechsler Adult Intelligence Scale (WAIS), which measure an individual's IQ, or Intelligence Quotient. Wechsler's original IQ tests were comprised of two scales intended to measure verbal and nonverbal abilities. The fourth edition of the WISC and fourth edition of the WAIS are still two of the most widely used IQ tests today. The current Wechsler scales are comprised of four major indexes: verbal comprehension, perceptual reasoning, working memory, and processing speed.

While Wechsler focused on intellectual abilities, in 1943 he suggested that non-intellective abilities were also essential for predicting one's success in life. He stated:

> I have tried to show that in addition to intellective there are also definite non-intellective factors that determine intelligent behavior. If the foregoing observations are correct, it follows that we cannot expect to measure total intelligence until our tests also include some measures of the non-intellective factors (Wechsler, 2008, p. 103).

Several decades later, Howard Gardner made major strides toward the goals that Wechsler alluded to in 1943. Gardner, who believed that the traditional definitions of intelligence were too narrow, introduced the theory of multiple intelligences in his 1983 book *Frames of Mind: The Theory of Multiple Intelligences*. He proposed seven basic realms of intelligence: linguistic, logical-mathematical, musical, bodily kinesthetic, spatial, interpersonal, and intrapersonal (Gardner, 1983).

Influenced by Gardner, psychologists Peter Salovey and Jack Mayer developed their own definition in the article, "Emotional Intelligence" (Salovey & Mayer, 1990), which appeared in the *Journal of Imagination, Cognition and Personality*. They defined the term *emotional intelligence* as "the subset of social intelligence that involves the ability to monitor one's own and others' feelings and emotions, to discriminate among them and use this information to guide one's thinking and actions" (Salovey & Mayer, 1990, p.189). They divided emotional intelligence into five main domains:

1. Knowing one's emotions. This domain represents essentially emotional self-awareness and involves recognizing and monitoring emotions as they occur.

2. Managing emotions. The ability to deal with emotions in an appropriate manner represents the second domain. Managing emotions allows one to rebound from difficulties in life.

3. Motivating oneself. This domain reflects the ability to harness one's emotional energy to move towards personal goals.

4. Recognizing emotions in others. Empathy is the ability to "put oneself in someone else's shoes." Recognizing and responding appropriately to others' emotions are crucial skills.

5. Handling relationships. This domain refers to managing emotions in relationships. By dealing effectively with one's own and others' emotions, we can engage in relationships with others (Salovey & Mayer, 1990).

In 1994, Salovey and Mayer refined their definition of emotional intelligence as "the ability to perceive, accurately appraise, and express; the ability to access and/or generate feelings when they facilitate thought; the ability to understand emotion and emotional knowledge; and the ability to regulate emotions to promote emotional and intellectual growth" (Mayer & Salovey, 1997, p. 10).

In Goleman's 1994 bestseller, he recognizes Salovey and Mayer's original definitions (Goleman, 1994, p. 43). By 1998, Goleman refined his own definition of emotional intelligence to include five aspects: Self-Awareness, Self-Regulation, Motivation, Social Skills, and Empathy.

In the 2001 publication *The Emotionally Intelligent Workplace*, Cherniss and Goleman present an updated model of emotional intelligence that includes twenty competencies in four clusters. The clusters and examples of the competencies include:

• Personal Competence/Recognition: This includes self-awareness competencies, such as emotional self-awareness, accurate self-assessment, and self-confidence.

• Social Competence/Recognition: This includes social awareness competencies, such as empathy, service orientation, and organizational awareness.

• Personal Competence/Regulation: This includes self-management competencies, such as self-control, adaptability, and drive.

• Social Competence/Regulation: This includes relationship management competencies, such as influence, conflict management, and teamwork.

The uses of theories on emotional intelligence have continued to expand. Emotional intelligence remains an important concept in psychology, education, and business. Authors have expanded on the topic in books on everything from instructing parents on how to raise emotionally intelligent children (*How to Raise a Child with High EQ*, Shapiro, 1998) to utilizing emotional intelligence in corporate America (*The EQ Interview: Finding Employees with High Emotional Intelligence*, Lynn, 2008). There are even programs certifying educators, therapists, and business executives as providers of emotional intelligence training (ex., Talentsmart.com).

With so much research and so many theories on what emotional intelligence is and how important it really is, trying to understand emotional intelligence can be a cumbersome task. This is where the three Keys to Success become useful. The Keys to Success provides an easily understandable and usable definition of emotional intelligence. It allows practitioners and participants to use a shared language and set of concepts and provides the underlying approach to all the activities in this book.

The Three Keys to Success

Eight years ago, during a group session with emotionally and behaviorally disordered teens, I asked a question. At the time, it didn't strike me as a particularly profound question, but I have made a point of asking it of many groups since. The question was, "What are the most important factors in determining success or failure in life?" While some kids talked about grades and high school diplomas, most identified less academic skills and characteristics, such as respect, confidence, persistence, and communication skills. Even though most of these kids only demonstrated these characteristics occasionally at best, somehow they still understood the importance of these attributes. On that day, and many times since, my groups have acknowledged that there were many "unsuccessful smart people" because they lacked these characteristics. Without realizing it, these teens were identifying emotional intelligence as a cornerstone for success in life.

I created the three Keys to Success to help kids (and adults) understand emotional intelligence and the emotional and behavioral factors that seem to contribute most to determining success or failure in all aspects of life. What are these three Keys to Success? Emotional awareness, behavioral control, and skills in building positive interpersonal relationships. Each key builds on the skills emphasized in the previous key. I convey to my students that if they master the three Keys to Success, they are far more likely to find success and happiness in their lives.

This approach incorporates the basic tenets of emotional intelligence into an easily understandable, memorable, user-friendly format that translates well into group counseling sessions or for use across entire organizational cultures. When possible, I introduce the three Keys to Success to prospective group participants prior to the start of the group. This can be done individually in an interview, if you have the luxury of interviewing potential clientele for your group. If this is not possible, I generally introduce the concept during the group's first meeting. I have used the Keys to Success as the theme of a group (much as you might use depression support or anger management as central themes). When the group is centered upon another theme, such as leadership development or anger management, I introduce the Keys to Success in such a way as to connect to the central theme of the group.

In the following sections, you will find additional information about each of the Keys to Success. You will also find suggestions as to how to introduce each key to groups with various themes.

Key 1: Emotional Awareness

Key 1 refers to our awareness and understanding of the range of emotions that we experience as humans. This includes understanding the labels for emotions (such as mad, frustrated, and sad) and knowing how to recognize our own emotions and those of others.

The Vocabulary of Emotions

There are hundreds of words to describe the emotions we experience. My experience has taught me that most emotional descriptors fall into one of four basic categories: happiness, fear, sadness, and anger. Many other descriptors are variations on or levels of these basic terms for emotions. For example, *thrilled* can be viewed as a more intense version of happiness and *content* as a milder version. *Terrified* is a stronger version of fear, whereas *anxious* may be a lesser version. Some emotions can be thought of as either positive (those that make you feel good) or negative (those that don't make you feel good), while some, such as surprised, can be either. Still, other emotions seem more distantly connected to the basic four, such as loved, jealous, or confused. Finally, we can question whether certain words describe an emotion versus a state of being, such as tired or inferior. All of these complexities contribute to the weaknesses evident in so many children's and teens' emotional vocabularies. Additionally, it is rare that anyone directly teaches young people to identify and understand their true feelings; however, a vocabulary of emotions is an important ingredient in developing emotional intelligence.

Emotional Awareness of Oneself

Many of the kids and teens I have worked with over the years have had great difficulties identifying how they truly feel in any given moment, often confusing emotions for thoughts or behaviors. My conversation with "John" following his confrontation with a peer highlights this issue:

> **Me:** "John, how do you feel right now?"
>
> **John:** "I want to kill that kid."
>
> **Me:** "I understand, but that is a thought. How do you feel? What emotion are you feeling?"
>
> **John:** "I already told you! I want to kill that kid!"

While I can assume that John is angry, he struggles to identify the emotion by name. When people are overwhelmed by emotions such as anger and rage, their ability to think clearly diminishes and often prevents them from gaining insight into their own feelings. Add this lack of clarity to an already weak emotional vocabulary, and it's a potentially troubling situation. Without the ability to accurately identify the emotion, these kids and teens are left dealing only with thoughts and behaviors.

Emotional Honesty

Emotional honesty refers to being honest about what you are feeling. While being honest about emotions to others is important, being honest about your emotions to yourself is even more important. Often people deny the experience of certain emotions. Sometimes, it is because they truly don't recognize the emotion they are experiencing while other times, they avoid experiencing it by suppressing the emotion. Take the example of an adolescent male being confronted by a menacing peer. His body kicks into high gear as a result of the "fight or flight" response. Adrenaline surges throughout his body, increasing his heart rate and giving him more power and speed. While fear is a likely culprit in triggering the response, anger may be the more likely expressed emotion, verbally and behaviorally. In my experience, many adolescent males will deny ever having felt fear. This may be attributed to our society making it somewhat unacceptable for males, particularly adolescent males, to experience or display fear.

Denial of emotions for males or females can have negative consequences. Take the example of an adolescent girl I'll call "Kate" that I work with. Kate, who lost her mother a year ago, has significant learning disabilities. She was removed from her uncle's home and placed in foster care. After failing a test, she appeared distraught. Everything was catching up to her. After venting for 5 minutes, she suddenly declared that she was fine and wanted to return to class. After trying unsuccessfully to help her recognize that she was still too emotionally distressed to go back to class, I reluctantly wrote her a pass and sent her on her way. Five minutes later, I received a phone call from the assistant principal informing me that Kate had gotten into a physical altercation. Her attempt to stifle her emotions was unsuccessful and resulted in aggression when triggered by a peer. Beyond simple recognition, emotional awareness includes the ability to admit to ourselves the existence of the emotions we experience.

Empathy and Identifying Other's Emotions

According to the Merriam-Webster Online Dictionary, empathy is "the action of understanding, being aware of, being sensitive to, and vicariously experiencing the feelings, thoughts, and experience of another of either the past or present without having the feelings, thoughts, and experience fully communicated in an objectively explicit manner" ("Empathy," 2013). Simply put, empathy is our ability to emotionally (and metaphorically) put ourselves in someone else's shoes. This is one of the keystones to developing social skills. Children who have deficits in their abilities to empathize often struggle socially. The first step in developing empathy is being able to identify what another person is feeling.

Through our own socialization, most of us are fairly adept at integrating nonverbal cues (such as body language, facial expressions and tone of voice), verbal cues (the words being spoken), and observable behaviors into a cohesive understanding of another person's emotional state. A minority of people have difficulties doing this. Those diagnosed with disorders such as Asperger's syndrome, autism, and nonverbal learning disabilities struggle to comprehend this complex emotional communication system. The result is impairment in social relationships.

If we are able to recognize others' emotions, we are better able to understand the best ways to respond. If we can relate to another person's emotional experience (empathize), we can respond in a way that is appropriate and may help that person cope with what he or she is feeling. If we fail to connect with another's experience, we may demonstrate inappropriate reactions that trigger negative responses from others. Consider the following example:

On Fridays, our alternative high school competes against other schools in various sports. While coaching an interscholastic basketball game several seasons ago, my team was leading by over 20 points at the end of the first half. Our team was older, bigger, and far more talented. Sensing the frustration and humiliation the other team's players were feeling, I sat out my starters and played my bench players for the second half. My star player was irate. He demanded to be put in the game. My explanations as to why he wasn't playing were to no avail. Due to his behavior, he ended up being removed from the gym and suspended for the next game.

This student's lack of empathy for the other team's players led to his negative behavioral response. He simply couldn't comprehend the emotional experience of the other team's players. In turn, my player's behavior led to a negative consequence for him.

Key 2: Behavioral Control

The second key refers to our ability to control our behavioral reactions to our emotions. Ask a teenager, "What happens when you get angry?" The most likely response will involve behaviors: yelling, swearing, hitting a wall, crying, holding emotions in, etc. For many, the emotion is defined solely by the behavioral response.

Behavior is an observable and chosen response to stimuli, what goes on outside as well as inside of us. Defining emotions by their behavioral response prohibits us from recognizing the internal factors that play a major role in what behaviors will be displayed in a given situation. When we experience any emotion, our brain triggers chemical reactions within our bodies. For example, the neurotransmitters norepinephrine, dopamine and endorphins are believed to be chemicals released when we feel happy. We know that norepinephrine and adrenaline are responsible for the fight-or-flight response triggered when someone is scared or angry. The release of these neurotransmitters triggers changes in our bodies as well as in our thoughts. We have vastly different thoughts when we are happy than when we are angry or scared.

In addition to the chemical aspect of emotions, personal history and experience play a role in determining what behaviors we will demonstrate in response to a particular emotion. When something happens in our environment, we may react in a very different way from the person next to us. Our personal history acts as a window through which all new experiences are viewed and, in turn, interpreted. Cognitive behavioral therapy (CBT), one of the most common therapeutic approaches used to help people regulate emotions and behaviors, operates on the theory that our thoughts and perceptions, not external events, cause our behavioral reactions. This influences the biochemical process, which in turn affects our thinking and behavioral reactions. Understanding this principle can be central to changing behavior.

Post-traumatic stress disorder (PTSD) provides an extreme case example of how our personal experiences factor into our behavioral reactions to our emotions. When someone suffers from PTSD, previously neutral events become triggers for intense fear. For example, a soldier who has returned from war may have a significantly higher stress reaction to fireworks than someone who was not in a situation in which those types of sounds were linked with danger and death. Prior to the combat experience, the sound of fireworks was a neutral event. After combat, it has become a trigger.

The lack of understanding that many teens have about how their emotions and behaviors are connected can contribute to poor behavioral choices. This Key to Success is about making better behavioral choices when experiencing negative emotions. It is essential to have an understanding of how our emotions trigger physiological changes, which impact our thought patterns and influence our behavioral choices.

Many activities in this book can trigger emotions such as frustration, confusion, anxiety, and anger. Many of the clients with whom you will be working struggle to effectively deal with these emotions and often display this through negative behaviors. This will provide you with direct opportunities to help your clients identify the currently maladaptive ways they deal with their negative emotions and develop new, more adaptive coping strategies.

Key 3: Establishing and Maintaining Positive Relationships

The third key refers to our ability to establish and maintain positive relationships with other people. Emotional awareness and understanding (Key 1) and the ability to control our behaviors in response to our emotions (Key 2) are prerequisites to establishing and maintaining positive relationships with other people. While Keys 1 and 2 are essential skills, they are not the only ingredients necessary to create successful relationships. Communication skills, empathy, open-mindedness, integrity, and trust are all important in fostering successful relationships.

Communication Skills

Communication can be conceptualized in several ways. It can be understood as an exchange of information, as in expressive or receptive communication. Expressive communication is the outgoing message, the information one organism is trying to convey to another. Receptive communication refers to the incoming messages, the information received by one organism from another or from the environment. Communication can be verbal or nonverbal. Albert Mehrabian (1971) in his studies on communication came to the conclusion that only about 7% of communication is based on the actual words we use. The rest is based on nonverbal aspects of communication, such as tone of voice (38%) and body language (55%).

Receptive Communication

As humans, we are constantly receiving messages from our environment. Through the lens of our previous life experiences, we assign meaning to the information, which allows us to gain a better understanding of our world. Receiving information through any sense requires us to pay attention.

Attention. Focused attention is a prerequisite to all forms of receptive communication. Failing to pay attention to what is happening around us can result in our missing essential information, sometimes with disastrous results. Many of the students you work with likely have deficits in their ability to maintain focused attention. Disorders such as attention deficit hyperactivity disorder (ADHD) do not mean that individuals cannot attend to stimuli in their environment but that they have a difficult time focusing and maintaining their attention to relevant stimuli. Filtering out irrelevant stimuli is often difficult. Many of the activities in this book emphasize the "Be Here" principle. This refers to the fact that we need to be not only physically present but also mentally and emotionally present. To fully "be here" requires focused attention. In all likelihood, these activities will illuminate difficulties your clients have with focusing their attention. These situations will provide you with an opportunity to help your groups learn how to better focus their attention and to inhibit their impulses. Additionally, most of the activities in this book are multimodal and highly engaging, making them appealing to kids with attention deficits.

Listening. According to Merriam-Webster.com, one definition of *listen* is "to hear something with thoughtful attention." To "hear" something is only part of the definition. The other part is to apply oneself using "thoughtful attention," mentally processing what is heard and assigning meaning to it. Many times I have heard colleagues accuse students or clients of not listening. Sometimes this is true. Other times, the students are actually listening, but the meaning they assign to what was communicated differs from the intended meaning. Using the activities in this book, you are likely to encounter both scenarios: students not really listening and students listening but interpreting what you say differently than you intended. There are many factors as to why this happens. Frequently students with attention deficits, learning problems, or emotional difficulties miss nonverbal messages. On the other hand, the nonverbal aspects of communications can confound meaning. If a high percentage of human communication is nonverbal, what you are saying is not always as important as how you are saying it and what facial expressions and body language are accompanying your words. Personal history may also play a role in how one interprets or misinterprets information. Two people are prone to interpret incoming information differently due to differences in personal experiences. These topics can be explored when issues arise during group activities that expose weaknesses in listening or interpreting incoming information.

Expressive Communication

Verbal communication refers simply to the words we use when we communicate. When working with clients who have social and emotional difficulties, you are likely to encounter extremes of verbal communication: those who don't speak and those who don't stop talking! In my experience, many professionals often don't confront these problems for fear of embarrassing or hurting the feelings of the kids they work with. Direct confrontation of these issues can be truly uncomfortable. Fortunately, this is not your only option. Facilitators can help guide participants and convey how much or little communication is appropriate to share in the group. Appendix I provides a few tips for facilitators working with participants who speak too often or not enough.

Nonverbal Communication

In addition to nonverbal sounds, tone of voice, the volume and cadence of speech, nonverbal communication includes what is sometimes called body language—one's facial expressions, posture, gestures, and overall physical appearance. All of these nonverbal aspects of communication provide information about a person's emotional state, thoughts, and intentions. Nonverbal communication can also confuse verbal expression. Saying words with a different tone of voice, volume, or cadence can convey completely different meanings. (Try this exercise: say the words "I like you." Try it putting an emphasis on the first word, then the second, and finally the third. Add a questioning tone at the end of the words. Snicker after you say the line. Change your facial expression as you speak. You'll find that by varying these aspects of communication, these simple words can carry many meanings.)

Many activities in this book focus on expressive communication, both verbal and nonverbal. In using these activities, you will be given opportunities to discuss communication and help your clients to better understand the messages they are sending to others.

Empathy, Open-Mindedness, and Integrity

Each of these characteristics is important in establishing and maintaining healthy interpersonal relationships. Empathy allows us to step outside ourselves and see the world from somebody else's perspective, connecting with others on an emotional level. This is an essential component for creating meaningful relationships that dive deeper than a superficial level. Many clients with emotional and behavioral disturbances struggle with empathy. This will likely arise throughout your time in group.

A poster in my office about open-mindedness has the following caption: "Minds are like parachutes—they only function when open. –Thomas Dewar" We all see the world in our own way. Successful relationships require some level of open-mindedness. Resistance to considering other people's views, ideas, and opinions will result in difficulties with relationships. The activities in this book provide ample opportunities for creative problem solving or "thinking outside the box." Any closed-mindedness on the part of your participants will become evident as they attempt to work out collaborative solutions to the activities you present. This will provide you as the facilitator with opportunities to help them become more open-minded.

Integrity and Trustworthiness

Integrity and trustworthiness are integrally connected. Those who demonstrate integrity are generally more well respected and trusted by others. As Stephen Covey states in *7 Habits of Highly Effective People* (2004): "One of the most important ways to manifest integrity is to be loyal to those who are not present. In doing so, we build the trust of those who are present" (p. 196).

Many activities in this book place students in a position where they have the choice to be honest or dishonest. Some activities will require the entire group to restart if one member makes a mistake. The group will be making decisions (either overtly or covertly) as to whether those mistakes will be exposed or covered up. These are excellent opportunities for facilitators to address the issues of integrity and trust.

Chapter Summary

Emotional intelligence refers to the ability to understand and cope with our own and other people's emotions, control our behavior, and develop and maintain positive relationships. The Keys to Success provide a simple, easily understandable common language for identifying and speaking about emotional intelligence.

The three Keys to Success are:

1. **Emotional Awareness.** This includes recognizing, accurately identifying, and verbalizing one's emotions and recognizing and empathizing with other's emotions.

2. **Behavioral Control.** This refers to understanding and controlling our behavioral responses to our own and others' emotions.

3. **Establishing and Maintaining Positive Relationships.** To have positive relationships, people must demonstrate the first two keys (Emotional Awareness and Behavioral Control). Other skills needed for building positive relationships include communicating effectively, acting with integrity, being trustworthy, showing trust in others, and demonstrating open-mindedness.

CHAPTER

3

The Full Value Commitment

When any group of people gathers, whether it's in a counseling group, classroom, or local government meeting or even among 30,000 Red Sox fans at Fenway Park, a set of behavioral norms is in place. These norms can be spoken or unspoken, written or unwritten. For example, it's not written anywhere that I know of that in the seventh inning stretch at Fenway Park, you have to sing along (as best you can) with Neil Diamond's "Sweet Caroline." That behavior is specific to the park and its patrons, but if you are there for the first time, you catch on pretty quickly. Even though it's not written anywhere, it's just "what you do." In the counseling groups with which most of us work, there are both unspoken norms as well as a set of explicit rules. Most classrooms have them. Town governments create ordinances, and the larger society implements laws that we must obey. These rules are put into place to create a set of behavioral expectations that will help maintain safety and allow for the pursuit of happiness for all.

This program's approach calls on facilitators and participants to create a set of behavioral norms that all participants agree to comply with, norms that are contained in the Full Value Commitment (FVC). The commitment is based on the Full Value Contract developed by the early Project Adventure staff and originally documented in a manual to Project Adventure programs, *Islands of Healing* (Schoel, Prouty, & Radcliffe, 1988). While the original term is *contract,* I prefer *commitment.* (For me, the term *contract* sounds too formal and legally binding. It also implies that there may be major legal ramifications for noncompliance. The word *commitment* on the other hand, suggests what the participants are willing to dedicate themselves to. A commitment does not imply perfect adherence but a willingness to dedicate one's best effort towards something.)

The FVC is the cornerstone of Project Adventure programs, and it is central in my groups utilizing the Keys to Success approach. It lays the groundwork for everything that happens during a group. Like rules or laws, the FVC sets out behavioral expectations. These expectations can be changed when necessary but do have consequences when broken. Unlike most rules or laws, the FVC is not created by a single leader, such as a classroom teacher or a small group of elected officials. The FVC is created by all group members, the participants and the facilitator. While rules are generally monitored and enforced by an authority figure, the FVC is meant to be enforced by the group members themselves. Finally, while many rules are unspoken, the FVC is typically reviewed after virtually every activity. It provides the basis for understanding and interpreting behavior as well as connecting it to the participants' outside lives.

While the specifics of FVCs vary from group to group, there are certain essential components that should be included in all FVCs. As the title implies, the FVC requires each participant to value all members fully. Everyone counts equally and should have a say in all aspects of the group's functioning. No one has the right to devalue others or oneself. Toward these ends, the FVC should aim to create norms that ensure the physical and emotional safety of all group members. The norms need to be agreed upon by all members of the group, and each member must accept responsibility for personally upholding and maintaining these norms to the best of his or her ability.

With these characteristics of FVCs in mind, I usually try to guide my group to include some version of the following five principles: Be Here, Be Safe, Speak Your Truth, Hear the Truth, and Have Fun.

1. **Be Here.** This principle refers to being both physically and mentally in the here and now. Being focused on the present is essential for individual and group progress. As we all know, the events in our lives may creep into our minds at inopportune times such as during work hours. Many of the kids and teens with whom we work have problems in their lives that usurp their ability to stay focused on school or other environments that demand focused attention. Groups will be no exception. In order to stay focused, members will have to put aside emotions and thoughts that could interfere with their participation. Connected to this understanding of the principle Be Here, many facilitators use the term *commitment* in their FVCs.

2. **Be Safe.** Most people automatically associate this principle with physical safety. This includes the expectation that members will not intentionally harm each other physically and will monitor their own bodies and behavior to keep themselves and their peers safe. For example, play fighting and horsing around are not allowed. However, the other aspect of safety is emotional safety. This includes respect and the expectation that group members will not put each other down or verbally insult or assault other group members. Physical and emotional intimidation will not be tolerated. Many facilitators use the word *respect* to help summarize emotional safety.

3. **Speak Your Truth.** This tenet of the FVC encourages members to verbalize thoughts and feelings. Speaking one's truth must be done in a way that protects other group members' physical and emotional safety. If safety is maintained, members can feel free to express themselves. If one group member has negative feedback to offer another member, it should be conveyed in a way that doesn't violate emotional safety.

4. **Hear The Truth.** Hear the Truth is about listening to others. During regular group time, members should focus their attention and actively listen to directions and anything other group members have to say. It also means that if one group member is offering feedback to another about his or her behavior, the person receiving the message is expected to at least listen to what the speaker has to say.

5. **Have Fun.** All these actions must be accomplished in the name of fun. Adventure and experiential groups take fun very seriously! We learn best when we are in a positive mindset. The activities used in experiential groups are aimed at keeping things enjoyable. I tell my participants that if they make sure to work on the first four tenets of the commitment, I will work very hard to ensure the fifth!

Using the Full Value Commitment with the Keys to Success

You may have noticed a similarity between the commitment participants agree to and the Keys to Success I've outlined. In fact, the group commitment should reinforce the skills and program goals the participants are working toward. The table below describes how the FVC aligns with elements of the Keys to Success. While connections drawn in the table are the most natural relationships, it's important to keep in mind that all aspects of the FVC connect with all parts of the Keys to Success.

Keys to Success's Alignment with the Full Value Commitment

Full Value Commitment	Keys to Success
Be Here (physically and mentally)	Emotional Awareness and Behavioral Control
Be Safe (physically and emotionally)	Emotional Awareness and Behavioral Control
Speak Your Truth	Positive Interpersonal Relationships
Hear the Truth	Positive Interpersonal Relationships
Have Fun	Emotional Awareness, Behavioral Control, Positive Interpersonal Relationships

It is important to recognize that, in addition to behavioral expectations, both the FVC and Keys to Success are goals towards which all members are striving. Group members will not meet the FVC at all times either individually or collectively as a group. Members will not demonstrate proficiency in all aspects of the Keys to Success throughout their time together as a group. If they meet these criteria all of the time, they probably don't need to be in your group.

Violations of the FVC present opportunities for skilled facilitators to intervene and guide the group toward essential learning and growth. Reviewing the FVC after each activity allows the group to reflect upon its actions and determine where the group has upheld the contract and where improvement is needed. This is not to say that major safety violations should be tolerated as learning opportunities; they cannot be. For example, physical aggression, blatant disrespect, or repeated violations of either physical or emotional safety should be addressed directly and immediately by the facilitator. Group members will be looking to you to determine if they will be physically and emotionally safe in the group. If participants do not feel safe, the group will not progress. If the group is in an earlier phase of its development, you will need to decide the fate of members who engage in serious violations of safety. If your group has become a more highly functioning unit, the group as a whole may be able to control the destiny of members who have committed major safety violations.

As stated above, the Keys to Success are also goals for the group to reach. With the support of the FVC, group members develop the Keys to Success skills. As conflicts arise in groups, you will notice that weaknesses in Keys to Success skills are at the heart of these conflicts. Bringing these underlying issues to the surface within the safety net of the agreed-upon behaviors and values of the FVC pushes individuals and groups towards new and better ways of thinking and behaving.

Creating an FVC for Your Group

One of the first decisions to make about the FVC is whether it will be a finished product that is presented to the group by the facilitator or created by the group itself. In my view, whenever possible, it is ideal to have the group create the FVC. The process of creating the FVC helps participants feel a sense of ownership and creates a higher level of "buy-in" to the behavioral expectations. However, one main factor that needs to be considered when creating an FVC is how long the group sessions will run. When I have a group for a brief period of time, I am more likely to present to them a ready-made FVC, as the process of creating a meaningful FVC can be quite time-consuming. Longer-term groups are usually given the task of creating an FVC.

A second factor I consider in making this decision is the cognitive or emotional limitations group members may have. If group members have significant impairments in these areas, they may lack the ability at the onset of the group to successfully develop the FVC. At times, I have begun such a group with a FVC laid out and modified it later as the group members developed their skills. When such modifications are made, I review them with the group and check for clarity and agreement amongst all members.

A final factor I weigh into this decision is whether the group is mandated or voluntary. Mandated groups often have a lower level of investment in the group. Being required to attend a group can lead participants to opt out of creating a FVC or even sabotaging the process. However, there can be great benefits in struggling to create the FVC with a mandated group. Often, over time, these groups of mandated participants can and will become increasingly responsible for monitoring their own behavior.

The process of creating the FVC can be just as important as having the actual FVC itself. Creating an FVC can be accomplished in many ways, ranging from simply brainstorming a list to using decision-making processes that may span several sessions. Several options for creating an FVC are covered in the "Beginning Group Activities" chapter, including the activities Character Card FVC (p. 67) and The Body (p. 73). Choosing the ideal approach will depend upon your preference as a facilitator and your assessment of the needs of your group. However you choose to develop the FVC, you should make it clear at the start of the group sessions how the FVC differs from a simple set of rules.

Participant Choice in Challenges

Different activities pose varying levels of challenge to different group members. As facilitators, we encourage our clients to grow as individuals from the experiences we provide. We ask them to stretch their personal limits and, hopefully, move beyond self-perceived limitations. Nevertheless, participants should determine their degree of participation in the activities. They should determine what level of challenges they are willing to accept. Within Project Adventure, this concept is called Challenge by Choice®, and it finds its basis in the FVC. Allowing participants to have the final say in what level of challenge they will accept provides the sense of value that the FVC attempts to create and protect.

Additionally, challenge by choice fosters the message that participants will be safe within the group. Forcing or coercing participants to participate at a level beyond what they are freely willing to do will not promote growth. Participants, however, need to experience a degree of challenge in order to grow and succeed within the program.

I often highlight this concept of Challenge by Choice with the activity Comfort Zone (p. 218). The activity identifies three specific zones within which we can find ourselves functioning:

- Comfort Zone (totally comfortable with the activity)
- Stretch Zone (not totally comfortable but not likely to panic, optimal for personal growth)
- Panic Zone (completely uncomfortable, on the verge of panic).

If an activity is likely to place participants within the Panic Zone, it is up to them to Speak their Truth. If clients spend most of their time in their personal Comfort Zones, they will not grow as individuals. Ideally, we want our clients to be functioning within the Stretch Zone.

Challenge by Choice does not provide participants with an excuse to sit on the sidelines and watch. If a client is not comfortable with a particular activity, the facilitator can modify the activity to help the client be more comfortable or find a different way for the client to participate with the goal of helping the client find value and grow from the experience. I often tell my clients that while they have the right to choose their challenge, I have the right to challenge their choices if I believe they are simply avoiding the activity.

Chapter Summary

The cornerstone of experiential counseling, the FVC puts into place a set of behavioral expectations that will help maintain safety and allow for the pursuit of happiness for all. Unlike traditional rules, the FVC is often created by the group, monitored by the group, and spoken about often, not just when a particular aspect of the contract is broken. The basic FVC presented in this chapter includes five components and asks group participants to:

1. Be Here physically and mentally.
2. Be Safe physically and emotionally.
3. Speak Your Truth, that is, speak your mind in an appropriate way.
4. Hear the Truth and listen respectfully to what others have to say.
5. Have Fun. If the group abides by the first four commitments, the fifth one will happen.

The FVC can either be created by the facilitator(s) or the group itself. Several factors including group members' abilities and willingness can help guide the facilitator's decision about how to approach developing the FVC.

While the FVC and Keys to Success are both sets of expectations, they are also goals to be strived for. Expect violations and facilitate for growth. That is not to say, however, that major violations should go without consequences. Ideally, monitoring of the FVC will slowly shift from the facilitator to the participants.

A related concept, Challenge by Choice, allows participants to set the level of challenge they are willing to accept and that places them in a position for optimal personal growth. Facilitators can modify activities or offer alternative ways for members to participate to help foster their personal growth.

CHAPTER
4

Phases of the Activity

When facilitating experiential groups using the Keys to Success approach, program leaders discover that each activity has three distinct yet interconnected phases: the introduction, the activity itself, and the group reflection or discussion on the activity. Project Adventure calls these the briefing, the activity, and debriefing phases. In their book *Islands of Healing*, the developers of Project Adventure training call this activity format the Adventure Wave: "The ongoing Adventure process of Briefing/Activity/Debriefing [that is] in operation throughout the Adventure experience" (Schoel et al., 1988, p. 31). Like a wave, the level of activity builds slowly and peaks during the activity phase, ebbing as the activity phase moves into the debriefing phase.

The Adventure Wave provides a metaphor through which facilitators can understand the progress of an activity and a format or plan for facilitating activities for participants in the adventure experience.[1] I have developed the guidelines on facilitating activities presented in this book with these three distinct phases in mind. Conceptualizing activities in this way will allow facilitators to help their clients engage in the activities and reflect on how the activities connect to their lives and the skills and goals they are working toward. This chapter provides information on how to understand these phases of an activity and use them when running an activity. It also provides examples of how to facilitate activities using the briefing, action, and debriefing format.

The Briefing

The briefing is the facilitator's introduction of the activity to the group. It should provide basic information and a metaphor for understanding the activity. When I am briefing a group about an activity, I keep several things in mind:

- **The Three Keys to Success.** This philosophy of emotional intelligence underlies almost everything I do with my groups, and it is an important driving factor in creating the metaphor, or artistic portion, of the brief. Which key or keys does the activity focus on? During the briefing, I often ask questions that focus on the skills involved with the main key or keys that I am hoping to address with that particular activity.

- **The Focus of the Group.** What type of group is this? Is this a leadership group? Depression support group? An anger management group? This will help me tailor my briefing to connect with the primary issues to be addressed within the group.

---

[1]In-depth analyses of the Adventure Wave are available in *Islands of Healing* (Schoel, Prouty, & Radcliffe, 1988) and *Exploring Islands of Healing* (Schoel & Maizell, 2002).

- **The Goals of the Group.** This includes the group's stated and unstated goals. I take into account the overriding goal that the group has set out to accomplish as well its more immediate goals, as determined by my assessment of where the group's current level of functioning seems to be.

The two main components of the briefing, or introduction, I call the technical and artistic components.

The Technical Component

The technical aspect of the introduction involves giving group members basic information about an activity including its title, directions on how to carry out the activity, and the activity's beginning and end points. The introduction may include a stated goal as well. This aspect of the introduction remains fairly constant for any given activity. Almost all activities will have this technical component.

The Artistic Component

Creating the artistic component of the introduction is where facilitation evolves from a job to an art form. By presenting metaphors for the activity, the facilitator sets up how he or she would like the group to perceive the upcoming activity and connect it to specific life skills or real life experiences. Some facilitators call this process "frontloading." The metaphor has a direct impact upon how the members of the group will perceive that activity while they are engaged in it. Changing this component allows facilitators to use the same activity with different groups that have differing goals. The introduction also sets up how the activity will be discussed afterwards in the debriefing.

If you have some familiarity with adventure activities, you may have heard some of the typical metaphors used, such as crossing a peanut-butter swamp, traveling to alien worlds, and technology gone awry. While these explanations generally add to the fun, they don't always provide much in the way of guiding your group towards specific goals. Since the three Keys to Success underlie most of what happens during my groups, I often incorporate them into the artistic portion of the introduction. This helps bring these skills into the consciousness of the participants during the activity. During the debriefing, we can then reflect upon skills discussed during the brief, how these played out during the activity and what this means for the participants.

By changing this component of the introduction, most activities included in this book can be adapted to fit a wide array of groups. The activity Path to Success (p. 321) serves as an example of how varying the introduction can allow the same activity to be used for two very different types of groups. In the Path to Success activity, group members use a trial-and-error method of walking across pads on the ground to determine the correct path from one end of the "maze" to the other. They will know if they make a correct move by the facilitator's immediate feedback. The activity is usually done in silence. For anger management groups, I often introduce the activity as follows:

> "In front of you is the Forest of Rage. Where you are standing is a dark place where anger reigns supreme. Everything is affected by this anger. On the other side is a much brighter place where the anger may still lurk but there is also light and happiness. On that side, you get to

choose to spend your time in the light or find that dark anger. Today, you will be attempting to cross from one end to the other. What skills do you use to get through your own "darkness"? How do you think these might help you today?"

This way of introducing the activity includes a metaphorical aspect (Forest of Rage) but also calls for participants to focus on the skills they are in the group to develop. During the debriefing, participants will reflect on how they used the skills they identified during the briefing.

I also use this activity for groups that are working on leadership skills. For a leadership group, I might introduce the activity as follows:

"In front of you lies the Path to Ultimate Leadership. Unfortunately, there is only one correct path to becoming a leader. All other paths will leave you behind, doomed to be a follower for the remainder of your days. Choosing the correct path will not be easy. If you can successfully determine the correct path as a group, you will arrive on the other side of your quest with the ultimate leadership skills. What skill do you think might await you on the other side? What skills can you use to help your group find the right path?"

These two very different ways of introducing an activity set up how members will perceive it. In the second group, the skills identified for leadership development may be the same or different than those identified for anger management. Even if participants identify the same skills, they may be viewed differently in each group. Take the skill patience for example. This skill may be viewed differently by someone working on anger management than it is by someone working on leadership development. The person in the former group may relate it more to patience with friends and family without losing one's cool. In the latter group, patience may have to do with being patient with those you are leading. In both cases, the skill is directly connected to the three Keys to Success. In this case, Keys 1 and 2: emotional awareness and behavioral control.

The introductions to activities also set up the debriefing discussion that will follow the activity, or Action phase. The Action phase of this activity will be similar with either introduction; however, what each group learns and takes away from the activity will be determined by the artistic component of the introduction and the follow-up debriefing.

The Action

You've given the directions, tailored your introduction to set up how you want the group to perceive the activity, and now it's underway. This is the action phase of the activity. During this phase, you, the facilitator, are constantly assessing the group's progress and taking mental (and sometimes written) notes on the group's dynamic and interactions. As the facilitator, you can step in at any time and make adjustments as needed. Your decisions as to how much and in what ways to get involved during the action phase will depend on a variety of factors. Facilitators that are monitoring an activity will want to consider:

- what stage of development the group is in,

- how ready group members are to monitor their own adherence to the FVC,
- what the group's goals are, and
- what behaviors you observe.

There are no hard-and-fast rules as to when a facilitator should intervene during the activity phase. It may not be an easy decision. Some situations, such as major safety violations, should never be overlooked. If a group is in the early stages of development, I tend to intervene sooner than I do with groups that have already demonstrated the ability to work through some level of conflict and have already shown that they are willing to call each other on FVC violations.

There are times when conflict erupts, but the group appears to be dealing with it effectively. If, however, the group seems to be stuck and unable to navigate the conflict, forward motion may be halted. In this case, I tend to intervene in the least invasive way possible. At times, simply asking a question—such as, "I'm just curious, but are you all actually listening to each other or just talking?"—can help. I might simply offer a reflection, such as "I have heard many good ideas but I don't think most of you have heard them because you seem to be talking more than listening." At times, a more intensive intervention may be needed. I may stop the action, call the group to circle up, and ask them if they notice any violations of the FVC. I may also ask them to reflect upon whether or not they are utilizing the skills they identified at the onset of the activity.

The facilitator's involvement in the action phase can include modifying the activity based on how difficult or simple the group finds the activity. Facilitators might also find that they'll want to adjust the activity's rules. For example, if the activity seems to be too easy, the facilitator can change some aspect of the rules to increase the level of challenge. Blindfolding members, restricting some members' use of a sense or ability, or placing obstacles in the way of an activity can all increase the challenge level. Likewise, activities can be made simpler by removing obstacles or granting an extra power or extra chance to participants. A word of caution: if in introducing an activity, you forget to mention a rule and the group finds the "loophole," it is usually not a good idea to implement that rule mid-activity. Allow the group activity to move forward. If the group completes the activity with ease, you can have the group repeat it with the rule you had left out.

The Debriefing

At its most basic, the debriefing is a discussion about what happened during an activity and what it meant. By raising questions, the facilitator guides the debriefing process. At times, especially with simpler warm-up activities, little or no debriefing will be required. During a debriefing, the facilitator's questions generally focus on the following:

- perceptions, thoughts, and emotions
- behaviors
- skills
- success versus failure
- connecting

Following the activity phase, I like to find out how my participants perceived the activity. What thoughts and feelings did they experience before, during, and at the conclusion of the activity? Did these perceptions, thoughts, and feelings change during the activity? Why and how did this connect with their actions or behaviors? The group should reflect on how their behaviors were in alignment with or violation of the FVC. Group members should reflect upon the skills they used during the activity and how they related to the three Keys to Success. Ultimately, did the group's choices lead to success or failure for the group? At some point, most groups will be called upon to come up with their own definitions of success and failure. All of this discussion should help participants grow as individuals and push the group to a higher level of functioning. Have participants spell out how what was discussed will help them in future activities. Help them draw connections to their lives outside of the group.

Each activity in the book includes specific debriefing questions. Additional debriefing tools are included as well within the appendices.

Putting It All Together

As you gain more experience in facilitation, the three parts of the activity (Introduction, the Action, and Debriefing) will begin to flow more smoothly. In the following pages, I provide case examples of activities through all three phases.

Example 1

Without any outward signs of conflict, my depression support group of eight members has successfully navigated through name games, get-to-know-you, and icebreaker activities during the first three sessions. There have been no signs of conflict. While it may appear that they are a group in a more-advanced phase of development, in all likelihood, they are still politely feeling each other out. To nudge the group towards growth, I need to choose an activity that offers a higher level of challenge, knowing this may produce some level of conflict. Towards this goal, I present Cross the Great Divide (p. 356), which is easily adaptable, provides a fair level of challenge, and can be revised, depending upon the group's progress. After setting up the activity, I gather the group in a circle and give the following briefing:

> "Well, you guys have done a great job so far with your commitment to each other (the FVC). I think you're ready for a bit more of a challenge. That being said, I want you to look over here (pointing to the "River," the area between the start and finish points). Between this shore here and that one there lies the River of Despair! It is not a pleasant place. I know that many of you have been there. Some of you may even feel like you are there now. I also know that most of you have felt very alone in that river. However, today you have something different. You have several resources. One of those resources is each other. Today you will be able to rely on each other to get across that River of Despair. What traits or skills do you bring to this challenge today that will allow you to be a support to your teammates in getting across that River?"

As the group members state their individual characteristics and skills one at a time, I hand them one of the "steps" needed to cross the river. Often, members will say things such as, "I'm a good listener" or "I have good balance." If a member gets stuck and can't think of what they bring to the group, I will sometimes ask the group what skills or talents they've observed that member to possess. Be sure that you can trust the group members to make positive statements before asking their opinion on this.

Once all members have their steps, I explain how to carry out the activity and how this resource works. The participants then begin the activity, and we move into the Action phase. During this phase, the group starts off laughing and clearly having fun, temporarily forgetting most of what we just talked about. After losing a few steps for violations of the rules of the game (such as not keeping in contact with a step), they become more serious, realizing that the activity has now become much more difficult. As they go, I notice who is most vocal, who is quiet, who speaks, and who listens. I see some members sharing ideas and not being heard, and I mark this for later discussion. I also notice some members blaming others for losing the steps. The emerging conflict signals to me that they have begun to enter an important new phase of group development. I don't intervene, as the group seems to be moving on without any major violations of our FVC. Tension rises as the participants near the end of the challenge. With some more careless errors as they near the goal, they lose several more steps, making completion of the activity even more difficult. The group really pulls together, however, and finishes the activity. They high-five and cheer each other for conquering the task. I praise them and gather them back into the circle.

There are several ways to approach the debriefing to the completed activity. The facilitator could ask participants very open-ended questions, such as "So, what happened?" The facilitator could also be more directive and ask questions such as, "So, what skills did you find you needed to use to get across the River of Despair?" This approach would link the debriefing directly to the briefing.

In this case, I opt for the more open-ended approach and ask for their thoughts on what happened, and the members immediately launch into recalling the actual events of the activity. They talk about how they lost some steps but stuck together. Taking their lead, I ask how they felt when those first steps were lost. Someone states that they felt like they were doomed to failure. I then ask, "In real life, what happens when one piece of your support system disappears or fails you? Do you feel that way too?" By connecting the feeling elicited by the activity to a real-life situation, the group begins to share stories and thoughts about feeling of abandonment in their real lives.

After some conversation about this, I guide the discussion back to the FVC, asking the group to assess how they did in the activity. Some members state that they felt the group met all the commitments. No one argues, but after having observed some violations in listening and blaming during the activity, I push the topic. "As I was watching you guys, it seemed that some people assumed leadership roles and others hung back a bit. I also noticed that the ideas the group used were the ones put forth by the most vocal leaders. Was there anyone else who had an idea that wasn't used?" I may not get a taker on this bait, but it's worth putting out anyway. One of the members speaks up and says that another member verbalized an idea but the group moved right past it. An air of tension fills our circle. As a facilitator, there may be a temptation at this point to steer the boat in a different direction. The storm is coming. If the group is ready, steer into the storm! This period of conflict can provide an opportunity for personal and group growth.

Without openly blaming each other, we discuss how it feels to not be heard. Most of the group members can relate to this feeling from other aspects of their lives. I guide the discussion towards solutions. The group offers ideas to make sure everyone gets heard in future activities.

Example 2

On the second of three full days of working with a group of 14 young adolescent counselors in training for a local summer camp, I note that some conflicts have arisen but were resolved by the day's end. The participants have experienced some level of conflict, and it's time to see what they have learned from the experience. The stated goals of the program are for the counselors in training to build trust and camaraderie and improve the decision-making skills they will need as camp counselors. As the facilitator, the more immediate goals are to see how well they can manage the emotion of frustration and its impact upon their behavior and interactions. I choose the activity Field of Distraction (p. 372), a challenging initiative that will be likely to trigger their frustration and challenge them to maintain positive interactions with each other. For the activity, the group is broken into pairs. Each pair is given a stuffed animal. One member of each pair is blindfolded. The sighted partner remains stationary outside the playing area while verbally guiding their blindfolded partner through the playing area filled with obstacles and other blindfolded people. This area is about 60 feet across, and pairs are spread out evenly around the perimeter. The goal is for each pair to retrieve their stuffed animal, which the facilitator has placed within the playing area. If the blindfolded partner touches any other participants or obstacles, a facilitator would guide that person back to the place outside the playing area where his or her sighted partner stands. The pair would then restart.

After giving the technical briefing on the activity, I give the artistic component, which captures how I want the participants to see the challenge:

> "You guys are counselors in trainings. That means you hope to be counselors for the camp next summer. The stuffed animal represents that goal. There will be many obstacles that can set you back and prevent you from reaching your goal. You have a support system in each other. Don't forget that you are each other's resources. What obstacles might you encounter in becoming a counselor? What skills will you use to reach your goal today?"

After a brief discussion, the group begins the challenge. To make the activity more difficult, I have placed each pair's stuffed animal as far away from the pair as possible. As the blindfolded participants move further into the circle, it becomes increasingly difficult for them to hear their partners' directions. Several pairs need to restart the activity because blindfolded participants touched other participants or obstacles, and the frustration level is rising. After several minutes, with no "goals" being obtained, it becomes clear that the group is no longer being productive as they begin to blame each other and push the limits of the FVC. I stop the group and have them circle up. I ask, "What's happening here?" Immediately, members begin to launch into a litany of reasons why their partners are at fault: "He doesn't speak loud enough," and "She's not listening to me." I bring the discussion back to some of the skills participants mentioned during the introduction: communication and teamwork. I also remind participants that each member of the group is considered a resource. I ask the group to move on and discuss some new ways to approach the task. After some discussion, one asks me if sighted partners can talk to blindfolded participants that are not their assigned partners.

"I never said you couldn't," I reply. Suddenly, the group realizes that they can use each other as communication resources. They work out a plan that has sighted members sharing responsibility for all blindfolded members in the circle based on who is closest to each of them. The sighted partners decide to communicate with each other by passing messages around the circle from one sighted participant to the next. The group makes a second attempt and is successful. I invite the partners to switch roles, and they complete another round of the activity.

During the debriefing, the group members acknowledge that their frustration led to them blaming each other for the initial lack of success. They also discover that during the first round, they had seen other group members as distractions, while during the second round, they were redefined as resources. I guide the group to discuss how issues of blame and getting caught up in focusing on the problem rather than solutions could interfere with being an effective camp counselor. We also discuss how negative events or "distractions" can be redefined to help a group. By the end of the debriefing, the group realizes that by thinking creatively and focusing on possible solutions as opposed to only the problem, the group was able to work cooperatively towards successfully completing the task. It allowed participants to view other pairs as resources, a viewpoint that will be essential when they become camp counselors.

Example 3

We are in the third session of a conflict prevention program with 18 high school-aged participants. After reviewing the FVC and Keys to Success, I set up an activity called Knot My Issue (p. 350). For this activity, I simply give participants the technical briefing before the first phase. The basic instructions are that each group of six students will hold the ends of three crossed ropes and, without letting go, create a knot. The group ties their knots and the time stops. I say to the group:

> "Well, now you've created quite a mess. Has anyone here ever had a conflict that created a mess in their lives?" Most members raise their hands. "Has anyone ever had a conflict that created a mess in their lives and left it for someone else to fix?" Giggling, most members again raise their hands. "How nice it is," I continue, "to create a mess and leave it for someone else! Well, you get to do that now!" I instruct the groups to place their knotted ropes on the ground and move to the knot to their right, leaving their mess for another group to deal with. Each participant must pick up the end of the rope in front of them and, without letting go of the end of the rope they pick up, untangle the knot created by the group that was there before them. Groaning and laughing, the groups move to the new knots and untangle them. The group is then given a second chance to create a knot. Most groups assume they will be moving to a different knot again and create a much more difficult knot the second time.

When they are done, I say, "What happens when we leave our messes for others to clean up?" Several members offer responses. One participant says that the messes get worse. "Well, often, our messes do get worse. And who is left to clean them up?" Without me saying it, many group members suspect that they will be untying their own knots. I then ask them to untangle the knot they've just made. Once they untie their own knots (which is far more challenging), we move into the debriefing.

I open the debriefing by simply asking: "What happened?" The group launches into a discussion. Participants quickly realize the main message that if you leave your mess for others to fix, you will end up with a bigger mess that you need to fix! We then discuss how to prevent conflicts from becoming bigger than they need to be and emphasize how important it is not to ignore the conflict but to deal with it when it's small.

Facilitators should use their creativity to tailor introductions and metaphors to the goals of their group and its stage of group development. Debriefing questions should invite reflection and lead participants to draw connections between the activity and the group's and their own personal goals. I almost always include the following approaches in my debriefings:

1. An open ended question, such as, "How did that go?" or "So, what happened?"

2. A check in with the FVC: "Did we, as a group, meet our commitment to each other?"

3. Questions and comments that overtly or less obviously link the group's experience to the skills underlying the three Keys to Success.

4. The invitation to transfer lessons learned in the group to members' real lives outside the group. I generally ask questions such as, "So how does what you just said about this connect with your real life?"

In this book, you'll find activities and suggestions for debriefing questions. Each activity includes guidance on the following components of an activity:

Briefing (or what I will call in the activities the Introduction/Metaphor). This section includes suggestions for the artistic component of the introduction to the activity.

The Action. The exercises include descriptions of the activity for the technical component of the introductions as well as other information to help readers set up and facilitate the activity.

Debriefing. This section presents questions and comments that will help you link the activity to the FVC and Keys to Success and help you guide the group members to relate the insights they've gained to their real life situations. What I offer in these pages are suggestions, not hard, fast rules.

Chapter Summary

The Adventure Wave, identified by Schoel, Prouty, and Radcliffe in the book *Islands of Healing* (1988), provides a tool for facilitators to understand and, in turn, plan the adventure experience for participants. Basically, each activity consists of three distinct yet interconnected phases. First is the introduction, which is made up of two parts that I refer to as the technical and artistic components. The technical aspect includes the basic information needed for participants to engage in the activity: directions, rules, beginning and end points, and goals. The artistic component (sometimes referred to as frontloading) includes metaphorical or implied connections between the activity and real life. It helps set up how participants will perceive the activity and facilitates their connecting it to real-life experiences. By changing this part of the introduction, activities can be modified to fit a wide variety of themes and groups.

The second phase of the activity is the action phase. This is the time when the group is engaged in the actual activity. During this time, facilitators may refer to the introduction when needed or incorporate aspects of the third phase: the debriefing. During this phase, facilitators help participants draw connections between what happened during the activity and the participants' lives. This chapter concludes with several examples demonstrating the way these three aspects of the Adventure Wave play out together.

5 Preparing for Your Group

Preparing for a group begins well before the group's first meeting. If you are working with a new group, before participants even arrive, you will be making decisions based upon the information you have about the members. With experiential groups, programs follow a general sequence of activities, moving from simpler activities that generally require lower levels of cognitive and emotional investment to more complex activities that require a higher level of group cohesion and trust. While each group has its own goals (which may be predetermined by you or others or created within the early stages of the group), all experiential counseling groups seek to help the participants grow as individuals in the skill areas that comprise the three Keys to Success. How quickly a group progresses from the simpler to more complex activities can vary greatly based upon the individuals in the group and the group dynamic. Flexibility is essential for facilitators, as they will need to adapt expectations and may need to change what they are doing at any point based on what they are observing. The more facilitators know about their participants prior to the start of the group, the more prepared they will be when the group first convenes. With that in mind, there is certain basic information I like to have before a beginning a new group.

Information about Group Members and Format

- How long will I be working with this group?
- How many people are expected to attend?
- How old are they? If they are not adults, what type of supervision will there be?
- Do they know each other and if so, how well? Are they from an established organization?
- What types of activities would they like to do? Would they like the experience to be more active or passive?
- Have they been involved in any adventure programming as a group or as individuals before?
- Does anyone coming have any physical limitations or medical issues of which I should be aware?

Information about Group Goals

- What are the group's stated goals? In other words, what do members want to get out of the experience or what are the expectations of those referring or bringing the group members?

- Is the group mandated or voluntary? Mandated groups often come with predetermined goals.

Discovering the answers to these questions will help you decide how to best facilitate your group.

Tailoring Activities to Group Members

Deciding which activities to try and how to present them will be based mostly on your understanding of your participants and their goals. How familiar are they with experiential counseling or adventure programs? How well acquainted are they with each other? What are the goals of the group? If this is a themed group, such as anger management or leadership development, the overall goals may be already established. I still find out early in the group's time together what members hope to get out of the experience: Do they have their own, more specific goals relating to the theme? I sometimes find that participants have goals that are only distantly connected to the theme of the group.

Consider How Long the Group Will Run. Depending on whether you will be working with a group for one hour or a full day or for one session versus eight sessions, you should weigh the length of the sessions into your choices for activities. This is where activity sequencing truly comes into play. For short programs, you may proceed through the sequencing stages quite quickly or you may choose to focus on simpler activities that don't involve a great deal of trust or a high level of teamwork. Pushing into more emotionally or cognitively demanding activities before a solid basis of trust and cohesion is built can lead to participants shutting down or demonstrating negative behaviors out of discomfort or anxiety. For longer-lasting programs, you have the luxury of really working with sequencing, spending time developing trust and cohesion within the group before moving to more demanding activities. As a facilitator, keep in mind that your sequencing plan may need to be adapted as your group shows you what they are ready to attempt. For further information on sequencing activities, see Chapter 7.

Consider the Group's Size and the Age of the Participants. With a little bit of creativity, many activities can be adapted or modified to work with smaller or larger groups and with younger and older populations. Some are better for larger groups; some are better for smaller groups. The activity write-ups in this book include information on the optimal numbers of participants for each activity and the typical age ranges for participants. These numbers are suggestions based on my experience. They are not definitive. For example, many tag games are a natural fit with younger groups that have a great deal of energy. Activities such as Peek-a-Who (p. 96) may work best with groups that are smaller so that each participant has more chances and remains engaged. With modifications, however, most activities can be adapted to fit younger or older populations and for use in groups of varying sizes. For instance, tag games can be great with the right group of older participants. Likewise, facilitators can run several games of Peek-A-Who at once giving participants plenty of chances to play.

Take into Account the Desired Level of Activity. Whether a group desires a more active or passive level of participation in a program will also weigh into your decisions. Some groups want (or require) activities that are high energy. Some don't. Generally, younger group participants require more fast-paced activities to sustain their attention. Older groups or groups with participants that are higher functioning in terms of Keys to Success skills can often deal with more cognitively demanding activities that require a lower level of physical activity.

If members of your group have documented physical limitations or medical conditions, you may have to modify activities to include them. Project Adventure publications such as *Islands of Healing* (Schoel et al., 1988) offer a great deal of information about incorporating individuals with disabilities in adventure programs. On some of occasions, you might need to rely on your own ingenuity. I once had a group session in which I planned to do the activity Web of Life (p. 307). When my group arrived, one of the kids had a broken foot. As I was about to change my plan entirely, I realized that we all had chairs with wheels. We decided to try the activity sitting in the chairs to incorporate the injured student. The added challenge of navigating in rolling chairs led to outcomes that far surpassed my expectations!

Consider the Relationships of Group Members. How well group members know each other and whether they will continue a relationship beyond your first meeting with them should also factor into your decisions on what activities to run. If they know each other well, you will likely want to spend little time on name games and get-to-know-you activities; however, I have worked with groups that, despite having been together other for extended periods of time, don't really know all that much about each other. In this case, get-to-know-you activities can be quite enlightening and fun for your group. Likewise, name games can be used to reinforce existing connections.

Incorporate the Group's Goals. Facilitators' selection of activities will be influenced by the group's goals. The goals may be predetermined by the group theme or by those referring the participants, decided by group members or both. Is the main goal bonding? Is it acquiring skills in conflict resolution? general team building? improving social skills? While most activities in this book can be adapted, some will be a more natural fit for certain themes or group goals than others. For example, Knot My Issue (p. 350) is a natural fit for conflict or decision making where situations can become "messy." Bull Ring (p. 368) is a natural for groups that need to develop patience and focus and to really function as a team. Facilitators should plan ahead of time to make their presentation of the activities coincide with the group's goals. Appendices A through D discuss how to facilitate groups on specific themes or for specific participants.

Equipment and Props

When I facilitate adventure groups, I often carry some of the more common props with me, such as gym spots, bandannas, raccoon circles or ropes, some toss-able items such as yarn balls or stuffed animals, markers, and index cards. This basic kit gives me the option to run many different activities if my plans need to be changed. In the activity sections of this book, the specific props for each activity are listed.

Co-Facilitating Groups

Generally speaking, when I am working with groups of emotionally or behaviorally disordered youth, I have either a co-facilitator or another staff member (such as a teacher) working with me. There are several advantages to co-facilitation. No matter how observant you are, when facilitating a group, your attention and energy are divided, and a second pair of observant eyes will notice things that you miss. Having a second facilitator also allows you to address situations without having to leave the group unattended. This can be helpful if you need to deal with any serious safety violations during an activity. Like the adage says, "Two heads are better than one." I often find that planning with a co-facilitator leads to a synergistic relationship where one idea triggers another which triggers another and so on. Having a co-facilitator allows me to think outside my own box. When co-facilitating a group, there are very few times that I don't learn something new. After co-facilitating a group, I generally debrief with my co-facilitators. This process allows me to receive feedback about my own facilitation, which, in turn, allows me to continually grow as a facilitator. It also gives me the opportunity to reflect back to others how I viewed their performance, which allows them to grow.

There are, however, a few disadvantages to co-facilitating groups. The main one is inconvenience. Co-facilitation does take more effort than facilitating alone when you don't have to discuss or compromise your plans. It can also be a problem when co-facilitators don't share a mutual respect for each other as people or facilitators. There have been times when I co-facilitated with people who had very different philosophies about adventure programming than I did, which created a less than ideal situation. Usually, the extra effort of co-facilitation reaps rewards. In general, if you have the option, co-facilitating with someone you trust and respect is best.

Organizing a Session

In organizing a session in experiential counseling, I offer a piece of advice: over plan. In my experience, whether it's a group of people you've never met before or kids you've known for years, a day or session very rarely goes exactly as planned. While this may be an anxiety trigger for you as a facilitator, try to view it as an opportunity. Usually, the group indicates, often nonverbally, what direction it needs to go, and that direction may not be what you had planned. When this happens, it's best to be prepared to change direction. Adaptability is a core characteristic of good facilitation. For a typical school-group session of one period (45 minutes to an hour), I may have four or five activities ready to go. These may include a warm-up or two and a few options for more challenging activities. Through my assessment of the group, I will determine which of the activities I am prepared to facilitate will work best.

Chapter Summary

This chapter examines the basic information you should have prior to beginning any group. How to choose particular activities should be based on the information facilitators have on group members, the group format, and group members' goals. The chapter presents information on equipment and offers some considerations on co-facilitation of adventure counseling programs. Tips on organizing a day of experiential group work are also offered.

CHAPTER 6

Assessing and Monitoring Your Group

No matter how much you plan ahead for your group, rarely will everything go according to your plan. When bringing individuals together as a group, a unique and unpredictable dynamic is created. There is no definitive way to predict how an activity, a day, or group will turn out. I have had what seemed early on to be highly functioning groups crumble in conflict at the slightest push towards more challenging activities. Likewise, I have had groups whose individual participants had many emotional and behavioral problems, but they pulled together as a functioning group. While preparation is important, it is equally as important to be able to continually assess and monitor your group's progress. Dynamics can shift quickly and unpredictably. Taking the pulse of the group as you go will help you decide your next course of action. Towards this end, there are several ways to monitor and assess your group as you facilitate.

Tuckman's Five Stages of Group Development

For counselors, Tuckman's four-stage model (1965) of group development is probably the most widely known and most applicable theory in group work. According to the model, groups develop across several stages, moving first from formation through conflict and then to interdependence as a team. Tuckman defines the stages as forming, storming, norming, and performing. Eventually, a fifth stage, called adjourning, was added (Tuckman & Jensen, 1977).

Making use of Tuckman's model can be helpful in evaluating and responding to your group's needs as a facilitator. It wasn't until I was in graduate school that I was able to connect my psychology coursework with life and had the opportunity to see how the theory of group formation translated into reality. I offer the following overview of Tuchman's model with the hope that it might help you when applying your training and experience in managing your groups' dynamics.

Forming

When groups first come together, members often get to know one another on only a somewhat superficial level. Generally, members want to be accepted and liked; therefore, conflicts and deeper emotions are often avoided. At this time, the forming stage, group members are learning more about each other and assessing themselves in relation to the rest of the group. While this phase is usually "happy" and "comfortable," not much true growth occurs. This growth begins to occur when members start to push against the perceived limits of the group.

Storming

During the storming stage, the group members begin testing the limits of the facilitator and of each other. True feelings are brought to the surface, and conflicts are likely to arise. Sometimes the conflicts may lie just below the surface. Sometimes they may be out in the open. Members will differ in their reactions to these developments. Some may move head first into this phase while others may try to keep the peace that was characteristic of the forming phase. Often, a pecking order is being established, and for groups of people who already know each other, previously established pecking orders become more defined. Skilled facilitators will view this stage as an opportunity for growth. How behavior is handled during the storming stage is crucial for healthy group development. It is important for facilitators to recognize that conflict is not a bad thing but a necessary ingredient for true growth in a group and its members.

Norming

What comes out of the storming stage is an understanding about how members of the group should treat one another. If the storming phase is resolved successfully, group members will emerge with a greater understanding and acceptance of each other and their strengths and weaknesses, and they will show an increased level of trust. Group norms will have been developed and agreed upon (though you are likely to be the only one in the group aware that this is happening). Members are beginning to work more harmoniously.

Performing

This stage is characterized by a state of interdependence and flexibility. Members know each other well enough to work together with a trust level that fosters independence and support at the same time. The group and its members can quickly change roles and adapt to changing situations as needed. Members are both task and people oriented and group identity, loyalty, and morale are high. Not all groups will achieve this "flow state." It's important to note that if you feel like your group has moved into this stage quickly, without any "storming," it's possible that your group is actually in a phase more akin to "forming."

Adjourning

Last, members who are joined in one project can enter a stage that Tuchman calls adjourning. At this stage, the group has completed its task and gets ready to let go and move on. They can reflect upon what they have accomplished in their time together. Often there is pride mixed with sadness that their time together is ending. Connections between the experience in the group and their lives outside the group are now clear.

Using the Five-Stage Model

We typically think of our groups as beginning in the forming stage. While this is often true, it is not always the case. If you are working with a group whose members know each other well, previously established social norms may exist that you are unaware of. This does not necessarily mean that they are on the fast path to the performing stage. Often, these groups have somewhat dysfunctional relationship norms. Most of the time, there is a definitive pecking order with both established leaders and folks at the bottom. This order can be defined by official positions (such as bosses and workers, principals and teachers) or unofficial ones, as is often the case with kids and teens. When this occurs, it's important for you as the facilitator to be aware of it. If the group has been together for some time, it's very likely that they have established some norms already, and these norms may not be healthy. This will often become evident early on in your group through their interactions.

Watch for these signs:

- One or more members talking down to or ordering other members around. This will clue you in to the top and bottom of the pecking order.

- Members clustering together. Often the top dogs will stay with the other top dogs while the middle of the group may gravitate to like level members, and the lowest will either stick together or sometimes stand alone.

- Members who speak and those who don't. Those at the middle and bottom may not verbalize much in the beginning. Leaders may also not verbalize much, but in this case, the rest of the group will likely follow this lead.

- A group "attitude" that seems to follow the attitude of a particular member. This may be more subtle, less based in language and more based in nonverbal communication.

When you find that your group has these established norms, as a facilitator, you need to consider in what direction the group needs to move. This type of group may appear to function at the performing stage, accomplishing tasks with little or no conflict; however, this appearance may be a mirage. The situation may be that the leader or leaders are directing the group by being authoritarian. If the group members do not seem to feel safe enough to express their thoughts, the group is not really at the performing stage.

As a facilitator, more than likely, you will need to get this group back to the forming stage. Just as metaphors are an important part of connecting activities to our life experience, I will throw one out to you about these types of seemingly highly functioning groups: If you build a house and the foundation was done incorrectly, to fix it, you need to rebuild it from the bottom up. Participants' established roles will need to be broken down so that new roles can be developed safely. There are numerous approaches and tips as to how to accomplish this task. First, I find it very important to identify the leaders in the group. If they seem to be folks who can be positive leaders (that is, people who can encourage development of the FVC and Keys to Success behaviors), they may be viewed as assets for the facilitator. If, on the other hand, there seem to be more negative and oppressive leaders, these participants will need to be absolved of their leadership role by removing their power within the group. This is not an easy task and usually dictates that the facilitator take a highly directive role early on and strictly enforce the FVC, challenging the established leaders' authority when they challenge the facilitator or violate the contract. If members realize that you are the true "top dog," they will begin to feel safer knowing that you will protect them from the negativity of their perceived leaders. This will take time and commitment.

A second goal is to find ways to elevate members who are lower in the pecking order to a position of equality. This is where knowing how to select and present appropriate activities and how to modify them as necessary for your group becomes so important. Some simple techniques that help in these situations include giving certain people certain powers and removing powers from others during an activity. For example, if the only one who can talk during an activity is a quiet kid and you've banned all the loud kids from talking through the metaphor presentation, roles will have to shift. Creating disequilibrium within such a group is the optimal way to begin to shift these roles.

For groups that are truly forming and whose members don't know each other, facilitators will likely be working with groups at the forming stage. Assessing groups during this phase involves observing participants while engaging the group. As the facilitator, you should seek to identify natural leadership abilities, those who are likely to want to rise to the top and those who are more likely to want to sink into the background. In a newly formed group, it is the responsibility of the facilitator to enforce the FVC early on.

GRABBS Assessment

One excellent tool for the ongoing assessment of your group is the GRABBS model (Schoel et al., 1988). Developed by Project Adventure facilitators, this handy tool lets facilitators assess groups as they are happening. The GRABBS acronym stands for goals, readiness, affect, behavior, body, and setting. It represents what facilitators should assess when observing the group dynamic.

Goals

As facilitators, we have our own vision of what we want our group to accomplish. They are our goals for the group. While it's important to keep these in mind, it is also important to recognize that the group's own goals, which may be unstated, matter as much as, if not more than, the facilitator's goals and agenda. What is the group trying to and needing to accomplish?

Readiness

As a facilitator, you need to consider whether the group is ready for what you have planned. Is the activity a match for their current phase of group development? Is it a match for their age or maturity level?

Affect

What is the mood of the group as a whole? Are they eager and determined? Are they apathetic? Are they just plain ticked off? The answers to these questions will give you a great deal of information as to the group's level of readiness, as well as what the group's goals need to be at that time. This information will help guide you in your activity selection.

Behavior

What is the behavior of group members saying to you as the facilitator? Are they violating safety? Are they communicating? Who is "in" and who is "out" within the group?

Body

What is the physical condition and state of the group members? Are they healthy? Are there any disabilities that need to be taken into account? Are they hungry or tired or satisfied and energetic?

Setting

Look around the area that will serve as the group's physical setting. Will there be other people or other distractions? Are there boundaries? Is it indoors or outdoors? Are there any dangerous areas or objects that need to be addressed?

Chapter Summary

Tuckman and Jensen's five stages of group development (1977)—forming, storming, norming, performing, and adjourning—provide a valuable tool for facilitators for assessing group dynamics and group health. While the stages are presented in a sequential fashion, a group may not move through all stages and may not move through stages sequentially. The chapter presents ideas for handling situations in which a new group comes to you (the facilitator) with established—and frequently unhealthy—norms.

The GRABBS assessment model (Schoel et al., 1988) is derived from the work of Project Adventure facilitators. GRABBS is an acronym for goals, readiness, affect, behavior, body, and setting. Attending to these features will help you make the most sensible decisions about how to proceed with your group.

7 Activity Sequencing

Just as the Adventure Wave provides a framework and sequence of events for each activity, the sequence of activities should convey a logical, coherent process. The sequence of activities generally moves from simpler exercises (such as name games, tag games, and warm ups) to those that are more physically or mentally challenging and involve an increased level of trust, such as low- and high-level initiatives or trust-building activities. In the course of the group, activities build upon each other with increasing difficulty to provide a consistent and appropriate level of challenge for participants, which promotes growth. Sequencing activities in this manner also allows the group to take on increased responsibility for monitoring and enforcing the FVC.

The shift of control from facilitator to participants reflects what I term "control to empowerment." This shift in authority promotes healthy development in teens just as does a parents' decision to grant increased freedom to their teens when they can demonstrate increased levels of personal responsibility. It is also evident in many classrooms where teachers early in the school year maintain tight control over the classroom environment but allow for more freedom as students demonstrate the ability to handle freedom responsibly.

As with many other aspects of adventure programming, there are no hard-and-fast rules about how to sequence activities; however, choosing activities at random can have negative effects upon a group's performance and development. Giving the group a more challenging activity before participants are ready often results in negative behaviors or members shutting down. The chapters in the activity sections of this book are arranged in a general sequential order, presenting first the activities that are most typically used early in a group's time together and then moving to the activities used when the group dynamics are better developed.

For a group comprised of several one-hour, weekly sessions (a format many school-based counselors will use), I typically begin the first session with fun activities aimed at getting the group warmed up and helping members learn each other's names. This will likely take most, if not all, of the first session. Typically, over the next session or two, I will shift to activities that aim to help participants get to know one another better and increase their level of trust. During the second session, I will also begin (and possibly finish) having the group create its own FVC. As the group progresses, using the information from my ongoing monitoring and assessment, the group will progress into more complex, challenging activities. Below are some questions and guidelines facilitators should consider when choosing an activity.

At What Stage of Development Is My Group?

Groups just coming together will often begin with activities from the chapters Beginning Group Activities and Name Games. Facilitators will also use activities from the chapters Icebreakers, Get to Know You, and Tag Games early on with a group. These activities allow group members to learn names and begin to get to know one another. They also allow the group members to gain an initial understanding of what will be expected during group while having a whole lot of fun. Many of these activities focus on the Be Here aspect of the FVC and are aimed at bringing participants into the group both physically and mentally. Generally, there is minimal debriefing during this phase of development (as is reflected in the Debriefing section of these activities). Engaging in more complex activities or in-depth debriefings too early in a group's time together can actually inhibit personal sharing and commitment. At this early stage of group development, facilitators will maintain a tight reign the on group's behavior and be the primary person monitoring the FVC. Facilitators should directly address breaches of the commitment early on. This is essential for creating an environment in which the group members will feel safe to express themselves. (A detailed description of Tuckman's Stages of Group Development is contained on p. 41.)

The Storming Stage

As group members begin to test limits, facilitators should choose activities that allow the group to experience conflict while providing opportunities to work towards resolutions. Often, groups need to come to the brink of disaster before they can pull together and successfully navigate through the storm. A wide range of activities can be used during this phase. Many of the initiatives, such as Turn Over a New Leaf or Cross the Great Divide, are activities that will challenge any group and are likely to create conflict within a controlled environment. Facilitators should also consider what type of conflict the group is struggling with and how introductions and metaphors for activities can be tailored to help the group move forward. For example, if I have a group that is struggling to develop trust among the members, I might use the activity Full-Value Hog Call (p. 268) in which blindfolded partners must find each other by shouting out aspects of the FVC. I'd introduce the activity with a brainstorming session about what behaviors the group needs to demonstrate in order to increase the level of trust. If the behaviors the group decided upon for its FVC were honesty, forgiveness, and encouragement, I might divide the group into smaller groups of three people each. Each smaller group would choose one person to represent honesty, one to represent forgiveness, and one to represent encouragement. I would then send all participants representing the same FVC aspect to a designated area within the field. I would then have the group members find each other according to the typical Full-Value Hog Call directions. The debriefing portion of activities becomes extremely important during the storming phase. My debrief for this activity would focus on what actions each person took during the activity to foster the three behaviors the group chose to focus on.

The Norming and Performing Stages

During these stages, activities that provide a higher level of challenge, such as trust activities and initiatives, are generally called for. Keep in mind that these activities can sometimes bring about conflict in groups that are in the norming and performing stages. With your guidance, the group can resolve these conflicts in a positive manner, paving the way for further growth. It's important to understand that the higher-level activities can be mentally and emotionally draining. It is often a good idea to incorporate some icebreakers, tag games, or other less-intense activities into your sessions with higher-performing groups to afford them a break from the intensity of the higher-level activities. Keep in mind that groups don't necessarily move through these stages in a sequential fashion. A group may function in more than one phase at a time. Continually monitoring your group using the GRABBS assessment can provide you with direction as to which activities are appropriate at any given time.

What Is My GRABBS Assessment Telling Me?

As a facilitator, you don't have to set aside activities once they have been completed. You can choose appropriate activities based on your assessment of the group's current status and needs. There will be times when even your best-performing group is getting tired and hungry. That is not the time to push forward with high-level initiatives when a light, fun icebreaker is more appropriate before breaking for lunch. I begin most group sessions with a simple, fun activity just to get the participants warmed up. These activities also provide me with some insight as to how the group is functioning at the moment. If the group struggles with the easier activities, I toss aside my plans to engage them in more advanced activities until my GRABBS assessment tells me that they are ready. If a group is demonstrating unsafe behaviors, I will not engage them in a complex trust-building activity. If there seems to be a grouchy affect to the group, a fun, engaging icebreaker may be a good choice.

Does the Group Need a Break?

Sometimes, especially if a group has been together for a while, changing the type of activity is a good idea. For example, if my high-performing group is tackling challenge after challenge for weeks on end, I might do some simpler activities just to give them a break. In my position as a school psychologist, many groups I work with meet on a weekly basis for the entire school year. I tend to alternate activity-based sessions with talk sessions so as to avoid activity burnout. This keeps the activity-based group sessions fresh. There are also times that a group may prefer to just talk. Using my GRABBS assessment, I try as much as possible to take my cues from the group.

Activity Sequences That Work Well

After facilitating adventure programs for a while, you will find that some activities flow well together, particularly activities used early in a group's development that are shorter and don't require a great deal of debriefing. It's likely that you will use these sequences over and over. One of the things that amazes me most about the best facilitators I have worked with is the seamless flow of their activities. Here are some examples of activities that I find flow well one to the next:

- **Listen Up, Trigger Finger, Do As I Say.** For the first activity, I tell the group that I am working on getting them to listen. For Trigger Finger, I inform the group that I want their brains and bodies working together. For Do As I Say, I indicate that I want them to be listening and having their words, thoughts, and actions matching up.

- **Two Person Trust Leans, Three Person Trust Leans, Wind in The Willows, Levitation.** This sequence allows trust to build incrementally by moving from a simple two-person trust activity to activities that involve the entire group lifting someone off the ground.

- **Left In, Concentric Circles, Take a Stand.** These three activities allow group members to get to know each other quickly while having fun.

- **Name Whip, Cross Circle Names, Love Those New Red Potatoes, Peek-A-Who.** Stringing together a series of increasingly challenging name games can keep this learning process fun.

- **Name Whip, Warp Speed, Group Juggle.** These activities allow group members to learn names in a fun way while facing some lower-level teambuilding challenges.

Chapter Summary

In experiential counseling and adventure programs, the sequence of activities generally moves from simpler exercises (such as name games, tag games, and warm-ups) to those that are more physically or mentally challenging and involve an increased level of trust, such as low- and high-level initiatives and trust-building activities. Deciding which activity should be used during any particular session should be based on what stage of group development your group is in and how participants are performing in the moment, according to your GRABBS assessment. Certain activities, particularly those used early in the program, can be woven together to create a seamless flow. Facilitators will find their own combinations of activities over time. Finally, taking a break from more complex activities or even activities in general is appropriate.

8 Beginning Group Activities

In his Business Know-How article "How to Make a Strong First Impression: Seven Tips That Really Work," Bill Lampton maintains that within 7 to 17 seconds people form an opinion of those they meet (www.businessknowhow.com). According to Lydia Ramsey, author of *Manners That Sell,* it only takes 7 seconds (www.mannersthatsell.com). In her article on About.com, Michelle T. Sterling, founder of Global Image Group, suggests that an opinion has already been formed within 3 seconds!

Whatever the amount of time, first impressions are made quickly and are not easily changed. This holds true for facilitators that are facilitating adventure-based counseling groups as well. Setting the right tone in the first minutes of the first group session is important for creating an atmosphere that will foster success within the group. If you aspire to create a safe, trusting, open atmosphere where members can take risks and accept the invitation to step outside of their "comfort zones," your first activities must be chosen carefully. Additionally, as the facilitator, you must model the behaviors and attitudes you want your group to adopt.

As a group gathers for its first session, the members will be looking to you to understand what this experience will be like. Members will bring anxieties and fears, expectations, and personal goals, their outside issues, and personal agendas. They may ask themselves: Will this be a safe place? Will it be a place where I can express myself without fear of retribution? Will it be boring? Fun? What will be expected of me? Will I be embarrassed or humiliated in front of everyone else? Will I make mistakes? These questions will undoubtedly be on the minds of your group members. It is your job as the group facilitator to make it clear from the beginning that this will be a safe, enjoyable, and meaningful experience in which members will be able to learn about themselves and each other in an environment that fosters growth.

What can you do to create this atmosphere? Begin with your own behaviors and appearance.

- Be energetic and positive
- Portray confidence
- Speak loud enough for your group to hear you
- Speak slowly and clearly (but not too slowly!)
- Move as you speak
- Speak with your hands and body not just your mouth. Be dramatic!
- Be organized and have the instructions for your activities memorized

- State the expectations for behavior early on
- Be willing to engage in the activities, accepting the risk of looking silly

In addition to your own appearance and behaviors, certain activities will help create the tone for your group. The Beginning Group Activities are aimed at creating a safe, fun environment where group bonding can begin to take place. These activities will help your group find its unique identity and create an individual culture with experiences that are all their own! Many of these activities are designed to be used throughout the group's sessions and sometimes beyond!

Group Handshake

During my first job as a school psychologist, I worked with a fifth grade student who had difficulties connecting with others. One day, we decided to make up our own handshake, one that only we would know. Each time we met after that we added a new part to the handshake. By the end of the school year, the handshake, which now looked more like some outrageous dance, lasted for nearly 2 minutes. The handshake created a unique, personal connection between me and the student and created a solid groundwork for the therapeutic relationship to develop. By having your group create its own handshake, it can begin developing its own unique identity right away.

Target Group: Any size

Size of Group: Any age

Props: None

Objectives

Activity Goal: Creating group cohesion, bonding, and identity. The longer the group is together, the more impact this activity has the potential to make.

Main FVC Connection: Be Here

Key to Success Connections: Behavioral control, building positive relationships

Facilitator Guidelines

Introduction/Metaphor

I like to introduce this activity by drawing a comparison to athletes who have their own celebratory handshakes. To introduce the activity, you could say something like, "Maybe you've noticed teams or athletes who have their own unique gestures or handshakes with their teammates. Clubs, fraternities, and sororities also have their own secret handshakes. Why do they create these handshakes? Generally they create a bond, make them feel special and unique and part of something bigger than they are." Beginning early in the group's experience, let the participants know that, as a group, they will be creating a secret handshake that will "grow" over time.

The Action

By drawing numbers or counting off participants, organize the group in a random order. The first person will create the first step in the handshake. The next person will create the next step. During each successive session, another group member adds a new move to this continually developing handshake. By the end of the group, the handshake will likely have become a dance!

Variation 1

Use the tenets of the FVC as the basis for the handshake. For example, have the first step of the handshake represent Be Here, the second step Be Safe, and so on (or whatever the components are for your group's FVC). Start again with the first tenet once you've gotten through them all. This variation works best with a higher-functioning group.

Variation 2

Have the group work in pairs to create a handshake. Reconvene the group. Have each pair teach its handshake to the rest of the group. If the group is not too large, you can combine these handshakes into one group handshake.

Debriefing

I generally don't debrief this activity; however, facilitators should keep in mind that the Group Handshake helps groups begin to create a sense of identity.

Question for When the Focus Is on Behavioral Control

- How did you come up with your part of the handshake?

Questions for When the Focus Is On Building Positive Relationships

- How did you and your partner work together to develop the handshake? Did you have to compromise?

Seeds of Change

Plants are constant reminders about the need to focus on goals. Without attention and vigilance, they won't survive. This activity is ripe for metaphors (pun intended). It translates well to themes of change and growth, working towards goals, and learning how to take care of ourselves, others, and our environment. This activity begins during an early session in a group's time together and should be revisited frequently.

Target Group: Any age range

Size of Group: Any size group as long as membership has been stable and will last at least one month.

Props: plant pots, planting soil, flower/plant seeds, tool to scoop and pat dirt, paper, and writing utensils.

Objectives

Activity Goal: Create a focus on personal goals and growth

Main FVC Connections: Be Here, Speak Your Truth (Members must put goals into words and be ready to discuss how they are progressing.)

Keys to Success Connections: Emotional awareness, behavioral control

Facilitator Guidelines

Introduction/Metaphor

If the focus is on personal change, the facilitator can ask, "Does personal change happen quickly or slowly?" In gardening, as in life, we sow seeds, water our plants, and weed our gardens. I often introduce this activity by reading and discussing the following quote: "It is the height of absurdity to sow little but weeds in the first half of one's lifetime and expect to harvest a valuable crop in the second half" ("It is the height," 2004).

The Action

Each group member receives a plant pot, which they should decorate and personalize.

Ask participants to write at least one goal that they would like to accomplish during their time in the group.

After making sure members have written an appropriate goal, have each member place his or her goal in the pot and cover it with soil.

Group members should then plant their own seeds.

Members will be in charge of watering their seeds and caring for their plants as they grow. This will be an ongoing metaphorical reminder to "feed and water" their goals with positive choices and behaviors. Facilitators can check in with group members each time they meet to discuss the progress of their plant and their goals.

Debriefing

The debriefing of this activity may happen over the course of the group's time together as the seedlings grow (or fail to thrive). When the seeds are first planted, the debriefing can consist of a brainstorming session about caring for the plants and "growing" goals by following the same principles. For each debriefing, facilitators should connect the process of growing the plant to the member's goals.

Questions for When the Focus Is on Emotional Awareness

- How do you feel about the progress of your plant? How about the progress of your goals?

- How does it feel to be responsible for another life?

Questions for When the Focus Is on Behavioral Control

- What are you doing to make sure your plant survives? Are you doing the same for yourself and your goals?

- Is your strategy successful?

- What do you need to change in order to make your plant healthier? How about making yourself healthier?

Tribal Names

Use this activity with a group that will be together for an extended period of time (at least several sessions).

Target Group: Any group old enough to understand the concept and mature enough to take it seriously

Size of Group: Maximum of about 20

Props: Pieces of paper with everyone's name and one bag or container to hold the papers

Objectives

Activity Goal: Group cohesion and bonding, developing observation skills and helping participants focus on the actions of others (as opposed to only themselves)

Main FVC Connections: Be Here (Using powers of observation helps bring members into the here and now), Speak Your Truth (Group members have the opportunity to express opinions through the task of giving names to their peers), Hear the Truth (Participants gain insight as to how they are viewed by others through the names they are given.)

Keys to Success Connection: Building positive relationships

Facilitator Guidelines

Preparation

Before the group begins, write each member's name on separate pieces of paper, fold them, and put them in a bag or other container. If you don't have all the names ahead of time or are unsure of who will actually show up, have members write their own names on a piece of paper as they enter group. Fold these pieces of paper once you collect them and place them in the container.

Introduction/Metaphor

Explain to group members that in many Native American cultures, names reflect the person's personality or characteristic actions. Names could be subject to change based on a person's actions. Tell your group that they will be giving each other tribal names. The names should reflect something that describes the person or his or her actions in the group.

The Action

Collect in a container all the slips of paper with the group members' names.

Tell participants about Native American tribal names and how they are earned. Indicate that your group will be just like a tribe and that each group member will receive a tribal name.

Have each member pick a name from the bag. If members select their own names, they should fold the paper, return it to the bag, and pick a new name. Make sure members don't share whose name they have!

Tell participants that each group member will observe the person whose name they picked for the remainder of the day (or over several sessions if the group format is short sessions) and create a tribal name for this person. Emphasize that the names should be appropriate and highlight positive aspects of that person.

At the end of the day (or second day if the group will be long term), the group members will reveal who they were watching, what name they have chosen for that person and why.

Encourage the group to refer to the other members by their tribal names during the group's time together. The tribal name can be adjusted to incorporate behaviors that may come after the initial naming.

Debriefing

Questions for When the Focus Is on Emotional Awareness

- How do you feel about the name you were given? Is it accurate?

Questions for When the Focus Is on Behavioral Control

- What does your tribal name say about your actions so far? Is it a name you hope to keep or one that you hope will change? What do you need to do to keep it (or change it)?

Questions for When the Focus Is on Positive Relationships

- How did you come up with the name you gave out?
- What was it like to have to observe someone else while they didn't know you were watching them?
- What was it like to be observed without knowing exactly who was watching you?

Listen Up

This is an excellent activity to get a distractible group focused quickly. It is one of my absolute favorite activities. I learned it by being an unwitting victim of someone else's fun--and long before I discovered experiential counseling! This activity is particularly difficult for impulsive individuals as the quickest answer is often incorrect. To be "successful" at outwitting the facilitator, participants must manage these impulses and discriminate between essential and nonessential information.

Target Group: Any group old enough to understand the purpose of the activity

Size of Group: No more than about 30 participants

Props: None

Objectives

Activity Goal: Behavioral control and focus

Main FVC Connection: Be Here (The challenge of outwitting the facilitator brings participants into the moment.)

Keys to Success Connection: Behavioral control

Facilitator Guidelines

Introduction/Metaphor

Introduce this activity by questioning the attention span, focus, or listening skills of the group in a tongue-in-cheek sort of way. Indicate that since you don't think they are focused, you would like to conduct a little "test" of their listening skills.

The Action

Tell the group that you will say a word and then ask group members to repeat the word five times, speaking it along with you. Tell the group that you will ask a question and they are to answer out loud as quickly as possible.

Check for understanding. You might ask group members to repeat the rules, or you can ask if any of them know the test. (If you have someone who has clearly done this activity before, you can ask this person to not give away the rest.)

Tell them that the first word is *silk*. Say, "Ready...set.... Silk, silk, silk, silk, silk" followed immediately by "What do cows drink?" Most people will confidently respond "Milk!" after which you will share with them that cows generally drink water. Now, express some mock concern about how poorly they seem to listen and note that you have another word for them.

The second word is *most*. Instruct the group to repeat this word five times with you. Once they repeat it with you, ask, "What do you put in a toaster?" Many people will answer "toast," though some participants will have caught on and after some hesitation correctly answer "bread." Point out that most people do, in fact, put bread in their toaster (unless they like burnt toast).

Acknowledge the group's improvement and let them know you want to repeat the activity with one more word to make sure they are all "with" you.

The third word is *spot.* Have the group repeat this five times, and ask them, "What do you do at a green light?" Many people will say "stop" at which point you inform them that they should "go" at a green light and that you will certainly avoid driving behind them when they get their license!

Debriefing

Questions for When the Focus Is On Behavioral Control

- What happened just now when you found yourself "acting without thinking?" What happens in your life when you act without thinking?

- How important is focus for this activity? How important is focus in real life?

- Is it difficult to figure out what is important information in life versus what is not important? Do you ever get "sidetracked" by the less important things in life and lose your focus on the most important things?

Trigger Finger*

Be sure to practice the Trigger Finger gesture before doing this activity with a group. You have to make the movement look easy!

Target Group: Any

Size of Group: 2 to 30

Props: None

Objectives

Activity Goal: Maintaining focus and attention

Main FVC Connection: Be Here (Once you've got the participants trying this, trust me…they can't focus on anything else!)

Keys to Success Connection: Behavioral control

Facilitator Guidelines

Introduction/Metaphor

As the facilitator, you might want to launch this activity by saying something like the following: "It's important for us to make sure our minds and bodies are working together today. This next activity will help me see if that's the case with this group."

The Action

Have your group stand in a circle.

Ask the participants to point with their left index finger at someone standing across from them in the circle. Since everyone in this group is pretty cool, have participants give that person a thumbs up with their right thumbs. While still pointing at the person across from them, participants should say, "You're cool!"

Demonstrate the Trigger Finger maneuver to your group, insisting that no one try this until they've watched you. You and the participants start from the same position with your left index finger pointing ahead and your right thumb pointing thumbs up. The maneuver is to switch finger gestures from one hand to the next: The left pointer finger comes in as the left thumb goes up while the right thumb goes down and the right index finger points out. Sounds easy, right? Try switching back and forth a few times!

---

*The first time I did this activity was at the National Challenge Course Symposium in Boulder, Colorado.

Debriefing

For me, this activity is about getting the brain and body working together. When our actions and thoughts match, things tend to go smoothly. When our actions and thoughts are in conflict, trouble is sure to follow.

Questions for When the Focus Is on Behavioral Control

- Was this activity difficult? Was it harder than it looked? Why?
- What happens when your actions and thoughts don't match up?
- Did your thoughts and actions match up better with practice?
- When you found it difficult, did you give up or keep trying?

Bus Driver

Many of us may remember playing this game in second grade...enough said! This activity can be used to launch into a discussion about listening, attention, or focus.

Target Group: Best with younger groups, as many older kids and adults may be familiar with this activity

Size of Group: Fewer than 20 participants

Props: None

Objectives

Activity Goal: Practicing focus and listening skills

Main FVC Connections: Be Here (Participants can get taken up with counting even as you speak), Speak Your Truth (This activity affords participants the opportunity to take a small risk in answering the question at the end.)

Keys to Success Connection: Behavioral control

Facilitator Guidelines

Introduction/Metaphor

You can introduce this activity by questioning—in a tongue-in-cheek sort of way—the attention span, focus, or listening skills of the group. Indicate that since you don't think they are focused, you want to conduct a "little test" of their listening skills.

The Action

Before starting this activity, you should tell the correct answer to one member of the group. Tell that member to listen, as you will state that "You" are driving the bus. Ask this member to keep the answer secret until the end of the game. At the end of the game, the other participants may not believe you began the introduction with the fact that "you" are driving the bus. Having a witness helps convince them!

Begin your story by saying, "So, you are driving a bus."

Continue your story by telling how many people get on and off at each bus stop. For example, you might say, "At the first stop, four people get on. At the next stop, three get on but two get off." Continue the story this way for several more bus stops. The students will be busily adding and subtracting in their head.

At the end, ask the group, "So, who was driving the bus?" Your accomplice will likely be the only one who knows the correct answer. Make sure they don't give it away!

After watching your group members suffer for a little while, you can tell them who was driving, and your accomplice can attest that you really did tell them that they were the bus drivers!

Debriefing

Questions for When the Focus Is on Behavioral Control

- Why did you miss the most relevant information and end up focusing on the less relevant information? Does this happen in real life? What is the result?

- How can we help ourselves focus on the real important stuff rather than the less important stuff in our lives?

- What are some things that distract you from the most important things in your life?

Line Up by Number 1.0*

For facilitators, this is a good activity to observe group dynamics in action. Watch for emerging leaders as well as those who seem to distance themselves from leadership roles.

Target Group: This activity is best used with higher-functioning groups; however, it can be modified and used with virtually any group at any time. (See below for variations on this activity).

Size of Group: 6 to 20

Props: Blindfolds (optional)

Objectives

Activity Goal: Practice group cooperation

Main FVC Connections: Be Here (This activity requires all group members to participate in the solution). Be Safe (If blindfolds are used, all group members must take care to keep the blindfolded members safe.)

Keys to Success Connections: Emotional awareness, behavioral control, positive interpersonal relationships

Facilitator Guidelines

Introduction/Metaphor

For the basic version of this activity, there is no introduction, just a launch into the action.

The Action

When your participants arrive for their first group session, simply tell them to "line up by number" or "line up in number order." You will be met with curious expressions and demands for more information. By refusing to provide any further information, the group members will eventually get the message that they are to determine what "line up by number" actually means. Line up by birthdays? height? or in random order? I have witnessed many solutions!

Once group members have followed your instructions and placed themselves in a line, ask someone to explain the criteria they used to complete the task. They should stay in the line they've created when answering your question.

Ask them to line up by number once again. The groups can use different systems by which to rank the group.

Of course, if the group needs help in setting up a new line, you can also offer them other criteria by which to line up! Some typical criteria include birthdates, ages (choose this

---

*An early version of this activity appears in Rohnke, K. (1984). *Silver Bullets*. Covington, GA: Project Adventure. It appears under the name Chronological Lineup.

one wisely), alphabetical order by first name or last name or even middle name, or numerical order by distance from home, that is by how close or far they live from the spot in which they are standing. Be creative! You can also vary some other aspects of this activity.

From this point, you can extend the activity and ask participants to divide into groups or pairs. For example, you can create pairs by having group members at one end of the end of the line walk to the other end of the line so that, each group member is facing another. You can also simply split the line in half at the midpoint to create two groups, or you can count off group members and divide as needed.

Variations on the Action

Take note that most of these variations should not be done when you are first meeting a group as they are somewhat more complex and require that the group has demonstrated that they can work well together.

Variation 1. Don't allow participants to speak.

Variation 2. Blindfold half the participants.

Variation 3. Blindfold all but one of the participants.

Variation 4. Blindfold everybody (but not the facilitators!).

Variation 5. Time the effort and have the group try to beat its personal record.

Debriefing

Questions for When the Focus Is on Emotional Awareness

- How did you feel when given such vague directions? How did you react to that? Are you someone who needs things to be "black and white" or can you deal with things not being exactly spelled out for you?

Question for When the Focus Is on Behavioral Control

- How did you react to the directions?

Questions for When the Focus Is on Positive Relationships

- As a group, how did you decide which criteria to use?
- Did anyone emerge as a leader during this activity? How? Why?
- Did you feel you were able to participate in creating the solution?

If using variations that deprive participants of certain senses, you might ask:

- How did not being able to see or talk impact the process and outcome of the activity?

Character Card FVC

At a leadership camp several summers ago, I began using the GivaGeta Character Cards to create the FVC. My co-facilitator Mike Kakalow and I have continued to mold the process ever since. This activity has become a standard activity each year we run the program. Jim Cain of Team Work & Team Play and Jim Cantoni, co-founder of GivaGeta, created the GivaGeta Character Cards as part of the collection called The World's Kindest Playing Cards. You can find out more about Jim Cain at his website Team Work & Team Play (www.teamworkandteamplay.com). Jim Cantoni's website is www.givageta.com.

Target Group: Any

Size of Group: Maximum of 30

Props: Character and Debriefing Words (see p. 467) or GivaGeta Character Cards, sticky notes, and writing utensils

Objectives

Activity Goal: Creating the FVC

Main FVC Connections: Be Here, Speak Your Truth, Hear the Truth. Since this activity is designed to help the group create the FVC, it should connect to all aspects of the FVC.

Keys to Success Connections: Behavioral control, building positive relationships

Facilitator Guidelines

Introduction/Metaphor

If you are using the GivaGeta Character Cards, note that each card has one large character word, several quotes relating to that word as well as a "Big Question." Each card has one of 12 possible character words. One card is blank. On this card, I often place a blank sticky note so that if participants choose to, they can add a characteristic that is not already included in the deck. You can begin the activity by introducing the cards and explaining the character words on each. Explain that these cards represent the characteristics successful groups need to have. Tell the group that they are to use the cards to decide which are the three (or four or five) most important characteristics of a successful group.

The Action

For this activity, divide your GivaGeta Character Cards deck into four smaller subsets, organizing by character words. Each subset of cards should have one each of the 12 character words and one blank card. On the blank card, place the blank sticky note.

Divide your larger group into smaller groups of up to five members. If you have more than four smaller groups, you will need more than one deck of cards. Give each smaller group one subset of the GivaGeta Character Cards and one writing utensil. For the first phase of the activity, have each group review the character words and decide on the three (or four or five) most important characteristics that the group will need to function well during their time together. The group should then choose these character cards.

Once each group has chosen its cards, reconvene the larger group to discuss each subgroup's choices. Have group members spread out the cards their group has chosen. Each smaller group should have one member tell the group why they chose the cards they did. Most likely, there will be some overlap in choices.

For the second phase of the activity, ask the entire group to come to a consensus as to which are the five most important characteristics. These character traits will serve as the basis for the FVC. When debriefing future activities, you can use the cards by simply placing them at the center of a circle at the onset of the debriefing.

Debriefing

In all likelihood, since there is often a great deal of discussion during this activity, you will be debriefing as you go. If you choose to debrief this activity at the end, you can focus on the process involved in creating the FVC from the cards. Note that the smaller groups will often become fairly attached to the cards they have chosen. The second phase of this activity can be fairly intense and takes some time.

Questions for When the Focus Is on Behavioral Control

- Did you have to compromise to accomplish the task? Was that difficult for you?
- Did you have to "negotiate?" What does that really mean? What skills does it require? When else in your life have you had to use these negotiation skills?

Questions for When the Focus Is on Positive Relationships

- How did you come to a consensus within the smaller groups as to which were most important?
- How did the whole group come to a consensus? What was difficult about this process?

Learning Style FVC

This activity is simply an engaging way to get your group members acclimated to the behavioral expectations the group will have during their time together. I use this activity with groups that I have never met but plan to be with for at least a full day or a few sessions. While presented differently, this was the very first FVC I learned at my very first Project Adventure workshop.

Target Group: Any age group

Size of Group: Any size

Props: None

Objectives

Activity Goal: Set behavioral expectations for group activities

Main FVC Connections: Be Here, Be Safe, Speak Your Truth, Hear the Truth, Have Fun

Keys to Success Connections: Emotional awareness, behavioral control

Facilitator Guidelines

Introduction/Metaphor

Survey your group about what learning style suits them best. You can ask them, "Is it auditory (hearing), visual (seeing), or kinesthetic (doing)?" while briefly explaining each. Introduce the concept of the FVC (see pp. 21–22): "Since we have many different learning styles in this group, we are going to learn the FVC using all three learning styles: visual, auditory, and kinesthetic."

The Action

Have your group stand in a circle.

Introduce the activity by explaining that the FVC is important to the success of the group and that they will be learning the elements of the FVC by using all the different learning styles: auditory (hearing), visual (seeing), and kinesthetic (doing).

Explain that you will show them a gesture that is to represent a commitment of the FVC (i.e., Be Here, Be Safe, Speak Your Truth, Hear the Truth). Simultaneously perform the gesture while yelling that commitment.

The gestures I use are:

Be Here: Jump about a foot forward with both feet while pointing to the ground.

Be Safe: Yell "Safe" while showing the baseball umpire movement for safe.

Speak Your Truth: Lean forward, cupping your hands around your mouth to create a makeshift megaphone.

Hear the Truth: Lean forward and cup your hands behind your ears as if trying to hear something quiet.

After demonstrating the gestures representing each commitment, tell the group that you would like them on the count of three to join you in saying and demonstrating the commitments. Count to three and have the group yell the commitment and perform the sign along with you. Make sure they are loud (unless you are using a library).

As a variation on the activity, to launch the group into the gesture for each commitment, have a member of the group count to three in a different language.

Follow this pattern for all the commitments except for Have Fun. The group must determine what sign will represent Have Fun. Once the group does, invite one group member to lead the rest of the group in demonstrating the movement and sound for Have Fun.

Debriefing

Generally, I don't debrief this activity other than checking for clarity and questions before moving on.

OK Tag

In this game, each participant tries to "tag" the others by getting them to glance at their half-hidden OK signs. I was introduced to this ingenious game in college. My roommates and I had a yearlong game going. After becoming pretty good at avoiding being "caught," we got quite creative. My favorite episode was when my roommate Jim taped a small piece of paper to the driver-side handle of my car door. As I bent down to look at it before getting into my car, I saw a picture of the OK sign on the paper with "Gotcha!" written under it! Little did I know, this game also appears as Basic Killer in *Silver Bullets* (Rohnke, 1984).

OK Tag is an ongoing, open-ended game more than an on-site activity. It can begin at any point in a group's time together and can literally last through the group or beyond (or at least as long as the members last)!

Target Group: Any group, teens and older, that will be together for an extended period of time

Size of Group: Any size

Props: None

Objectives

Activity Goal: Encourage fun and bonding among group members

Main FVC Connection: Be Here (This activity actually brings the fun of group to the outside world.)

Keys to Success Connections: Behavioral control, build and maintain positive relationships

Introduction/Metaphor

You can have fun introducing this game. You might want to present it as a sinister, ongoing game that will plague the members for the rest of their shared time together—whether it's group time, school time, or social time!

The Action

To start, show participants the OK Tag gesture by making a circle with your pointer and thumb (like the OK symbol). Hold this symbol below your waist.

Explain that each player is trying to get another player to look at his or her hand gesture. You might ask someone else (who knows the game) to help demonstrate. If they look at your OK sign, you've got them! If they don't look, you didn't get them.

Let participants know that this can be an ongoing game.

Have group members start the game. Once group members have been playing for awhile (during group, in the halls, at parties), they begin to get more creative with their OK symbols as members become more wary...almost paranoid!

Debriefing

I generally don't debrief this activity. I allow it to develop a life of its own among the group members. At times, with less-mature group members, the activity may become overused or played at inappropriate times (such as during math class). There is also the risk of having "sore winners" and "sore losers." Address these issues if they arise.

The Body*

This activity is about creating a physical and metaphorical representation of the group and its behavioral expectations, the FVC. (See pp. 21–22 for a description of the FVC.)

The Body activity has two phases. During the first phase, the group brainstorms two lists of behaviors, one that details the behaviors expected of the group members and another that lists behaviors they hope to keep out of the group. The second part of the activity involves one group member drawing the body by tracing the outline of a volunteer group member onto paper. The group members will write down the desired behaviors inside the traced figure and the undesired behaviors outside of it.

Target Group: Higher-functioning pre-teen through adult participants

Size of Group: 20 or fewer

Props: Large pieces of paper (large enough to trace people on), markers, flip charts or large boards, paper and pencil or pens for individuals or subgroups to write notes

Objectives

Activity Goals: Promote an understanding of the FVC and help groups create one

Main FVC Connections: This activity is about creating the FVC and, therefore, connects to all FVC concepts.

Keys to Success Connections: Emotional awareness, building positive relationships

Introduction/Metaphor

Begin with a discussion about what community means, such as being part of a larger group, living and working together and striving to reach common goals. (Reviewing titles on community can help you with this. One excellent one is "From Group to Community" by Scott Peck, which appears in *Gold Nuggets: Reading for Experiential Education* (Schoel & Stratton, 1990).

You might begin by explaining that all communities employ a set of behavioral norms to promote their members' safety and happiness. Typically, these norms are known as rules and laws. Introduce the FVC and emphasize what it has in common with and how it differs from rules and laws.

The Action

Have the group brainstorm two lists of behaviors: one that details the expected behaviors and another that lists behaviors that should be kept out of the group. Facilitators may

---

*I learned a similar activity called The Being at an advanced adventure-based counseling workshop at Project Adventure. The activity appeared in the workshop manual and was created as a way of "physicalizing" the FVC. According to Jim Schoel, the idea came from Barry Orms, Buddy Orange, and Lou Polese of Boys Harbor in New York City.

want to create smaller subgroups to better accomplish these tasks. Each can be assigned to create one of the two lists, or both groups can spend some time on making each list.

Reconvene the larger group and have each subgroup share what they came up with.

During the discussion, summarize the information as best you can, combining similar statements such as "Be kind" and "Be nice." In the end, you should have a list of expected behaviors and a list of behaviors the group wishes to keep out of their time together. These can be compiled on a flip chart, whiteboard, or notepad.

Ask the group to start the second part of the activity: tracing the outline of one volunteer group member onto the large tracing paper. Carefully monitor the appropriateness and safety of behavior during tracing! The outline on the paper will be the Body.

Once this is accomplished, have group members write the expected behaviors for the group inside the outline of the body outline. They should write unwanted behaviors outside the traced outline of the body. All members should take part in this activity.

The Body can be further decorated and should be given an actual name. Encourage group members to refer to The Body by its name.

All members should sign the paper containing the tracing of the Body. Their signatures will be their commitment to the behavioral expectations described. The Body should be present at every group meeting.

Variation 1

Have the group draw another object, making sure there is a clear boundary marking inside and outside of the object. One creative group I worked with drew a fish tank. Inside the fish tank, they each drew a fish with their own name and one of the expected behaviors. Outside the tank, they listed all of the behaviors to be avoided during group time.

Variation 2

Using a blank Community Puzzle (available from Training Wheels, http://www.training-wheels.com), have group members design puzzle pieces that contain each of the behavioral expectations. If you will be working with a group for a long period of time, you may wish to leave some pieces blank to add new behavior norms at a later time, if the group adopts them.

Variation 3

Depending on the group, you may skip the brainstorming phase and give them the FVC concepts to write down inside the tracing of the body. You can discuss what the tenets of the FVC mean to them. (Chapter 3 gives more information about the FVC.)

Debriefing

Typically, this activity does not require any debriefing as it is designed to address emotions, behaviors, and relationships during the activity.

Group Power Clap

A power clap is a multisensory affirmation that can be used throughout the group members' time together. It is simply a single, synchronized clap given by the entire group when something good happens. Typically, one member will count to three (in whatever language they wish). On three, the entire group claps once, loudly, together. For really good things, you may want more power claps.

Target Group: Any

Size of Group: Any

Props: None

Objectives

Activity Goal: Learn a tool to communicate with members, create positive messages, and promote group bonding

Main FVC Connections: Be Here (Celebrating accomplishments keeps the group in the moment.), Speak the Truth (Members are given an opportunity to recognize individual and group efforts.)

Keys to Success Connections: Emotional awareness, positive interpersonal relationships

Facilitator Guidelines

Introduction/Metaphor

You can begin by discussing how it feels to be appreciated or recognized. You may want to survey your group for stories of when members were appreciated or recognized. You can then introduce the Power Clap and explain that it is meant to be a celebratory gesture.

The Action

Explain that the power clap is a single, synchronized clap given by the entire group when something good happens. Typically, one member will count to three (in whatever language they wish). On three, the entire group claps once loudly together.

Demonstrate the clap.

Explain that for really good things, you may want more power claps. In this case, for example, you can call out, "a power clap of three." In this case, the counter counts down, and the group claps hard together three times.

Facilitators can demonstrate by giving an example: (i.e., "Johnny, you did an awesome job on that element. How about a power clap of three for him? Uno, dos, tres!").

Explain that members can also call for power claps (i.e., "I thought we worked like a real team...power clap of five!"). It can happen after activities as part of debriefing (especially to close the debriefing) or when an individual accomplishes something that this person felt was challenging.

Debriefing

The power clap is often used as part of a debriefing and does not require any separate debriefing. It connects with the Keys to Success in that this activity can be a powerful way of affirming the value of the group's members. Affirming others, or a group as a whole, can be an essential, often overlooked ingredient in the recipe for successful relationships.

FVC Team Memory*

Use this activity to ask your group to brainstorm the behaviors that should be expected during the time the group is together. You can ask them, "How should we treat each other?" The answers create the groundwork for the FVC. If you have already created the FVC, you can use the behavioral expectations designated by your FVC for this activity. If you need more behaviors for this activity than you have listed in your FVC, you can have your group break down the commitments into more specific behaviors.

Target Group: Higher-functioning groups, generally middle school aged and older

Size of Group: 6 to 25 participants

Props: Index cards or GivaGeta Character Cards, pen or pencil, and two boundary markers such as webbing or rope

Objectives

Activity Goal: Promote an understanding of the FVC

Main FVC Connections: All aspects of the FVC, but especially: Be Here (Members must stay focused on the action, even when it's not their turn. If they don't, it will quickly become apparent to the group.), Speak Your Truth, and Hear the Truth (At some point, most groups realize that the person turning over the cards should be communicating with the rest of the group behind the starting line.)

Keys to Success Connections: Emotional awareness, behavioral control, and building positive relationships

Introduction/Metaphor

Ask your group "How should we treat each other?" Brainstorm the behaviors that should be expected during the time the group is together. "Remember the Memory game you played as a kid, where cards are placed face down and you turn them over two at a time to find matches? Well, here's the group version of that game!"

The Action

Have your group brainstorm behavioral expectations

Or spell out behavioral expectations based on each of the FVC tenets. For example, if you have Be Safe on your contract, you can ask what behaviors does that include? Be respectful, have self-control, be considerate and so on.

---

* Several years ago at the National Challenge Course Symposium in Boulder, Colorado, I learned a version of this activity called Team Memory from Michelle Cummings of Training Wheels. It appears in her book *Playing With a Full Deck* (2007). A similar version of this activity called Character Cards appears in the book *Essential Staff Training Activities* (2009) by Jim Cain, Claire-Marie Hannon, and Dave Knobbe.

As the group members share the their thoughts with you, write each behavior on two separate index cards. You should end up with a pair of matching index cards listing the expected behaviors. (For example, "raise your hand" would be written twice, once on each index card.) You may want to solicit group members' help in writing down the thoughts, so you don't get bogged down.

Once you have gotten enough behaviors (you determine what "enough" is but you should have no fewer than five behaviors written on ten cards), the game can be set up and played.

Designate a starting line about 20 feet from the playing area.

Have the group stand behind the starting line.

Shuffle the index cards. In the playing area, arrange the cards with the writing face down in a rectangular or square shape, as you would in the classic memory game cards.

Explain the rules of the game. Instruct the group that one at a time, members will go from the starting line to the playing area and flip over two cards. If the cards are a match, participants can continue flipping over two cards at a time until they don't get a match. The participant should bring the pairs back to the group. If the cards are not a match, participants must turn them face down again and return to the starting point. Only one person may be in the playing area at any given time. All other members must stay behind the starting line. Each person must have a turn before any group member goes twice. This will create an order that is repeated throughout the challenge. Give the group little or no time to plan before their first attempt.

You can offer the group a time limit to accomplish this task, such as 4 minutes. You can also simply time the group to establish a baseline time to beat on successive attempts.

Most groups will not get all of the matches in the allotted time. If you have a particularly high-functioning group, you may want to decrease the time limit or erase it all together and simply see how long it takes the group to accomplish the task.

After the first try, debrief with the group and offer them an opportunity to improve their performance on a second attempt. This time, allow them some planning time. You can determine how many attempts the group will get.

Variation 1

You can play Team Memory with any topic, not just the FVC.

Variation 2

Accomplish the task without speaking.

Debriefing

During this activity, I often find that some team members work harder than others. That can trigger frustration in the ones working hardest. If you observe this, address it during the debriefing. Find out how people responded emotionally and how that translated into behavior.

Questions for When the Focus Is on Emotional Awareness

- Did you believe you could meet the goal time? Why or why not?

- How did you feel knowing the time was ticking away?
- How did you feel during this activity?

Questions for When the Focus Is on Behavioral Control

- How did you respond to the time pressure as individuals and as a group?
- What did you do that helped your group succeed?
- What did you learn after the first attempt? How did you use that knowledge?

Questions for When the Focus Is on Positive Relationships

- How did you work together to accomplish the group goal?
- Did anything interfere with your ability to work as a team?
- How was communication important during this activity?
- Did anyone seem to take charge?

Virtual Photo Album

This is a great large-group closing activity, with each member sharing one mental snapshot that they have gathered that day. In smaller groups, members can often share more than one snapshot. This activity sets up a wonderful closing at the end of each session. It can also be used as a termination activity for the group.

Target Group: Any age range

Size of Group: 24 or fewer participants. In groups larger than 25 or so, the activity becomes cumbersome.

Props: None

Objectives

Activity Goals: Review group activities and debrief

Main FVC Connections: Be Here (The photo album helps members stay in the moment throughout the day, as they must consciously work to mentally record information images, feelings, and things learned throughout the day. Facilitator reminders throughout the session help!), Speak Your Truth and Hear the Truth (Group members are given the opportunity to share salient aspects of the day with each other. What participants recall and choose to share can provide unique insights as to each member's motives and personality.)

Keys to Success Connections: Emotional awareness, behavioral control, building positive relationships

Introduction/Metaphor

You can begin this activity by saying, "When we go on a vacation or a journey, we usually bring a camera to capture visual images that we want to remember. Today we'll be taking a journey as well. We don't know what will happen so we must be ready at all times to capture the special moments. To do this, we will use our "mental cameras." These mental cameras have some important differences from the real cameras you bring on vacation. While those cameras only capture visual images, our mental cameras can capture images, feelings, and lessons learned. Throughout the day, I would like you to be taking mental pictures and recording things that happen, feelings you have, and lessons you learn. You will have the opportunity to share some of these mental photos later in the day as we create a virtual photo album."

The Action

Let participants know that the Action takes place throughout the day.

Remind them that at the end of the day, the group will create a virtual photo album by verbally sharing their mental snapshots.

Emphasize that snapshots should be shared with respect and attention to emotional safety. This is not an opportunity to make fun of each other or air grievances.

Debriefing

This activity is a debriefing. Below are some questions you can use during the activity to help group members connect their experiences to the Keys to Success.

Questions for When the Focus Is on Emotional Awareness

- Why do you think that particular experience stuck out to you?
- How did you feel when that happened?
- How do you think the other person felt when that happened?

Question for When the Focus Is on Behavioral Control

- What impact did that event have on the group?

Question for When the Focus Is on Positive Relationships

- Did that event help the group bond?

Place Card

If you have a fairly large group coming together for a first time and have everyone's name in advance of the first session, try this introduction activity! For several years, I facilitated a single-day indoor adventure workshop for middle school-aged kids at Manchester Community College in Connecticut. One year, I decided to try this activity since I had everyone's name ahead of time. I thought it would be a great way to immediately break up any pre-existing cliques and nudge the participants out of their comfort zones a bit. I used different colors and added numbers and letters to the cards to make dividing participants into random subgroups quick and easy later in the program. It worked like a charm!

For this activity, you must have the names of all participants ahead of the first group meeting.

Target Group: Teens or adults who don't yet know each other

Size of Group: Any size

Props: Oversized index cards or other cards to function as place cards, pen or marker to write down each group member's name

Objectives

Activity Goals: Introduce participants to fellow group members, begin practicing Keys to Success skills

Main FVC Connections: Be Here (What better way is there to bring members into the moment than place them in a situation to find and meet a specific person?), Speak Your Truth and Hear the Truth (Group members get to share information about themselves and hear about others.)

Keys to Success Connections: Emotional awareness, behavioral control, positive interpersonal relationships

Facilitator Guidelines

Preparation

Using oversized index cards, write one person's name on one side of a card and another person's name on the flip side. Create two identical versions of each card. For example, if you have written Mary Jones's name on one side of a card and Jim Smith's on the other, make sure you create a second identical card with Mary Jones's name on one side and Jim Smith's on the other. I write one name in one color and the other in a different color, making both cards exactly the same. The different color inks can be used to divide the group for other activities later on.

Introduction/Metaphor

This activity begins when you greet participants and instruct them to find the cards with their names on them. This activity can be coupled with other activities.

The Action

Place the cards on a table near the entrance of the area in which you will be facilitating. Each participant's name should be showing on a place card. For example, Mary's name should appear face up on one card, and Jim's name should appear face up on another.

As you greet participants, instruct them to find the card with their name on it.

Have them enter the room with their card and gather in a circle.

Once everyone has entered the room, instruct participants to find the person whose name is on the back of their card. Tell them that they should introduce themselves and find out some interesting facts about each other. You may want to give some groups (particularly younger groups) specific questions to ask or information to gather rather than leaving the conversations open-ended.

Have the group reconvene. If the group is small enough and time allows, have members introduce their partners and the information they've gathered about them.

Transition to Other Activities

This activity easily transitions into many other introductory activities.

- Use the color of place-card names as a basis for dividing your group into smaller subgroups. Use more than two colors of ink when writing names on the place cards to create criteria for dividing a large group into several subgroups.

- Include numbers on the place cards to set up subgroups for later activities. If you put the number 1, 2, 3, or 4 on each card, you can use the numbers to divide the group into four subsets for other activities, including See Ya (p. 202). To organize these activities, simply ask group members to get together with all the participants who have the same number on their place cards. Or ask group members to make smaller groups consisting of those with place cards containing each number 1 through 4 (that is, there should be one and only one of each number represented in the subgroup).

- Include letters or numbers on the place cards, writing them in different ink colors to give you additional criteria for creating different groupings later in the session. For example, when I run this activity, I may put one letter on each card, either A, B, C, or D. This gives me four groupings. If I write half of each group of letters in blue ink and the other half in red, I have eight groups.

- Use the place cards instead of gym spots, when setting the activity Left In (p. 212). If you include yourself in the activity, there will be the correct number of places designated by the cards.

Debriefing

This activity is about connecting with others and using basic social skills. When the group reconvenes, encourage people to speak loudly and clearly when sharing information about each other and about other members. Also, make it clear that it's OK for partners to ask each other about information they've forgotten or are unclear about but would like to share with the group.

Questions for When the Focus Is on Emotional Awareness

- Did anyone feel anxious coming into the group today? Do you feel differently now than when you first arrived? Why?
- Did anyone feel anxious when given the first task?
- Did this activity help you feel more comfortable?

Questions for When the Focus Is on Behavioral Control

- How did you go about finding the person on your card?
- How did you decide what questions to ask?

Questions for When the Focus Is on Positive Relationships

- What did you find out about your partner?
- Did you find anything that you and your partner have in common?

CHAPTER
9
Name Games

The first step in establishing a positive relationship with another person (Key to Success #3) is learning his or her name. I am amazed at how often the high school kids I have worked with didn't know their teachers' names half way through the school year! To me, it speaks volumes about the relationship between these students and their teachers.

In group work, especially when working with larger groups, facilitators often rely on nametags. While this may be necessary at times, I prefer to avoid using nametags whenever possible. In my opinion, they offer a convenient excuse to avoid learning the names of the group members, which, in turn, fosters superficial relationships. Some people claim that they have terrible memories for names; I am one of these people. However, it amazes me how quickly even I, through the use of games, can learn all of the names of a fairly large group of people.

When a group comes together, the members may or may not know each other's names. If they don't, then name games are a great place to start! If they do know each other, you can still use name games as introductory activities by varying the activities slightly. For example, you can use middle or last names or names backwards: such as my name, Ttocs.

The games listed in this section allow members to learn each other's names while starting to break down inhibitions. It is sometimes difficult for older kids, kids with emotional issues, and adults to let down their guard and allow themselves to be transported back to a time when they were children and less inhibited. It's possible that your participants have never had the opportunity to be that uninhibited child, growing up in an environment that forced them to be "adults" too quickly. For these individuals, dropping their defenses may be an extremely difficult task. These early activities can be very therapeutic. Often, when working with groups whose members may have emotional and behavioral difficulties, you may find yourself using name games, de-inhibitizers, and low-level challenges for longer than expected. I have facilitated groups that never moved past these types of activities. In general, the more inhibited the group members, the longer you will focus on these introductory activities. For most groups, however, these games will be a fun, engaging gateway into activities that pose greater challenges and provide more opportunities for personal growth and group development.

Name Whip

I first discovered this activity when attending my first introductory workshop on adventure-based counseling. I almost always use Name Whip as a preface to other names games such as Toss a Name, Group Juggle, Warp Speed; Love Those New Red Potatoes; Cross the Circle Names; Peek-a-Who; and Whamp 'Em.

Target Group: Any age group

Size of Group: No more than about 30

Props: None

Objectives

Activity Goal: Introduce group participants to one another and encourage members to learn each other's names. Begin practicing Keys to Success skills.

Main FVC Connection: Be Here

Keys to Success Connection: Establishing positive relationships

Facilitator Guidelines

Introduction/Metaphor

A Name Whip is simply an activity where all participants take turns stating their names. Generally, this happens when everyone is standing in a circle early in the group's formation.

The Action

Have participants stand together in a circle and let them know you'd like each to state his or her name for the group to hear.

Ask one group member to state his or her name and then the next group member, moving around the circle each taking turns. Make sure that group members state their names loudly and clearly enough for the other participants to hear them. If needed, group members can ask for names to be repeated.

If the group members took turns around the circle in a clockwise direction, have them reverse it for a second go around, stating their names and taking turns in a counter-clockwise fashion around the circle. For larger groups, you may want to go around several times.

Encourage group members to remember as many of the names they hear as possible. To add a bit more fun and challenge to the activity, have group members state their names as quickly as possible when taking turns around the circle.

Debriefing

This activity generally does not require a debriefing.

Toss a Name, Group Juggle, Warp Speed

These three different, independent activities can be used separately but also work well in combination with one another. These activities can work as name games, but they can also be used later in the sequence of group activities as initiatives. Begin these activities with Name Whip.

Target Group: Any age group

Size of Group: No more than about 20 or so

Props: Small, soft or padded toss-able items (These are items that can be tossed without injuring other people, such as yarn balls and stuffed animals without hard parts.) Have as many toss-ables as there are participants in the group.

Objectives

Activity Goal: Introduce group participants to one another and encourage members to learn each other's names. Begin practicing Keys to Success skills.

Main FVC Connections: Be Here (Each of these activities calls for a heightened level of focused attention. The challenge portion tends to keep the attention of even the most distractible participants!), Be Safe (Any time items are being tossed, you must emphasize safe throwing methods to prevent participants from firing fast balls at each other. A fast-moving stuffed bear can still hurt!)

Keys to Success Connections: Emotional awareness, behavioral control

Facilitator Guidelines

Introduction/Metaphor for Toss a Name 1

As facilitator, introduce a toss-able item to the group. Explain that group members will be using the item in a name game. Toss the item to a group member (someone who is not to your immediate left or right) and call that person's name. That person should respond by thanking you by name and then tossing the item to someone else (again, not someone to the immediate left or right). The recipient thanks the thrower by name, and the toss-able continues around the group until everyone has gotten it. Make sure you receive it last.

Tell group members that they must remember who they received the toss-able from and who they sent it to. This pattern will establish a set order in the activity.

The Action of Toss a Name 1

Let the group know that you are starting the activity. Begin by lobbing the toss-able to a participant in the group.

Have group members move the toss-able around the group while calling out participants' names.

If it's a large group, I ask members to raise their hands or cross their arms after they've received and thrown the toss-able to indicate that they've already had their turn. Remind group members that they must remember whom they received from and tossed to. Make sure that you are the last one to receive the item.

Once the group has successfully created the pattern, go through it once again to reinforce it. You might press the group to complete the pattern of tosses more quickly or with fewer drops of the toss-able.

At this point, you can either move to the activity Toss a Name 2, Group Juggle (Version 1), or Warp Speed.

Introduction/Metaphor for Toss a Name 2

Put aside the first toss-able and introduce a second toss-able item. Explain to group members that this one will follow the established order of tosses, only in reverse. Each person will throw to the person they had previously received from. For example, if during Toss a Name 1, John threw to Betty, and Betty threw to Dave. Dave will now throw to Betty, and Betty to John.

Explain that this first toss-able had its pattern, but this new, second toss-able will travel in its own pattern in reverse of the first.

The Action of Toss a Name 2

Have the group practice with the second toss-able.

Make sure the group has the new, reversed order established by practicing it several times. Once they seem fairly secure with the new order, bring the first toss-able back into play. The goal is to have both toss-ables going around at the same time, one with the forward pattern and one with the reverse pattern.

See how long it takes group members to complete a cycle of both items. Allow the group several opportunities to improve upon their time.

Introduction/Metaphor for Group Juggle (Version 1)

Let members know that they are ready for a little more action. "Let's add a few more toss-ables! Keep passing them along and calling out your receiver's name."

The Action of Group Juggle

Following the sequence established in Toss a Name 1 (p. 87), prepare to toss in a new item while the original item is making its way through the group in its already established pattern.

As the first item goes to the first person then the second and third, throw a second item to the person to whom you threw the first item. That person continues by throwing it to the next person in the sequence. When the items return to you, simply keep them moving along the sequence.

You can add a third item and a fourth, fifth, or more items, until the group crumbles in laughter, unable to keep up with the items. Once you notice the group struggling to throw and catch multiple items, drop the items by your feet as they make their way back to you, ending the round.

Ask the group how many toss-ables the believe they can move around the group with no drops. Challenge the group to see if it can send each item around twice without dropping it. You can also set a time challenge for the group to complete a round or two within a certain time limit.

Allow the group several attempts (with planning in between) to improve upon their efforts. You can continue for a designated number of attempts or continue until they make an attempt in which their time does not improve.

Introduction/Metaphor for Group Juggle 2

Have each member choose a toss-able and stand in a circle. State that what goes up, of course, must come down. Instruct the group that when you say "go," they are to toss their item into the air (at least 3 feet higher than the tallest person's head) and try to catch a different item as it returns to earth. Tell them that if an item falls to the ground, it is to remain there until you tell them otherwise. Emphasize the need to be careful as many people will be moving at once to catch items while looking up.

The Action of Group Juggle 2

On your call, your participants will toss their items in the air and attempt to catch an item that is not theirs. On the first try, many items will end up on the ground. Count the number of items caught. Have your participants pick up the items that fell and divvy them up so that everyone has one (it doesn't have to be the one they started with). Give the group some time to create a plan that affords them the ability to catch more items than in Round One following the same rules. Can they catch all items on the second or third attempt?

Introduction/Metaphor for Warp Speed

After Toss a Name 1, time the group to see how long it takes the item to get back to the person who began with it. Inform the group how long it took and ask them to beat this time. After a few tries, tell them that you think they can do this in under 10 seconds (5 seconds for smaller groups, 20 for larger ones). You can also ask the group to set a goal for itself.

The Action of Warp Speed

Ask, "Who is with me?" Most likely, they'll be eager to accept the challenge you've set for them. Then, state the rules: "The object has to continue in the already established order, person to person, until it gets back to me, the person who launched it. You must continue to state the name of the person it's going to, and the item must leave your hands to go to someone else's." The group will eventually realize that they might be able to move—or members will ask if the participants have to stay in the same order they are currently in. The answer to that question is, "Staying in the same physical group order was not stated in the directions." The group may reorganize the circle, as long as the item goes through the same order of participants.

Variation

You can also transition from Group Juggle 1 into Warp Speed. After determining the highest number of items that went around the group successfully, try Warp Speed. You can also try using multiple toss-able items for Warp Speed.

Debriefing

Questions for When the Focus Is on Emotional Awareness

- Do you feel that you were able to share your thoughts and contribute to the solution?
- Are there times in your life when you have not felt "heard" by others?
- How did it feel to have to perform with the time pressure? How do you perform under time pressures in other areas of your life?
- How did it feel to accomplish the goal (or not accomplish the goal)?

Questions for When the Focus Is on Behavioral Control

- Did certain members take the lead? Why?
- For those who felt stressed out by the pressure to accomplish the goal, how did it affect your performance? How does stress affect your performance in other aspects of your life?

Questions for When the Focus Is on Positive Relationships

- Did effective "teamwork" play a role in the group's success? How?
- What role did communication play in your group's success?
- How many of you can name each person in the group at this point?

Love Those New Red Potatoes*

This name game can be used following the Name Whip activity.

Target Group: Any age group

Size of Group: 8 to 25 people

Props: None

Objectives

Activity Goal: Learn the names of group members while having fun

Main FVC Connection: Be Here

Keys to Success Connection: Emotional awareness

Facilitator Guidelines

Introduction/Metaphor

Following Name Whip (p. 86), have your group circle up with you standing in the center of the circle.

The Action

Have the group go through the Name Whip activity a few times. Be sure to repeat several rounds with larger groups.

If someone speaks too quietly to hear, group members can ask them to repeat it louder.

Explain the rules of Love Those New Red Potatoes. Tell your group that the person in the middle will point and look directly at another group member standing in the circle (who we will refer to as the "appointed" person). The pointer will say one of four things: You, Me, Left, or Right. The appointed person must respond by stating the correct name of the person as requested, that is, if the person pointing says "You," the appointed person must say his or her own name. If the person in the middle says "Me," the appointed person should name the person in the middle of the circle. For the request "Left" or "Right," appointed persons should name the person to their left or right.

While the appointed person is trying to state the correct name, the person in the middle of the circle says "Love Those New Red Potatoes!" If the person in the center finishes before the appointed person states the correct name, the two switch places. The new person in the center continues the game in the same fashion. If, however, the appointed person says the name before the person in the center finishes exclaiming "Love Those New Red Potatoes," the appointed person is safe, and the person in the center continues the process of challenging group members until he or she manages to get out of the center.

---

*I have seen this game played many ways with different names over the years. One version is called Bumpity Bump Bump and appears in *Cowstails and Cobras II* (Rohnke, 1989).

Either select a group member to enter the center of the circle and start the activity or begin with yourself in the center. If you start, you can afford the group a few practice rounds where no one will have to replace you in the center. This helps solidify the instructions.

It is sometimes necessary to limit the number of turns the person in the center can have to keep the game moving. Continue the game until folks seem to have a firm grasp of each other's names or until everyone seems ready to move on.

Debriefing

As with many name games, don't feel that you have to do much, if any, debriefing for this activity. However, if you choose to, the following are some interesting topics to discuss.

Questions for When the Focus Is on Emotional Awareness

- Did anyone feel frustrated when they were in the center? How did you deal with it?
- How did your response to frustration compare to how you usually deal with frustration?
- Did anyone experience confusion during this activity? How did you react to it? How did you make things clearer for yourself?

Questions for When the Focus Is on Behavioral Control

- What strategies did you use in the center to get out?
- What strategies did you use to stay out of the center?

See 'Em Say 'Em Names

This is a very simple name game when there's not much time for a more in-depth activity. Thanks to Nikki Currie-Huggard who taught me this activity while we were working at the Pine Lakes Ropes Course in Bristol, Connecticut.

Target Group: Any age group

Size of Group: 4 to 30 (However, the activity may take too long with larger groups.)

Props: None

Objectives

Activity Goal: Allow group members to get acquainted and learn each other's names

Main FVC Connections: Be Here

Keys to Success Connection: Emotional awareness

Facilitator Guidelines

Introduction/Metaphor

"Not only do I want to hear your names but I want to see your names!"

The Action

Have group members state their names and make a physical representation of each letter in their names. Some common methods of representing the letters are wiggling one's hips or moving arms and legs in the shape of the letters, tracing the letters on the ground with one's foot or in the air with a finger, using sign language, etc.

Debriefing

It's unlikely you will need to debrief this activity; however, being "silly" calls for a level of self-confidence. By acting silly, we risk bruised egos when others laugh at our actions. See which of your members take risks and who plays it safe, who gets more creative, and who settles for doing what other members do.

Cross the Circle Names

As I've mentioned, I don't use nametags for groups I facilitate. They provide an excuse to avoid learning names. I picked up this activity at one of my many trainings at Project Adventure, and it can be a fun way for group participants to learn each other's names. Facilitators should run this activity after having their group participate in Name Whip.

Target Group: Any age group

Size of Group: 8 to about 20

Props: Gym spots (Also known as poly spots, these are usually flat, round rubber spots used to mark off boundaries or locations in a field of play for gym games). The activity can also be done without these props.

Objectives

Activity Goals: Having group members get acquainted and learn each other's names

Main FVC Connections: Be Here, Be Safe (including physically safe)

Keys to Success Connections: Emotional awareness, positive interpersonal relationships

Facilitator Guidelines

Introduction/Metaphor

Spread the gym spots out in a circle and have each member stand on a spot. I often begin this activity by stating that I dislike nametags, and even though I am very bad at remembering names, I have learned ways to remember them. I tell participants that I know that the entire group can learn each other's names in 10 minutes. You may also want to mention that during the activity, people may experience some confusion. If they do, they should just laugh it off and keep moving!

The Action

Organize and run a few rounds of the activity Name Whip (p. 86). For larger groups, you may need to do a few more practice tries with this activity than you will with smaller groups. Remind participants to remember as many names as they can.

Begin Love Those New Red Potatoes by walking across the circle towards another group member while stating that person's name. (You should travel all the way across the circle, not just to your immediate left or right.)

Before you reach his or her spot in the circle, the person you called out must vacate his or her spot and move across the circle toward another group member while stating that person's name.

Take the spot of the person you called.

The person you called will take the spot of the other group member he or she called. This pattern continues through the activity.

At some point, as the facilitator, you can begin a second stream of people by walking toward another group member and stating his or her name. At this point, there should be two streams of people crossing the circle.

You can then start another stream. Continue adding new streams until your group is falling into chaos, which should be accompanied by a good dose of laughter!

Debriefing

Questions for When the Focus Is on Emotional Awareness

- Did anyone feel confused? How did you handle that confusion?

Questions for When the Focus Is on Positive Relationships

- Can anyone recall all the names of your group members? Have them state the names. This further reinforces name knowledge.

Peek-a-Who

This is one of my all-time favorite name games. Try this one once group members have spent some time learning each other's names. It can be used even later in a program when the kids already know each other well. If you have used the Tribal Names activity (p. 57), you can have group members use their tribal names instead of their real names. Last names and middle names are also fair game! A version of this game is also included in *The Bottomless Bag Again* (Rohnke, 1991).

Target Group: Any age group

Size of Group: No more than 20 people

Props: Medium to large tarp or sheet (the bigger the item, the more people you can accommodate), a music player (for Variations 1 and 2)

Objectives

Activity Goals: Get to know each other's names

Main FVC Connections: Be Here

Keys to Success Connections: Emotional awareness, behavioral control, positive interpersonal relationships

Facilitator Guidelines

Introduction/Metaphor

If you do not have a co-facilitator, have a member of the group help you set up the tarp for the activity.

The Action

Divide the group into two.

Have the subgroups gather on either side of a tarp you and your co-facilitator hold up to make a wall. If you don't have a co-facilitator, have one of the group members assist you in holding one end of the tarp. Rotate this group member after each round or two.

Ask each subgroup to secretly nominate one member to move to the front of the group and squat down by the tarp.

On the count of three, the facilitators quickly lower the tarp to the ground so that the two nominated members are revealed to each other.

Whoever is quickest to correctly name the other person wins the round. The losing participant crosses over to the other side and is now a member of the team that won that round.

Continue activity until everyone is on one side or the group seems ready to move on to another activity.

Variation 1

Lay out gym spots in two adjacent circles with the spots about a foot apart from each other. Between the adjacent circles, place a small hoop. Have members of each subgroup stand on one of the circles of gym spots. When you begin the music, each group should circle in a clockwise direction. When the music stops, the two people whose feet are in (or closest to) the hoop must turn to face each other. Whoever states the correct name of the other person first wins that person for their team.

Variation 2

For a fun hot weather version, add two water guns! Put the filled water guns next to the hoop. When the music stops, the players in the hoop each pick up the water gun that's closest and name their opponents as quickly as possible. Once they name their opponents, they squirt them with water!

Debriefing

Pay attention to who participates and who doesn't. Are there group members who seem to be coordinating the plan while others sit back and watch? Debrief based on your observations of the group dynamics.

Questions for When the Focus Is on Emotional Awareness

- Did anyone find this activity difficult? Why?
- When you were facing off, how did you feel? How did you react to that feeling?

Questions for When the Focus Is on Behavioral Control

- Were there times when someone inadvertently gave away information to the other team? Why did that happen? Did you change your actions after that?
- Since this activity was competitive, how did we as a group handle that competition?

Questions for When the Focus Is on Positive Relationships

- How did you decide who would go to the front and play each round?
- Were there people who came to the front more often than others? How did that impact the outcome of the activity?

Whamp 'Em

This activity can be run with any group whose participants have at least some familiarity with other group members' names. You may want to run a few rounds of the game Name Whip (p. 86) before starting this activity.

   I learned this activity at a Project Adventure workshop some years ago. A version of it also appears in *The Bottomless Bag Again* (Rohnke, 1991).

Target Group: Any age group

Size of Group: 7 to about 12 people

Props: Foam sword or pool noodle cut in half

Objectives

Activity Goals: Learn names of group members

Main FVC Connections: Be Here (Without focusing on the here and now, you will surely be swatted and won't be able to keep up with the pace. This game is a bit more challenging than most name games due to the time pressure.), Be Safe (Swatting the wrong body part too hard, even with a foam noodle, can still hurt.)

Keys to Success Connections: Behavioral control, establishing positive relationships

Facilitator Guidelines

Introduction/Metaphor

Invite your group to sit in a circle on the ground with their feet pointing towards the center. For this activity, you can also have them sit in chairs, placing their feet in front of them. Use one fewer chair than needed to seat everyone in the group.

   Standing in the center of the circle, demonstrate the power of your Whamp 'Em Sword by holding it high! (The foam noodle will serve as your Whamp 'Em Sword.) Explain that the person standing in the center of the circle holds this sword. By pointing it to another group member and saying his or her name, the game is begun!

   Make sure to demonstrate proper swatting technique by tapping group members only on the toes or knees if they are in chairs. Not too hard either!

   Emphasize that there is no Whamping of any other body parts.

The Action

As the facilitator, you can begin the activity by standing in the center of the circle and pointing the Whamp 'Em Sword at any one of the seated group members while stating his or her name. Or you can designate a person for the center of the circle.

Explain that the first person pointed to has a 3-second grace period to say the name of someone else in the group. If this person does not state someone's name in the 3 seconds allotted (as counted by the person with the Whamp 'Em sword), this person is open to be Whamped with the sword. If, however, this person does call out the name of another member in the group, the person in the center will attempt to swat the identified person before that person is able to name another group member. Each named person must call out another person's name before being Whamped. If the swatter is successful in Whamping a group member before that person can call out someone else's name, the swatter will exchange places with the swatted person, and the new swatter will point to a seated group member to begin, giving that person the obligatory 3 seconds to reply.

Start the activity.

(I generally don't allow group members to remain in the middle for more than 30 seconds to keep things fair.)

Debriefing

Questions for When the Focus Is on Behavioral Control

- Did the fast pace of the game affect your ability to recall and state other participants' names? Did it affect your ability to track down others to swat?

- Did anyone get frustrated during this game? What did you do about it? Did it help or hinder your performance?

- Did everyone "swat" safely?

Name Gesture Replay

In this activity, members of the group will introduce themselves by name and create a gesture that tells the group something about them. They will demonstrate the gesture while stating their name. Group members will repeat each person's name and gesture before introducing their own.

Target Group: Any age group

Size of Group: 4 to 12 people

Props: None

Objectives

Activity Goal: Learn names as well as something about each person

Main FVC Connections: Be Here, Speak Your Truth (Through nonverbal means, each member is communicating something about themselves.)

Keys to Success Connections: Emotional awareness, establishing positive relationships

Facilitator Guidelines

Introduction/Metaphor

For this game, I usually tell my group, "You are not only going to have the opportunity to introduce yourself but you also will let us know something about yourself—without using words!"

The Action

As facilitator, I generally demonstrate the activity first by stating my name and making a gesture such as casting and reeling an imaginary fishing rod or strumming an air guitar, both actions that tell a little about me. The next person must state my name and act out my gesture and then add his or her own. (You can start with someone other than yourself if you think that it would work best for the group, considering members' strong or poor memory skills or cognitive abilities.)

Also, as the activity is in progress, facilitators can ask questions based on the gestures your group members are demonstrating. For example, if someone acts out throwing a ball, I may ask what sport it is, how long they've played, what is their favorite team in that sport, etc. I also check to see if any other group members have questions for that person, based on their name or gesture.

Have the group members, one at a time, state their names and demonstrate a representative gesture.

Continue until the last person takes a turn and has to state all the names and do all the gestures of the group members before presenting his or her own. Ask if any other group members are willing to try to state all the names and demonstrate all the gestures!

Variation

In this version, each person presents only his or her own name and gesture rather than also including each previous name and gesture. After each person's turn, the entire group responds by repeating in unison that member's name and gesture. This version is much simpler!

Debriefing

Acting out a self-disclosing gesture to a group of people you don't know can be fairly intimidating and requires some level of self-confidence. You can tap into this fact during the debriefing, particularly if folks seem to struggle with this activity.

Questions for When the Focus Is on Positive Relationships

- What did you learn about each other?
- Who had the most easily identifiable gesture?
- Whose gesture was the hardest to understand?

CHAPTER

10 Tag Games

A few years ago, my wife and I, along with our three daughters, hatched a New Year's Eve plan. Each hour, from 7:00 p.m. to midnight, would be dedicated to an activity picked by one family member. My oldest daughter, who was approaching 8 years old at the time, chose flashlight tag. Anyone who lives in New England can tell you that December nights are not particularly conducive to outdoor tag games! However, we had said whatever reasonable activities the kids chose, we would do. While playing outside on a December night in New England might not be considered "reasonable," we went with it.

My daughter had never actually played flashlight tag before but heard about it from some friends at school. I remembered playing it as a child but couldn't recall the rules. After a quick Internet search, I relayed the rules to my family. Equipped with our flashlights, we headed into the chilly winter night.

Just shy of an hour later, our family tumbled through the front door, laughing and thoroughly wiped out from running around. The next day, we all agreed that this was the best activity of the night, and it's become a standard choice for our family New Year's Eve parties ever since.

As kids, some of the first games we learn are tag games. For many of us, childhood was the last time we played tag! The games included in this section are often referred to as "warm-ups" and sometimes "de-inhibitizers." Warm-ups refer to activities that get you ready for the more complex cognitively and emotionally demanding interpersonal interactions required by the higher-level activities, often referred to as challenges or initiatives. They also literally warm you up, sometimes too much if it's July!

De-inhibitizers, like warm-ups, get us ready for more challenging activities. But, as the word suggests, they also help free us up from our inhibitions. *Inhibit* is defined as "to restrain or hold back" (American Heritage Dictionary of the English Language, 1980). One of the amazing things about young children is their lack of inhibition. They are free and honest, almost to a fault. As children enter the middle and later half of what Erik Erikson called the School Age phase of development, when they're 6 to 12 years old (Erikson, 1950), they become more aware of themselves in relation to their peers. This gives rise to possible feelings of inferiority or superiority. These feelings shape their sense of identity in relation to their peers, an identity encouraged by the feedback or reinforcement their behavior receives from the environment (Bandura, 1977). As children learn what behaviors evoke positive responses and which ones evoke negative responses, they learn to inhibit those behaviors that evoke negative responses. This is healthy. However, as children grow into adolescence, their awareness of how they fit in with their peer group becomes even more integral to their identity, and for them, the ego-related consequences of taking social risks skyrockets. Many adolescents are unwilling to risk embarrassing themselves or looking silly in front of their peers. (The risk taking teens pursue is often more about seeking physical risks or engaging in dangerous behaviors, rather than taking risks on behaviors that might make them vulnerable or look silly.) This attitude often continues through adolescence and into adulthood. Most of us are far more inhibited than our young children are!

In my experience, tag games act as de-inhibitizers by allowing older children, adolescents, and adults to return to a more innocent time in their lives. While they might feel somewhat inhibited at the onset of the activity, most teens and adults will lose themselves in the fun of the activity once it begins. The opportunity to have this type of unbridled, uninhibited playtime is often a great release for those of us who have become more inhibited over time. As inhibitions fade, the doors open for participants to connect with each other on a more genuine level. These activities foster growth in relationships.

As a facilitator, it is essential that you are willing to drop your own inhibitions about looking silly. If you are a genuine example of how to be uninhibited, the group will likely follow your lead. But, beware! Teens are extremely good at exposing a fake. As a facilitator, embrace silliness! Embrace the chance to just have fun and lose yourself in the game. Of course, as you do this, make sure to maintain your facilitator role, especially as the guardian of the FVC. With good facilitation, you will likely get little resistance to these types of activities. If you do encounter resistance, it will likely be before the actual activity begins. Gently remind members of the FVC if they are showing signs of violating it. I don't recall ever having a group not enjoying tag games once they began despite the grumblings before the game. Most of the time, those grumblings are stemming from fear, self-consciousness, and other enemies of uninhibited fun.

Considerations When Planning Tag Games

As a side note, facilitators should be aware of the environment in which they are asking their group to play games such as tag. I learned the hard way that in the courtyard next to the school, adjacent to a busy road was not the place to ask high school students to play tag. In this setting, my group was far too self-conscious of the kids watching them from boring English classes or the glances they received from passers-by in their cars. These factors prevented them from dropping their inhibitions, and we got nowhere. The next week, I had the same group on a ropes course in the middle of the woods and they played like kindergarteners!

When planning tag games, facilitators should also consider what the group members are wearing. If you have a group of well-dressed kids, girls with high heels or short skirts, you may encounter valid resistance to tag. You should also be aware of factors such as time and weather. Trying to get a group of adolescents to play tag in an open field at 8 o'clock, on a steamy August morning is not likely to go over well. If they've just stuffed themselves with a huge breakfast of donuts and bagels, it may not be wise to play fast-paced tag games. Luckily, some of the activities listed here involve less physical activity than do others.

Finally, before launching a tag game, facilitators should find out if any group members have physical limitations that would prevent them from participating in the tag games as they are planned. If this is the case, you the facilitator have two options: don't play the game or alter the game to include everybody. Whenever possible, I opt for the second choice. If you have a high-functioning group, asking them to help you create modifications to the activity can be part of the growth experience!

So, tag away and enjoy!

Bears, Salmon, and Mosquitoes

This activity is a team tag version of Rock, Paper, Scissors. I learned it in my very first training at Project Adventure. A version of it also appears in *The New Games Book* (Fluegelman, 1976).

Target Group: Any group with the cognitive abilities to comprehend the instructions. If they can understand the game Rock, Paper, Scissors, they can understand this activity, as it is basically Rock, Paper, Scissors on a grander scale.

Size of Group: 10 or more people

Props: Three boundary markers (Facilitators can use ropes, gym spots, sticks, lunch bags, etc.)

Objectives

Activity Goals: Warm the group up, decrease inhibitions, enhance communication and group decision-making skills

Main FVC Connections: Be Here (The group members must pay attention to each other during planning to make sure they have the correct sign. If they don't stay present during the activity, they are sure to get tagged.), Be Safe (Each member is responsible for this or her own safety as well as that of group members.), Speak Your Truth, Hear the Truth (During this activity, members are encouraged to share ideas and come to a team consensus as they strategize about what sign is best for each round. Note who takes the lead, who simply listens and follows, and who tunes out all together.)

Keys to Success Connections: Emotional awareness, behavioral control, and establishing positive relationships

Facilitator Guidelines

Setup

Find an area that is free of debris or possible hazards.

Set up your playing area by creating a space with a centerline and two end-zone boundaries that run parallel to the centerline. The end-zone boundaries should be equal distance from the centerline, about 25 feet away. To measure the boundary line placement, walk 10 (or so) large paces from your centerline to one end-zone boundary. Repeat the process to mark the other end-zone boundary. You may also want to create a sideline boundary. When your boundaries are set, you've got something akin to a small football field with end zones, out-of-bounds markers, and a midfield line. See diagram.

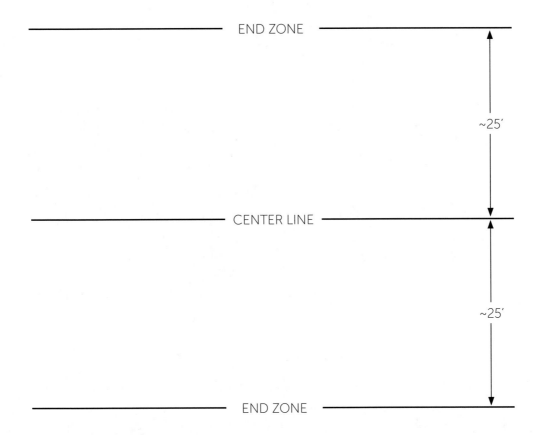

Introduction/Metaphor

This game is a tag version of Rock, Paper, Scissors, and it often helps to tell your group this when you begin explaining the rules. When introducing the game, check to see who knows the Rock, Paper, Scissors game in which Rock beats Scissors, Scissors beats Paper and Paper beats Rock. You may also want to remind the group of the hand signs that go with that game. The Bears, Salmon, and Mosquitoes activity also has three groups. In this activity, Bears eat Salmon, Salmon eat Mosquitoes, and Mosquitoes sting Bears. Each animal has its own physical sign, and each sign has its own power over another group. The game will be played in teams across from each other on a field.

I might introduce the game as follows: "This game is about survival of the strongest. Who's strongest, however, may not always be obvious. Sometimes it's the big guys who win out. Sometimes the bigger you are, the harder you fall!"

The Action

Split your group into two teams.

Review the game rules. When introducing the game, check to see who knows the Rock, Paper, Scissors game in which rock beats scissors, scissors beats paper, and paper beats rock. In this game, bears eat salmon, salmon eat mosquitoes, and mosquitoes sting bears. Each animal has its own physical sign.

Demonstrate the following signs to your group, allowing for some vigorous practicing of the signs. See the pictures below for the signs.

Bear: Hands held menacingly above your head as you growl and make mean faces.

Salmon: Hands together in front of you about chest height, pointing away from your body and wiggling like a fish while you make "fish lips." While salmon are generally very quiet, they can sometimes make a "blub, blub" sound.

Participants place their hands together at chest height to make the sign for Salmon.

Mosquitoes: Hands in front, chest height, wiggling your fingers like little bugs while making a resounding high pitch buzz.

Emphasize to your group that they are responsible for the safety of all group members, not just the members of their team. Because there is running, chasing, and tagging all happening simultaneously, the risk of injury is elevated.

Instruct the group members to huddle with their teammates and decide on a sign (Bears, Salmon, or Mosquitoes) and "back up" sign. The back-up sign will be used in the event of a tie, when both teams show the same sign.

Once everyone is clear about what their team's sign and back-up sign are, have each team line up parallel to the centerline and 1 to 2 feet away from it. The two teams are now facing each other at close range (no more than 3 or 4 feet apart), divided only by the centerline.

Let teams know that you will begin a countdown before they are to show their signs. Remind them that if both teams show the same sign, they are to wait for a new three count before showing the back-up sign.

On the facilitators count of three, each team will simultaneously perform its agreed-upon sign. All members should perform the same sign!

The team with the stronger sign will chase the team with the weaker sign towards its own end line. Any member of the weaker sign team that gets tagged before reaching the end line will become a member of the stronger sign team.

If the two teams show the same sign, the facilitator counts to three again, and the teams show their back-up sign.

The game continues until everyone is on one team and, of course, the players are all winners! Or you may end the activity when the group seems ready to move on.

Variation

You can change the animals! You can also make up your own signs!

Debriefing

Bigger is not always better – as we see in this activity when Bears face off with Mosquitoes. It's a great theme for the debriefing! Don't forget to check in with how the group members were able to maintain one another's safety. During the activity, you are likely to see breakdowns in communication as one team throws mixed signs. This can trigger frustration. Deal with this when it happens. You should also note who takes the lead in the activity, who simply listens, who follows and who tunes out all together.

Questions for When the Focus Is On Emotional Awareness

- Did anyone get frustrated during this activity? Why? How did you handle it?

Questions for When the Focus Is On Behavioral Control

- Were there times when you didn't know what was expected of you or you were unsure what the team's decision was? What did you do about it?
- How did you ensure your own safety?
- How did you keep others safe?
- Are there times in life when we have to consider someone else's safety over our own?

Questions for When the Focus Is On Positive Relationships

- How did you come to agreements with your teammates each round? What skills did you use?
- Was there anyone who got caught but didn't admit it? Why? Is integrity important in our group? Why?
- Were people sharing ideas and listening to each other?

Unity Tag 'n' Jelly Roll

I learned this activity in a Project Adventure training session. A version of this activity appears in *Silver Bullets* (Rohnke, 1984) as Add on Tag, although an earlier version called Blob also appears in *The New Game Book* (1976). Make sure your group is ready and comfortable with close physical contact and that the principle Challenge by Choice is followed in this activity. Use the "Jelly Roll" aspect of this activity only with groups that are truly ready for it.

Target Group: Any group comfortable with physical closeness

Size of Group: 8 to 24 people

Props: Boundary markers

Objectives

Activity Goal: Establishing group cohesion

Main FVC Connection: Be Safe

Keys to Success Connections: Emotional awareness, behavioral control, and establishing positive relationships

Facilitator Guidelines

Introduction/Metaphor

Create a circle or an area that is slightly smaller than the amount of space you would need for the entire group to stretch across while holding hands. Have a group member volunteer to be "it." To launch the activity, you might say something like the following: "What is 'Unity'? What does it mean to pull together with others and stand as one? Are there times when you felt as if you were one with a larger force?" Discuss these topics and add that "hopefully, Unity is something that we can create here today!"

The Action

Emphasize that since there will be a great deal of movement in a small space, everyone should be careful.

Present the rules for the game. "It" must move about the circle, trying to tag other members. Once tagged, the tagged person links arms with "It," and the two continue to chase members as a single unit, without breaking their connection. The pair will link arms with all they tag, eventually creating a chain of folks! As the "It" group grows, the others will have less and less room in which to escape. Play continues until everyone is "It," and the entire group is united into a single arm-in-arm unit. When the "It" group members lose their connection (as will inevitably happen during play), they may simply regroup and continue.

Variation

This variation is for more mature groups. Once the entire group is part of the "It" group, have group members remain linked while the original "It" person begins to walk around in a circle in the inner boundary of the playing area. Have the original "It" make progressively smaller circles. This, in turn, will begin wrapping the circle into a smaller and smaller unit until the line of players has wrapped itself up in a big 'ol jelly roll-shaped group hug!

Debriefing

Questions for When the Focus Is on Emotional Awareness

- How did it feel to be caught but not be "out" in this tag game?
- How did it feel to be connected to the entire group? Are there times in your life that you felt as if you were a part of something great? Are there times when you felt left out by a larger group? What was that like?

Questions for When the Focus Is on Behavioral Control

- What is the difference between "safe" or "acceptable" physical contact and "unsafe" or "unacceptable" physical contact? What should our ground rules be around physical contact?

Questions for When the Focus Is on Positive Relationships

- When you became part of the "it" group, was it difficult to stay connected? Why or why not? Is it difficult to stay connected to groups in your life?

Pairs Tag*

This tag game is an appropriate activity for a wide range of groups. In this version of tag, the person playing "It" will try to tag his or her partner only. The other partner will try to escape by running about the activity area, often hiding behind other group members. Once players are tagged, they must perform a predetermined, fun, and slightly silly task decided on by the group.

Target Group: Any age group

Size of Group: 8 or more people

Props: Boundary markers

Objectives

Activity Goal: Having fun while maintaining safety by becoming aware of and managing their own behaviors

Main FVC Connections: Be Here, Be Safe (Members must focus on their safety and that of all other group members.)

Keys to Success Connection: Behavioral control

Facilitator Guidelines

Setup

Create an area big enough for your group to run around without too much unnecessary contact but not so big that you'll tire your group out too quickly. If you are playing in a smaller space, make this a "walking only" tag game. Walking can be defined as moving without bending at the knees.

Introduction/Metaphor

Pairs tag is one of those games that can be renamed to fit a particular group. For example, if you are facilitating an anger management group, the activity can be called Anger Begone tag. For a leadership group, it can be called Get the Leader tag. The metaphor can be tailored to the type of group. When running the activity as Anger Begone Tag, you can begin by talking about how it's often difficult to control our own anger:

"No matter how you try, you can't quite get a grip on it and eliminate it. Sometimes, other obstacles are in your way and sometimes, that anger is just too quick!"

For a leadership group, you can talk about how becoming a leader sometimes means overthrowing another leader, which, of course, is not always so simple! Sometimes, there are obstacles interfering with getting rid of one leader and becoming a leader yourself!

---

*An early version of this activity appears as Pairs Squared in *Cowstails and Cobras I* and *II* (Rohnke, 1977; Rohnke,1989)

When something gets in the way of your goal (whether it's controlling anger or rising to a leadership position), you must be creative and search for solutions!

The Action

Explain the rules of the game. Within the playing area, the person who is "It" will try to tag his or her partner only. The other partner will try to escape by running about and hiding behind other group members. Once players are tagged, they must perform a predetermined task. Once the task is completed, they are to chase down their partners. (This task allows time for players who were formerly "It" to get away and make for a chase.)

Describe examples of what the predetermined task might be. The task can be something silly, such as turning around three times while singing Three Blind Mice or doing five jumping jacks.

Ask your group to determine what the task should be. Facilitators can also create a fun task for the activity, if this helps the group begin the activity.

Creatively pair up group members. If there's an odd number, you can jump in and play as well!

Remind members of group safety. When members are focused on catching their partners, they may not be focused on keeping others safe. If you are in a small space, watch for violations of the "walking only" rule. It may help for group members to keep their "bumpers up." This means participants should hold their hands palms out in front of themselves at about chest height to protect against nose-to-nose or head-to-head collisions.

Have one member of each pair start off by being "It."

Continue the activity until your group is exhausted or simply ready to move on!

Variation 1

When players are It, they must close one eye.

Variation 2

When players are It, they must shut one eye and make a spyglass with their other hand by bringing their thumb and fingertips together to create a circle. They'll place this hand over their open eye and peer through it—just as they would with a telescope or spyglass.

Debriefing

The debriefing of this game can be minimal; however, for facilitators who use a metaphor in the brief (such as ones for anger or leadership groups), it's worth debriefing based on that metaphor. For example, if you described anger in the brief, you can discuss how anger can be very quick and difficult to catch before it escapes. Was your partner difficult to catch? When you describe leadership in the brief before the activity, you can discuss and connect the activity to situations in which more than one person is vying for a single leadership position. One aspect of this game that can be included in all debriefs is how to reach a goal despite the presence of obstacles.

Questions for When the Focus Is on Behavioral Control

- What strategies did you use to catch fast partners? Can these strategies be used to chase down your goals outside of this group?

- What obstacles got in the way of tagging your partner? What obstacles are getting in the way of you reaching your goals in life?

Transformer Tag

Transformer Tag is one of the most adaptable activities in this book. In this game, group members will present hand signals or signs and tag those members using other hand signs. The person tagged is "transformed" into a member of the tagger's hand-sign group. Through the metaphors and introduction, this activity can be molded to fit just about any type of experiential-counseling group.

Target Group: Upper elementary-school-age participants and older

Size of Group: 8 to 25 people

Props: Boundary markers

Objectives

Activity Goals: The goal will depend to some degree on the metaphor chosen; however, the activity helps participants examine the themes of change, resistance to change, and maintaining one's identity in the face of those who may be trying to get you to change.

Main FVC Connections: Be Here, Be Safe (Participants need to ensure the safety of others in this fast-paced tag game.), Speak Your Truth (Members will disclose information about the way they handle conflict or other situations. Facilitators should be sure to acknowledge this.)

Keys to Success Connections: Emotional awareness, behavioral control, and establishing positive relationships

Facilitator Guidelines

Setup

Create an area large enough for your group to play a safe, fun game of tag but not so large that they will wear themselves out too quickly or be unable to tag the fastest members of the group.

Introduction/Metaphor

This activity can be adapted and introduced in such a way to fit just about any type of group. The activity relies on the concepts of change, transformation, and self-identity. Use these themes to tailor your introduction.

Facilitators should adapt their presentation of the game instructions to the needs of group members or the theme of the group they are facilitating. For example, if you are working with a group whose members typically make poor decisions (such as adjudicated youth or youth who are in anger management or alternative-to-suspension programs), you may want to begin by asking group members how they solve problems. Do they solve problems using their "heads," "guts," or "butts"? For example, those who solve problems with their "heads" use logic. "Guts" go on that first reaction while the "Butts," well, they just dig in and refuse to compromise. For each approach, there is a corresponding sign. To illustrate the signs for these approaches to problem-solving, you can say, "If you solve problems with your 'head,' simply place one hand on your head. If you solve with your 'guts,' place a hand on your abdomen. If you solve problems with your 'butts' (metaphorically speaking of course), put a hand on your butt."

For leadership groups, facilitators might ask group members if they are leaders who lead with their "head, heart, or hammer." Those leading with their "head" think though problems. Those leading with their "heart" rely on emotional reactions to lead while those using the "hammer" are leaders who believe they need to be strong, firm, and decisive above all else. Facilitators should show the corresponding sign for each: hand on head for "head," hand over heart for "heart," and a fist for the "hammer" style of leading.

Facilitators can alter the signs and their meanings to fit their own groups' needs. Discuss what each of these means in terms of problem solving or leading.

The Action

Ask members to decide on which approach best reflects them. Once everyone has decided, introduce the activity.

Group members should show their signs for either Heads, Butts, or Guts. They must use one hand to show and maintain this sign. Using their free hand, group members will attempt to tag another group member who shows a sign different than their own. Once someone is tagged, this person is transformed to a member of the tagger's group and must show the symbol of the person who tagged them.

Have group members show their signs and start the activity.

The game continues until all members of the group are showing the same sign.

Debriefing

The debrief for this activity will depend upon the introduction you've chosen and the type of group you are working with. For anger management groups, which may be the most common and likely use of this activity, the focus could be on how folks currently solve their problems or deal with their anger or other negative emotions and how they would like to in the future. Members will disclose how they respond or have responded to situations in their lives. Discuss the pros and cons of each coping strategy. In any group or when using any metaphor for the signs, you, the facilitator, can discuss the fact that others will try to change them.

Questions for When the Focus Is on Emotional Awareness

- How did it feel when people were trying to change you? How did you react?
- Have people in your lives tried to change things about you? How has it worked? Were they justified in doing this?

Questions for When the Focus Is on Behavioral Control

- Which was the most common way that members solved problems, as evidenced by the largest contingent at the beginning of the game? How does that way work in real life?

- Which group won? Is that the group that began with the most? If not, why did that group have the most at the end?

- Are there times in life that your behavior is influenced by the actions of others? When?

- Did you want to "be changed" in this activity? Why not? Do we ever hold on to our ways of dealing with problems even when they don't work for us?

Questions for When the Focus Is on Positive Relationships

- Are there times when you need to change things about yourself to maintain or improve a relationship? What is the best way someone can help you to change?

- Have you ever tried push someone else to change? How did you do it? What was the outcome?

Everybody's It*

Target Group: Any age group

Size of Group: 8 to 25 people

Props: Boundary markers

Objectives

Activity Goals: Break down inhibitions, promote self-expression, explore individuality versus assimilation

Main FVC Connections: Be Here, Be Safe emotionally and physically (Group members are disclosing something about themselves through their individual sign, and it may be difficult to let go of their individuality—even metaphorically—when tagged!), Speak Your Truth (Through the creation of individual signs, participants are sharing a piece of themselves.)

Keys to Success Connections: Emotional awareness, behavioral control, establishing positive relationships

Facilitator Guidelines

Setup

Set up a boundary area large enough for the group to run around but not so large as to exhaust them or allow the fastest members to never be tagged.

Introduction/Metaphor

"We each have our own, unique style and personality. Let's express our individuality by coming up with signs or signals that represent who we are. Each one of us will have our own, personal, unique sign." Continue highlighting the uniqueness of individuals by pointing out the fact that in our society, people are often under pressure to assimilate, or fit into different groups. Engage the group in a discussion of what groups or social standards they feel pressure to fit into. Ask them how they maintain their individuality under such pressure. Once everyone has chosen a sign, you can check in as to why they chose that particular sign.

The Action

Have members create a personal sign that will not interfere with running or tagging.

Explain the rules of the game. After the members have created their personal signs, instruct them that they will all be "it." At the start, each participant displays his or her

---

*The original version of this activity appears in *Silver Bullets* (Rohnke, 1984).

own personal sign. As group members are tagged, they are converted into the sign of the player that tagged them. They now must display that sign.

Before starting the activity, emphasize safety, as you do with all fast-paced tag games.

Have participants begin the activity.

Continue the activity until all members are displaying the same sign. If you choose to highlight the competitive aspect of this game, you can declare the person whose sign the group shows at the end of the activity the winner.

Debriefing

To create a fitting, personal sign, this activity calls for self-reflection. I often find that more emotionally disturbed kids have difficulties coming up with a sign. Sometimes asking others to offer a sign based on how they see that person is worthwhile. If you do this, emphasize and assess the group's level of commitment to emotional safety first.

On a deeper level, this activity explores the balance we all try to strike in maintaining our individuality while fitting in with other "groups" in our society. Allow this metaphorical connection to guide your debrief.

Questions When the Focus Is on Emotional Awareness

- Did you feel confused during this game? How does this relate to feelings of confusion outside this group when others are trying to influence you?
- Why did you pick the sign you did?
- How did it feel to give up your sign and take on someone else's?

Questions When the Focus Is on Behavioral Control

- What did you do to protect your sign? What do you do to preserve your identity in the world?

Questions When the Focus Is on Positive Relationships

- Is it sometimes good to allow yourself to be influenced or changed by others? Who has been that person in your life and how?
- How have you been an agent of change for others in your life?

Lions and Hyenas*

In this activity, participants form a circle around the facilitator and try to retrieve a dropped item in the center of the circle. The facilitator or person in the center can tag anyone who approaches the item and send him or her back outside the circle. I first learned this activity from my colleague and friend Blair Wolchowski, though I believe he used a different name and introduction. It has since become one of my favorites and a favorite of the kids I work with on a daily basis.*

Target Group: Any age group

Size of Group: 8 to about 24 people

Props: Rope or other objects (such as gym spots) to create a circular boundary, one stuffed toy animal

Objectives

Activity Goals: Explore themes of working alone versus working together to achieve a goal

Main FVC Connections: Be Here, Be Safe (All group members are responsible for their own safety as well as the safety of their peers.)

Keys to Success Connections: Emotional awareness, behavioral control, establishing positive relationships

Facilitator Guidelines

Introduction/Metaphor

I set this activity up with the following scenario: "Have you ever watched the National Geographic or Discovery channel? For those of us old enough to remember it, how about Mutual of Omaha's Wild Kingdom? It always seems like one of those big, tough lions is sitting down to enjoy a tasty antelope when those pesky hyenas show up and use all sorts of distracting tactics to steal the antelope from the king of the jungle. Usually, there's only one poor lion trying to enjoy dinner and a whole bunch of hyenas trying to ruin it. Well, that's the story behind this game."

Note: For some, this scenario of a lion eating an antelope and losing it to hyenas may be too gory. Use your judgment. If needed, change the name and introduction to this activity to avoid the subjects of predators and prey.

---

*The origin of this activity may stem back to an activity called Smaug's Jewels that appears in *The New Games Book* (1976).

The Action

Have your group form a circle around a boundary. The boundary lines should be set 10 to 15 feet from the person standing in the center of the circle. You, the facilitator, will be the person standing in the middle of the circle to start.

Let the group know that you are the lion, and all the group members are the hyenas. Show them your prey by holding up the object in your hand. (Preferably you will have a toy stuffed antelope, though teddy bears or any other toy stuffed animal will do.)

Explain that when the lion is holding the critter, all group members should be standing on the outside of the circular boundary. When the lion drops the critter on the ground, the hyenas (rest of the group members) may enter the circle and try to get it.

Let group members know that the lion can tag the hyenas, sending them back out of the circle and yipping into the night, not to be seen again until the next round of the activity. If the lion tags a hyena who has taken the critter, the critter is returned to the lion who restarts the activity. To restart the activity, the participants who are the hyenas should line up outside the boundary circle, and the lion can restart the game by dropping the critter. If, however, a hyena is able to take the critter and escape outside of the boundary lines without being tagged, this participant is safe and will replace the lion as the new king of the jungle. In the rare event that all hyenas are tagged without successfully stealing the critter, the lion is determined an ultimate king and may choose a new lion to take his or her place.

Let participants know that lions also have rules to follow. Once a lion drops an object, the lion cannot pick it up again unless it is returned by a tagged hyena. The lion should stand at least one foot away from a dropped object. The lion can stand over the object but cannot touch it, crouch over it, or guard it so closely that it becomes inaccessible to the hyenas.

Before launching the activity, carefully review safety rules as this tag game involves many people, moving quickly in a small space. Point out that with many people simultaneously launching towards a toy critter on the ground, there is a potential for head bumping. Emphasize that all group members are responsible for their own safety as well as the safety of their peers.

Debriefing

Questions for When the Focus Is on Emotional Awareness

- As the lion, how did it feel having so many people coming at you at once? How did you handle that? Do you ever feel like that in life, that everyone is coming at you?

Questions for When the Focus Is on Behavioral Control

- What strategies did you use as the lion to deal with so many hyenas? Do you ever feel like you are being overwhelmed like this in life? What strategies can you use?

Questions for When the Focus Is on Positive Relationships

- As hyenas, did you find yourselves working together at all? (This question could lead to a discussion about the "pack mentality.") If so, how did you communicate with the others? Would you have been successful in this game if you were the only hyena? How does that translate to accomplishing tasks outside of group?

- How did you balance cooperation with competition amongst the hyenas?

Knee Tag*

This activity is similar to Everyone's It (p. 118), except players in this game must try to tag each other on the knee. The designated playing area for this activity should be large enough for participants to move around in but not so large that participants move out too far to make the activity fun.

Target Group: Any age group. The activity works well with young and grown up children.

Size of Group: 8 to 50 people

Props: Boundary markers

Objectives

Activity Goals: Break down inhibitions, explore themes of playing it safe versus taking risks

Main FVC Connections: Be Here, Be Safe (Participants need to be aware of physical safety issues associated with tag, especially since in this activity, legal tagging takes place only "below the belt." Also, emotional safety is emphasized by giving participants choice in how they participate.), Speak Your Truth, Hear the Truth (Players who are working with time limits for the activity need to play fairly and be honest.)

Keys to Success Connections: Behavioral control and establishing positive relationships

Facilitator Guidelines

Introduction/Metaphor

For this activity, facilitators can keep it simple and just give group members the rules. However, if as facilitator, you would like to deepen the activity's meaning through metaphors, the theme of "choice" works well. This activity can bring the Challenge by Choice philosophy to life as players choose their level of participation in the action through the variations. It works well with the theme of healthy risk taking versus playing it safe.

The Action

Explain the rules for this game of tag. Everyone is It and tries to tag other participants. Participants can be tagged only on their knees, and anyone who is tagged must go down on one knee and is out for the round.

Let group members know there are rules around being tagged. To prevent being tagged, participants can guard their knees by placing their hands on them. When participants' hands are on their knees, they can't be tagged, but they also cannot move their feet. To

---

* I first learned this activity while working at the Riverfront Ropes Course in Hartford, Connecticut. Much later, I found a basic version of it called Knee Slap in *No Props, Great Games with No Equipment* by Mark Collard of Project Adventure (2005).

move, participants must take their hands off their knees and bring their hands to at least waist level. The participants must take at least three steps before covering their knees again.

The group can also create time limits. For example, they can allow participants to cover their knees only to a count of "five Mississippi," and they can require there must be a "fifteen second" period before players can cover their knees again.

Remind participants of the safety rules, as there is the possibility of bumping heads when two players go for each others' knees.

Start the game.

In a following round, facilitators can ask participants if they want to try a different variation.

Variation 1

I often use this pairs variation before the whole-group version described above. Have players choose a partner. Partners get into position and face off. Pairs should be close enough to each other that each can touch the other person's knees. Once in position they can no longer move their feet. They must try to touch their partner's knees with the rules that covering the knees protects them. Each knee touch counts as a point (if you want to keep score).

Variation 2

If players are tagged, active players can high-five a tagged player to get them back in the game.

Variation 3

If the player who tagged you gets tagged, you are back in the game!

Variation 4

If the player takes a knee after being tagged, that player can tag another's knee. This will get the tagged participant out and the player back in! Players can begin tagging from the kneeling position as soon as they take a knee.

Debriefing

If you are using the time rule, you may notice players violating this. I often let it go and see if other members notice, which invites a live demonstration of "Speak Your Truth" and "Hear the Truth." If they don't notice, I often bring up integrity during the debriefing. You may also observe other violations in the rules during this game.

Questions for When the Focus Is on Behavioral Control

- You had the choice of how to participate in this activity. If you just kept your hands on your knees, you didn't get tagged but likely didn't tag anyone else. Others may have taken more risks and possibly, reaped more rewards. How did you choose to participate and why?

Questions for When the Focus Is on Positive Relationships

- Even though this game is competitive, you had the opportunity to bring your competitors back into the game. Did you? Why or why not?
- Did anyone bring you back in? How did that feel? Did you return the favor?

Up Chuck*

This bombardment tag game is extremely active so make sure to take into consideration hot weather and any members with physical limitations. Facilitators should also make sure the soft objects participants use are without any hard parts. Facilitators should consider emotional safety of group members. Differences in athletic ability are highlighted during this activity. Additionally, this activity lends itself to the possibility of participants sticking with pre-existing cliques and ganging up on others.

Target Group: Any group about 8 years old and up

Size of Group: 10 to 35 people

Props: Boundary markers and one soft toss-able item per person that group members can toss at each other without inflicting injury. Fleece balls or soft stuffed animals with no hard parts work well for this.

Objectives

Activity Goals: Break down inhibitions, generate energy

Main FVC Connections: Be Safe (physically and emotionally)

Keys to Success Connections: Emotional awareness and behavioral control

Facilitator Guidelines

Setup

Facilitators should create an activity area with a boundary that is not so large that people will leave the heart of the game but big enough for some good, hardy running.

Introduction/Metaphor

I don't generally use a metaphor or brief on this activity but just go right to explaining the rules.

The Action

Gather your group in a circle.

Give each member a toss-able item. Make sure these toss-ables cannot cause damage when being hurled at participants. Inform your group that what they are holding is called a "chuck." When it is tossed in the air, it's an "Up Chuck."

Tell group members they will be using the chucks in a tag game. There are typically three phases to this game that will be introduced successively after each round. The rules for each phase should be explained right before that phase is played. Each phase begins the

---

*I learned this one on a warm summer day in Windsor, CT, from my colleague and friend, Rick Bosch. The original version of this activity appears in *Quicksilver* (Rohnke, 1994).

same way. Members stand in a large circle about an arm's length apart and facing away from the center of the circle. When a designated person yells "UP CHUCK!," participants toss the chucks over their shoulders and toward the center of the circle. Players then quickly leave the circle and try to grab a chuck.

Phase 1

Members can hold only one chuck at a time. Chucks are to be hurled at opponents but can land below participants' waists only! Group members who throw a chuck can pick up another chuck, one at a time, until they themselves are tagged with a chuck. Group members who are hit are down and must take a knee and wait for the round to end. (Catching the chuck also counts as being hit.) These participants must forfeit their chuck if they are holding one. The round ends when there is one player left.

Phase 2

The rules are the same as in Phase 1, except when the person who hit a participant gets hit, the first participant is back in the game! Don't know exactly who hit you? That's OK. Just pick someone you think tagged you, and when this person is hit, you are free.

Phase 3

In this round, tagged participants who are down can hold onto their chucks and re-enter the game by hitting active members. Active players can also deliver chucks to tagged-out participants. Inactive participants can also simply pick up chucks that land near them. Tagged participants must keep their toes planted in the spot where they went down and can only get chucks that are within reaching distance.

Debriefing

If you notice players ganging up or taking advantage of less athletic participants, you can address these issues during the debriefing.

Questions When the Focus Is on Emotional Awareness

- How did it feel to get hit?
- Which round did you enjoy the most?

Questions When the Focus Is on Behavioral Control

- This game called for you to work on the honor system about when and by whom you were hit. Were you honest?

Questions When the Focus Is on Positive Relationships

- Did you help anybody who was down during the last round? Were they already a friend of yours?
- Did anyone help you when you were down? How did you treat them after that?
- Were there any alliances created? How did that come about? Were you connected with those people before this activity?

- Did anyone feel like they were the target of an alliance? What did that feel like? What does it feel like to be the target of groups of kids in school?

Slow-Motion Tag

This is a new twist on a usually high-speed game. This activity requires participants to divide their attention between trying to keep the cup on their head, tagging others, and avoiding being tagged. Creating a successful balance of these three aspects of this activity is not easy!

Target Group: Any age group

Size of Group: 8 to 24 people

Props: One plastic or paper cup per person, boundary markers

Objectives

Activity Goals: Tag that has little to do with athleticism and more to do with focus and creating a balance between seemingly incompatible goals. It also helps participants realize that all is not as it seems!

Main FVC Connection: Be Here

Keys to Success Connections: Emotional awareness and behavioral control

Facilitator Guidelines

Setup

For this game, you should create a playing area that is big enough for your group to move freely but not so large that group members are more than a few feet apart from one another at any given spot within the boundary markers.

Introduction/Metaphor

Introduce Slow-Motion Tag by inviting participants to think about the activity they are about to start. You might say something like "When we think of tag games, we usually envision fast-paced mayhem. However, when we assume that something is a certain way because it's always been that way before, we may get let down. Even worse, if we respond to the situation the way we always have and fail to adapt, we may find ourselves in trouble! That is the case with this tag game. If you move quickly, you will not last long!" The tasks of this game (keeping a cup on your head and tagging others) are seemingly incompatible goals. You can create an introduction around this theme as well.

The Action

Give each participant a paper or plastic cup. Encourage your group to spread out within the playing area.

Explain the rules of the activity. Participants must try to tag each other and avoid being tagged while simultaneously balancing a paper cup atop their heads. Once the game begins, participants cannot touch the paper cup with their hands at any time unless it falls to the ground. Then, they may pick it up and place it back on their heads. Participants may not touch an opponent's cup. Participants get a strike for each time they are tagged or their cup falls to the ground for any reason. Once a player gets three strikes, they are out of the game.

Let participants know that each of them will keep track of their own strikes using the honor system.

Have participants place the paper cups on top of their heads.

Once everyone's cup is placed, announce the start of the activity.

Continue play until there is only one player left or until a time limit has elapsed, your choice.

Debriefing

This activity can produce frustration, especially with more impulsive kids who tend to move too quickly, causing the cup to tumble from their heads. You may want to discuss participant's tendencies to move quickly to avoid being tagged or when trying to tag someone else. Ask them, did slowing down help? Does it help when we move quickly in tenuous situations?

Questions for When the Focus Is on Emotional Awareness

- How did your experiences in past tag games help or hinder you in this tag game?
- Are there times when you have assumed something would be a certain way and found out you were way off base? How did you respond? What was the outcome?

Questions for When the Focus Is on Behavioral Control

- Was it difficult to divide your attention between so many aspects of the game (tagging, avoiding tags, balancing the cup)? Are there times in your life when you've felt like your attention was being pulled in many directions? How did you handle that? What did you learn from this activity about how you can handle those situations in the future?
- How was this different from regular tag games? How did that translate into your choices?
- How did the competitive nature of this activity impact your strategy?

The Evil Eye

In this game of tag, participants try to avoid the gaze of the Evil Eye. Thanks to Dick Hammond for showing me this activity at The National Challenge Course Professionals Symposium in Boulder, Colorado.

Target Group: Any age group

Size of Group: 8 to about 40 people

Props: Boundary markers

Objectives

Activity Goals: Break down inhibitions, build integrity

Main FVC Connection: Be Safe

Keys to Success Connections: Emotional awareness and establishing positive relationships

Facilitator Guidelines

Setup

Create a playing area. If you are in a classroom, the walls of the room will serve as the boundary. If you are using a large, open space, structure your boundaries to allow your group to move without bumping each other but not much larger.

Introduction/Metaphor

"Sometimes, words can't really describe how you feel. Sometimes, a dirty look or an evil eye can speak a thousand words! I don't like being on the receiving end of that look. For this activity, you will need to avoid the Evil Eye!"

The Action

Divide your group into pairs. Have each pair decide who will be the Evil Eye first.

Explain the rules, saying that one person in each pair will get to play the role of the Evil Eye. The Evil Eye will attempt to make eye contact with their partners. Partners must look straight ahead, not up or down, and they must keep moving. They cannot hide in a corner of the room or find a place where it would be impossible for their Evil Eye to succeed in making eye contact with them. If eye contact is made, the receiver becomes the new Evil Eye of the pair. The former Evil Eye is given a 5-second count to move away.

Let participants know to get ready to start the activity. Tell them that when you say, "Go," the game will start, and participants who are the Evil Eye should attempt to make eye contact with their partners.

Count down from five and say, "Go."

Continue the activity until your group is ready to move on to another activity.

Debriefing

Because this is a simple tag game, you may be able to simply "move on" to the next activity without debriefing. However, this activity can bring up issues about integrity, as partners must agree that eye contact was made while playing a competitive-type of game.

Questions for When the Focus Is on Emotional Awareness

- How much can you tell about how a person is feeling by their facial expressions?
- Who in your life has an effective "Evil Eye?"

Questions for When the Focus Is on Positive Relationships

- Were you and your partner always in agreement about when eye contact took place?
- How did you come to agreement when each of you "saw" the situation differently? What is a time in your life when you didn't see eye-to-eye with someone else?
- Which role was more challenging? The Evil Eye or the one avoiding it? How about in real life?
- Are you more likely to give someone an "Evil Eye" or use words or actions to convey negative feelings to another person?

Jedi Knight

In this tag game, each team has one Jedi Knight. Teammates work to keep their Jedi Knight safe from bombardment while trying to take out the other team's players and knight. Team members who are tagged with a toss-able are out, but Jedi Knights can use their light sabers to free them and sometimes find protection by stepping into a safety zone. I learned this activity when I got my first job as a ropes-course facilitator working on the Manchester Ropes Challenge Course in Manchester, Connecticut. Star Wars fan, Kevin Brophy, the challenge course coordinator, created it. Thanks Kevin!

Target Group: Any age group

Size of Group: 12 to 30 people

Props: 20 or more toss-ables, two foam swords or half-size pool noodles (these will be the light sabers), two Hula-Hoops, and boundary markers

Objectives

Activity Goals: Practice self-sacrifice, teamwork

Main FVC Connections: Be Safe, Speak Your Truth, Hear the Truth (Teams that communicate and use a coordinated effort tend to be more successful.)

Keys to Success Connections: Emotional awareness, behavioral control, and establishing positive relationships

Facilitator Guidelines

Setup

This activity requires a fairly large space. When setting up the activity, you should create a rectangular playing area with a centerline and two end lines. The end lines should be 20 to 30 feet from the midline. You will want to make sure the end lines are equal distance from the center About 5 feet in from each end line, you should place a Hula-Hoop. This is the Jedi Knight's safety zone.

Make sure to use toss-ables that do not have any hard parts that can hurt people when they're hurled at them.

Introduction/Metaphor

Check in to see who has seen Star Wars. What's special about a Jedi Knight? There's only a few of them. They have great powers and most of them use the force to defend good and triumph over evil. In this game, you have one Jedi Knight on each team. Each team's goal is to take out the other team's members and Jedi Knight by hitting them with their toss-ables. Teammates, though, should be sure to keep their Jedi Knight safe so their knight can help them conquer their evil foes!

The Action

Place your toss-ables along the centerline.

Divide your group into two teams with one team on each side of the centerline.

Explain the rules of the game:

In this activity, each team has one Jedi Knight, and all other team members are warriors. Teams try to tag out other team members by hitting them with a toss-able. If anyone is struck by a toss-able, that person is to take a knee and is temporarily out of the game. Players cannot touch any toss-ables in this position, and they must give up any toss-ables they were holding when hit.

Jedi Knights cannot throw anything. But Jedi Knights can knock down toss-ables with their light sabers, and they can free tagged-out teammates. (You can show group members the foam sword or half-size pool noodle you are using as the light saber.) Players who are temporarily out can re-enter the game if their Jedi Knight taps them with the light saber. But Jedi Knights need protection. Once they are tagged by a toss-able, they are out, and their team loses.

Explain that Jedi Knights can also take cover. Point out the Hula-Hoops placed about 5 feet in from the end lines. Explain that these are each Jedi Knight's safety zones. The Jedi Knight is safe when he/she is within the Hula-Hoop.

A team is declared the winner when:

1. A team member hits the other team's Jedi Knight with a toss-able, or

2. The only member left on the opposing team is the Jedi Knight

Have each team nominate its Jedi Knight for the first round.

Give the Jedi Knights their light sabers (the foam sword or half-size pool noodle).

Emphasize safety rules such as no swatting others with the light sabers (only light touches) and not trying to hurt opponents with the toss-ables.

Send all other participants, Jedi Knights and warriors, to their own end lines to begin the game.

Explain that on your command of "Go," the activity begins and warrior participants (but not the Jedi Knights) should race to the center to grab toss-ables. They can then begin to toss them at the members of the other team.

Once group members are ready, announce, "Go!"

Continue play until facilitators can announce a winner.

Variation

Play by the same rules but don't use a safe-space Hula-Hoop.

Debriefing

I like to focus on whether group members acted independently or tried to come up with a plan and coordinate efforts amongst their teammates. What were the outcomes of these approaches? This can be discussed between rounds if you notice a lack of team play. I also like to discuss "self-sacrifice." The Jedi Knight is the most important member of the team, and often group members have to risk their own safety in the game to protect their Jedi.

Questions for When the Focus Is on Emotional Awareness

- How did it feel to win this game? How about losing?

Questions for When the Focus Is on Behavioral Control

- Did you just throw the toss-ables or try to develop a strategy?
- How did you handle losing? How did you handle winning?
- Was it harder being the Jedi or the warriors? Why?

Questions for When the Focus Is on Positive Relationships

- Did you feel that all team members were working together?
- Did your team use a coordinated attack or was it each player for himself or herself?
- Did anyone have to risk his or her own safety to protect the team's Jedi? Are there times in life that you have to make personal sacrifices to help someone else?
- As the Jedi Knight, you are counted on to help your team and stay safe. What was it like to have that pressure on you? Are there times in your life you have to work under pressure? How do you handle it?

Rock Star and Bodyguard

In this tag game, a participant protects a fellow player from being hit with a toss-able (this could be anything as small as a fleece ball to a beach ball. Your choice in toss-able will change the feel of the game somewhat. It may be fun to try using one then the other).

Target Group: Any age group

Size of Group: 8 to 15 people

Props: a boundary marker, one large beach ball or a soft toss-able such as a fleece ball

Objectives

Activity Goals: Practice self-sacrifice, helping others, teamwork

Main FVC Connections: Be Safe (Even though the objects being hurled at group members are soft, members need to make sure to keep themselves and others safe.), Speak Your Truth, Hear the Truth (This activity can be seen as an individual endeavor or a teamwork exercise. If a group works together to get the rock star, the group is far more likely to be successful.)

Keys to Success Connections: Emotional awareness, behavioral control, establishing positive relationships

Facilitator Guidelines

Introduction/Metaphor

"How many of you have ever wanted to be famous? What would you want to be famous for? Have you ever noticed that those really big stars have bodyguards? What does a bodyguard do? What skills and attributes does a person need to have to be a great bodyguard (ex., dedication, self-sacrifice, trustworthiness)?

Setup

Lay out an external circular boundary with spot markers, rope, or raccoon circles (pieces of nylon webbing, usually 15 feet long). The distance from the center of the circle to the outer boundary should measure at least 10 feet. Make the distance larger for older, stronger groups. Begin with either one beach ball or a fleece ball.

The Action

Ask for two volunteers to come to the center of the circle. Have them decide who will be the rock star and who will be the bodyguard.

Let the group know that the group members standing around the circle are now the paparazzi. The paparazzi will try to hit the rock star with the beach ball (or the fleece ball). The bodyguard must keep the rock star safe from being touched by the ball. If the ball touches the rock star, the thrower of the ball comes to the center and chooses a partner.

The new pair decides who will be the new rock star and who will be the bodyguard. If the throw hits, is blocked, or caught by the bodyguard, the rock star is safe and play continues as the bodyguard tosses the ball back to someone in the circle. If a member of the paparazzi enters the circle to pick up the ball, this player must go back outside of the boundary before throwing the ball at the rock star.

If you choose to give the paparazzi a time limit in which to throw at the rock star, let participants know what it is.

Start the activity.

Variation 1

Add another ball (and maybe even another after that!)

Variation 2

Have more than one bodyguard, especially if there are numerous toss-ables being used in the game

Variation 3

Have several rock stars and several bodyguards

Variation 4

If you are running the activity outside and have a lot of room, widen your circle and use a jelly ball (rubber playground ball) that is to be punched towards the rock star. You can run this version of the activity with or without a bodyguard. The jelly ball should NOT be thrown!

Debriefing

I like to explore how well the participants worked together as a group when part of the paparazzi. Often, during the early rounds, bombardment is an individual activity. Once a highly successful pair enters the center, the group may start to realize that working as a team (for example, by throwing the ball across the circle to someone else who has a better angle) is preferable. If some members of the group are not invested in the activity, it will become obvious as balls fly past them, and they are charged with running to get it.

Questions for When the Focus Is on Emotional Awareness

- What position did you like best: paparazzi, rock star or bodyguard? Why? What do you think this says about you?

Question for When the Focus Is on Behavioral Control

- Did you just randomly throw the ball at the rock star or did you have a plan?

Questions for When the Focus Is on Positive Relationships

- Did you act alone in trying to hit the rock star or did you work together as a group? When did you start to work together as a group in trying to hit the rock star?

- Are there times in your life when you felt like you had do something on your own but realized that you had support?

Heads and Tails Tag*

In this fun game of "chase the tail," group members will be running while holding onto the person in front of them. This can create the potential for injuries. Instruct group members to let go of the person in front of them if needed to maintain everyone's safety.

Target Group: Any age group

Size of Group: Five to eight participants per team

Props: One bandanna per team

Objectives

Activity Goals: Break down inhibitions, use a strategy to accomplish a goal

Main FVC Connection: Be Safe (Members need to take steps to maintain everyone's safety in this activity.)

Keys to Success Connections: Emotional awareness, behavioral control, and establishing positive relationships

Facilitator Guidelines

Introduction/Metaphor

"When people say they feel like they are chasing their own tail, what do they mean? Generally, it means that you are busy but accomplishing very little. We are going to try an activity called Heads and Tails Tag. Today, when you chase your tail, you hope to accomplish something…catching it!"

The Action

Have your team(s) of five to eight participants line up single file with hands on the shoulders of the person in front of them.

Let participants know that the first person in the line is the head of the dragon. The person at the rear is the tail of the dragon. The tail has a bandanna hanging loosely from his or her back pocket. Give the bandanna to the player who is acting as the tail of the dragon.

Explain the rules: On your cue, the head will attempt to grab the bandanna from the tail's pocket without any members of the dragon losing contact with the persons in front of

---

*An original version of this activity called Catch the Dragon's Tail is published in *The New Games Book* (1976)

them. If the head is successful in catching the tail and capturing the bandanna, that player becomes the tail, and the next person in line becomes the head of the dragon.

Let group members know that they should let go of the person in front of them if they need to maintain safety. If someone lets go during the fun, the group members can just come back together re-form the chain.

Start the activity and continue until everyone has had a chance to try out each role.

Debriefing

Questions for When the Focus Is on Emotional Awareness

- Which role did you like best? Least?
- Which role was the easiest? Hardest?

Questions for When the Focus Is on Behavioral Control

- What strategies did you use as the head to catch the tail?
- What strategies did you use as the tail to stay away from the head?
- Are there times in your life when you feel like you are "chasing your tail?" How do you deal with it?

Questions for When the Focus Is on Positive Relationships

- If you were in the middle of the dragon, did you feel like you had much "say" in what was happening? How did that feel? What situations exist in your life in which you don't feel that you have say?
- If you were not at the head or tail spot, did you feel like you were helping one or the other succeed? How did you decide whom to help?

Tail Tag

T. J. Butcher of the Waterford Country School in Waterford, Connecticut, presented this activity to our Manchester Regional Academy staff at a training several years ago.

Target Group: Best used with older groups, as it drives home a specific point

Size of Group: 8 to 16 people

Props: One bandanna for each participant, boundary markers

Objectives

Activity Goals: Encourage empathy, explore concepts of "need" and "greed"

Main FVC Connection: Be Safe

Keys to Success Connections: Emotional awareness, behavioral control, and establishing positive relationships

Facilitator Guidelines

Setup

Create a playing area that doesn't leave a whole lot of free space for running.

Introduction/Metaphor

"This bandanna represents everything you could ever need or want. It is the key to your total happiness and fulfillment. Please place it in your back pocket or tuck it into the back of your belt. Try not to lose that bandanna or you'll have nothing and you will be out of the game. Ready? Set? Go!"

The Action

Give each player a bandanna and explain that it "represents everything you could ever need or want." Tell participants to place the bandannas in their back pockets or tuck it into their belts. Explain that they may not use their hands to guard their bandanna from being taken.

Ask group members to spread out at the onset of the activity.

Emphasize that participants should keep safety in mind.

Say, "Go!"

Once you say go, you may be met with looks of bewilderment. You may be asked questions as to what they are supposed to do. Just restate the fact that the bandannas represent everything they could ever want. Chances are pretty good that some members will attempt to steal the bandannas from other members. This usually triggers a chain reaction of participants grabbing others' bandannas while protecting their own. Eventually, some may realize that since each bandanna represents everything they could ever want, they already have everything they need so don't need any more bandannas.

Debriefing

I find it interesting to see how participants respond. Did they grab other group members' bandannas? Do they realize they don't need to? Do they try to protect their own? Do they give any bandannas to others?

Questions When the Focus Is on Emotional Awareness

- How did you feel when others tried to take your bandanna? What does this say about our nature and how we protect our resources and things we care about?
- How did you feel when you took someone else's bandanna?

Questions When the Focus Is on Behavioral Control

- After I gave the directions, what was the first thing you did? Why?
- Was there a point when you decided not to take anyone else's bandanna? Why?

Questions When the Focus Is on Positive Relationships

- Did you try to take anyone else's bandanna? Why?
- Are there times when you are willing to interfere with someone else's happiness to promote your own?
- Did you give any bandannas back to others?
- Are there times you are willing to sacrifice your own happiness for that of someone else?

11 Icebreakers

So your group members know each other's names now. Maybe you've exhausted them with tag games. Maybe you've opted to skip the tag games. Now what? The sequence of activities in experiential group counseling programs should guide members towards becoming progressively less inhibited and more open to cognitively complex and emotionally risky activities.

Icebreakers are activities meant to get the group moving and to begin to break down inhibitions. Also known as energizers or de-inhibitors, icebreaker activities are high on fun and relatively low on cognitive investment. The goal is to get folks moving, laughing, and simply enjoying themselves. These activities help individuals focus on the group, and focusing on the group rather than the individual helps members get involved without feeling embarrassed or as if they were the center of attention.

De-inhibitors are activities meant to do just what their name says, help members drop their inhibitions. To act "silly" calls for some level of emotional risk. For most emotionally healthy people, these activities serve the purpose of breaking down inhibitions without creating any significant anxiety. Kids or teens with emotional problems are often unaware that "silliness" involves emotional risk. Asking these kids or teens to act silly in front of their peers can stir up emotions such as anxiety, which may hover just below their awareness. Often, these internal emotional experiences trigger outwardly inappropriate behaviors such as avoidance or oppositional behavior. As the facilitator, it is important to watch for an increase in negative or avoidant behaviors during these early activities. This could signal a level of discomfort and anxiety about the activities. Being willing to model the silliness and fun you want your group to engage in goes a long way toward helping engage reluctant participants.

When choosing activities for your group, keep in mind that de-inhibitors can be emotionally risky for some people. If you are seeing resistance or other negative behaviors during these types of activities, this may be the reason. If this occurs, you can process it with the group if you feel it would be effective. If not, sometimes a switch of activity is your best option.

Icebreakers

I love ICE BREAKERS® mints. For a few years, I just kept tossing the empty containers in a bag, vowing to use them for something someday. Then it hit me: use them for icebreakers! The name said it all.

Target Group: Any age range

Size of Group: 8 or more

Props: Bag containing many empty ICE BREAKERS mints containers, each containing one icebreaker question written on a piece of paper

Objectives

Activity Goal: Help participants get to know each other and begin establishing interpersonal connections

Main FVC Connections: Speak Your Truth, Hear the Truth

Keys to Success Connection: Establishing positive relationships

Facilitator Guidelines

Setup

Before group meets, write icebreaker questions on pieces of paper. Fold them and place inside empty candy containers (one per container). For the questions, you can use general icebreaker questions (ex., If you could travel to any one country this year, which would it be?) or more group-specific questions (ex., Tell about the last time your parents/guardians made you mad). Appendix E has questions that you can use for icebreakers.

Introduction/Metaphor

I like to introduce this activity by admitting my addiction! "I have a serious addiction: ICE BREAKERS mints…particularly the blue ones. For quite some time, I saved the empty containers, vowing to use them in my group work somehow. Then it hit me…use them for icebreakers!"

The Action

Depending upon how many participants you have, divide the larger group into smaller groups of two to four.

Have each group choose one container.

Once each group has a container, have them open it and retrieve the paper inside.

Tell them that each group should discuss the question written on the paper. If you want, have each group share a bit about their discussion.

Once they are done, have them choose a new container and discuss again. You can also shuffle groups by having one member leave each group to join another after one icebreaker question.

Variation

Don't have participants partner up. If there are the right amount of participants (you can judge "right amount"), each one can take a container and read a question to the group. Either the reader can answer the question and then move on to another container and question or everyone can have the opportunity to answer each question read. Don't let participants open their containers until it's their turn. This builds suspense!

Debriefing

As this activity is based on discussions, I generally don't debrief it.

Frenzy*

This short, fast-paced activity ensures every group member meets everyone else.

Target Group: Any age group

Size of Group: Over 20 participants

Props: None

Objectives

Activity Goal: Quickly familiarize group members with each other

Main FVC Connection: Be Here

Keys to Success Connections: Behavioral control, establishing personal relationships

Facilitator Guidelines

Introduction/Metaphor and the Action

When your group is gathered, simply tell them that they have exactly two minutes to meet everyone in the room (if that's too tough, as many folks as they can). Encourage them to greet everyone genuinely, with a hearty handshake and an exchange of names.

Once the time limit is up, regroup in a circle. You can check in to see if everyone met each other. If not, encourage participants to take an extra minute to meet those they have not yet met.

Variation 1

Have group members share one interesting piece of information about themselves with each person they meet.

Variation 2

Have group members find someone they don't know and spend a designated amount of time with that person (e.g., 20 seconds) having a discussion, maybe finding commonalities. At the end of the time period, you say, "switch!" Participants will find another person to introduce themselves to and have another brief discussion. For smaller groups, continue until everyone has met everyone else.

Debriefing

No debriefing of this activity is required unless you would like to see if anyone can recall some of the names of the people they met.

---

*I learned this from Tom Leahy at NCCPS in Boulder Colorado. Jim Cain also uses numerous similar activities.

Front Back Switch

This icebreaker activity calls for participants to be focused on the "here and now" or find themselves left in the middle.

Target Group: Any age group

Size of Group: Nine or more group members, though an odd number is needed to play

Props: None

Objectives

Activity Goals: Decreasing inhibitions, create energy

Main FVC Connection: Be Here

Keys to Success Connection: Behavioral control

Facilitator Guidelines

Introduction/Metaphor

This is a simple icebreaker without any deep metaphorical meaning. It's best just to jump right in!

The Action

Creatively pair up your group members. This activity requires an odd number of participants, and one person will be left without a partner. This may mean that you, the facilitator, may need to play to create the required odd number of participants. If the group has an odd number of members, you may simply facilitate the activity.

Have someone volunteer to be the first one without a partner. In situations where you, the facilitator, are joining the activity, you may choose to be the first participant without a partner.

Once players are paired up and the lone player is selected, offer the group the instructions while demonstrating each command with a volunteer:

"In this game, there are three commands: front, back, and switch. When the caller at the center of the circle says 'front,' you are to face your partner. When the caller says 'back', you are to turn and stand back-to-back with your partner. When the caller says 'switch,' you are to find another partner as quickly as you can. The person calling out the commands will also be searching for a partner. In the end, one of you will be left without a partner. The person without a partner will be the next one to call out the commands."

Begin the activity and continue for several rounds until you determine it is time to add a new variation on the activity or to debrief.

Variation 1

After a few rounds, introduce a new instruction, such as the command "side," at which partners stand side by side. For each new round, have the person in the center add a new instruction.

Variation 2

Each time new partnerships are formed following a switch command, ask participants to have a brief discussion about a designated topic with their new partner. For instance, you might ask them to discuss a favorite family tradition or one food they could never live without.

Note: Sometimes participants will avoid partnering up with others so that they can be left in the center to call out the instructions. If more than one player is determined to be in the center, you will have several participants left in the end running away from each other. You may need to intervene. One way to intervene is to yell, "freeze!" Most participants know to stop and stand in place once they hear this command. Once participants have "frozen" in place, you can put the participants who are closest to each other together, leaving one person out to become the new caller.

Debriefing

This activity can be done with little or no debrief.

Questions for When the Focus Is on Emotional Awareness

- Did you like being the one calling the instructions or following the instructions? Why? What do you think this says about you?

Zip Zap Zoom 2.0*

This is a fast-moving game that needs no special introduction. It can be combined with other games such as Love Those New Red Potatoes. (See p. 91).

Target Group: Any age group

Size of Group: 8 to 25 people

Props: Gym spots

Objectives

Activity Goals: Create energy, decrease inhibitions

Main FVC Connection: Be Here

Keys to Success Connection: Behavioral control

Facilitator Guidelines

Introduction/Metaphor

I don't offer much of an introduction to this activity. Generally, I just stand in the middle and launch into the directions.

The Action

Gather your group in a circle with all participants standing on a gym spot except for you, the facilitator, who will be standing in the center of the circle.

Explain the rules of the activity:

The activity begins with the person in the center of the circle looking and pointing directly to a participant standing in the circle while saying, "Zip!" At that command, the person pointed to should immediately crouch down while the participants on either side of this person should turn to face each other with their hands together in "prayer" position. Once facing each other, each of these two participants extends their arms and points to the other and yells "Zap!" (See photo.) If any one of these participants fails to do his or her job quickly, that person comes to the center of the circle while the person in the center takes that participant's place. At any time, the person in the center may also yell, "Zoom!" At this command,

---

*A version of this game appears as Zip Zap in Mark Collard's book *No Props* (Collard, 2005).

everyone, including the caller in the center of the circle, switches to a new spot, leaving someone in the middle.

Begin the activity and continue for several rounds until you determine it is time to add a new variation on the activity or to debrief.

Variation 1

Introduce this activity after several rounds of Love Those New Red Potatoes. (See p. 91.) Play a few rounds of Zip Zap Zoom 2.0 then combine the two activities. In the combined activity, after pointing to a participant in the circle, the player in the middle has the option of using the commands and following instructions for either Love Those New Red Potatoes or Zip Zap Zoom 2.0.

Variation 2

Have two people act as command callers in the middle of the circle. With two command callers, there will be quite a bit more confusion as they may be calling different commands or commanding the same person to do two different things! This variation shouldn't last very long as it will become quite chaotic

Debriefing

I don't generally debrief this activity unless something happens that tells me I need to.

Do You Like Your Neighbors?

I learned this fun, simple icebreaker activity while working at a ropes course in Windsor, Connecticut. Years later, I found a version of it called Do you Love Your Neighbors in *Count Me In* (Collard, 2008).

Target Group: Any age group

Size of Group: 8 to 24 people

Props: Gym spots

Objectives

Activity Goals: Break down inhibitions, enhance self-expression

Main FVC Connection: Be Here

Keys to Success Connections: Emotional awareness, establishing positive relationships

Facilitator Guidelines

Introduction/Metaphor

This activity provides a simple, fun warm-up that doesn't really need any introduction beyond the rules.

Setup

Use the gym spots to create a circle. There should be one fewer gym spots than people in your group (ex., for a group of 12 participants, you should use 11 gym spots).

The Action

Stand in the center of the circle and ask each group member to stand on a spot. Being in the center, you will not have a spot of your own.

Explain the rules to the participants:

As the person in the center, you, the facilitator, will point to any player in the circle and ask the question: "Do you like your neighbor?"

That player must either respond "yes" or "no." If the player says "no," the two members on either side of the player must switch spots. These players can only take each other's gym spot and not any other. The player who said "no" will also be attempting to get one of these spots, resulting in three players vying for two spots. Whoever does not get a spot is the next person in the middle.

If, when asked the question "Do you like your neighbor?," the pointed-to player responds "yes," that person must follow with this statement: "But, I don't like people who…" The player can add a characteristic, such as "wear jeans" or "like punk rock music." Whoever the statement describes (for example, people wearing jeans or who do like punk rock music) must leave their spots and find another spot that is not to their immediate left or right. The person in the center of the circle will also attempt to find a spot. As a result, one person will be left without a spot. That person will be the next player to point and call out the "Do you like your neighbor?" question.

Begin the activity and continue for several rounds until you determine it is time to debrief or move to a new activity.

Debriefing

Generally, I don't debrief this activity unless issues arise that need to be addressed.

Clap-Stomp-Snap!*

This counting activity requires participants to quickly alternate between using the verbal and nonverbal portions of their brain. It also necessitates players to adapt quickly to changing expectations!

Target Group: Any age range

Size of Group: Two or more, even number of participants required

Props: None

Objectives

Activity Goals: Engage participants, foster teamwork and paired problem solving

Main FVC Connection: Be Here

Keys to Success Connections: Behavioral control, establishing positive relationships

Facilitator Guidelines

Introduction/Metaphor

"How hard is it to count to three? How about with a partner? Not too bad, right? This activity requires you to move between saying and doing. Listen closely because you may have to move quickly!"

The Action

Have your group pair up with partners facing each other.

Explain that in this activity, players will count to three, but in each of the five levels of the game, you, the facilitator, will give the instructions for each level. During each level, the partners will count to three, four times in a row. In each successive round, players will replace a number with a physical motion.

Begin the activity by starting with Level 1.

Level 1. Call out the rules for Level 1. Facilitators can say, "Count to three four times in a row by having each partner take a turn in stating a number. For example, if Johnny says '1,' Jimmy says '2,' and Johnny follows by saying '3.' Jimmy then says '1' and so on until they have counted to three four times."

Have the participants count to three as described.

Level 2. Call out the rules for Level 2. Facilitators can say "This time when counting, participants must replace the number 1 with a clap. So to count off, partners create the following pattern:

---

*I learned this activity from my friend and colleague Linda Williams at an improvisation workshop at the National Challenge Course Professionals Symposium (NCCPS) in Boulder, Colorado.

Johnny will perform a clap and Jimmy will say, '2,' followed by Johnny saying '3,' and Jimmy starting the second time through with a clap."

Level 3. Call out the rules for Level 3. Facilitators can say, "In this count, instead of saying '2,' replace it with a stomp."

Demonstrate that the new pattern is clap, stomp, 3; clap, stomp, 3, and so on, again with partners alternating. Explain that each partner alternates turns and the partners should count to three this way four times in a row.

Have the participants count to three as described.

Level 4. Call out the rules for Level 4. Explain that players will replace number 3 with a snap.

Demonstrate the count-off pattern: "clap, stomp, snap." Tell participants to repeat this count off four times in a row, with each partner alternating movements as before.

Have the participants count to three as described.

Level 5. Ask groups to combine so that there are four players in each group.

Have participants perform the three count described in Level 4, only this time alternating turns across the four players.

Debriefing

Questions for When the Focus Is on Behavioral Control

- Why were levels two through four so difficult?
- How do you respond in your life when the expectations keep changing; are you able to "adapt?"

Questions for When the Focus Is on Positive Interpersonal Relationships

- Did you and your partner make any mistakes during the activity? How did you each handle it?
- Did you and your partner figure out a way to support each other during this activity?

Hi Lo Yo

This is a game of gestures. I learned this activity at a workshop at Project Adventure. A similar activity, Ah So Ko, appears in *Funn Stuff* (Rohnke, 1995).

Target Group: Any group able to comprehend the rules

Size of Group: 8 to 16 participants

Props: None

Objectives

Activity Goals: Break down inhibitions, engage participants

Main FVC Connection: Be Here

Keys to Success Connections: Emotional awareness, behavioral control, positive interpersonal relationships

Facilitator Guidelines

Introduction/Metaphor

This activity provides an excellent metaphor for being able to accept mistakes, even appreciate their value. When taking this focus, I often introduce the activity with a discussion about how people are treated when they mess up. Does the way we treat people who make mistakes actually help them do better? Are there a better ways for us to handle other people's mistakes? Are mistakes ever "good?"

You might introduce Hi Lo Yo by saying, "In this activity, we are going to celebrate mistakes by cheering for anyone who makes one and allowing them to go first in the next round!"

This activity can also be connected to discussions about paying attention, thinking and responding quickly, and nonverbal communication.

The Action

Have your group stand in a circle.

Explain that participants will be taking part in a game of gestures. The gestures are Hi, Lo, and Yo.

- Demonstrate the gesture for Hi. Hold one hand palm down over your head. Your hand should be bent at the wrist and pointing to the person either to your left (if you use your right hand) or your right (if you use your left hand).

- Demonstrate the gesture for Lo. Hold one hand palm up, arm bent at the elbow and wrist, sweeping the arm across the body at waist level, again pointing to the left or right.

- Demonstrate the gesture for Yo. Place your hands at chest height, palms facing out, and extend your arms in the direction of another player in the circle. You should appear to be making a basketball pass. The Yo gesture should be made to any person in the circle, aside from those to the immediate right or left.

Explain the rules of the activity. The person beginning the activity will always start by saying "Hi" and using the corresponding gesture. The Hi is passed to the first person's immediate left or right, depending on which way the person points. The pointed-to-person now says and shows the gesture for Lo. The receiver of the Lo sign must then say and perform the Yo gesture. The person sending Yo must make clear eye contact with the receiver to avoid cross-circle confusion. The receiver of Yo must begin again with Hi.

The facilitator will be counting silently to "three Mississippi" during each pass. Anyone who takes longer than this to perform the gesture or does not accurately respond according to the instructions will have "messed up."

Remember, since we don't want to discourage others, the group should applaud and allow that person to begin the next round.

You can start the activity or simply ask for a volunteer to begin.

Variation 1

After several rounds, have the group do the activity in silence.

Variation 2

Add a No gesture. This is an alternative response to Yo. The person receiving Yo has a choice: Continue with Hi or cross their arms over their torso and tell the sending Yo person, "No." This gesture sends the action back to the Yo person who has to begin with Hi. You can also ask your group to add a gesture!

Debriefing

The debriefing will depend upon which introduction you choose: paying attention, non-verbal communication, or accepting mistakes. If you presented the activity in the context of accepting mistakes, you could ask the following:

Questions When the Focus Is on Emotional Awareness

- How did it feel to mess up and have people cheer and celebrate this? Would this approach make you more likely to try fixing mistakes?
- Are mistakes "good" or "bad?" Why?

Questions When the Focus Is on Behavioral Control

- What made this activity easy? What made it difficult?
- How important was being focused for this activity?

Questions When the Focus Is on Positive Relationships

- How can we support people in our lives when they mess up?

Gotcha*

This may be the most commonly played icebreaker I've seen. Success in this activity can be determined in two ways: catching a finger and avoiding having your finger caught. I often use this activity as the first icebreaker in my programs right after I've informed the participants that I want them to experience success in the group. In terms of safety, participants will be grabbing fingers and swinging their arms. I point out how, if people are not careful, these moves can result in hurt fingers and injured noses!

Target Group: Any age range

Size of Group: 6 to 50 people

Props: None

Objectives

Activity Goals: Warm up, experience "success," understand safety

Main FVC Connections: Be Here, Be Safe (This activity provides a great demonstration of how to keep each other safe, setting the group up for many of the more advanced team-oriented activities.)

Keys to Success Connections: Emotional awareness, behavioral control, positive interpersonal relationships

Facilitator Guidelines

Introduction/Metaphor

While this activity can be used as a simple warm-up, I usually use an introduction that pertains to success, failure, and mutual safety.

The Action

Have participants stand in a circle, shoulders about a foot apart.

Ask group members to hold up their left hands and wave to everyone in the group while saying a hearty "Hello!"

Have them extend their left hands, palm up, in front of the midsection of the person on their left. Once participants have their hands extended, invite them to join you as you point to the sky with your right hand and say, "Oh what a beautiful day!"

Instruct members to place their right pointer fingers in the palm of the hand in front of them.

---

*An earlier variation of this activity appears in Funn Stuff (1996) by Karl Rohnke.

Explain that when you say the word *Gotcha,* group members will perform two simultaneous actions: grab the fingers in their left palms while pulling their own right fingers away from the palms they're touching. Before starting, emphasize the need to keep everyone safe. This means when grabbing fingers, people should not try to break the other person's finger and when lifting fingers from a grasping palm, they shouldn't whack anyone in the nose. As facilitator, you can be the first to say the word *Gotcha.* Remind them of the special word (Gotcha) and state that the next time you say that word, they are to perform the grab and remove actions. I like to count "one, two, THREE!" Almost everyone will go on "three." I explain that the secret word is "GOTCHA!" at which time, they should perform the actions! Do a few more rounds, finding ways to keep the group guessing when you will say the secret word. You can then ask for volunteers in the group to be the one to call out "Gotcha!"

Then, try it while reversing hands (place right hands palms up and left index fingers pointing down) offering a chance for revenge on those next to you!

For the final round, have participants put either index finger in their own palms and try to grab their own fingers while also trying to escape. Either way, they will be successful!

Variation 1

Set up the basic Gotcha activity with participants extending their left hands palms up and their neighbors placing right forefingers in palms. This time, have participants reach across with their right hands to grab the pointer fingers touching their left palms. If this action is done correctly, no one will be able to catch any one else.

Variation 2, Gotcha Clap

Have group members place their left hands palm up in front of their neighbors to the left, just as they would in the Gotcha activity. This time, instead of extending their pointer fingers, have group members place their right palms facing down a few inches above their neighbors' left palms. On the three count, group members should attempt to bring their palms together (right hands moving down, left hands moving up) for a simultaneous group clap. When they've mastered a single clap, move to a double clap. You can then ask the group to try a series of claps, such as two claps, turn hands the opposite way (face up if it was face down and face down if it was face up) and clap twice, turn them back the original way and clap twice, and turn them once more for a final single clap. It should sound like, now-it's-time-to-have-some-FUN! You can have them say this while clapping too!

Variation 3, Gotcha Toes

For this variation, have group members turn their left foot towards the person on their left and hold it above that person's right foot. On "Go," group members will attempt with their left foot to tap the right toe of the person on their left while at the same time twisting their right foot away from the tapper on their right!

Debriefing

If you introduce this activity as a way to encourage success within the group, focus on this during the debriefing. You can also discuss how well the group maintained each other's safety and how safety will play an increasingly important role as the activities become more challenging.

Questions for When the Focus Is on Emotional Awareness

- How does it feel to do something successfully?
- What is one area in life in which you've experienced success? How did it feel?
- Were there times that you felt unsuccessful during the activity? How about in your lives?

Questions for When the Focus Is on Behavioral Control

- How did you determine success in this activity?
- How did you create your success?
- What did you do to make sure you kept your self and others safe?

Questions for When the Focus Is on Positive Relationships

- How did each of you contribute to the success of others in this activity (i.e., making sure not to hurt anyone)?
- Who is responsible for your safety? (The answer is everyone: facilitators, self, and peers)

Cross Town Connection

For this activity, you will be sharing fictitious "local" handshakes from various parts of the country or the world. For each handshake, group members will find a new partner, preferably someone they don't know. I generally use four or five handshakes during this activity. Participants have a difficult time remembering the handshakes and partners if you do more than five.

I learned a version of this activity from Jim Cain at a workshop some years ago, and it appears as Handshakes! in Jim's book *Essential Staff Training Activities* (2009), written with C. Hannon and D. Knobbe. A similar activity called Partner Handshakes is published in Mark Collard's 2005 book.

Target Group: Any age group

Size of Group: 8 or more people

Props: None

Objectives

Activity Goals: Break down inhibitions, increase group engagement

Main FVC Connection: Be Here

Keys to Success Connection: establishing positive relationships

Facilitator Guidelines

Introduction/Metaphor

Use this activity to focus on personal interactions. You could introduce the activity saying something like, "I have been lucky enough to travel to many places in my life. What I have found is that people in different places have different ways of greeting each other. Because I am such a nice guy, many people have let me in on secret handshakes that are unique to different parts of our country. So now, I am going to share these with you."

The Action

Tell the group that you will be demonstrating some handshakes used in different parts of the country or world. Introduce each handshake with a story. (While these are some of the most common handshakes that I have used, the variety of possibilities is only limited by your imagination.)

- Cape Cod: In Cape Cod, fishing is a big industry and favorite pastime. Cape Codders reflect this in their greetings to each other. When shaking hands, each partner extends his or her hand just like in a typical handshake. Instead of clasping hands, however, the partners extend their hands to the other person's forearm and slap it like a fish out of water.

- Maine: In Maine, there's lots of logging. The lumberjacks have a secret handshake too. Each partner extends his or her right fist, thumb up, towards the other person. Instruct group participants to grab their partners' thumbs with their left hands and move their hands rapidly back and forth like a huge saw.

- Seattle: Seattle is well known as the origin of the coffee and cappuccino craze. In the '90s, people were so into coffee and cappuccino, they sometimes drank two cups at a time! They couldn't even use their hands to greet each other anymore! What they did was raise the coffee in both hands to shoulder level and tap their shoes together, once on each foot, right toe to right toe then, left toe to left toe.

- Texas: In Texas, they love to square dance. Their greeting looks a lot like a dance step. Partners link arms at the elbow and twirl.
- Wisconsin: What is Wisconsin known for? Cows. Right! What comes from cows? Yes, milk. And in Wisconsin, what do they make with milk? Cheese! Right! For this greeting, one partner intertwines left- and right-hand fingers so that his fingers curl into his palms. He extends his arms and turns his hands, palms facing out and thumbs pointing down. The other partner, recognizing their similarity to a cow's udder, milks the fingers. I know... it's just wrong!

Demonstrate the first handshake with a volunteer.

Have group members divide into pairs. Once paired up, participants should exchange names and perform the first handshake. Remind group members to remember who their partners are for each handshake. Once you finish the first handshake, have your group reform the circle and point to their first handshake partner. Follow this pattern for each of the handshakes you use.

Let participants know that for the second part of this activity, group members will quickly find their partners based on which handshake you call out. For example, when you call out "Maine partners," group members should find their Maine partners and perform the Maine handshake.

Call the next handshake fairly quickly.

Continue for several rounds, creating a moderate level of chaos in your group! You can use the partnerships formed during Cross Town Connection for activities that call for pairs later in your program.

Debriefing

Questions for When the Focus Is on Emotional Awareness

- How do you feel when you receive a warm greeting from a friend or family member?
- How does it feel when people either don't greet you or don't respond to your greeting?

Question for When the Focus Is on Positive Relationships

- Why are greetings such as handshakes important?

Look Up, Look Down*

This activity can be used as a way to divide your group into pairs or simply as a warm-up.

Target Group: Any age range

Size of Group: 6 to 16 people

Props: None

Objectives

Activity Goals: Break down inhibitions, increase focus and group engagement

Main FVC Connection: Be Here

Keys to Success Connections: Emotional awareness, behavioral control

Facilitator Guidelines

Introduction/Metaphor

"Did you ever get that feeling that someone was looking at you? You look up and find you are staring into each other's eyes. How does that feel? Me? I just want to scream! In this activity, we'll be running a version of stare down."

The Action

Have your group circle up, standing shoulder to shoulder.

Explain that in this activity you will instruct them to look down. Tell them that when you say, "Look up," everyone should look up and stare into another participant's eyes. During each round of the game, each participant should only stare at one person and not change the direction of his or her gaze. If that person happens to be staring back, both members must yell and back out of the circle. If the person is not looking at them (and is looking at someone else), the participant is safe and remains in the circle!

Instruct the group to look down. Say "Look up" and begin the activity.

Continue until there are only two players left. These two will be the co-champions. If you have an odd number of players, play another until you end up with a single champion.

Variation

Beware: This one gets loud! When a pair finds themselves staring into each other's eyes, they should scream for as long as possible. The person whose single-breath scream lasts longest remains in the game!

---

*I learned this at my second workshop at Project Adventure. A version of the activity appears in *No Props* (2005) by Mark Collard.

Debriefing

Questions for When the Focus Is on Behavioral Control

- Did you use a strategy for this activity? Did it work?

Questions for When the Focus Is on Positive Relationships

- How do you feel about someone staring at you? Is it a challenge to you or a nonverbal compliment?

Group Thumb Wrestle*

I began using this activity a few years ago with great success! How do I measure success? No broken fingers! This activity aims to create a competitive yet fun atmosphere.

Target Group: Any age group

Size of Group: 4 to 32 people (The activity requires an even number of participants.)

Props: None

Objectives

Activity Goals: Break down inhibitions, increase engagement and focus, help participants deal with competitive activities

Main FVC Connections: Be Here, Be Safe (Emphasize that this is a "friendly" competition, not a win-at-any-cost scenario! Also winners should be graceful in their victories.)

Keys to Success Connections: Emotional awareness, behavioral control, establishing positive relationships

Facilitator Guidelines

Introduction/Metaphor

I generally don't give much of an introduction for this activity other than telling group members what they need to do.

The Action

Have your group stand in a circle and count off by twos.

Ask all of the Number Ones to cross their arms in front of their bodies.

Next, have all Number Twos link hands with the Number Ones "thumb-wrestling" style. Each participant will be holding the hand of the person on their left and right.

_____

*A similar activity called Thumb Wrestling in Stereo where two people compete using both hands appears in Mark Collard's book *No Props* (2005).

On the count of three, each person will engage in a two-handed thumb-wrestling match, with their right hand thumb-wrestling with one person and their left thumb wrestling with another.

A winner is declared when a person pins down another's thumb for a three count. (Pins must be made with the thumb only and without the use of other fingers.)

For fairness, after a round or two, have the Number Twos be the ones to cross their arms

Then, have everyone move to another spot in the circle, renumber, and have the group thumb wrestle with two new partners.

Debriefing

Questions for When the Focus Is on Behavioral Control

- Did we keep each other safe?
- Did anyone put someone else's safety at risk in order to win? Are there times when it is worth risking someone's safety to win?

Evolution

This is a classic activity I learned early on at Project Adventure. If you know Rock, Paper, Scissors, this activity should be easy to learn and a lot of fun for your group. A similar version of the activity, called Metamorphose, appears in *Funn Stuff,* volume 2 (Rohnke, 1996).

Target Group: Any age range

Size of Group: 8 to 24 people

Props: None

Objectives

Activity Goals: Bring awareness to interpersonal differences, promote acceptance, discourage cliques, and help create emotional safety

Main FVC Connections: Be Here, Be Safe (I like to connect this activity to emotional safety, focusing on how creating a "pecking order" leads to treating people differently.)

Keys to Success Connections: Emotional awareness, behavioral control, establishing positive relationships

Facilitator Guidelines

Introduction/Metaphor

In general, I view this activity as a great metaphor for how we as individuals (or as part of a collective) classify other people and treat each grouping differently based on these classifications. Who do we consider "below" us or "above" us? However, the activity can also be a way to think about cycles or progressions, growth and improvement. How you introduce this highly adaptable activity will change based on the group's goals and what type of group you are facilitating. For example, a group working on social awareness may progress through levels indicative of social classes, such as "impoverished" to "middle class" to "affluent." This allows the group to think about what it means to classify people. Where the emphasis is more on stages of change or skill mastery, a group dealing with anger management may be divided into groups identified as "uncontrolled rage" to "controlled rage" to "normal anger" to "full anger control." A friend and colleague of mine, Shawn Moriarity, uses group names that help students learn about food chains and ecosystems. Participants move through groups such as soil as a nutrient for grass, grass as a nutrient for plant-eating animals that are eaten by bigger meat-eating animals and excreted and eventually turned back to soil.

The Action

Check to make sure that everyone understands the game Rock, Paper, Scissors. If not, explain the rules to this game: rock beats scissors, scissors beats paper, and paper beats rock. Show the gestures that go with each and demonstrate how players count off together before they reveal their sign.

Once everyone understands the rules to that game, discuss the concept of "evolving change" (or metamorphosis when evolution is not appropriate), advancing from one stage to another, growing, gaining mastery, or improving as you go. For example, an egg becomes a chick, which becomes a chicken, which is not quite as majestic as an eagle.

Show the visual-kinetic sign that goes with each creature in this cycle. People representing eggs walk around holding their hands over their heads and cupping them together to form an oval shape. Chicks squat low and hold their hands up, pinching their thumbs and fingers together like a cheeping mouth. Those who are chickens wander about clucking and flapping their elbows like wings. Finally, the eagle soars gracefully on the swirling winds. These participants walk with their arms extended.

Explain that all participants will begin as the simplest life form, the egg in this case, and attempt to morph into the most complex form, the eagle, in our example.

Explain that to advance to another form, each group member will face off with another group member representing the same life form and play Rock, Paper, Scissors. The winner advances to the next "more advanced" life form, and the loser "devolves" to the next simpler life form. If the losing player is already at the beginning level, that player remains at that level. Following the showdown, the pair separates, and each participant finds a different member of their evolutionary group and plays Rock, Paper, Scissors again. Each member continues playing until he or she has reached the most advanced group, in this case the eagle group.

Have participants find partners for Rock, Paper, Scissors and start the activity. Play until the group seems ready to debrief.

Debriefing

The debriefing should relate to how you've introduced the activity and should build on this metaphor.

Questions for When the Focus Is on Emotional Awareness

- How did it feel for those who seemed to get stuck being one of the "lower" life forms?
- For those who were stuck as a "lower" life form, did you feel left behind? Have you ever felt that way before?
- How did it feel to reach the top of the evolutionary ladder? Who is at the top of our society's evolutionary ladder? Would you want to be there? Why or why not?
- In what ways are you driven in your lives to move forward, to evolve?

Questions for When the Focus Is on Behavioral Control

- Did you use any strategy to conquer your opponents?
- What skills and abilities do you need to be able to "evolve" in your own life?

Questions for When the Focus Is on Positive Relationships

- How did you treat those who were "lower" than you? How about those who were "higher" than you? Why?
- How can you help others in their personal evolution?
- How can others help you in your personal evolution?

Quick Link*

Target Group: Any age group

Size of Group: 8 or more people

Props: None

Objectives

Activity Goals: Highlight interpersonal commonalities, promote acceptance

Main FVC Connections: Be Here, Speak Your Truth

Keys to Success Connections: Emotional awareness and establishing positive relationships

Facilitator Guidelines

Introduction/Metaphor

Explain to group members that they will have to find out who in the group also shares the characteristic you, the facilitator, will call out. For example, who shares the same birth month? You might begin the activity by highlighting the activity's challenge to find connections:

"Looking around the room, you can see that we are all different from one another. That's the easy part. Let's find out some ways that we're alike."

The Action

Instruct your group members that as quickly as possible, they should get into groups based on the criteria you call out. Facilitators should make sure to be loud and clear when calling out the criteria! Some common criteria are birth month, number of siblings, color of pants, type of toothpaste you used this morning, favorite sport, first letter of first name. Be creative!

Call out the first criteria.

Debriefing

I often debrief this activity as it goes. For example, once the sub groups are formed in response to the criteria I have offered, I check in with each group.

Question for When the Focus Is on Emotional Awareness

- If you were ever alone in a group, how did that feel?

---

*This activity is derived from Categories, an activity in *Cowstails and Cobras II* (Rohnke, 1989).

Questions for When the Focus Is on Positive Relationships

- Did you learn anything new about anyone today?
- Did you find something you had in common with someone that you didn't know before this activity?
- Why is it important to find out what you have in common with others?

Elevator Air*

I learned this activity in my first training at Project Adventure. This activity helps participants focus on the atmosphere of group interactions, and I use it early in a group's time together to help set the tone. It calls for the participants to reflect on how it "feels" to be part of a group. It also helps participants envision how the group should progress.

The activity also brings to light each individual's feelings about closeness and interaction. While we might assume that group participants would be most comfortable with a "party" atmosphere, this won't always be the case. Some group members may be more comfortable with less closeness and may verbalize this during the activity. There is no right or wrong "atmosphere" for a group. It's important as the facilitator, to set the tone of acceptance for varying opinions.

Target Group: Middle school and older

Size of Group: 6 to 20 participants

Props: None, though you can use gym spots to create a circle, especially with more attention- and focus-challenged groups

Objectives

Activity Goals: Help set the tone and create a positive atmosphere for the group, help identify personal comfort levels

Main FVC Connections: Be Here, Be Safe

Keys to Success Connections: Emotional awareness and establishing positive relationships

Facilitator Guidelines

Introduction/Metaphor

Have your group circle up and introduce the experience you call "elevator air":

"How do we humans deal with elevator rides? Well, most of us (except those with an unrelenting desire for attention) stand there, quietly facing the doors without talking. We notice how stiff the atmosphere feels, almost stifling. The silence can be overbearing...when is this thing going to stop? I call that experience "elevator air."

The Action

Explain that in this activity group members will walk across the circle to take a new spot on the other side. Ask your group to imagine themselves in that stuffed elevator and that stiff "elevator air" as they walk across the circle to a new spot. Tell them that crossing through elevator air means avoiding eye contact, not talking, or touching.

---

*A version of this activity appears in Mark Collard's book *No Props* (Collard, 2005)

Have the participants cross to another spot in the circle, while imaging the experience of elevator air.

Once they've accomplished this simple task, check in about how it felt to walk through that group atmosphere, elevator air.

Next, tell them about "school hallway air" (or other type of moderately social environment, such as mall air, village air, downtown air). This should be "air" that is a bit warmer and inviting, but not overly so. This second type of "air" invites polite "hellos," maybe formal handshakes and greetings, nods and brief but shallow conversations.

Have the group participants cross the circle while imagining the experience of this group atmosphere, or "air."

Check in with the group about how it felt to walk through this particular air, especially in relation to the "elevator air."

For the finale, have the group members imagine walking through "Party Air" while crossing through the middle of the circle. This type of atmosphere calls for warm greetings, such as hearty handshakes, high-fives, or hugs and a general attitude of "long time no see!" People may even stop to dance!

Emphasize that participants should practice safe touching only. Tell the group that if someone is uncomfortable with someone else's version of a "party" atmosphere, they should speak up.

At the end of this circle crossing, talk about how it felt to be in each group atmosphere and discuss what type of "air" the group feels they have right now. What type of "air" would they like to have for the remainder of their time together?

Debriefing

Most of the debriefing is inherent in the actual activity and happens as the activity moves along, rather than at the end of the activity.

Questions for When the Focus Is on Emotional Awareness

- Which type of "air" were you most comfortable with? Why?

Questions for When the Focus Is on Behavioral Control

- What can each of us do to create a warm, caring, and safe atmosphere within our group?

Questions for When the Focus Is on Positive Relationships

- How can your mood impact other's moods?
- How can your mood impact the group mood?
- How can we work it out when people have differing visions as to how the group "atmosphere" should be?

Rock-Paper-Scissors Olympic Trials

This activity tests your group participants' skills in competitive rounds of Rock-Paper-Scissors. If you don't know the rules of this game, rock beats scissors, scissors beats paper, and paper beats rock. Each is represented by a hand gesture. Scissors is represented by the peace sign turned sideways (to look like, well, you guessed it... scissors). Players represent rock by balling their hands up into a fist, held with the thumb on top, and paper is represented by extending one's open hand palm down. Competing players face off and say, "Rock, paper, scissors, shoot!" in unison. At "shoot," each player shows his or her hand gesture, resulting in either a tie or one player winning.

I first learned this activity as Entourage. While I usually don't say it in the introduction, this activity is about being a good sport.

Target Group: Any group

Size of Group: 12 to 45 people

Props: None

Objectives

Activity Goals: Generate energy, increase group engagement, encourage healthy competition and good sportsmanship

Main FVC Connections: Be Here, Be Safe (Emotional Safety)

Keys to Success Connections: Emotional awareness and behavioral control

Facilitator Guidelines

Introduction/Metaphor

"Who thinks they are a top notch Rock-Paper-Scissors player? Well, Rock-Paper-Scissors will be the newest Olympic sport in the next spring Olympics and I've been hired as the coach! One of my jobs is recruiting. So, today, I am looking to find a champion Rock-Paper-Scissors player. To do this, we will have an RPS tournament!"

The Action

Begin by dividing your group into pairs.

Make sure that everyone knows the rules for Rock-Paper-Scissors.

Tell your group that the loser of each first round will be so in awe of the person who won that the losing player will become the winner's adoring fan and cheering section. The losing player will stand behind the winner and cheer as the winner takes on another player. Whoever wins that round inherits their opponent's cheering section as well as their defeated opponent, and these players join the cheering section. The cheering section gathers around the player and cheers him or her on in the next round of RPS. This process continues until there are only two players left with about half the group routing for one and half for the other.

Begin the first round of Rock-Paper-Scissors.

Continue the rounds until there are only two players left. At this point, as facilitator, I often run a best of five series, with the first player to win three rounds becoming champion.

At the end of the activity, all hail the champ and newest member of the next Olympic RPS team!

Debriefing

While this activity can be a simple warm-up with no processing, it does offer some interesting opportunities to create a more significant, meaningful experience. There is more to being a "winner" or "loser" in this activity in that group members are required to support the people who just beat them! How hard is that to do? This activity is about competing, supporting others, and losing gracefully.

Questions for When the Focus Is on Behavioral Control

- Did anyone use a particular strategy while playing?
- Did you find it difficult to cheer for the person who beat you?

Questions for When the Focus Is on Positive Relationships

- How did it feel to have to cheer for someone who just defeated you? Was it easy or hard? If it was easy, are there times in your life when supporting an "opponent" would be needed and may be more difficult for you? Why?
- How did it feel to have so many people cheering you on?
- In this activity we are "fickle." Our allegiance shifts after each round. Have you had real life experiences where people kept shifting their allegiances?

Identity Theft

I learned this activity from Heather Wlochowski when we were co-facilitating a Manchester High School leadership group at Manchester Community College in Connecticut.

Target Group: Any group of participants middle school age or older

Size of Group: At least a dozen and the more the merrier

Props: None

Objectives

Activity Goals: Break down inhibitions, get to know each other, increase frustration tolerance

Main FVC Connections: Be Here, Speak Your Truth, Hear the Truth

Keys to Success Connections: Emotional awareness, behavioral control, establishing positive relationships

Facilitator Guidelines

Introduction/Metaphor

"These days, identity theft is a big problem. Today, we are going to steal each other's identities and see what happens! If you lose your own identity, you better have someone else's!"

The Action

Have your group members think of three things about themselves that other group members probably wouldn't know. Tell them they are not to share this information with anyone just yet. Once everyone is ready, inform group members that they will exchange identities with three other group members.

Explain that, on your cue, members should find partners and share with their partners their names and the three facts about themselves. As the partners part ways, each will assume the identity of their partner. When each finds a second partner, that person will share the name and three facts that his or her previous partner shared. After the second meeting, each group member assumes the identity of the second partner and seeks out a third meeting with a new partner. At the third meeting, group members will share the name and facts that their previous partner shared with them.

Tell participants that once they've shared their information and assumed the identity of the third person, group members should return to the circle and try to remember only the last identity they were given. Once everyone is back in the circle, group members will share with the group their last identity, starting with the name and following with the three facts. Rarely will this information have been conveyed accurately through so many folks. The real person can fill in the details!

Debriefing

Most of the debriefing is inherent in the sharing of information at the end of the activity. Facilitators seeking to get more mileage from this activity may want to consider the topics of maintaining focus, organizing rapidly delivered and changing information, and the courage it takes to share a piece of yourself with others.

Questions for When the Focus Is on Emotional Awareness

- How did it feel to share personal information with others, especially knowing it was going to be conveyed to someone else by someone else?

Questions for When the Focus Is on Behavioral Control

- What made this task difficult?
- Did you use a strategy to remember the important information?
- How did you remember all the information you needed to remember?
- Are there times in life when it's tough to keep track of important things because of competing incoming information?

Question for When the Focus Is on Positive Relationships

- What was one cool thing you learned about someone today?

Hot Categories

This activity requires participants to quickly retrieve information from long-term memory and verbalize it. Simply put, you've gotta think on your feet! Facilitators can alter categories called out in the activity to fit the theme of the group. This activity can also be used as a classroom exercise and a fun way to review for a test.

Target Group: Middle school age or older

Size of Group: 8 to 16 participants

Props: Hot Categories list (See Appendix E)

Objectives

Activity Goals: Break down inhibitions, increase group engagement

Main FVC Connection: Be Here

Keys to Success Connections: Emotional awareness, behavioral control

Facilitator Guidelines

Introduction/Metaphor

Ask the group, "What does thinking on your feet mean?" Discuss how well they do it and what skills it takes to do this. "For this activity, you will need to think on your feet!"

Setup

To prepare for facilitating this activity, you can use the list of categories from page 439. Feel free to add or subtract from this list, or if you think you can do better, create your own!

The Action

Have your group sit in a circle.

Explain that you will be announcing a category and that each participant will take turns calling out an item that belongs in that category, moving clockwise around the circle. For example, if I call out the category of "fruit," participants can call out things such as lemons, apples, pears, etc.

Tell the group that once you've announced the category, each person has a "three Mississippi" count after the previous person responds to give their own response. If a correct response is not delivered within that timeframe, the person is out. Any response already given cannot be repeated.

Explain that when a player is ruled out of the game, you, the facilitator, can either continue calling out the same category or you can change it if you feel it has run its course.

Begin the game and continue until there is a single winner! Don't allow answers to be repeated and you are the final judge and jury as to whether an answer is correct or not.

Variation

Allow the group to decide through majority vote if an answer is correct or not. This can lead to interesting discussions.

Debriefing

This activity is difficult for people who struggle with anxiety or dealing with time pressures. It's also an activity that can expose differences in funds of general knowledge and cognitive abilities. If you use this activity, be aware of how group members who struggle with this activity are handling it as well as how others are treating those who struggle. Aside from difficulties that may arise due to these issues, I generally don't debrief this activity. If your slower players are willing to speak, it can be a forum for them to express how it feels to not be able to keep up with others. They may experience this frustration in other areas of their lives as well.

Questions for When the Focus Is on Emotional Awareness

- What was easy about this activity? What was difficult?
- How did the time pressure in this activity make you feel?
- Were there times that you felt I was wrong or unfair as the judge? How did you handle that?

Question for When the Focus Is on Behavioral Control

- How did you respond to the time pressure?

Question for When the Focus Is on Positive Relationships

- How did you treat those who had a difficult time with this activity?

Dictionary Definitions

This game goes way back to an old parlor game called Dictionary. It has been popularized and mass produced as a board game under different names over the past few decades. For this version, all you need is a dictionary, some paper, and writing utensils.

Target Group: Middle school age and older

Size of Group: 6 to 12 participants

Props: Dictionary, paper, writing utensils

Objectives

Activity Goals: Decrease inhibitions, increase engagement, encourage creative thought

Main FVC Connections: Speak Your Truth, Hear the Truth

Keys to Success Connections: Emotional awareness, establishing positive relationships

Facilitator Guidelines

Introduction/Metaphor

"How good are you at acting? How about lying? Are lying and acting similar? How so? How are they different? We may find some answers to these questions in this activity."

Setup

Cut the paper into pieces just large enough to write a sentence on. Give each member of the group several pieces of the paper and a writing utensil. If possible, have participants use identical writing utensils (i.e., all pencils, all blue pens, etc.).

The Action

Tell the group that in this activity, the group will be making up word definitions and trying to fool one another into believing them. A "Dictionary Definer" will find a word for the group, and each participant will write down a definition for it that they think other group members would truly believe is the correct definition.

Have a volunteer become the first "Dictionary Definer." The Definer will scan the dictionary for a word that he or she believes no one else will know. (The definer does not have to know the word either.)

The definer reads the word aloud, but NOT the definition.

Each group member creates and writes down a definition for that word and his or her name.

The Definer writes down the correct definition and collects all the other definitions.

Ask the Definer to silently read over each one to make sure the group's definitions are legible.

Ask the Definer to mix up the definitions and then read all the definitions out loud.

Once they are all read, call for a vote. Members must vote for the definition they believe is correct.

Count up the vote and ask the Dictionary Definer if the definition with the most votes is the correct one. If not, check to see if the next most popular one is and continue until the correct definition is stated.

After the first round, ask for a volunteer to be the new Dictionary Definer.

Debriefing

Questions for When the Focus Is on Behavioral Control

- Was it difficult to come up with believable sounding definitions? How did you do it?
- As the Dictionary Definer, was it difficult to not give away the correct definition when you were reading the definitions aloud? How do people who are lying give themselves away verbally and nonverbally?
- What strategies did you use to figure out which definition was the correct one?

Questions for When the Focus Is on Positive Relationships

- For this activity, nonverbal communication can be helpful. How important is nonverbal communication in your daily lives? Give some examples.

Count Me Out (and Count Me In)

I learned this game while at NCCPS in Boulder, Colorado, some years ago. Many kids I work with know a basic version of this activity as a game called Taps.

Target Group: Upper elementary-school-age participants and older

Size of Group: 4 to 8 people

Props: None

Objectives

Activity Goals: Increase engagement, promote healthy competition

Main FVC Connection: Be Here

Keys to Success Connections: Emotional awareness, behavioral control, establishing positive relationships

Facilitator Guidelines

Introduction/Metaphor

"Is it better to give or receive? When is it better to give? When is it better to receive? In this activity, giving is definitely better than receiving. In fact, if you receive too much, you expire! But, choose wisely who you give to!"

The Action

Have participants stand in a circle.

Tell them that the game's action will move clockwise around the circle.

Instruct players to put both their hands into the middle of the circle with just their index (or pointer) fingers extended.

Explain the rules: The first person will begin by tapping any other player's hand with one of their pointer fingers. In doing this, the first player "gives" the second player another finger. The tapped player must now extend two fingers on the hand that was tapped. Moving clockwise from the player who began the round, the next player in the circle takes a turn by tapping any other player with one of his or her fingers. If a player who is holding out two fingers is tapped by a player holding out one finger, the tapped player now has to hold out three fingers. Once a tap causes a player to extend exactly five fingers, that hand is out of the game. However, if a tap adds up to more than five fingers, players will reset to the amount of fingers beyond the five. For example, if a player extending four fingers is tapped by someone holding out two fingers, giving them a total of six, the tapped player would hold out only one finger (or one over the five).

Start the activity and see that it continues around the circle. Each time a hand is tapped, the number of fingers to be extended should be equal to the total number of fingers both players are showing at the time of the tap.

Have participants continue going around the circle until there is only one player left and a winner is declared.

Variation, Count Me In

This variation of the activity has the opposite goal: group members work to keep everyone in as long as possible.

Set the game up the same way as in Count Me Out.

Tell participants that this time, as they tap hands, they should try *not* to give other players exactly five fingers. Again, the action moves clockwise.

See how long the group can go without losing anyone from the circle.

Debriefing

Questions for When the Focus Is on Emotional Awareness

- Did you enjoy the first version or the second version more?
- Were there times in the game in which you felt "ganged up" on? How did that feel?
- Did you take part in ganging up on someone else?

Questions for When the Focus Is on Behavioral Control

- How were you successful in this game?
- Why were you not successful in this game?
- Did you plan your moves?

Questions for When the Focus Is on Positive Relationships

- When is giving good? When is it not so good?
- When is it good to receive? When is it not good to receive?
- Did you feel any particular alliance to someone else in the game? Why? What was the result? What are the results of forming alliances with others in real life?
- Are there times in your life you've been involved in ganging up on others?
- Are there times in your life you've been on the receiving end of people ganging up on you?

King of the Jungle

This activity requires participants to remember and quickly perform other participants' physical signs when cued. This requires focused attention and activation of the working memory. I believe this activity has its roots in less-than-therapeutic settings as an activity called Thumper, historically played in college dorm rooms.

Target Group: Any age range

Size of Group: 6 to 12 people

Props: None

Objectives

Activity Goals: Increase engagement, promote healthy competition, highlight how we treat those we perceive as "below" us

Main FVC Connection: Be Here

Keys to Success Connections: Emotional awareness, behavioral control, establishing positive relationships

Facilitator Guidelines

Introduction/Metaphor

"In *The Lion King*, Simba sings, 'I can't wait to be King!' Why does he want to be king? What does it mean to be at the top? How do you get there?"

Setup

Each member of the group should choose an animal and a kinetic or visual (possibly even auditory) sign to represent their animal. For example, if I choose Crocodile, I might extend my arms out in front of me to represent the crocodile's jaws and snap them together. Once everyone has chosen an animal, have the group members one by one demonstrate their signs. You may want to go around a few times for larger groups.

The Action

Explain that the goal of the activity is to become the King of the Jungle. Participants will try to travel around the circle and take the king's spot. Participants move counterclockwise around the circle. Whoever starts the game is declared the reigning King of the Jungle. (I like to give the King a throne-like chair, if possible.)

Explain the rules: The king will begin the activity by displaying his or her sign followed by someone else's sign. The person whose sign is displayed must then show his or her own sign, followed by the sign of another group member. Continue this pattern until someone makes a mistake. If a participant doesn't show the correct sign within the facilitator's silent count to "three Mississippi," that player must move to the immediate left of the King of the Jungle. This participant will have to work all the way around the circle counterclockwise to reach the king's spot. If the person playing the King is wrong, that participant moves to the last place spot (or to the left of their original spot when King), and the person to the King's right becomes the new King. Anyone who makes a mistake must move one spot to their left, leaving that player one place further away from being King.

Have the participant playing the king begin the activity.

Variation 1

For a possibly simpler version, facilitators can use numbers.

Assign each player a number, one through however many people are playing.

Begin a beat with your hands. (This pattern could be as simple as slap the thighs and clap the hands).

Have players say their own number followed by someone else's number while keeping within the beat.

Variation 2

You can also keep a beat while participants display the animal signs.

Debriefing

In addition to encouraging participants to be focused, this activity nicely highlights social status and how people treat each other within a pecking order. It also demonstrates that it doesn't take much to get knocked down from a lofty status.

Questions for When the Focus Is on Emotional Awareness

- How did it feel to become king or move towards becoming king?
- How did it feel to get knocked down to the bottom of the order?

Questions for When the Focus Is on Behavioral Control

- How were you able to be successful in this activity?
- What was difficult about this activity?

Questions for When the Focus Is on Positive Relationships

- How did you treat those above you? How did you treat those below?
- How did people above you treat you? How were you treated by those ranked below you?

Your Add*

This activity involves the ability to quickly calculate without pencil and paper. Facilitators shouldn't use it with groups whose members who would find this extremely difficult.

Target Group: Middle-school-age participants and older

Size of Group: 4 to 24 participants

Props: None

Objectives

Activity Goal: Increase engagement

Main FVC Connection: Be Here

Keys to Success Connection: Emotional awareness, behavioral control

Facilitator Guidelines

Introduction/Metaphor

I generally use this activity as a time filler, without using any specific introduction.

The Action

Have your group divide into pairs.

Have the paired group members face each other with hands held behind their backs.

Tell participants that on their count of three, each member of the pair will hold out both of their hands and show anywhere from no fingers to ten fingers. Both participants will then attempt to add up and say as quickly as possible the total number of fingers being shown. The first person to say the correct answer is the winner of that round.

Have participants begin the activity.

Variation 1

Facilitators can run this activity as a tournament, where the winner of each match takes on the winner of the next match until a champion is crowned. Encourage the defeated members to root for the member who beat them or the member who beat that person.

Variation 2

This activity can also be done in groups of three or more.

---

*A version of this activity appears in *The Bottomless Bag Again* by (Rohnke 1991).

Debriefing

Questions for When the Focus Is on Emotional Awareness

- Did you feel that you were "outmatched" in this activity? How did that feel? What are your strengths?

Chosen Few*

This activity encourages participants to step outside themselves and gain awareness of others. For many kids with emotional problems, this is difficult. The activity also helps participants find commonalities with their peers.

Target Group: Any upper elementary-school-age group or older

Size of Group: 6 to 12 participants

Props: None

Objectives

Activity Goals: Increase engagement, increase awareness of others and environment, shift focus from self to others

Main FVC Connection: Be Here

Keys to Success Connections: Emotional awareness, behavioral control, building positive relationships

Facilitator Guidelines

Introduction/Metaphor

"This is a test of your detective abilities. What skills does a detective use to solve a case? You will need those abilities for this activity!"

The Action

Have your group sit in a circle.

Ask one member to stand in the middle of the circle and think of something that he or she has in common with at least one other member of the group. Make sure participants choose something that others would be able to identify and guess. You can let them know that the shared trait could be that you both are wearing white shoes, have a brother, have a last name beginning with the letter *B,* are both over 5 feet tall, etc.

Once ready, have the person in the middle of the circle ask all members who share that characteristic to stand.

Let group members, including those standing, know that they must then guess what the common characteristic is. Whoever guesses it first will be the next one to come to the middle and decide the shared trait.

In the case that the group doesn't guess the correct characteristic, have a player from the circle replace the person in the middle and begin the activity again.

---

* A version of this activity called Me Too aka Chosen Few appears in *Back Pocket Adventure* by
  Karl Rohnke and Jim Grout (1998).

Variation

The person identifying the common trait does not have to stand in the center of the circle and does not have to share the trait they are thinking of. In this case, the person simply asks the participants who do share the trait to stand.

Debriefing

Questions for When the Focus Is on Emotional Awareness

- Have you ever been in a group of people and felt they had nothing in common with you? What was that like?

Questions for When the Focus Is on Behavioral Control

- How did you figure out what you had in common? What strategies did you use?
- When you were in the middle of the circle, how did you determine what common features you were going to focus on?

Questions for When the Focus Is on Positive Relationships

- To form friendships, is it important to find things you share in common? What are the most important common traits you share with your friends?
- Can you be friends with someone who doesn't have much in common with you?

Change-Up

Change-Up can be used as a simple icebreaker or processed at a deeper level. The activity is about being observant and aware of details in our environment. A basic building block of social skills is empathy, or the ability to step outside ourselves and experience life from someone else's perspective. Those who lack this ability are often not tuned in to their environment. Kids who have social-skill deficits may not tune into the nonverbal information coming their way from others.

I learned this activity at a Project Adventure workshop. A version of the activity called Last Detail appears in *Quicksilver* (1995) by Karl Rohnke.

Target Group: Elementary-school-age participants and older

Size of Group: Two or more; there must be an even number of participants to run the activity

Props: None

Objectives

Activity Goals: Increase engagement, increase awareness of others and the environment, shift focus from self to others, help understand detail-oriented versus whole-picture thinking

Main FVC Connection: Be Here

Keys to Success Connections: Emotional awareness, behavioral control, establishing positive relationships

Facilitator Guidelines

Introduction/Metaphor

"How detail oriented are you? Are you the person who sees the 'forest' or the 'trees?' Do you have keen powers of observation? In this activity, you will find out!"

The Action

Divide your group into pairs.

Instruct partners to study each other for about a half minute. Encourage them to take note of as many details as possible.

Explain that, on your cue, the partners should stand back-to-back.

Once they are back-to-back, instruct them to change one thing about their appearance.

When everyone has done this, have the pairs turn and face each other and try to figure out what their partner has changed.

Continue the rounds by having the partners change two things the next time and three things in the next round. Or have participants switch partners.

Debriefing

Beyond an icebreaker activity, the Change-Up can be used as activity to reflect on being observant and aware of details in our environment, an important skill toward building social awareness and empathy. It should also be noted that sometimes kids who reside in more dangerous environments are hyper-aware of the details they see. They may notice everything. For example, a group of inner-city youth may be able to relate to the feeling of needing for their own safety to tune into every possible visual cue. Facilitators should take this into account.

Question for When the Focus Is on Emotional Awareness

- How did it feel to be "studied"?

Questions for When the Focus Is on Behavioral Control

- In your life, when are powers of observation and noticing details important?
- For what types of jobs might these abilities be important?
- Has there ever been a time when your not noticing details caused you problems?

Questions for When the Focus Is on Positive Relationships

- Is noticing details important to maintaining positive relationships? How so?

One Up, One Down

Unfortunately, this game can only be used once with any particular group. The activity requires group members to carefully observe the actions of the group and listen to the feedback of the facilitator to discover the underlying "rules" of the game.

Target Group: Middle-school-age or older participants

Size of Group: Any size group

Props: None

Objectives

Activity Goals: Increase engagement, increase observation skills and awareness of environment

Main FVC Connection: Be Here

Keys to Success Connections: Emotional awareness, behavioral control, establishing personal relationships

Facilitator Guidelines

Introduction/Metaphor

Have your group sit in a circle and say to them: "Pay careful attention to me. I will say one of three things: 'One up, one down,' 'two up,' or 'two down.' Then moving clockwise around the circle, each person will have to decide which of those three things to say. I will tell you if you are right or wrong. As the game goes on, if you figure out what 'rule' I am playing by, show it with your actions but don't tell others what you have figured out. Simply test the theory with your actions and words."

The Action

Begin with one of the following statements: "one up, one down," "two up," or "two down." If you say "one up, one down," you will also have to place one hand above the other. It can be under your chin, on your shoulder...anywhere that would be considered "up." The other hand must be below the other or "down." It can be on the ground, in your lap, etc. In the same vein, "two up" would be two hands up. "Two down" represents two hands down.

Ask the person to your right to say one of the three statements. You will tell them if they are right or wrong based on where their hands are placed. For example, if the next person says "two up" but has his hands in his lap, he's wrong. If he says "two down" and has placed both hands in his lap, he's right!

Continue this pattern around your circle, each person stating one of the three possible statements and receiving feedback from you about whether they are right or wrong.

At first, make your movements very covert. As the game wears on and some members are struggling to figure it out, exaggerate your movements to clue them in.

Debriefing

This activity tends to produce frustration; be prepared to debrief this emotion and its resulting behavior.

Questions for When the Focus Is on Emotional Awareness

- How did you feel when you were told that you were wrong or right?
- As others started to catch on, how did it feel to those of you who still hadn't caught on?
- Are there times in your life when you feel like everyone else "gets it" and you don't?
- How did it feel to not understand what was going on?
- How did it feel when you finally caught on?

Question for When the Focus Is on Behavioral Control

- How did you deal with not knowing what was going on?

Question for When the Focus Is on Positive Relationships

- For those who caught on first, did you do anything to help your peers get it?

Famous People

For some groups, this is simply a fun activity that requires no in-depth debrief. However, being able to ask and answer questions and use the information you receive are important relationship-building skills.

Target Group: Any group old enough to know your list of celebrities

Size of Group: 8 or more people

Props: Name tags or index cards (enough for one per person), tape

Objectives

Activity Goals: Increase engagement, promote positive interpersonal communication skills

Main FVC Connections: Speak Your Truth, Hear the Truth

Keys to Success Connections: Emotional awareness, behavioral control, establishing personal relationships

Facilitator Guidelines

Setup

Prior to your session, create a list of famous people that the members of your group are likely to know. Write each name on a name tag or an index card.

Introduction/Metaphor

"What would it be like to be famous? Today, you will receive a new identity, that of a famous person. But, you won't know exactly who that is. It's your job to figure out, who you are!"

The Action

During group, tape a card to each member's back so that he or she cannot see the card. Instruct members not to tell their peers the name of the persons on their backs.

Have group members mix and mingle, asking each other yes-or-no questions about the person whose names are on their cards. Instruct the group that the questions should be those that can be answered only by saying, "yes" or "no" or "maybe" and "I don't know."

Let participants continue guessing until they figure out who it is. The number of questions and guesses are unlimited unless you, the facilitator, see any reason for there to be limits.

Debriefing

Many kids with social skill deficits don't bother asking questions to learn more about other people. Those skills are highlighted in this activity. Also, this activity can be difficult for cognitively limited kids who can easily become targets of their peers if they have difficulty with the questioning and deductive reasoning aspects of the activity. Finally, the last person to finish the activity is at risk of standing out in a negative way. Facilitators should be aware of the reaction of these participants' peers.

Questions for When the Focus Is on Emotional Awareness

- Did you find this activity easy or difficult? Why?

Questions for When the Focus Is on Behavioral Control

- Did you find that each question you asked guided your next question? Why?
- Have you ever had to deal with a life-situation in which asking questions was necessary?

Questions for When the Focus Is on Positive Relationships

- What questions did you find to be the most important? How does this translate to real life relationships?
- Is it important to ask people questions? Why?

The Way I See It...*

During this activity, the facilitator gives a single set of directions to all members. Even though everyone hears the same thing and attempts to follow the same directions, the results often look quite different in the end. This provides an excellent metaphor for how we all interpret our worlds differently.

Target Group: Any age group

Size of Group: Any size group

Props: One sheet of paper per participant

Objectives

Activity Goal: Understand perspective and how we all interpret our worlds differently

Main FVC Connections: Speak Your Truth, Hear the Truth

Keys to Success Connections: Emotional awareness, behavioral control, establishing positive relationships

Facilitator Guidelines

Introduction/Metaphor

"'We don't see the world as it is but rather, as we are.' What does this quote mean? Let's see how differently we interpret our world."

The Action

With your group seated, give one piece of paper to each participant.

Request that your group members do not look at each other or at what their peers are doing during the activity. If possible, arrange them so that they are not facing each other and cannot easily see each other's papers.

Ask them to fold their papers in half. Sometimes, participants will question which way to fold their pieces of paper to which I respond, "yes."

Next tell them to tear off the upper right-hand corner of the paper. Again, you may hear requests for clarification. Resist answering!

For the next step, ask them to fold the paper in half again and tear off the upper right-hand corner of the paper.

Repeat these directions for a third time.

Have group members unfold their papers and compare them with those of the other participants.

---

*A similar activity called You Tear Me Up appears in Karl Rohnke's book *The Bottomless Bag Again* (1991).

Debriefing

Questions for When the Focus Is on Emotional Awareness

- Did you feel confused at all during this activity? How did you deal with that?

- How does it feel when someone else doesn't seem to understand your point of view?

- Why do we interpret things differently than other people?

Questions for When the Focus Is on Behavioral Control

- How did you decide what I meant by "fold your paper in half?" Why did you decide that? Why did you not all do it the same way?

- Did you look at what others were doing (or were you tempted to) during this activity? If so, why?

Questions for When the Focus Is on Positive Relationships

- How does having different interpretations of our worlds play out in relationships with other people such as parents, friends, boyfriends, or girlfriends?

- Is it ever beneficial that we all interpret our worlds differently? How can this contribute to developing relationships?

12 Get To Know You

"So, tell me about yourself" may be the most common job interview request, and for many, it's also the presumed, stereotypical first question that "shrinks" ask their patients. It conjures up images of a Freud-like man, gently stroking his beard while awaiting the nervous answer from his couch-bound patient. For many people, prompts such as "tell me about yourself" are difficult to respond to. In my experience, when posing an open-ended question such as this to teens, I am often met with shoulder shrugs, responses of "I don't know," or simply silence. How would one start to respond to this question?

The activities in this section go beyond name games, warm-ups, and icebreakers. They provide a safe framework for participants to take social risks and share personal information. The prompts to elicit information often offer closed-ended but playful questions and are generally easier questions to respond to. Which would be easier for you to answer: "tell me about yourself" or "if you could have any super power, what would it be"? Which answer would be more fun to hear? In both cases, the questioner learns something about the person.

The activities are also fun. While they are engaging and entertaining, the activities also help develop a platform of trust among group members. If participants can share information about themselves and still feel accepted, they will be willing and able to tolerate the higher levels of challenge required of more advanced activities.

Many of these activities focus on Speak Your Truth and Hear the Truth elements of the FVC. Most of the activities also connect with the third Key to Success: building and maintaining positive interpersonal relationships. These activities break down social barriers and foster increased feelings of empathy amongst the group members. Since self-disclosure requires an atmosphere of safety, the facilitator must be sure to fully enforce the tenets of the FVC.

Take a Stand*

What's the difference between arguing and debating? This activity helps participants figure that out by teaching them how to debate an issue without allowing it to become a full-blown conflict. It can also be used to help a group of people find commonalities and differences among each other and, in turn, help build trust and acceptance within the group.

Target Group: Any age group

Size of Group: 6 or more participants

Props: None

Objectives

Activity Goals: Differentiate between debating and arguing, build trust and acceptance within the group

Main FVC Connections: Speak Your Truth, Hear the Truth

Keys to Success Connections: Emotional awareness, behavioral control, establishing positive relationships

Facilitator Guidelines

Introduction/Metaphor

"What's the difference between arguing and debating? Which one is 'productive' and which is 'destructive?'"

The Action

Have your group line up single file, facing you.

Tell participants that you will be calling out words and that members must immediately decide which one they prefer and move to the side that you designate. For example, you can say "hamburgers" while pointing to your left and "hot dogs" while pointing to your right. People who like a burger better than a dog will go to your left, while those who prefer a dog will move to the right.

Once they are in place, tell them to look around to see who is with them. Have members point out their observations. You can do the same!

Variation 1

Ask questions that have three or four possible answers, such as whether participants prefer winter, spring, summer, or fall. Offer four possible places to move to.

---

*A similar activity known as The Bus appears in *The Revised and Expanded Book of Raccoon Circles* by Jim Cain and Tom Smith (2007).

Variation 2

Once the members have chosen their sides, each group has 1 minute to come up with reasons why its choice is the best! Each side nominates one person to debate the issue with the representative from the other side. Facilitate a 1-minute debate and, if you'd like, choose winners based on how well they debated as opposed to argued.

Debriefing

During the activity, I often stop between rounds and point out differences I note in the sides people chose. I generally only debrief after the activity if I use the debating component (Variation 2).

Questions for When the Focus Is on Emotional Awareness

- How did it feel to be the person debating? Did it feel different from the conflicts you typically have in life? How so?

Question for When the Focus Is on Behavioral Control

- What was the difference between what we just did and arguing or fighting?

Questions for When the Focus Is on Positive Relationships

- Conflict is normal in relationships. How can the activity we just did help you with conflicts in your relationships outside this group?
- Did you learn anything surprising about any of your group-mates?

See Ya*

This activity is a great one to start a program. It combines physical movement with fun ways for participants to begin getting to know each other.

Target Group: Any age group

Size of Group: 12 to 50 participants

Props: None

Objectives

Activity Goal: Get to know each other

Main FVC Connections: Be Here, Speak Your Truth, Hear the Truth

Keys to Success Connection: Establishing positive relationships

Facilitator Guidelines

Introduction/Metaphor

I don't have any particular way to introduce this activity. I generally just launch into the directions.

The Action

Divide your larger group into smaller groups of four to six people.

Once the smaller groups are formed, tell the participants that each group will always have the same number of people.

Give each group a topic to discuss for 2 minutes (or whatever time limit you would like to use). Some suggested topics are favorite movies, places you would like to travel to, the place where you grew up, the type of music you like best, favorite family tradition, etc.

When the 2 minutes are up, have one member leave each group and find a new group. To determine which member will depart, give the group a certain criterion such as the person with the longest hair, the person who lives the farthest away, or the person who's got the longest left thumb.

When it is determined who is leaving, the group says, "See ya!" to that person and then, with exuberance, repeatedly calls out "over here!" until another person joins the group.

Continue for several rounds.

---

* I learned this activity from Jim Cain at an annual Connecticut Experiential Education Association (CEEA) conference. Jim, along with Tom Smith, have it written up as See Ya in their book *The Revised and Expanded Book of Raccoon Circles* (2007). In the description, Jim credits Chris Cavert for sharing the activity with him. It also appears as Over Here in Cain's book *Essential Staff Training Activities* (2009), co-authored by Claire-Marie Hannon and Dave Knobbe.

Debriefing

This activity requires discussion all along and generally requires no debriefing. You may want to check in to see if people learned anything interesting about anyone else.

Prompts

In this activity, prompts are aimed to elicit interesting personal stories that may otherwise remain buried in the recesses of memory.

Target Group: Any age group that is cognitively and emotionally ready for it

Size of Group: 4 to 16 participants

Props: None

Objectives

Activity Goal: Share personal stories as a way to get to know each other

Main FVC Connections: Speak Your Truth, Hear the Truth

Keys to Success Connections: Emotional awareness, behavioral control, establishing positive relationships

Facilitator Guidelines

Preparation

"Tell me about yourself." If you've ever asked this question of a teenager, you may have been met with quizzical looks, shoulder shrugs and "I don't know." Freely recalling our own personal history can be difficult, and kids may feel put on the spot. Many of us find it easier to respond to direct questions: "How old are you?" "How many siblings do you have?" In this activity, be aware that prompts can trigger emotionally laden stories. Make sure to maintain an emotionally safe environment for sharing.

Introduction/Metaphor

"Sometimes it's difficult to remember personal events and stories from your life. Often a prompt helps. In this situation, a prompt will be something that may trigger a memory from your past, something that you can share with this group. Don't worry if the rest of us don't understand the connection to the prompt. It only has to make sense to you!"

The Action

Gather your group members in a circle.

Offer them one (or more) prompts, such as numbers, colors, summer, times they felt embarrassment or anger. Any topic will do.

Ask each member to think of a personal story to go with one of the prompts. For example you may say, "The prompt is a color," then each member must tell a personal story that relates to a color.

Members share their personal stories with the group.

If group members are having difficulty retrieving memories, give them several prompt options. For example, "Your prompt choices are colors, sounds, and verbs. Tell a story that has to do with one of these."

Debriefing

Discussion is an integral part of this activity, and it generally does not require debriefing after the activity.

Not So Missing Link*

Target Group: Any age group

Size of Group: 6 to 20 participants

Props: None

Objectives

Activity Goal: Create a sense of connectedness

Main FVC Connections: Speak Your Truth, Hear the Truth

Keys to Success Connections: Emotional awareness, establishing positive relationships

Facilitator Guidelines

Introduction/Metaphor

"In looking around at our group, I can see lots of differences. I can see that John has blue eyes and Jim has brown eyes. I can see Tara wearing jeans and Jenny wearing shorts. Sometimes, it's tougher to tell what we have in common."

The Action

Ask for a volunteer.

Your volunteer should make a statement about himself or herself that is true.

If the statement is also true about someone else in the group, that person should link to the first person arm in arm.

The second person makes a statement that is true about himself or herself and is joined by a third group member.

If the statement is true about more than one group member, only one may link arms with the person who made the statement.

Continue until all members are linked. The last person must make a statement about himself or herself that is also true of the first person. This may take several attempts.

Once the first and last persons find their commonalities, they link arms to create a full circle, which represents the connectedness of the entire group.

Debriefing

Questions for When the Focus Is on Emotional Awareness

- How does it feel to be connected to others?
- How does it feel when we are not connected to those around us?

---

*Thank you to Dick Hammond for showing me this one at the NCCPS in Boulder, Colorado.

Questions for When the Focus Is on Positive Relationships

- Are there times in your life when you've felt disconnected or "different," only to find that you have more in common with those around you than you first realized?

- Are there times when you thought you had a lot in common with someone but found out that you were more different than alike?

- Can you have a relationship with a person who has different views than you do? Are there any personal views that you cannot tolerate?

Spectrum*

This activity helps folks determine where they stand in contrast to their peers.

Target Group: Any age group

Size of Group: 4 to 20 participants

Props: Raccoon circle, piece of rope or tape

Objectives

Activity Goal: Group members see where they stand in contrast to others and, in the process, get to know each other better and gain experience in conflict resolution, negotiation, and compromise

Main FVC Connections: Be Safe, Speak Your Truth, Hear the Truth

Keys to Success Connections: Emotional awareness, establishing positive relationships

Facilitator Guidelines

Introduction/Metaphor

"Spectrum can be defined as 'the distribution of a characteristic in terms of quality or quantity.' Most phenomena in life can be characterized by where they fall on a spectrum. For instance, intelligence: Some people are very smart, some pretty smart, still others, unfortunately, are not smart at all. Virtually any personal characteristic, mood, talent, weakness, or strength can be characterized in relation to other people using the spectrum concept. This activity helps folks determine where they stand in contrast to other group members."

The Action

Lay out your rope in a curved line.

Inform the group that they will be arranging themselves along the rope according to a certain criterion. For example: "Arrange yourselves according to the darkness of your eyes." Some criteria can be basic, without much emotional risk, such as number of siblings, how close you live to where you are standing, etc. You can work your way up to more complex criteria such as level of happiness or ability to lead others.

For each criterion, the group members will be able to line up from one end of the rope to the other. The round is complete when all members agree that the order they are in is correct. The more meaningful the criterion, the more likely it will spark lively discussion and possible conflict about where people belong.

---

*A version of this activity appears in *No Props: Great Games with No Equipment* (Collard, 2005).

Debriefing

Debrief participants in this activity as you go along. Point out your observations between each round. This activity holds the potential for conflict in that group members may not agree where they belong along the spectrum, especially for topics that require more emotional investment. This can provide an ideal opportunity to help them learn conflict resolution, negotiation, and compromise skills.

Questions for When the Focus Is on Emotional Awareness

- Were there any times when you didn't agree with others about where you belonged on the spectrum? How did you feel about that? How did you handle that?

Questions for When the Focus Is on Positive Relationships

- How did you figure out where you fit on the spectrum? Was this more difficult for certain criteria than for others?

- Was it easier when the statement was something simple that you can see (such as height) versus something that you can't see (such as happiness)?

Concentric Circles*

This versatile get-to-know-you activity can be used for a variety of topics. As presented here, it helps participants get to know each other.

Target Group: Any age group

Size of Group: 12 or more participants (an even number is required)

Props: None

Objectives

Activity Goal: Help group members get to know one another

Main FVC Connections: Speak Your Truth, Hear the Truth

Keys to Success Connection: Establishing positive relationships

Facilitator Guidelines

Introduction/Metaphor

"One of the best methods of communicating with a group is to have the group stand in a circle. For this activity, we are actually going to create two circles!"

The Action

Have your participants gather in a circle. Include yourself in the circle if you have an odd number of participants.

Have the group count off by twos (one, two, one, two, etc.).

Ask all of the "twos" to look at the person on the right, take one large step into the circle, and turn and face that person.

At this point, you should have an outer circle facing in, an inner circle facing out, and each person facing a partner.

Give the group a topic or task that each pair should discuss or perform together while still remaining in the circle. The task can be something fun and/or challenging.

Once the task is completed, have members of the outside circle move two (or three or four) people to their right. Have the new partners introduce themselves and engage in a new task.

Debriefing

Discussion is an integral part of this activity, and it generally does not require debriefing.

---

*A somewhat similar activity, Palm Springs Circuit, appears in *Zip Lines* (Winter 2001, No. 42) and was submitted by Mary Henton. I learned this activity at Project Adventure during a workshop.

Questions for When the Focus Is on Positive Relationships

You can check in with the group after each round and ask if anyone would like to share information that was discussed or explain how the pairs accomplished their tasks.

Left In*

This fun warm-up activity helps group members see how they are connected to other members. I've heard this activity called so many other names, including Have You Ever?, Switcheroo, and Categories. I like the name Left In because, as I tell my groups, no one wants to feel "left out." This activity is about making folks feel included, or left in.

Target Group: Any age group

Size of Group: 8 to 30 participants

Props: Gym spots, one fewer than the number of participants in the activity

Objectives

Activity Goal: Create a feeling of connectedness and inclusion

Main FVC Connections: Speak Your Truth, Hear the Truth

Keys to Success Connections: Emotional awareness, establishing positive relationships

Facilitator Guidelines

Introduction/Metaphor

"How many of you have felt left out before? How did that feel? Well, we don't want anyone feeling left out so we are going to play an game called left in!"

The Action

Place the gym spots in a circle, a few feet apart from each other.

Have participants stand on the spots. There should be one fewer spots than there are participants.

The person with no spot (presumably you in the first round) will stand in the middle of the circle, being "left in."

That person will make a statement that is true about himself or herself. For example, left in the middle I might say, "I play a musical instrument."

Anyone who plays a musical instrument must quickly find a new spot in the circle that is not to the immediate left or right of the spot they are leaving. The person in the middle will also try to find a spot.

This will leave a new person left in the middle.

Once everyone is in place again, the person in the center will state something that is true of himself or herself and so on.

---

* The earliest written version of this activity I can find is called Have You Ever in *Quicksilver* (Rohnke & Butler, 1995).

Variation 1

After a few rounds, inconspicuously remove one spot. This will leave two people in the middle. The task is for them to find one thing they have in common and state it to the group. Again, they should try to find spots, leaving two new people in the middle. Continue to remove spots until five or six (or more) people are in the middle.

Variation 2

Some participants may not like being left in the middle with the pressure of making their "left in" statement. You can offer the group a "zoom" option. Anytime the person in the center says, "zoom!" everyone must find a new spot.

Variation 3

If your participants are a bit too shy to be "left in" the middle, use the same number of spots as participants and designate one of the spots in the circle as the "left in spot." The person who ends up on this spot will make the next statement. This variation offers a higher level of choice for participants.

Debriefing

If you choose to debrief, you can focus on how we connect with others and how we can embrace each other's differences.

Questions for When the Focus Is on Emotional Awareness

- Have you ever felt as though you didn't have anything in common with those around you? How did that feel?
- How do you feel when you are spending time with people you feel connected to?

Questions for When the Focus Is on Positive Relationships

- Is it important to find commonalities with others to form relationships with them? How do we do this?
- Can we have positive relationships with people who are very different from ourselves? How?

Jenga 5.4*

I have always liked creative ways of offering icebreaker questions. For quite some time, I have used Jenga® during group sessions. It's one of those games that seems to engage just about everyone. I created the 5.4 version to add a therapeutic twist to traditional Jenga. This activity can be tailored for virtually any topic you can imagine! The list on p. 437 offers some great general questions and conversation starters; however, feel free to create lists of your own that fit the group you are working with. Your introduction may be based on the list of questions you choose to use.

Target Group: Any age group

Size of Group: 2 to 12 participants

Props: Jenga set with each piece numbered 1 through 54, and list of 54 questions

Objectives

Activity Goal: Get to know each other through conversation

Main FVC Connections: Speak Your Truth, Hear the Truth

Keys to Success Connection: Establishing positive relationships

Facilitator Guidelines

Setup

Set up the Jenga game as directed in the game's instructions. If you have five or fewer group members, they can play as singles. If you have more than five, divide the group into two or more teams. I would suggest no more than four teams of three people.

In determining how high a tower is, I count the levels of Jenga pieces. Three pieces will create a full level. Less than three is a fractional level. So, if you have 22 full levels and two more pieces on top when the tower topples, the level is 22⅔ (22 levels and 2 of the 3 possible on the next level).

Introduction/Metaphor

Facilitators' introductions can be based on the list of questions they choose to use. I often indicate that in addition to learning about each other, the group's goal is to create the highest possible tower. This removes the competition between teams and creates a sense of common purpose.

The Action

Choose the order in which teams will take their turns.

Have each team determine who will go first, second, and so on.

---

*JENGA® & ©2013 Hasbro, Inc. Used with permission.

On each player's turn, that player will choose a piece just as he or she would in regular Jenga®.

Once players pull their pieces, players should inform you of the number on the piece. The number corresponds with a question on your list.

Before putting their pieces back, players must answer the question. If players simply cannot answer the question, they place their pieces back and their team loses its next turn.

If players get a question they've already had, they can choose a different number between 1 and 54 and respond to that question.

Variation

For each question answered, give the team a point. If the team doesn't answer a question, it doesn't get a point (rather than losing a turn).

Debriefing

This activity is discussion based and generally requires no debriefing; however, if you have the group focus on working together to build the highest tower possible, you can inquire about the teamwork involved.

Questions for When the Focus Is on Emotional Awareness

- Did you feel a sense of cooperation or competition with the other groups?
- Did you feel a sense of pressure as the tower increased in size and became more unstable? Did you find yourself hoping that someone would knock it down before your next turn?

Questions for When the Focus Is on Behavioral Control

- Did you try to help the other groups or did you attempt to sabotage them?
- Did you encourage your teammates? How?

The Whole Truth*

This icebreaker activity is a huge hit with my groups!

Target Group: Middle school age and older participants

Size of Group: 8 to 20 people

Props: Paper and pens or pencils

Objectives

Activity Goal: Get to know each other

Main FVC Connections: Speak Your Truth, Hear the Truth

Keys to Success Connections: Emotional awareness, behavioral control, establishing positive relationships

Facilitator Guidelines

Setup

You may have group members who are not willing to come to the front of the room for one reason or another. Gently encourage them but allow them to make the final decision.

Introduction/Metaphor

"Acting or lying? What's the difference?"

The Action

Have all members of your group write down three facts about themselves that they don't think other people in the group would know (or maybe not even believe!). I encourage everyone to use similar pens or pencils so that the lists are more difficult to differentiate for prying eyes. Each participant should write his or her name on the paper.

Collect all of the papers.

Choose three or four papers. Ask the participants whose papers were chosen to step to the front of the room.

You will read one statement from the papers you've selected. Therefore, what you read will be true of only one person standing in the front of the room.

Participants standing in the front of the room should act as though the statement read was written by them.

The rest of the group has five questions (or more or fewer, as you see fit) it can ask of the members up front. I generally require that the group ask questions of specific players, not general questions for all players.

---

*I found a version of this activity in Project Adventure's *Zip Lines* magazine (Summer 1999, No. 50). It was submitted by Adam Clark.

After the five questions are asked, take a vote to see which player each audience member believes wrote the question.

Debriefing

Generally, I debrief as I go with this activity. It's interesting to hear the stories behind the statements.

Question for When the Focus Is on Emotional Awareness

- How did it feel to be up here, on the spot, trying to convince us that the statement was yours?

Questions for When the Focus Is on Behavioral Control

- What did you do to convince the audience that statements were about you when they really weren't?
- What did you do to convince the audience that statements weren't about you when they actually were?
- Are there times when it is OK to lie?

Questions for When the Focus Is on Positive Relationships

- Why do people lie?
- How important is honesty in positive relationships?

Comfort Zone

This activity helps us understand the "comfort zones" of others as we discover our own comfort zones.

Target Group: Middle school age or older

Size of Group: Maximum of about 40 people

Props: Boundary markers, spots, or ropes that can be used to create a circle

Objectives

Activity Goal: Identifying the limits of our comfort zones while becoming aware of others'

Main FVC Connections: Be Safe, Speak Your Truth, Hear the Truth

Keys to Success Connections: Emotional awareness, behavioral control, establishing positive relationships

Facilitator Guidelines

Setup

Create an area with an inner circle (Hula-Hoop size or a bit larger) and an outer circle. Leave about 3 feet of space between the inner and outer circles. These circles may need to be bigger with very large groups.

Create a list of situations people encounter in life that elicit varying levels of anxiety. I encourage you, the facilitator, to create lists based upon the needs of your particular group. Start off with general situations such as the examples mentioned below.

Introduction/Metaphor

"We all have different 'comfort zones.' I may be comfortable with something that you are not. This next activity helps us define our own comfort zones while providing us with an understanding of the comfort zones of others. It also helps us identify our 'growth zones' and 'panic zones.' What might those mean?"

The Action

Explain that inside the inner circle marker represents those things that participants are totally comfortable with. For example, I am completely comfortable with speaking in public so I will stand in the center circle. This is called the Comfort Zone.

Explain that the area between the two circles represents the Growth Zone. This area is where participants will stand when you call out situations in life that they are not totally comfortable with but might be willing to try. The Growth Zone is where most of our personal growth occurs. We are uncomfortable in this zone, but not so much so that we are in the Panic Zone, which is outside the outer circle and represents those things or situations that would trigger a panic response. For me, skydiving is within the Panic Zone.

Call out a situation from your list, something that would create varying levels of anxiety. For example, holding a baby, petting a dog you don't know, or speaking in front of a group. Have group members move to the zone that best represents how they feel about what you say.

Encourage participants to look around each time a situation is called out and notice where people are standing. This often sparks mid-action debriefings.

Based on the reactions from group members, make statements more meaningful (and likely more intense). For example, "how comfortable are you admitting you are afraid" or "how comfortable would you be if you were asked to lie to your parents by a friend?"

You can also include the members by asking them if there is anything they would like to know about their peers. If so, call it out!

Variation 1

If you don't have props with you, you can do this activity using the center of the room as your Comfort Zone and moving to the walls, which are the most extreme point of the Panic Zone. Closer to the center represents more comfort.

Variation 2

If you have a small space, create the Comfort Zone on a table and have each participant respond to questions by placing a personal icon on the spot on the table to represent their answer.

Debriefing

I generally open discussion during this activity by pointing out observations after each statement or question. This allows members to examine where their comfort levels are in relation to their peers'. Keep in mind that revealing fears can be an intimidating task for anyone!

Questions for When the Focus Is on Emotional Awareness

- What does it feel like to be in situations in which you are in the Panic Zone? Growth Zone? Comfort Zone?
- Did you take a risk in this activity by disclosing how you feel about particular situations? How did it feel to do that? How did people respond?

Questions for When the Focus Is on Behavioral Control

- What behavior would we see if you were doing something in your Panic Zone? Growth Zone? Comfort Zone?
- What would life be like if you never tried anything outside your Comfort Zone?
- What is one activity in your life that began in the Panic Zone but has moved? How about one that began in the Growth Zone but moved to the Comfort Zone?

Questions for When the Focus Is on Positive Relationships

- Who in your life helps you when you are operating outside your Comfort Zone?
- How will you support each other in the Growth Zone or Panic Zone?

Commonalities Shuffle*

This activity helps group members find commonalities that are deeper than surface level. Finding commonalities that go beyond appearances creates a sense of belonging and helps the group begin to form an identity.

Target Group: Any age group

Size of Group: 10 to 40 participants

Props: Radio, CD player, or media player with speakers; Hula-Hoops or raccoon circles

Objectives

Activity Goal: Finding commonalities in each grouping that go beyond appearances

Main FVC Connections: Speak Your Truth, Hear the Truth

Keys to Success Connections: Emotional awareness, establishing positive relationships

Facilitator Guidelines

Introduction/Metaphor

"When we meet someone new, we immediately begin to draw conclusions as to how similar or different they are from ourselves. We gather this information based on what they look like, what they wear, and the way they speak. This activity helps find the commonalities we have with others that go beyond the surface!"

The Action

Spread out several Hula-Hoops in your playing area (about one for every five people).

Tell your group that when the music is on, they are to "shuffle" around the playing area. Shuffling can be dancing, hopping, skipping, or simply shuffling—basically anything besides standing still.

When the music stops, participants should quickly make their way to the closest hoop. There should be at least two participants per hoop so adjust as necessary.

Once the music has stopped and the members have found a hoop, have each subgroup determine one thing the members all have in common that cannot be determined simply by looking at them. Have each group share the commonality it has found.

Once each group has shared, turn the music back on to begin the next round and slyly remove one hoop.

Again, when the music has stopped and members have formed subgroups in the hoops, have them find one thing that they all have in common that you cannot tell by looking

---

*I learned this at Project Adventure. A similar activity is written up as Moving Toward Extinction in *Teamwork and Teamplay* (Cain & Jolliff, 1998).

at them. It needs to be different than anything anyone in the hoop came up with during round one.

If you want to increase the challenge, you can ask them to find two commonalities during the second round and increase the number of commonalities they must find each round by one.

Continue removing hoops each round until there is only one hoop remaining, at which point the participants must find one thing (or two, or three…) that the entire group has in common that cannot be determined just by looking at them.

Debriefing

Since the activity includes discussion as it goes, I generally don't debrief afterward.

Questions for When the Focus Is on Emotional Awareness

- Have you ever felt like you didn't have anything in common with those around you? How did that feel?
- How do you feel when you are spending time with people with whom you feel connected?

Questions for When the Focus Is on Positive Relationships

- Is it important to find commonalities with others to form relationships with them? How do we do this?

Human Treasure Hunt

This activity allows group members to learn new things about each other that they may have never discovered otherwise.

Target Group: Any age group

Size of Group: 8 to 20 participants

Props: Treasure Hunt Sheet, pens or pencils

Objectives

Activity Goal: Learn new things about one another

Main FVC Connections: Speak Your Truth, Hear the Truth

Keys to Success Connections: Behavioral control, establishing positive relationships

Facilitator Guidelines

Setup

You can use the Treasure Hunt Sheet (p. 440, Appendix E) or create one appropriate to the group you are working with.

Introduction/Metaphor

"'He who finds a faithful friend, finds a treasure' (Jewish proverb). We are going on our own treasure hunt to begin down that path to friendship. This treasure hunt will help us all learn about each other."

The Action

Each group member receives a Treasure Hunt Sheet and writing utensil.

The goal is to complete the sheet by writing in the names of group members who meet the criteria of each statement.

If there are enough participants, no group member's name should be written in for more than one category on any given sheet.

Debriefing

I like to have group members share some stories that go along with the more interesting statements on the Treasure Hunt sheets.

Question for When the Focus Is on Behavioral Control

- Was it easy or difficult to approach others and ask them questions about themselves?

Questions for When the Focus Is on Positive Relationships

- Did you learn anything new about anyone today?
- What was the most unusual thing you learned about a fellow group member today?

Snowball

This activity provides a fun way for members to express themselves, learn about each other, and blow off some steam. I have always enjoyed it.

Target Group: Any age group, as long as participants have shown the ability to be mature enough to handle the activity

Size of Group: 4 to 12 people

Props: Paper and pencil or pen for each member

Objectives

Activity Goal: Get to know other group members

Main FVC Connections: Be Safe, Speak Your Truth, Hear the Truth

Keys to Success Connection: Establishing positive relationships

Facilitator Guidelines

Introduction/Metaphor

"Isn't it a blast when on those snowy days, a snowball fight erupts with your friends? What's so fun about snowball fights? With this activity, you will be getting to know each other better as well as blowing off some steam with an indoor snowball fight."

The Action

Give each group member a pencil and piece of paper.

Ask group members to write some specific information about themselves. For example, have participants write about their biggest fear, their greatest achievement, and what their life will be like in 20 years. Group members should not put their names on their papers.

Once finished, members will crumple the papers.

On your cue, they should begin a "snowball fight" with the crumpled papers.

After a minute or so of this craziness, have each member get a snowball, unravel them one by one, and read them aloud.

After each one, group members must try to guess who the writer is.

Variation

This activity can be used in combination with Three Truths and a Lie (p. 229), in which the information is written, crumpled, and thrown. If using this variation, you should have participants write their names on their papers.

Debriefing

Since the activity is based on self-disclosure through writing and discussion, I generally don't debrief at the end.

What I Like About You

This activity works with groups who already know each other. I often use it as a closing activity. It can also be used as an activity to bring together a group that has forgotten that they actually like each other! However, do not use this activity with groups that will see it as an opportunity to violate the emotional safety of other members.

Target Group: Any, as long as participants have proven themselves trustworthy enough to handle the task responsibly

Size of Group: 6 to 20 people

Props: One piece of paper per person, tape, one writing utensil per person (markers work best)

Objectives

Activity Goals: Share positive perceptions, get to know each other, provide positive affirmations to others

Main FVC Connections: Be Safe, Speak Your Truth, Hear the Truth

Keys to Success Connections: Emotional awareness, behavioral control, establishing positive relationships

Facilitator Guidelines

Introduction/Metaphor

"What does it mean to give someone a positive affirmation? How often do you do this? Are there people in your life who give you those positive messages? Today, you will offer positive affirmations to each other."

The Action

Tape an 8½ × 11-inch piece of paper to each participant's back. On top of the paper should be written, "What I like about you is…."

Give each member a marker. Each group member should write one thing they like about each other group member on the paper taped to that person's back. I usually allow participants to post their messages anonymously.

Once each group member has written on the other group members' papers, have the participants remove the paper from their backs and read what others wrote. If you choose, you can have each person read aloud what was written.

Debriefing

With smaller groups, I like to have each member read his or her list out loud. With larger groups, I ask group members to read one or two of the statements written about them that stick out to them.

Questions for When the Focus Is on Emotional Awareness

- How did you feel about what was written about you? Do you agree or disagree with anything that was said?
- Would you add anything to what was written?

Questions for When the Focus Is on Behavioral Control

- Is it difficult for you to hear positive things said about you? How about negative things?
- Was it difficult to find positive things to say about others?

Question for When the Focus Is on Positive Relationships

- Why is it important to recognize and tell people about positive things you see in them?

Three Truths and a Lie (or Four Truths and a Lie)*

Target Group: Middle school age or older participants

Size of Group: 4 to 12 people

Props: None, though paper and pencil for each member can be helpful

Objectives

Activity Goals: Get to know each other better, explore how it feels to lie and to be lied to

Main FVC Connections: Speak Your Truth (and non-truth!), Hear the Truth

Keys to Success Connections: Emotional awareness, behavioral control, establishing positive relationships

Facilitator Guidelines

Introduction/Metaphor

"Can you tell when someone is lying? How? Do you think you can hide it when you are lying? Did anyone ever tell you about something they did that you just couldn't believe? Today, you are going to tell people four things about yourself. While what you say about yourself may be unbelievable, one of the statements should be a lie while the others are to be true."

The Action

Have group members come up with three amazing truths about themselves and one lie. Encourage participants to make it challenging for group members to differentiate between their truths and their lie.

One at a time, have group members state their three truths and single lie.

The rest of the group must figure out which statement is a lie. You can give the group 5, 10, or 20 yes-or-no questions to try to figure out what is truth and what is lie. Or don't allow them to ask any questions; it's up to you!

Encourage the person whose turn it is to act as though all the statements are true, even during the inquisition.

Variation

Create a list of 10 questions and print multiple copies. Cut up the questions on strips of paper that provide enough space for writing the answer. Give each member a copy of each question. Once participants answer the questions, have them fold their question-and-answer strips and put them in a box or bag. A volunteer goes first by picking out one folded piece of paper and reading the question and answer on that paper. Group

---

*This is one of those activities I learned during college as a party game. A version of it is written up in *Cowstails and Cobras II* (Rohnke, 1989) as Truth Is Stranger Than Fiction.

members should make sure not to let on if the Q and A is theirs. Group members guess who they believe wrote the answer. Once all have guessed, the true responders can admit their authorship.

Debriefing

Question for When the Focus Is on Emotional Awareness

- How do you feel when people lie to you?

Question for When the Focus Is on Behavioral Control

- What did you do to convince the rest of the group that the lie was true? Did you do or say anything to make the group believe your truths were lies?

Questions for When the Focus Is on Positive Relationships

- How were you able to determine if people were lying?
- Why is honesty important in fostering positive relationships?
- How does it impact your relationships with others when they lie to you?

Playing Card Introductions*

This card game is another one-on-one activity to help group members get to know each other.

Target Group: Any age group

Size of Group: Any size

Props: Deck of cards (or multiple decks if it's a really big group)

Objectives

Activity Goal: Get to know others by sharing personal information

Main FVC Connections: Speak Your Truth, Hear the Truth

Keys to Success Connection: Establishing positive relationships

Facilitator Guidelines

Introduction/Metaphor

I generally just start this activity without an introduction.

The Action

Have each member of the group take a playing card. You can pass the cards out, let participants pick one, or simply toss the cards on the floor and have folks safely grab a card. By matching either the suit, the number on the card, or the color of the card, group members must find a partner.

Once each person has found a partner, participants are to share amazing facts about themselves with their partner. The number of facts participants will share is determined by the number on their cards (face cards are 10 facts, the ace is 11).

Once group members have shared with their partners, have them do a blind card shuffle (hold cards face down and switch with at least three other people).

On your cue, they are to find a new partner and again share information based on the number on the card they are holding.

Debriefing

At the end of this activity, I generally ask participants to share any truly interesting facts they discovered about other group members.

---

*Michelle Cummings, M.S., of Training Wheels (www.training-wheels.com) created the original version of this activity. It is copyrighted in her book *Playing with a Full Deck* (2007).

Silent Interviews*

This activity helps demonstrate the importance of nonverbal behavior in communication.

Target Group: Any age group

Size of Group: 2 to 20 participants

Props: None

Objectives

Activity Goal: Help participants get to know one another better and illustrate effectiveness of nonverbal communication

Main FVC Connections: Be Here, Speak Your Truth, Hear the Truth

Keys to Success Connections: Behavioral control, establishing positive relationships

Facilitator Guidelines

Introduction/Metaphor

"What does the phrase 'actions speak louder than words' mean? How about 'a picture is worth a thousand words?' Both phrases remind us that we can communicate more information nonverbally than we do with the words we use. With this activity, you will be able to let your actions speak rather than your words."

The Action

During a group's first meeting, have members partner up.

Tell participants they have 2 minutes to interview their partners. Interviewers can ask questions verbally. The interviewee must respond nonverbally through physical gestures, facial expressions, etc. No use of words, spoken or unspoken (such as written or mouthed), is allowed.

At the end, gather your group in a circle and have all members share what they learned about their partners during the interview.

The partner should feel free to comment and correct the interpretations being stated.

Variation 1

To make it easier, allow the interviewer to write down what they believe his or her partner is communicating. You can choose whether or not the interviewer can show the partner what is written.

---

* I learned this at a training many years ago. A similar activity, It Ain't Me, Babe, is written up in *Cowstails and Cobras II* (Rohnke, 1989).

Variation 2

To make it more difficult, don't allow the interviewer to say anything. The direction would be for partners to spend two minutes nonverbally telling each other about themselves.

Variation 3

Give participants specific information that they should share nonverbally, such as one thing they like doing, one thing they dislike, and their favorite food.

Debriefing

Question for When the Focus Is on Behavioral Control

- How did you tell someone else about yourself without using words?

Questions for When the Focus Is on Positive Relationships

- Was it difficult to understand what your partner was trying to communicate?
- How much can you learn about someone without even talking to them?
- This activity calls for you to draw conclusions about someone based on nonverbal information only. Is there ever a risk in doing this?

Tiny Teach

This activity emphasizes personal competence and the idea that everyone has something to contribute.

Target Group: Any upper elementary-school-age or older participant

Size of Group: About 6 to 20

Props: None

Objectives

Activity Goal: Demonstrate that everyone has something to teach others

Main FVC Connections: Be Here, Speak Your Truth, Hear the Truth

Keys to Success Connections: Emotional awareness, behavioral control, establishing positive relationships

Facilitator Guidelines

Setup

This activity gives your participants the opportunity to teach each other and, in turn, the rest of the group, something new. However, for many kids it can be anxiety producing to be put on the spot to teach others. You may need to assist participants in coming up with ideas of what they can teach someone else.

Introduction/Metaphor

"When we hear the word teach, we often envision a 'teacher' teaching a 'student.' Sometimes, however, teachers can learn from their students, and of course, students can learn from each other."

The Action

Divide the group into pairs.

Instruct the group members that they will teach their partners something. What each member will teach is completely up to the participant. It can be verbal, action-based, or both.

Have partners decide who will go first.

Give a specific amount of time for participants to teach their partners something. I often demonstrate the concept of this game first by teaching the group something simple like a tae kwon do front kick or an old tongue twister.

Once partners have taught each other something, have the group circle up.

Each person will now teach the rest of the group what that person learned from his or her partner.

Debriefing

While this activity can be completed without any debriefing, I sometimes check in about what it was like to be in the "teacher" role.

Questions for When the Focus Is on Emotional Awareness

- How did you feel about having to teach something to someone else? Have you ever had to teach someone how to do something before?
- Was it more difficult to teach or learn?
- Was it more difficult to teach to one person or the whole group?

Questions for When the Focus Is on Behavioral Control

- How did you go about teaching something to someone? What was challenging about it?
- What does competence mean and how does it relate to this activity?

Question for When the Focus Is on Positive Relationships

- Who are the people who have taught you important things in your life?

CHAPTER
13 Low-Level Initiatives

Just like the icebreakers, these activities serve to get group members involved in the action and enjoying themselves while at the same time breaking down participants' inhibitions. Unlike icebreakers, however, these activities present an added element of "challenge" for the group. This challenge necessitates increased communication and group problem solving. Cognitive investment is increased, but the focus is still on fun. Participants must become more individually involved in the activity. For that reason, I call these activities "low-level initiatives."

For many groups, these activities can be interchangeable with the simpler icebreakers. Other groups may not be quite ready for the challenge component of these activities at the onset of a group session. If you are unsure, assess your group during the first few activities to determine whether they are ready for the increased level of cognitive investment.

Who's Next?*

The goal of this activity is to have your group recite the alphabet from A to Z. Of course, there's a catch. This activity illustrates the importance of communication in teamwork.

Target Group: Any group that knows the alphabet or that can count to the number of group members present

Size of Group: 5 to 25 participants

Props: None

Objectives

Activity Goals: Increase engagement, cope with frustration

Main FVC Connection: Be Here

Keys to Success Connections: Emotional awareness, behavioral control, establishing positive relationships

Facilitator Guidelines

Introduction/Metaphor

"Some things seem so simple, like the alphabet. My three-year-old breezes through with accuracy and ease! How about a group of very intelligent, honor-roll high school students? Not so easy!"

The Action

Before giving them any information about the task at hand, ask your group members to scatter themselves around the playing area.

Once they find a spot, ask them to sit down and close their eyes.

Now, explain that in this activity they are to recite the alphabet from A to Z, following these rules:

- Only one member at a time can say a letter.
- No one can say anything but a letter of the alphabet.
- If more than one person says a letter at the same time (overlapping in any way), the group starts over at *A*.
- All participants must keep their eyes closed for the entire activity.

Variation 1

Allow participants to keep their eyes open (which makes the activity easier).

---

*A similar activity called Count Off can be found in Karl Rohnke's book *The Bottomless Bag Again* (1991).

Variation 2

Stay in a circle (which makes it easier for participants).

Variation 3

Have the group count to ten or to the number equal to the number of members in the group. You can also use other sequential criteria such as months of the year or animals starting with each letter in alphabetical order (i.e., ant, bat, cat, etc.).

Debriefing

The removal of our typical forms of communication actually highlights the importance of communication in group problem solving for this activity.

Question for When the Focus Is on Emotional Awareness

- How did you feel when you had to restart?

Questions for When the Focus Is on Behavioral Control

- How did you decide when to speak out or not?
- Which variation of this activity was easiest and why? Which was most difficult and why?

Questions for When the Focus Is on Positive Relationships

- Without planning, you seemed to come up with a strategy to complete this activity. What was your strategy and how did it come about?
- How did keeping your eyes closed affect you or the group in this activity?

Pencil Ninja

Remember that old game where you balanced quarters on your elbow and tried to catch them as you swung your arm forward? Why not try it with pencils balanced on the back of your hand? The different phases and variations of this activity each call for somewhat different skills. The first phase is about focus and determination. Many times, participants will exceed the goals they set for themselves. Sometimes, they will fall short. In later phases and variations calling for team partners, participants must work together to be successful.

This activity has been evolving as I use it with my groups in school.

Target Group: Upper elementary-age or older participants

Size of Group: Any size group

Props: A lot of pencils, preferably without points

Objectives

Activity Goals: Increase engagement and focus, work with partners toward a common goal

Main FVC Connections: Be Here, Be Safe, Speak Your Truth, Hear the Truth

Keys to Success Connections: Emotional awareness, behavioral control, establishing positive relationships

Facilitator Guidelines

Setup

Have at least 20 pencils ready to go for each participant, even more if possible.

Introduction/Metaphor

"Ninjas are known to be stealthy. They move quickly and accurately. Today, you are going to test your ninja skills using pencils!"

The Action

Phase 1

Instruct group members to hold out their hands palms down and place a pencil on the back of their hands. The pencil can be placed pointing in any direction.

When participants are ready, ask them to flip the pencil into the air (flip being loosely defined) and attempt to catch it with the same hand.

Once they are successful with this challenge, have them add a second pencil. This time, they must flip and catch both pencils at the same time.

Begin the activity and let it run for multiple rounds.

During these rounds, as facilitator, you can ask participants to state how many pencils they believe they can catch successfully. As they are successful, keep adding pencils. Encourage participants to try and establish their personal record. You can challenge the group to come up with a total group goal for how many pencils can be caught successfully when adding each participant's best total.

Phase 2

Have participants pair up.

Have one partner balance a pencil on the back of his or her hand, as in Phase 1.

Tell the second partner to extend a hand below the partner's hand with the pencil, placing this hand palm down.

Explain that when the pencil is flipped, the second partners are to catch it with their hands continuing to be palm facing down. Have participants keep adding pencils as they are successful.

Begin the activity and let it run for multiple rounds.

Check in with participants to see how many pencils they believe they can catch while working in pairs.

Have partners reverse roles and continue the activity.

Variation 1

Have one person flip the pencils from the back of both their hands with the partner trying to catch both at the same time.

Variation 2

Same as Variation 1 except, working in groups of three, have one person flipping a pencil from each hand with each partner trying to catch one of the pencils.

Variation 3

Gather the group in a circle.

Have participants balance a pencil on the back of their right hands and be ready to catch them with their left hands, which they hold open palms up. The pencil will fall from the right hand of the person to their left. For even more challenge, have catching partners keep their catching hands turned palms down.

See if the group can catch all the pencils. (This variation of the activity is very challenging.)

Debriefing

Questions for When the Focus Is on Emotional Awareness

- What role did focus play in being successful? How about determination? How do you use these traits in your life?

Questions for When the Focus Is on Behavioral Control

- What abilities did you need to tap into to be successful in this activity?
- Did you meet or exceed your stated goals? Were your goals set too low or too high? What does this say about you?

Questions for When the Focus Is on Positive Relationships

- How did you and your partner find success in this activity? What cooperative skills were needed?
- Did you and your partner create a plan? How did you incorporate both people's ideas?

Antelope Cantaloupe*

There are times when groups display internal conflict. Members start acting like enemies rather than allies. This hinders their ability to reach common group goals. This activity highlights how internal conflict can sabotage the group's goals. Rarely do I plan to use this activity, but when the moment calls for it, it's ready to go.

Target Group: Teens and older. This activity can also be used with high-functioning preteen groups that can comprehend the metaphorical meaning of the activity.

Size of Group: 8 to 16 people

Props: Two pens or other small objects

Objectives

Activity Goal: Help a group realize and work through internal conflict

Main FVC Connection: Be Safe

Keys to Success Connections: Emotional awareness, behavioral control, establishing positive relationships

Facilitator Guidelines

Introduction/Metaphor

Since this activity is usually used when a group is in conflict, at times, this will call for discontinuing another activity that seems to be falling apart. I will tell the group that the current activity doesn't seem to be going so well, so I would like to try something different.

The Action

Have your group circle up.

In your hand, you should have two pens or other small objects. As facilitator, you will seat yourself between the people you will ask to start passing the pens around the circle.

Explain to the group that each person will be passing a pen to the next person on the team by following a specific dialogue and set of actions. The exchange should go as follows:

Person 1 to Person 2: "This is an antelope."

Person 2 to Person 1: "A what?"

Person 1 to Person 2: "An antelope."

---

*I learned this activity at an advanced Adventure Based Counseling workshop at Project Adventure. I later discovered similar activities written up as Hustle and Bustle in *Silver Bullets* (Rohnke, 1984) and as This is a What?, contributed by Bart Crawford in *Zip Lines* (Summer 1998, No. 36).

At this point, Person 2 says, "Oh! An antelope," and takes the pen.

Person 2 next turns to Person 3 and extends the pen, saying "This is an antelope."

Person 3 says to Person 2: "A what?"

Person 2 to Person 1: "A what?"

Person 1 to Person 2: "An antelope."

Person 2 to Person 3: "An antelope."

Person 3 takes the pen, saying "Oh, an antelope!"

Each time, the questions go all the way back to the person who began the process.

Explain that the second pen will go the opposite way around the circle following the same script except the word *antelope* will be replaced with the word *cantaloupe*.

Inform group members that they are now on two teams competing to see who can get the pen back to the facilitator the quickest

Start the activity: "Let's see which team's pen will get back to me first. Ready...set...go!"

When the pens are back to you, declare a winner and find out who the members of each team were. By this point, your group should be figuring out that they were all on the same team. If members tried to sabotage the "other team" by slowing down the passage of the pen, they were really sabotaging themselves.

Debriefing

Groups that are supposed to be working together often don't due to interpersonal conflicts. At times, the group's collective reason is overrun by individual desires and feelings of vengeance, which can negate any progress a group makes. This group self-sabotage can happen consciously or subconsciously. These types of behaviors are characteristic of the "Storming Stage" of group development; however, they can appear during other stages as well.

The debriefing for this activity can include discussion of many of these topics, depending upon how your group reacts to the activity itself.

Questions for When the Focus Is on Emotional Awareness

- What has been the mood of the group today? How did we get there? What has been the impact of this?

Questions for When the Focus Is on Behavioral Control

- Are there times when you have found yourself sabotaging your own progress, maybe to get back at someone else?
- When our group is in conflict, what are some actions you can take to help move us towards resolving the issues?

Questions for When the Focus Is on Positive Relationships

- How did we move from cooperative to competitive? What has been the result of this shift?
- How can we bring this group back to being a team that works together?

- Have you ever been part of a group before in which conflict kept you from achieving your goals?
- What are the characteristics of a highly functioning team? Are we displaying them? Why or why not?
- What skills have you used to resolve conflicts in other relationships in your life?

Don't Touch Me*

Target Group: Upper elementary--school-age participants or older

Size of Group: 8 to 16 people

Props: Hula-Hoop or other similar-sized circular boundaries or gym spots (optional)

Objectives

Activity Goals: Understand the concept of "personal space," coping with confusion, group goal setting, improving communication and group problem-solving skills

Main FVC Connections: Speak Your Truth, Hear the Truth

Keys to Success Connections: Emotional awareness, behavioral control, establishing positive relationships

Facilitator Guidelines

Introduction/Metaphor

Introduce the activity with a brief discussion about personal space. What is it? Why do we need it? How much personal space do you need? Note that people often get into our personal space. The activity also lends itself well to metaphors about dealing with negative emotions when we don't want people around.

You could introduce the activity by saying something like the following: "How many of us just want people to keep their distance when we are feeling angry or upset? Sometimes we just need to take a little space. Sometimes we say something to them and sometimes we don't. Today, you get to say something!"

The Action

Have your group stand in a circle and place a Hula-Hoop in the middle of the circle. Explain that the goal of the activity is for each member to cross the circle to a spot on the opposite side. Tell group members the rules for crossing the circle:

1. A group member must touch the area inside the hoop at the same time as one other group member who is also passing to the other side of the circle.

2. Only two group members may touch the ground inside the hoop at any given time.

3. Players cannot touch any other player.

4. As players cross the circle, they must call out "Don't touch me!"

---

*I learned this activity in a workshop in Connecticut during my first introduction to adventure-based counseling. A version of it appears in *Quicksilver* (Rohnke & Butler, 1995).

Tell participants that this is a timed activity.

Without giving the group time to ponder the instructions, say, "Go."

Time participant attempts to cross, adding 5 seconds for each rule violation you see.

Continue the activity.

Typically, in the first rounds of this activity there are a whole lot of folks heading for the other side, stepping in the hoop, bumping into each other. In other words, there is a lot of invading of personal space.

After running the activity for a period, stop the action and give the group some time to plan and have them try again. I usually ask the group to tell me a "goal time" for how long they think it will take to successfully accomplish the task. Give them at least three attempts to meet their goal.

Debriefing

Metaphorically speaking, this activity really hits home with Keys 1 and 2: dealing with our emotions and the behavior emotions trigger.

Questions for When the Focus Is on Emotional Awareness

- How did it feel crossing the middle of the circle, not being able to touch anyone?
- How did it feel to yell out that no one should touch you?
- When you are upset, do you like people around or prefer to be alone? Do you tell people what you need when you are upset?
- How do you feel when your personal space is invaded?

Questions for When the Focus Is on Behavioral Control

- When you are feeling like you might just snap on someone, do you take the initiative to make sure that doesn't happen? What do you do?
- How do you react when someone invades your personal space?

Questions for When the Focus Is on Positive Relationships

- How did you arrive at your solution to this challenge?

- When you assert yourself in order to have your needs met, does it impact relationships with others? How does it?

Impulse*

Target Group: Middle-school-age and older participants

Size of Group: 8 to 24 people

Props: A table and chairs. If there is no table, the activity can be run with participants lying flat on the ground with their hands extended towards the center of the circle.

Objectives

Activity Goals: Develop teamwork skills, promote healthy competition while working together

Main FVC Connection: Be Here

Keys to Success Connections: Behavioral control, establishing positive relationships

Facilitator Guidelines

Introduction/Metaphor

"Now, more than ever, we are all connected to each other. Sometimes it's through phones and texts. Sometimes it is through the Internet, and sometimes it is just through being in the same class or group. It seems like it should be easy to send messages from one person to another, but that is not always the case. Sometimes, getting information through all these complex lines of communication is difficult."

The Action

Have your group sit around a table with you.

Have one participant (Person A) place his or her left hand in front of the person to the left (Person B) and his or her right hand in front of the person on the right (Person C).

Tell Person B, the participant to the left of Person A, to do the same, thus placing his or her right hand over Person A's left hand. At this point, Person B's hand will be in front of Person A.

Ask Person C to place his or her left hand under Person A's right hand.

Begin the activity by tapping your right hand once on the table. Explain to the group that the goal is to send taps or an impulse clockwise around the circle without anyone taking turns out of order. This means that the person B will tap the table (or ground) with their right hand, followed by your left hand, followed person B's left hand, then person C's right hand and so on.

---

*I first learned this activity co-facilitating a counselors-in-training group on the Manchester Ropes Challenge Course. A version of it is written up in *Silver Bullets* (Rohnke, 1984).

Start the activity. If anyone messes up, just laugh and let that person start the impulse.

Once your group accomplishes the goal of sending the taps, or impulse, once around the circle, time how long it takes to travel once around the circle. Time it to see how quickly the group can get the impulse around without errors.

Variation 1

After these rounds, you can add the following rule: If someone double taps, the tap sequence, or impulse, reverses and travels counterclockwise around the circle. Another double tap will reverse it again. To prevent a two-person tap battle, create a rule. For example, you can say that players can only double tap with each hand once. You can also make up your own variations.

Variation 2

Add an elimination component. If someone messes up, their hand is out and play continues. The removal of hands will change the order of taps. Once a player has both hands out, that player is out of the activity.

Debriefing

Questions for When the Focus Is on Behavioral Control

- How was focus important in this activity?
- What made this activity difficult?

Questions for When the Focus Is on Positive Relationships

- How did you work as a group to be successful?
- What can this activity tell us about communication?
- How do you connect with others?

Clap Wave*

This activity requires participants to stay focused and inhibit impulses that would cause them to clap out of sequence.

Target Group: Any age group

Size of Group: 8 to 20 participants

Props: None

Objectives

Activity Goals: Increase group engagement and focus, increase commitment to a group goal

Main FVC Connection: Be Here

Keys to Success Connections: Behavioral control, establishing positive relationships

Facilitator Guidelines

Introduction/Metaphor

"Have you ever been to a sporting event and done the Wave? That's when a zealous crowd manages to stand up and raise their hands, moving section by section so that it appears as if a wave is moving around the arena! Amazingly, this all happens without any verbal communication to organize it. It's truly a great example of synchronicity. In this activity, we'll be making a wave but with clapping instead of hand waving.

The Action

Gather your group into a circle.

With your group circled up, have all members get into "clap position." That is, they should stand hands extended in front of them a few inches apart, ready to clap.

Tell the group that after you clap once, the person to your immediate left should clap once and the person to that person's left should follow with a clap and so on until the clap wave has gone all the way around the circle without anyone clapping out of sequence.

Launch a clap wave.

Once the group is successful, try the following challenges, possibly adding an elimination component when someone messes up:

1. Reverse the clap.

2. Add in a double clap, which sends the clap back the way it came.

3. Add in a two-handed finger snap, which causes the sequence to skip the next person.

4. Send the clap wave in both directions at the same time.

_____

*A version of this activity appears in *The Bottomless Bag Again* (Rohnke, 1991)

5. Alternate claps. For example, you start; the person two folks over to your left claps then it goes back to the person next to you followed by the person two to their left and so on.

6. Clap in a pattern. For example, assign each person in the circle a number, starting with you as number 1. Call out a sequence of numbers, indicating that each person called should clap. You might try calling "123, 234, 345" and so on.

Debriefing

If you observe impulsivity interfering with group members' success at any point, this issue may be worth debriefing.

Questions for When the Focus Is on Behavioral Control

- What was the most difficult variation?
- What did you have to do to contribute to the success of the group in this activity?

Question for When the Focus Is on Positive Relationships

- How did the group work together to accomplish this activity?

Night at the Museum

I learned this activity when co-facilitating a group with my colleague and friend Heather Wlochowski. It's about the powers of observation, patience, and impulse inhibition. It can also relate to integrity and honesty, depending on how the night watchmen call out the museum characters. Do these participants call out only people they aren't friends with?

Target Group: Any age group

Size of Group: 8 to 24 participants

Props: Nothing other than a fairly large space. An oversized classroom is the smallest space you would want to use.

Objectives

Activity Goals: Increase group engagement and focus, integrity

Main FVC Connection: Be Here

Keys to Success Connections: Behavioral control, establishing positive relationships

Facilitator Guidelines

Introduction/Metaphor

"If you've seen the movie *Night at the Museum* you know that museum characters move when the museum is closed. That poor, unsuspecting new night watchman is so baffled when he discovers the museum relics actually come to life at night! In this activity, it is the job of the night watchperson to keep the animals and people in the displays from leaving the museum. He or she must keep a very watchful eye as those museum characters can be sneaky!"

The Action

Explain that the group will be re-enacting *Night at the Museum* and that the goal of the activity is for the museum characters to escape without the watchperson catching them moving. The watchperson will be constantly scanning the group to see if anyone is moving. If players move and the watchperson doesn't actually see the movement, they are safe. If participants are seen moving, the watchperson calls them by name, and they are out for the remainder of the round.

Ask for a volunteer to be the first watchperson and have this participant stand in the center of the playing area. The remainder of the group members will be museum characters.

Ask the participants who are museum characters to should spread out over the playing area.

Have play run for a prescribed amount of time, say 3 minutes or until there's only one or a certain number of players left. (It's almost impossible to get it down to one player.)

Debriefing

Questions for When the Focus Is on Behavioral Control

- As a museum character, how did you decide when you would move?
- As the watchperson, did you use a strategy?
- What skills did each role call for? How else can you apply these skills in life?

Questions for When the Focus Is on Positive Relationships

- As the watchperson, were you completely honest about who was in and who was out?
- As museum characters, did you do anything to help other characters' movements not be detected?

Who's in the Lead?*

This activity has group members focus on what it means to be a leader. It can also be used to focus on what it means to observe closely and be perceptive.

Target Group: Any age group

Size of Group: 8 to 26 people

Props: None

Objectives

Activity Goals: Identify characteristics of leadership, determine roles of leaders—and those who need to follow a leader, using powers of observation

Main FVC Connection: Be Here

Keys to Success Connections: Emotional awareness, behavioral control, establishing positive relationships

Facilitator Guidelines

Introduction/Metaphor

There are two ways I like to introduce this activity. The first focuses on Leadership. To ask the group to consider leadership, you can start by reading the following quote and discussing its meaning:

> A leader is best when people barely know he exists; when his work is done, his aim fulfilled, they will say: We did it ourselves.—Lao Tzu

Determining the leader in this activity won't be easy.

The second introduction focuses on perception. Ask the group members how perceptive they think they are. Do they notice the small details? Are they tuned into their environments so much that they notice even the tiniest of changes? Ask for a volunteer that believes he is very perceptive. This volunteer will be the activity's Detective

The Action

Gather your group in a circle and introduce the activity.

Ask for a volunteer. (If you are using the introduction that focuses on perceptiveness, you will ask for a volunteer who believes he or she is very perceptive.)

Explain that in this activity, there will be one leader starting an action that the rest of the group will follow. It will be the Detective's role to figure out who the group leader is. The Detective has three guesses and 1 minute to figure out who the Leader is. (Facilitators

---

*The earliest version of this activity I have found is called Detective and appears in the book *New Games for the Whole Family* (LeFevre, 1988).

can give Detectives 5 guesses and 2 minutes to discover the leader, or whatever seems appropriate.)

Tell your volunteer to be the Detective and instruct this participant to leave the area

During this participant's absence, designate one person in the group to be the Leader (or have the group designate a leader). The rest of the group will be Followers.

Explain that the Leader's job is to start a group action (for instance, clapping hands, rubbing bellies, etc.) that will slowly morph into another movement. The Followers will do whatever the leader does but try not to allow the Detective to figure out who the Leader is.

Have the Detective return and let the action begin.

Run the activity until the Detective identifies the Leader. If the Detective is able to correctly identify the Leader, that player can join the group and the former Leader is now the Detective. If the Detective doesn't correctly name the Leader, well, you probably still want them to rejoin the group and find yourselves a new Detective and Leader.

Debriefing

Question for When the Focus Is on Emotional Awareness

- How did it feel to play each of the three roles: Leader, Follower, Detective?

Questions for When the Focus Is on Behavioral Control

- As Detective, what skills did you need to figure out who the leader was?
- As Leader, how did you try to keep your identity hidden?
- What were effective "leadership" skills in this activity? How do these compare with effective leadership skills in real life?
- As Followers, how did you help protect your leader's identity?
- Have you ever had to be dishonest to protect someone else?

Questions for When the Focus Is on Positive Relationships

- As a Follower in this activity, you are protecting the Leader's identity. Are there other situations in your life when you have to place someone else's safety above your own? What actions might this lead to?

Instant Impulse*

Even though it's competitive, this is one of my favorite games!

Target Group: Any age

Size of Group: 8 to 16 people

Props: Coin and an item to grab such as a fleece ball or stuffed animal

Objectives

Activity Goals: Increase group engagement, build teamwork, promote healthy competition

Main FVC Connection: Be Here

Keys to Success Connections: Emotional awareness, behavioral control, establishing positive relationships

Facilitator Guidelines

Introduction/Metaphor

"Have you ever felt truly part of a team? I mean, really connected? Today, you will be totally connected to your team. How well connected you are will determine your success!"

The Action

Divide your group into two equal teams.

Have the teams sit on the ground, forming two lines facing each other. Team members should sit side by side, holding the hands of the teammates next to them. Their legs should extend straight out in front of them, with their feet sole to sole with a member of the opposing team.

Stand at one end of the line (the Front). At the other end, place the fleece ball (or other item) halfway between the last members of each team and within each person's reaching distance.

Explain the rules of the activity: All team members except two nearest you, one from each team, will close their eyes while you flip a coin. If the coin lands tails up, the two watching are to do absolutely nothing. If it shows heads, the two team members are to pass an "impulse" down the line by squeezing the hands they are holding. The next person squeezes the

*Another version of this activity can be found in *Quicksilver* (Rohnke & Butler, 1995).

next hand and so on, sending the squeeze from the front of the line to the end. When the last member of the team receives the "impulse," that person is to reach for the fleece ball or critter without opening his or her eyes (you could use blindfolds for the team members at the end of the line). The team whose member grabs the critter is the winner of the round and that person will move to the front of the line. The rest of the team shifts one position down towards the end of the line.

Once participants are ready, instruct all members on both teams, except the two in front by you, to close their eyes.

Flip the coin, while the first person in each line watches you.

Continue play until one team's original first person is back to the first spot.

If an impulse is sent incorrectly on a "tails" flip, the team must send its first person to the back of the line and have each member move up one spot towards the front. Of course, no group member is allowed to give verbal cues when an impulse is being sent.

Debriefing

The competitive nature of this activity often offers fodder for the debriefing. Otherwise, the total reliance on teamwork to achieve a goal is an area to focus on.

Questions for When the Focus Is on Emotional Awareness

- How did the competitive nature of this activity affect you?
- How did it feel to be completely reliant on the person ahead of you in line for the cue to take action? How about being totally responsible for getting that impulse to the next person?

Questions for When the Focus Is on Behavioral Control

- How come there were times that a team sent an impulse on tails?
- What skills allowed you to be a good team member in this activity?

Questions for When the Focus Is on Positive Relationships

- Did any conflict arise during the activity? How was it resolved?
- What led your team to be successful?
- What could your team have done better?

Whatta Life Saver

This activity lends itself well to metaphors about a group of people needing to pull together and accomplish a task to save the world, kind of like Bruce Willis and Ben Affleck in the movie *Armageddon*.

Target Group: Any age range

Size of Group: 6 to 15 people

Props: Toothpicks, Life Savers candy (the type with holes in the middle)

Objectives

Activity Goals: Increase group focus and teamwork

Main FVC Connection: Be Here

Keys to Success Connections: Emotional awareness, behavioral control, establishing positive relationships

Facilitator Guidelines

Introduction/Metaphor

"Why do they call Life Savers, Life Savers? Of course, it's because they are shaped like the old-fashioned lifesaving flotation devices you can see on ships of yore. But can these Life Savers really save lives?"

The Action

Have your group sit in a circle.

Give each member one toothpick. Place the Life Saver on one of the toothpicks.

Explain to the group that in order to remain safe and maintain its lifesaving powers, the Life Saver must never hit the ground. It also must never touch any part of humans: the oil in our skin can destroy it instantly. Finally, the Life Saver must keep moving clockwise around the circle, going tooth pick to tooth pick without touching any person or the ground.

Start the activity.

Variation 1

Have two Life Savers going in opposite directions.

Variation 2

Move the entire package of Life Savers around the circle without any of them being touched or dropped to the ground.

Variation 3

Make three (or five or ten) passes around the circle as quickly as possible.

Variation 4

Have the group make successive attempts to improve the time it takes to pass the Life Saver around the circle.

Debriefing

Questions for When the Focus Is on Emotional Awareness

- Did this activity become frustrating at any time?
- How did you feel when someone messed up?

Questions for When the Focus Is on Behavioral Control

- How did you respond when someone messed up? Did your response help?
- How did you contribute to your team's success (or failure)?
- Did anyone cheat?

Questions for When the Focus Is on Positive Relationships

- How was your team successful?
- How was your team unsuccessful?
- Did your team communicate well?

Do As I Say*

Target Group: Any age group

Size of Group: 6 to 30 people

Props: None

Objectives

Activity Goals: Enhance group focus, demonstrate the importance of our words and actions matching up, coping with confusion

Main FVC Connection: Be Here

Keys to Success Connections: Emotional awareness, behavioral control, establishing positive relationships

Facilitator Guidelines

Introduction/Metaphor

"Having our thoughts, words, and actions all be in line is important. What happens when our thoughts, words and actions are not in line with each other?"

Setup

Facilitators will lead the group through four phases of this activity, but they should not let group members know what each phase entails ahead of time. Facilitators will instead call out the instructions just before starting that phase of the activity. In Phase 1, the group members will repeat what you, the facilitator, says and do what you say to do. For example, if you say, "Step forward," they will repeat this and step forward. In Phase 2, the group members will repeat what you say but do the opposite. For example, if you say, "Step forward," they should say "step forward" but actually step back.

In Phase 3, the group will say the opposite of what you say but actually do what you say. If you say, "Step forward," the group members are to say "step backward" but actually move forward. In the last phase, Phase 4, the group will say the opposite of what you say and do the opposite action. If you say, "Step forward," the group will say, "step backward" and follow their words.

The Action

Have your group stand in a circle.

Tell them that you are going give them some very simple directions that they are to immediately repeat aloud and follow. The four basic directions you will be giving are:

---

*I first learned this activity while co-facilitating a program in Connecticut with friend and colleague Rodney Brown. A version of it appears in *Count Me In* by Mark Collard (2008).

Step forward

Step backward

Step left

Step right

Begin Phase 1 by telling the group members that you will say the directions they are to follow.

Call out the directions (either Step forward, Step backward, Step left, or Step right) and have the group repeat the directions and follow them. After a few directions, inform the group that you're starting Phase 2. The group is to repeat what you say but do the opposite. Explain that if you say, "Step forward," the group should say "step forward" but actually step backward.

Begin Phase 2 and have the group try out the activity this way for several rounds.

Tell the group that you're starting Phase 3. In this phase, the group should say the opposite of what you say but actually do what you say. Explain that if you say, "Step forward," the group members are to say "step backward" but actually move forward.

Begin Phase 3.

After the group has tried the activity this way for several rounds, announce that you're starting Phase 4. Explain that in this phase the group will say the opposite of what you say and do the opposite action. If you say, "Step forward," group members will say, "step backward" and follow their words.

Begin Phase 4. Call out several commands at each phase until the group members begin to show some improvement.

Variation

The facilitator holds an arrow sign to indicate up, down, left, and right. Group members first say and do what the arrow sign indicates as the facilitator changes its direction. This phase is followed by the group saying what the sign shows and doing the opposite, then saying the opposite of what the arrow directs but doing what the sign indicates, and finally, doing and saying the opposite of what the sign directs.

Debriefing

In debriefing this activity, you will almost always find that the group feels the first and last phases were easiest and the middle ones most difficult. This is because the middle two phases require participants to do one thing while saying another; their actions and words don't match up. During the first and last phases, their words and actions are consistent. I generally try to help the group discover this for themselves and allow the discussion to flow about how life is much more difficult when our thoughts, actions, and words are not consistent

Question for When the Focus Is on Emotional Awareness

- How would you describe the way you felt during this activity?

Questions for When the Focus Is on Behavioral Control

- Which was easiest? Which was most difficult? Why?
- What happened when our words and actions didn't match? What happens in life when our words and actions don't match?

Questions for When the Focus Is on Positive Relationships

- Have there been times when you had problems because your actions and words did not match?
- Have there been times when someone else's words and actions not matching caused you problems?
- How does this activity relate to trustworthiness and integrity?

Full-Value Towel Toss

This activity is a fun, kinesthetic way to reinforce the Full Value Commitment (FVC) or other concepts.

Target Group: Any age group

Size of Group: 6 to 15 people

Props: Towel or several bandannas tied together

Objectives

Activity Goal: Solidify the FVC in the minds of the participants

Main FVC Connections: Be Here, Be Safe, Speak Your Truth, Hear the Truth

Keys to Success Connections: Emotional awareness, behavioral control, establishing positive relationships

Facilitator Guidelines

Introduction/Metaphor

Begin by reviewing the tenets of your FVC.

The Action

Have your group sit in a circle with you standing in the center.

Explain the activity: Say that you will hand a group member the towel and count down from three. While you are counting, the person with the towel must say one part of the FVC and toss the towel to another group member. That person must state a value from the commitment and toss the towel to someone else. As the person in the center, you are trying to get out of the middle. There are three ways the person in the middle can escape the center.

1. Catch the towel mid-flight. The person who threw the towel will become the person in the center.

2. Tag the knee of the person holding the towel before it is tossed. That person will be the new person in the center of the circle.

3. Leave after a minute expires and the person has not gotten out any other way. Ask for a volunteer to be in the center.

Once you've given the group the instructions, hand one person in the group the towel and count down from three.

Variation

Use this activity to promote discussion of other topics. For example, when using Full-Value Towel Toss in an anger management group, you might ask group members to name physiological responses to anger, such as adrenaline surge, flushed skin, tensed muscles, rapid heartbeat, quick breathing, and sweaty palms.

Debriefing

I generally don't debrief this activity as it is a review of the FVC. I may ask what was challenging or ask if the members used strategies to avoid going into the middle or for getting out of the middle.

Gunners and Cannons*

This game is about trust and mutual responsibility for safety. It also requires clear verbal communication.

Target Group: Any group responsible enough to handle the activity without trying to hurt each other, participants about 8-years-old and older

Size of Group: 8 to 24 people (an even number of participants is required)

Props: Blindfolds, toss-ables that won't hurt when folks are hit with them (one for every two people), a fairly large playing area, and boundary markers

Objectives

Activity Goals: Enhance trust among group members, promote healthy competition, encourage shared responsibility for personal safety

Main FVC Connections: Be Safe, Speak Your Truth, Hear the Truth

Keys to Success Connections: Emotional awareness, behavioral control, establishing positive relationships

Facilitator Guidelines

Setup

Facilitators should set up this activity in a space large enough to allow for some good movement but not so large that participants will never be close enough to play. Facilitators should set up the boundaries of the playing area before running the activity.

Introduction/Metaphor

This activity is about trust and shared responsibility. I often start this activity with a discussion about these topics. "What behaviors make it more likely for you to trust someone? What behaviors make it more difficult to trust people?"

The Action

Divide your group into pairs.

Give the instructions for the activity. Tell participants that in this activity players are either cannons or gunners. The cannons are the only ones who can touch the cannonballs. Gunners will be verbally directing their partners as to where to go, what to pick up, and when to throw. The gunners cannot touch the cannonballs or the cannons. The goal is for the cannons to launch their cannonballs at other cannons. If they hit another cannon, that cannon is out of the game for the remainder of the round. When launching, cannons

---

*An early version of this activity, called Ready, Aim..., appears in *Quicksilver* (Rohnke & Butler, 1995).

must tuck their arms against their sides and throw from the elbow, keeping their upper arms tucked against their bodies.

Give each pair a blindfold and have them determine which partner will be blindfolded and which will be sighted. The blindfolded partner is the "cannon," and the sighted partner is the "gunner."

Give each pair a toss-able, which will be the "cannonball."

Have pairs spread out across the playing area.

Begin the activity. Play continues until only one team is left. Be sure to have partners switch roles at least once after a first round. As the facilitator, monitor for safety.

Debriefing

Questions for When the Focus Is on Emotional Awareness

- How did it feel to be blindfolded?
- How did it feel to be the one responsible for someone else's safety?
- Which did you feel was more important as the gunner, launching cannonballs, avoiding cannonballs, or staying safe? How did you deal with these three goals at one time?

Questions for When the Focus Is on Behavioral Control

- When you were the cannon, did you listen to your gunner and act in a safe manner?
- Were there any violations of the throwing rules?
- What did you do as the gunner to keep your cannon safe?

Questions for When the Focus Is on Positive Relationships

- Was it difficult to trust your partner?
- What behaviors did your partner display that allowed you to trust this person?
- What behaviors did your partner display that prevented you from trusting this person?
- As the cannon, did you tell your partner what you needed from him or her?

Full-Value Hog Call*

The original version of this activity (called Hog Call) has partners find each other by calling out words that go together, such as "peanut butter and jelly" or "baseball and bat." This variation has partners using words from the FVC tenets instead of random pairings of terms. The increased challenge of this activity comes when there are several pairs that choose the same words, making it more difficult for partners to find each other.

Target Group: Any age group

Size of Group: 8 to 30 people

Props: A playing area that is larger than a classroom

Objectives

Activity Goals: Reinforce the FVC, enhance trust amongst group members, promote shared responsibility for personal safety, help in coping with confusion

Main FVC Connections: Be Safe, Speak Your Truth, Hear the Truth

Keys to Success Connections: Emotional awareness, behavioral control, establishing positive relationships

Facilitator Guidelines

Setup

The playing area should be larger than a classroom and up to half the size of a football field. When running this activity, make sure that participants walk with their arms or "bumpers" up and don't run and that facilitators are within the playing area to protect the participants' safety.

Introduction/Metaphor

"You know the FVC tenets: Be Here, Be Safe, Speak Your Truth, Hear the Truth, and Have Fun. With your partner, decide which of these tenets you will focus on during this next activity."

The Action

Have participants pair up.

Tell partners that they should pick one of the guidelines of the FVC and then choose which word each of them will represent. For instance, one partner might be "Speak" and the other "Your Truth."

---

*The original version of this game called Hog Call can be found in *Silver Bullets* (Rohnke, 1984).

Instruct each partner to move to opposite ends of a playing area and either put on blindfolds or close his or her eyes. Let participants know that on the facilitator's cue, partners should navigate the space by calling out one of the matching words until the pair comes together somewhere in the middle of the playing area.

Variation

You can use other topics and word or pairings for the Hog Call. Some possible examples include opposite emotions (Confused/Clear, Stressed/Calm) or leadership characteristics (creative, smart, confident).

Debriefing

Question for When the Focus Is on Emotional Awareness

- How did it feel to be blindfolded on the field?

Questions for When the Focus Is on Behavioral Control

- Did you stick with your original plan or did you have to modify it as the activity went along?
- Did you do anything that would be considered unsafe during this activity?
- During this activity, there was "interference" as other voices may have made it difficult to reach your goal. What types of interference are in the way of you reaching your goals in life? How do you overcome this interference?

Questions for When the Focus Is on Positive Relationships

- Did you and your partner have a plan? Did it work?
- Did your partner do anything to help you feel safer?

CHAPTER 14

Higher-Level Initiatives

German neurologist and psychiatrist, Kurt Goldstein introduced the term self-actualization in his 1934 book *The Organism,* defining it as "the master motive an individual possesses to meet his or her potential" (Goldstein, 1995). Goldstein holds that, as humans, we are driven toward self-actualization. The term has since become virtually synonymous with psychologist Abraham Maslow, who popularized the concept as part of his "hierarchy of human needs" (Maslow, 1943). Maslow saw it as the final level of human psychological development. Once the basic needs, such as food, shelter, and water, are met as well as one's need for belonging and self-esteem, a person can then strive toward achieving self-actualization, or becoming the best person they can become. Maslow's concept of the hierarchy of needs can also be applied to groups in the adventure counseling realm. Once group members' need for a sense of security is met, they can begin to seek challenges. As groups move through initial activities of name games, tag games, get-to-know-you and lower-level initiative activities, a sense of safety and trust develops within the group. Individual members become increasingly comfortable with one another. Participants begin to express themselves without fear of being shamed, insulted, or minimized. The progress of individual members pushes the whole group forward toward becoming the "best it can be." In sync with the individual members, the group strives toward its own "self-actualization." This progress is most often reflected in the norming and performing stages of group development.

Healthy individuals who are moving toward self-actualization seek out experiences that challenge them physically, mentally, or otherwise. Less psychologically healthy individuals often avoid challenging situations. For them, challenging situations may pose a threat to the ego through the possibility of failure. For many of these kids, to try and not succeed is more psychologically damaging than to not try at all and fail by default. If too many individuals within a group share this underlying belief, the group itself can become stuck in a pattern of avoidance. On the other hand, healthy groups, reflecting the natural inclination of the healthy individuals, seek out increasing levels of challenge. To reach this point in group development represents marked success for group members and facilitators alike.

The groups we work with are often made up of individuals who are struggling to reach or hang onto the lower rungs of Maslow's hierarchy. These teens are not getting their basic needs met or feel tossed aside by their school, community, or even their families. The earlier activities can provide a sense of belonging and help pave the path toward their individual, self-actualizing journeys. As this happens, the group becomes more able to tackle the challenges of the intense high-level initiatives and trust-building activities.

This section contains activities aimed at providing that higher level of challenge to groups that are truly ready. Before using these activities, facilitators need to make sure that they have thoroughly assessed their group's readiness, taking into account the group's stage of development as well as the results of the ongoing GRABBS assessments. The group needs to be meeting success in lower-level challenges and upholding the FVC. By this point, the group will likely have successfully navigated through some struggles or conflict and appear to be stronger as a unit as a result. Emotional safety is being maintained, and you observe your participants taking healthy risks. As facilitator, when first beginning these activities, you may notice a tendency to revert to the group's previous stages of development. Individuals may try to rely on old coping strategies and behaviors as the challenges mount. Your job as the facilitator is to help the individuals and, in turn, the group to surmount these roadblocks and to continue moving forward. This may necessitate returning to less-challenging activities at times. Have some ready to go. It also requires that you, the facilitator, accept that not all activities will go as planned. These moments are often fantastic opportunities for growth. Rather than simply following the easy path of conflict or frustration avoidance, use creative debriefings to dive into these situations. A group that can work through roadblocks will come out stronger in the end.

Activities in this chapter are grouped according to the space required to conduct them. The groupings are

- Initiatives Designed for Small Spaces. These initiatives are generally well suited for smaller spaces, such as classrooms or counseling offices.

- Initiatives Designed for Medium-Sized Spaces. Medium spaces, loosely defined, are larger than a small room and smaller than a gymnasium. In general, these initiatives are set up to be easily facilitated in a classroom-sized space or larger.

- Initiatives Designed for Larger Spaces. These activities are intended for spaces larger than a classroom, such as gymnasiums or outdoor locations.

With modification, many of these activities may be suitable for use in different size spaces as well.

Initiatives Designed for Small Spaces

Survivor

This is a simple, no-prop indoor activity that involves only the brain, paper, and pencil.

Target Group: Any

Size of Group: 3 to 12

Props: Paper and pencil or pen

Objectives

Activity Goals: Experience consensus-building in the face of a challenge, creative problem solving

Main FVC Connections: Speak Your Truth, Hear the Truth

Keys to Success Connections: Emotional awareness, behavioral control, establishing positive relationships

Facilitator Guidelines

Introduction/Metaphor

"You and your group will soon be dropped into the heart of the Rocky Mountain wilderness and challenged with the task of surviving for one month. You are allowed to bring 10 items in addition to the clothes you are wearing. The entire group must agree on the 10 items."

To build consensus, the group will need to utilize effective communication strategies, debate and compromise without fighting. You can begin with a discussion about the differences between arguing and debating. What skills will the group need to build consensus?

The Action

Give the group the task of developing a list of 10 items (more or less, depending on your group's functional levels) that they would want to have if they were stranded in the Rocky Mountains.

Variation 1

Vary the amount of time the group will be stranded.

Variation 2

Change the environment: stranded on a deserted island, the jungles of South America, or the middle of the ocean.

Variation 3

Vary the type of challenge. For example, the group has to come up with a set of 10 laws that will guide a new civilization. Compare this to the group's FVC!

Debriefing

Questions for When the Focus Is on Emotional Awareness

- Did you feel like your opinion counted? How did that feel?

Questions for When the Focus Is on Behavioral Control

- Did you have to compromise? When have you had to compromise in your real life?

Questions for When the Focus Is on Positive Relationships

- Did the group take into account personal strengths and weaknesses when deciding what items the group would need?
- What skills are needed for a leader to build consensus amongst a group? Did anyone in the group show these skills?
- Often we play certain roles in group situations. Some people are leaders. Some are followers. Some try to keep the peace, while others try to stir things up. What role did you play? Is that a typical role for you?

Weighing In

In this group decision-making activity, all members must weigh in to reach consensus.

Target Group: Middle school and older

Size of Group: 2 to 12 (can do with multiple groups)

Props: 78 pennies, 12 empty film canisters or similar-sized containers, small blank white labels, narrow-pointed marker

Objectives

Activity Goal: Build group consensus through communication and consideration of various opinions

Main FVC Connections: Speak Your Truth, Hear the Truth

Keys to Success Connections: Emotional awareness, behavioral control, establishing positive relationships

Facilitator Guidelines

Introduction/Metaphor

To weigh in means to voice your opinion on a matter. Ask your group: "When an important decision is being made amongst your friends, do you generally weigh in or stay quiet? How about when it's your family? Your school? Your town? For this activity, you will need to weigh in for your group to be successful."

The Action

Prior to your session, divide your pennies into the film canisters in the following manner: One canister will have one penny, the next will have two and so on, with each canister having one more penny than the previous one so that the final canister has 12 pennies. Place the covers on the canisters.

Write the letters *A* through *L* on 12 labels and randomly place the labels on the canisters, taking care not to create a clear pattern for the letters (i.e., don't label them A, B, C and so on in order of how many pennies are in each!). Make sure to write down the correct sequence of letters that denote the canisters in order of their contents from one to 12.

The goal is for your group to determine how many pennies are in each canister without opening them. The final decision must be consensus, meaning everyone agrees with the final answer—not "majority rules."

Check for correctness. If needed, provide feedback (more or less, depending on your group).

I generally give the group three tries to find the correct sequence, telling them how many are out of sequence after each attempt.

Variation 1

Don't label canisters. Allow the group to open the canisters once they feel they've gotten the correct order. They only have one chance to get it right in this variation.

Variation 2

Don't label canisters. Once the group has given you their final order, open the canisters one at a time with great drama!

Variation 3

Give each member of the group one canister (or more if there are fewer than 12 participants). Each player may touch only his or her own canister.

Variation 4

Same as Variation 3 but don't allow the group members to talk or otherwise communicate verbally (i.e., no writing).

Debriefing

Questions for When the Focus Is on Emotional Awareness

- Did this activity create any level of stress for you? How did you respond?
- Did you feel any pressure to agree with the rest of the group when you believed the order was not correct? How did you cope with that?

Question for When the Focus Is on Behavioral Control

- When you felt that someone was leading the group in the wrong direction, how did you respond?

Questions for When the Focus Is on Positive Relationships

- Did you feel that you had equal input for the answer?
- Did one person have more influence over the group than others?

Priorities

This activity grew out of discussions I had with teen groups about priorities.

Target Group: Middle school and older

Size of Group: 3 to 15

Props: A marker, several index cards for each person, large writing surface (optional)

Objectives

Activity Goals: Illustrate the impact of priorities on our lives, help participants see discrepancies between their stated priorities and actual choices in life

Main FVC Connections: Speak Your Truth, Hear the Truth

Keys to Success Connections: Emotional awareness, behavioral control, establishing positive relationships

Facilitator Guidelines

Setup

Prior to the session, print the terms *love, money, school, family,* and *friends* on large index cards or pieces of paper.

Introduction/Metaphor

I generally lead into this activity by opening up a discussion about priorities. What does priority mean? What influences how we develop our priorities? Do they remain constant or change over time?

The Action

Instruct your group that they should carry out the initial portion of this activity in silence; there is to be no discussion.

Give each group member five blank index cards and a marker. Instruct them to number the index cards 1 through 5 and write his or her first name on each (include last initial or name if you have several students with the same name).

On the floor or a large table, lay out your index cards with the five terms listed above.

Ask participants to determine in what order of priority these terms would fall for them. For example, the most important of these words would rank a "1" and the least important to them would be a "5." Each participant should place a numbered card in a column under each priority category. The cards should be placed so that they can be seen clearly.

Once everyone has placed their cards, discuss the results.

Variation

You can use different priorities. You can also increase or decrease the number of priorities used. Other terms I have used include *physical health, electronics,* and *popularity.*

Debriefing

Questions for When the Focus Is on Emotional Awareness

- Why did you put these in the order you did?
- What influenced your choices?
- What order would you have put these in five years ago? Why?
- What order do you think you will put these in 10 years from now? How about 20 years from now? Why?
- What order do you think your parents would put these in?

Questions for When the Focus Is on Behavioral Control

- How do these priorities impact your choices in life?
- Do your choices and behaviors in life actually reflect the priorities you shared today? For example, do you always act as if your displayed number one priority really is your number one priority?

Questions for When the Focus Is on Positive Relationships

- Does the order of your priorities ever lead to conflicts with others, such as parents?
- Do you think your parents would believe that your priorities are as you say they are here? Why or why not?

Silent Team Checkers

This problem-solving activity shows the importance of using communication to continually adjust strategies.

Target Group: Middle school and older

Size of Group: 4 to 8

Props: Checkers set, blindfolds

Objectives

Activity Goals: Strategize as a group in difficult situations, develop nonverbal communication and group problem-solving skills

Main FVC Connections: Speak Your Truth, Hear the Truth

Keys to Success Connections: Emotional awareness, behavioral control, establishing positive relationships

Facilitator Guidelines

Introduction/Metaphor

"Most of us have played checkers before. Very few have played as a team. Even fewer have played it blindfolded or without speaking. This activity is about communication and problem solving more than determining who is the ultimate champion checker player."

The Action

Set up a checkerboard according to the traditional rules.

Divide your group into two teams.

Decide which team will go first and the order in which team members will take their turn. All turns throughout the game must be taken in this predetermined order. The predetermined player takes the turn for the team on the team's turn.

All but one player on each team should wear a blindfold. You can have more than one person without a blindfold if you choose. The player without a blindfold can never touch the checkers.

Once the game has begun, none of the participants may speak to each other. You can offer the group planning time before each round of the activity. As the facilitator, you will decide how much feedback to provide as the game progresses.

Variation 1

For a simpler version, do not implement the "no speaking" rule. Or, only the blindfolded members may speak but the sighted player (or players) cannot speak.

Variation 2

Everyone is blindfolded and can speak.

Variation 3

The ultimate challenge: Everybody is blindfolded and no one can speak!

Debriefing

Questions for When the Focus Is on Emotional Awareness

- How did it feel to not be able to speak?
- How did it feel to not be able to see?
- Which version was the most challenging for you?
- Did you get frustrated at all? How did you handle that?

Questions for When the Focus Is on Behavioral Control

- How did you know what the best move was? Did you take into account information from your teammates?

Questions for When the Focus Is on Positive Relationships

- Did the planning time help?
- What strategies did you use to communicate each round? Did the strategy have to change each round? Do you ever have to change the way you communicate with people? What factors influence how you will communicate with others?
- How difficult was it to figure out what your teammates' plans were when you couldn't talk? Have you ever been in a situation in which you were trying to figure out why someone was doing what they were doing and you couldn't communicate with them about it?

Transmitter and Receiver

In this activity, participants will rely solely on verbal communication to accomplish a task.

Target Group: Middle school and older

Size of Group: 2 to 16 (even numbers work best)

Props: Pencils, paper, designs

Objectives

Activity Goal: Understanding the limitations of verbal communication without visual cues

Main FVC Connections: Be Here, Speak Your Truth, Hear the Truth

Keys to Success Connections: Emotional awareness, behavioral control, establishing positive relationships

Facilitator Guidelines

Introduction/Metaphor

"What percentage of communication is considered verbal (the words we use)? Amazingly, only 7%! That means that 93% of communication is not about the words we use. In all forms of communication, there is the Transmitter (sender of the message) and the Receiver (receiver of the message)."

The Action

Divide your group into pairs and have each pair decide who will be the Transmitter and who will be the Receiver. Have partners sit back-to-back so that they cannot see each other.

Give a piece of paper and pencil to each Receiver.

The Transmitter is given one of the designs. The Transmitter must verbally describe the design to the Receiver, who will try to draw the design based on the Transmitter's words. This must be completed without either partner seeing each other's paper.

When all pairs finish, have partners compare the original designs with the ones drawn by the Receivers.

After some discussion, have the partners switch roles and try new designs.

Variation 1

The Receiver may not talk.

Variation 2

Have one Transmitter for multiple Receivers.

Variation 3

Use designs that are not abstract (such as a star, smiley face, cartoon character), but don't allow the Transmitter to indicate verbally what the picture is. In other words, they must describe the picture as if it were an abstract design.

Debriefing

When visual cues are removed, verbal communication becomes more difficult. It is also more difficult to listen passively without being able to ask for clarification. For many students with emotional and behavioral problems, asking clarifying questions in school is too much of an emotional risk for an already fragile self-esteem. In this activity, not asking these questions can produce confusion and frustration and lead to designs that are way off base. This is an excellent metaphor for what happens in situations that produce confusion when people don't ask for clarification.

Questions for When the Focus Is on Emotional Awareness

- Which variation was easiest? Which one was most difficult? Why?

- How did you feel when you were not able to ask clarifying questions? Are there situations in your life when this has happened?

Questions for When the Focus Is on Behavioral Control

- How did you deal with the confusion you experienced during this activity? Was that effective?

- On the first try, what did you learn about communication? How did this help improve the second attempt?

Questions for When the Focus Is on Positive Relationships

- Why did you have difficulties creating the exact design your partner was describing?

- How are the communication difficulties you experienced in this activity similar to ones in real life? How do they impact your relationships with others?

Telephone

This game has been around longer than I have. I learned it as a child but found it has great use as a communication activity! As a group activity, you can use a longer, more complex message to pass on. For example, in working with an Anger Management group, I once told the first person, "The physiological aspects of anger may be the most important ones to regain control of for one's emotional well-being." While I don't recall exactly what the final message was, it had certainly changed quite a bit!

Target Group: Any age group

Size of Group: Minimum of 8 to 20 (can use with multiple groups)

Props: None

Objectives

Activity Goals: Highlight the fact that miscommunications can be related both to the one who delivers the message as well as the one who receives it, promote understanding about the social ramifications of rumors and other ways that communication issues lead to conflicts among kids and teens

Main FVC Connections: Be Here, Speak Your Truth, Hear the Truth

Keys to Success Connections: Emotional awareness, behavioral control, establishing positive relationships

Facilitator Guidelines

Introduction/Metaphor

"Has a miscommunication ever caused problems for you? How about misunderstandings or 'he said, she said' stuff? Have you ever been the victim of a vicious rumor? Have you ever perpetuated a rumor about someone else? How do these communication problems happen? Well, we're about to find out! Just because you played it as a kid doesn't mean it can't be used to learn important communication skills!"

The Action

Arrange your group in a straight line.

Give the person at the front of the line a verbal message. While you can give them any message you choose, I generally create a message that relates to the particular group. The message should be somewhat complex and long enough to be difficult to remember. It may even be difficult to understand!

Have the first person relay the message to the second person, the second to the third, and so on.

Have the last person in line recite the message as they received it.

Variation 1

Don't allow the message recipient to ask the message deliverer any clarifying questions about what they heard (or didn't hear!).

Variation 2

Use a list of unrelated words as your message and compare the results with a more meaningful message.

Debriefing

Questions for When the Focus Is on Emotional Awareness

- How did you feel when the message came to you? Were you confused? How did you deal with that?

Questions for When the Focus Is on Behavioral Control

- When you couldn't ask questions of the person giving you the message, did it change your approach to the task?
- Did the message change as it traveled? Why?

Questions for When the Focus Is on Positive Relationships

- Was the person giving the message more responsible for the message changing than the person receiving it? Thinking about situations in your life, is the one sending the message more at fault for miscommunication or misunderstanding than the person receiving the message?
- How do communication problems impact relationships?

Three Read

Today's teens must deal with the influences of peers, the media, and their parents. Making decisions can become quite difficult with all the information coming in. In thinking of a way to experientially demonstrate how we can become overwhelmed by incoming information from various sources, I came up with Three Read!

Target Group: Middle school and older participants

Size of Group: 4 to 12 (works best in multiples of 4 but can be altered to work with other numbers of participants)

Props: Three Read passages (p. 441) or other short reading passages you choose

Objectives

Activity Goals: Promote understanding of how various environmental influences can impact our ability to utilize good judgment and make decisions; explore the influence of parents, peers and the media on today's teens

Main FVC Connections: Be Here, Hear the Truth

Keys to Success Connections: Emotional awareness, behavioral control, establishing positive relationships

Facilitator Guidelines

Setup

Make sure your readers are comfortable reading out loud. I usually ask that if they are uncomfortable reading aloud for any reason, they simply become a Listener, no questions asked.

Introduction/Metaphor

This activity is an excellent metaphor for making decisions when there is a great deal of external information entering our brains from various sources.

"Have you ever sought advice for a difficult decision? Who do you seek advice from? What other factors weigh into the choice you will make? How about simple daily decisions such as what to buy and wear and what music to listen to? What influences these decisions? Parents? Friends? Media? Sometimes, with all of these influences, it's even harder to make sense of things and make a good decision!"

The Action

Divide your group into fours (some groups of five are OK too).

Have one member volunteer to be the Listener. If you have more than four in a group, you can have multiple Listeners.

Each of the other three people in the group, the Readers, should get one of the Three Read passages (p. 441). You can also choose three passages of your own that are relevant to the group. For example, I facilitated this activity with a parenting group once using passages on three different parenting styles.

When you say, "start," all the Readers begin reading their passages at the same time to their Listener(s).

The Listener's job is to try to comprehend each story as they are read to him or her simultaneously.

Debriefing

Questions for When the Focus Is on Emotional Awareness

- As the Listener, how did you feel when the passages were being read to you? When have you felt this way in your life?

- As the Reader, how did you feel reading your passage while the others were being read at the same time? When else have you felt this way?

Questions for When the Focus Is on Behavioral Control

- As the Listener, how did you cope with the overload of information? What strategies did you use?

- As a Reader, did you use any strategy to make sure your listener understood your information?

- Are there situations in your life when you feel overwhelmed with incoming information? How do you deal with these situations?

Questions for When the Focus Is on Positive Relationships

- How do you deal with situations in which you are receiving different advice from different people?

- Are there times it's good to seek out advice? Are there times when it's not a good idea?

- Who are the people in your life that influence your decisions?

Blindfolded Jenga*

This was created during a group at Manchester High School in Connecticut. We were playing Jenga® as a group in a conference room. In the same room, I stored a bunch of experiential gear. My blindfolds happened to be out and one of the students asked what I use them for. Somehow, that led to trying our game with blindfolds!

Target Group: Any age group

Size of Group: 2 to 8

Props: Jenga, blindfolds

Objectives

Activity Goals: Illustrate the importance of others to attain one's goals, enhance communication, build frustration tolerance

Main FVC Connections: Be Here, Speak Your Truth, Hear the Truth

Keys to Success Connections: Emotional awareness, behavioral control, establishing positive relationships

Facilitator Guidelines

Introduction/Metaphor

"Have you ever been in a position where you had to rely on someone else in order to accomplish your own goal? Have you ever been counted on by someone else to help that person accomplish a goal? During this activity, you will have to rely on someone else to achieve your own goal and vice versa!"

The Action

The object is to not be the team that knocks the structure down.

Set up the Jenga game. Have group members partner up.

Give each pair one blindfold. Ask partners to decide which of them will be blindfolded first. That person is the Player. The sighted partner is the Manager.

Following regular Jenga rules, have the Manager verbally direct their blindfolded partner (the Player) to remove and replace the Jenga pieces. At no time can the Manager touch the Jenga pieces or the Player.

After the first game, offer partners the opportunity to switch roles.

---

*JENGA® & ©2013 Hasbro, Inc. Used with permission.

Variation

Instead of having the teams compete to see who can avoid knocking the tower down, go for the largest tower the entire group can build. A 54-piece Jenga® set has 18 rows to start. You can count each row as you go.

Debriefing

Questions for When the Focus Is on Emotional Awareness

- How did you feel during that activity? Was it easy or difficult? Why?
- Which role was more difficult for you, Player or Manager? Why?

Questions for When the Focus Is on Behavioral Control

- As the Player, were there times when you moved too fast? What happened? Has there ever been a time in your life when moving fast caused you problems?
- As the Manager, were there times when it was difficult to hold back from touching the player or the game pieces? Tell about a time in your life when you had to use self-restraint.

Questions for When the Focus Is on Positive Relationships

- Given the rules, could either of you have successfully completed this activity alone? How did it feel knowing you had to rely on someone else to reach a goal?
- Was it easy for partners to communicate? How did you work to improve communication as the game went on?

Don't Get the Right Card

Target Group: Any age group

Size of Group: 2 to 12 participants

Props: A deck of playing cards

Objectives

Activity Goals: Experience the process of developing a team strategy, group problem solving

Main FVC Connections: Speak Your Truth, Hear the Truth

Keys to Success Connections: Emotional awareness, behavioral control, establishing positive relationships

Facilitator Guidelines

Introduction/Metaphor

"Is it difficult to predict the future? Are there things in life that are more predictable than others? Like what? Today, as a group, you will try to figure out how to predict what will not happen!"

The Action

Inform the group that you will be turning over the cards from the deck one at a time. Their job is to guess which card will not be next.

For this activity, suits are irrelevant (except for planning purposes). So, before I turn over the first card, the group must decide what they believe that card will not be. For example, the group decides it will not be an 8. I turn over the card and it's a Jack; they are correct.

If the group is correct, repeat the process for the next card and so on until they accidentally guess the "correct" card.

While there is quite a bit of luck involved in this activity, there are strategies the group can use to increase the odds of correctly guessing what will not be the next card.

If the group accidentally guesses the correct next card, count the number of cards they have successfully turned face up, shuffle the entire deck and allow the group to strategize.

Use the variations below for different rounds and see how the variations impact the outcome. If the group is tuned in, they will realize that once they have seen four cards of any given number, they can safely guess that number card through the rest of the deck.

Variation 1

Only the person whose turn it is may speak.

Variation 2

Group members may not communicate with each other in any way during a player's turn.

Variation 3

Group members may not communicate with each other at all.

Variation 4

Once all four cards of a number have been shown, the group can no longer guess that number.

Debriefing

Often, the strategy that affords your group its best chance of success is not immediately evident. Many times, I have observed groups using an opposite strategy such as guessing cards they have not yet seen. It's always interesting to find out how the group discovers their best strategy, how it is communicated and how well it worked.

Question for When the Focus Is on Emotional Awareness

- How did you feel when someone guessed the "correct" card and forced the group to start over?

Questions for When the Focus Is on Behavioral Control

- What strategy worked the best? Why?
- How did you come up with different strategies?

Questions for When the Focus Is on Positive Relationships

- How did you communicate the strategy to others? Was this easily done?

Initiatives Designed for Medium-Sized Spaces

Culture Shock

This is a great activity to highlight communication differences. Because we all communicate differently, miscommunications and misunderstandings are common in relationships.

Target Group: Middle school and older

Size of Group: 6 to 15 participants

Props: Culture Shock Instruction Lists for each group and a message each group needs to communicate to the other groups. (See Appendix E.)

Objectives

Activity Goal: Help participants understand that we differ in the ways we give, receive, and interpret communication. This understanding helps build tolerance and empathy for interpersonal differences.

Main FVC Connections: Speak Your Truth, Hear the Truth

Keys to Success Connections: Emotional awareness, behavioral control, establishing positive relationships

Facilitator Guidelines

Introduction/Metaphor

"You've travelled far and finally landed on a beautiful island. At first, you think it's deserted, but some of the island natives are coming to greet you. There appear to be two groups coming, one from the east and one from the west. Luckily, they seem happy to see you! As they come closer, you realize that they speak the same language as you, but there seems to be something odd about the way they try to communicate."

The Action

Divide participants into three groups.

Give each group one of the three Culture Shock Instruction lists. The instruction lists explain how group members prefer to communicate. Some indicate group members communicate only if they are a specific distance apart or only if they make no eye contact. (See Culture Shock Instruction Lists in Appendix E.)

Tell participants that they can in no way tell the other groups what their instructions say. They can only follow their instructions to the best of their ability.

Give each group a message to convey or have each select one. The messages can be something related to the type of group you are facilitating. For example, if it's an anger management group, you may have one group communicate to others what triggers their anger. The second group may communicate ways they currently deal with their anger, while the third group can try to relate how anger has caused them trouble in the past.

Have each group attempt to communicate its message to the other groups in the manner stated in the directions given to them. Allow the attempted communication to go on for a few minutes before calling a stop to the action. At this point, have each group guess at what the other groups' instructions stated.

Debriefing

Questions for When the Focus Is on Emotional Awareness

- How did you feel when you tried to communicate with others who did not communicate as you do? Has this happened in real life?

- How did you feel when others tried to communicate with you in ways that went against how you like to communicate? Has this happened to you in real life?

Questions for When the Focus Is on Behavioral Control

- How did you respond to those trying to communicate with you? How do you respond to others who may not communicate the way you do?

Questions for When the Focus Is on Positive Relationships

- Can you establish a relationship with someone who communicates differently than you?

- Who in your life communicates in a different manner than you do?

- Do you feel like your "culture" influences how you communicate? Does it bring you into conflict with others who are not part of your "culture"?

Stump Jump*

This activity requires a great deal of trust that the person in front of you will jump at the right time. This can only be accomplished with group synchronicity, serious planning, and total commitment!

Target Group: Any age group

Size of Group: 6 to 20 participants

Props: Gym spots (one per participant)

Objectives

Activity Goal: Problem-solve using planning, trust and commitment to the group

Main FVC Connections: Be Safe, Speak Your Truth, Hear the Truth

Keys to Success Connections: Emotional awareness, behavioral control, establishing positive relationships

Facilitator Guidelines

Introduction/Metaphor

"In the Florida Everglades, great big fan boats cruise sightseers across the swamps in search of crocodiles. Your group has boarded one of these boats, and in the most crocodile-infested area, you have crashed! The boat has sunk. There are just enough stumps sticking out of the muck for each of you to stand on one. Your only route to safety is to carefully walk along the tops of these stumps to shore."

This activity is about commitment. Without full commitment, the group cannot be successful. You can forgo the fantasy introduction above and open up with a discussion about commitment.

The Action

Arrange your gym spots in a circle about a foot and a half apart.

Have each participant stand on a spot. The goal is for the entire group to cycle clockwise through the spots until they end up on the same spot they started.

While doing this, participants cannot touch the ground or each other, and no stump may be occupied by more than one person at any given time.

To accomplish the task, group members must jump simultaneously forward to the stump in front of them.

They must do this successfully for as many times as it takes for each member to return to his or her original stump!

---

*A version of this activity appears in *Teamwork and Teamplay* (Cain & Jolliff, 1998) and *Team Challenge: Introduction to Low Initiatives Training* (Fark, 1994).

Variation 1

To make this easier, have group members step from one stump to the next. Only two feet may be on a stump at any given time. A bit more challenging may be only one foot at a time. You can add that no stump may be completely unoccupied at any time. You can use this version as a prequel to the version above.

Variation 2

Allow the group to practice off the spots before trying the actual activity.

Debriefing

Questions for When the Focus Is on Emotional Awareness

- Did your stress level rise at any point during this activity? Why?

Questions for When the Focus Is on Behavioral Control

- Did anyone mess up? How? How did the group react?

Questions for When the Focus Is on Positive Relationships

- How did commitment play into this activity? Where in your life have you had to make a total commitment?
- How was trust important to your group's success?
- How did you create and implement a successful plan?

Get 20*

Target Group: Upper elementary-age and older participants

Size of Group: 4 to 30 people

Props: Deck of cards (face cards removed)

Objectives

Activity Goals: Group communication and problem solving, examining different roles in solving a problem as a group

Main FVC Connections: Speak Your Truth, Hear the Truth

Keys to Success Connections: Behavioral control, establishing positive relationships

Facilitator Guidelines

Introduction/Metaphor

I generally give out the necessary cards and have the group just launch right into this challenge.

The Action

Divide your group into smaller groups of four or five participants. Give each participant one card.

The goal for each group is to use its cards to create a math equation that equals exactly 20. Participants can use any mathematical operations they want (such as addition, subtraction, division, multiplication). It is almost always possible to accomplish this task with four or five cards. For example, if my group had the numbers 1 (ace), 2, 6, 8, and 9, we could create the following problem to equal 20: 9-2-1+6+8=20. This activity is always possible with five cards as long as each card has a different value.

Variation 1

To make this easier, give each group seven or eight cards of which they can only use five.

Variation 2

If your groups are getting 20 quickly, challenge them to see how many different equations they can come up with equaling 20!

---

*Michelle Cummings, M.S., of Training Wheels (www.training-wheels.com) created the original version of this activity. It is copyrighted in her book *Playing with a Full Deck* (2007).

Debriefing

Question for When the Focus Is on Behavioral Control

- How did you go about solving this problem as a group?

Questions for When the Focus Is on Positive Relationships

- Did everyone take part in creating the solution? How about implementing it? Is it always desirable to have all members take part in planning a solution to a problem?

Group Blackjack*

Target Group: Middle school-age and older participants

Size of Group: 8 to 30 people

Props: Deck of cards

Objectives

Activity Goals: Examining group identification and allegiance, individual versus group goals, group communication and problem-solving

Main FVC Connections: Speak Your Truth, Hear the Truth

Keys to Success Connections: Emotional awareness, behavioral control, establishing positive relationships

Facilitator Guidelines

Introduction/Metaphor

"Has anyone here played blackjack? If so, what are strong blackjack hands? This is a team version of blackjack. The entire group is in this one together!"

The Action

Give each participant a card that the player is to hold but not look at. On your cue, the participants must hold their cards face out on their foreheads so that they cannot see their own number but others can.

The participants are to get into groups of two or more where all group members' cards add up to strong blackjack hands (19, 20, or 21). This activity is to be done in silence.

If one or more groups do not have cards equaling a good blackjack hand, the group must reshuffle itself until they are able to achieve the goal of each small group having a strong hand with all members included in the solution.

Variation 1

To make this easier, allow members to look at their cards.

Variation 2

To make the activity even easier, allow members to speak during the activity.

---

*Michelle Cummings, M.S., of Training Wheels (www.training-wheels.com) created the original version of this activity. It is copyrighted in her book *Playing with a Full Deck* (2007).

Debriefing

During this activity, once participants find their small group, there is a tendency to stop actively participating in the solution. Often, participants will be reluctant to shuffle the groups when necessary. If you observe this, it's interesting to investigate why this happens.

Questions for When the Focus Is on Emotional Awareness

- How did you feel when you found a group to be with? How did you feel when you realized that groups needed to be reshuffled?

Questions for When the Focus Is on Behavioral Control

- Once you found a group, did you do anything to help other groups? Why or why not?

Questions for When the Focus Is on Positive Relationships

- How did having a whole group goal impact the strategy you used?
- Were there times you had to sacrifice your nice, comfy spot in a group to help the larger group reach a goal? How did that impact you? How did it impact your group?
- Are there times in life when you've gotten so focused on your part of a task that you lose sight of the larger goal?

Body Language*

To be successful in this activity, the group must blend nonverbal and verbal communication!

Target Group: Any

Size of Group: 8 to 24

Props: List of short words (3 to 4 letters)

Objectives

Activity Goals: Explore verbal versus nonverbal communication, group communication and problem solving

Main FVC Connections: Speak Your Truth, Hear the Truth

Keys to Success Connection: Establishing positive relationships

Facilitator Guidelines

Setup

Create a list of words relevant to your group, generally words five letters long or shorter

Introduction/Metaphor

"What is the difference between verbal and nonverbal communication? Verbal communication is about the actual words we speak. Nonverbal communication is not about the words but how the information is conveyed. This activity blurs the line between verbal and nonverbal communication. Without speaking, you will need to communicate words to your fellow group-mates."

The Action

Divide your group into smaller groups of four (five will work if the numbers don't allow all groups to have four).

Give your first group one of the words from the list. The group has a set amount of time (I like 1 minute but, depending on your group, they may need a bit longer) to physically create the word in letters using their bodies. (This is not charades; the words are not to be acted out but actually spelled out physically in some way.)

The other group (or groups) tries to guess the word. The group that guesses quickest gets a point (if you want to keep score) or the entire group gets a point if the word is successfully conveyed.

When the first group has taken its turn, move on to the other groups.

---

*A version of this activity, called Body English, appears in *Silver Bullets* (Rohnke, 1984).

Variation

You can use longer words and make larger groups. Use a list of words that relates to the topic of your group. For example, if I am using this activity with a social-skills group, I might give them the words *Look, Listen, Smile, Talk,* etc.

Debriefing

If you customize the list of words to go with the theme of the group, debrief how these words fit in with the group's goals.

Questions for When the Focus Is on Positive Relationships

- How did your group decide how you would go about demonstrating your word? Was there one leader?

- Was it challenging to communicate words with your body? How else do we communicate with our bodies?

Turn Over a New Leaf*

Target Group: Any age group upper elementary age or older that has shown the ability to be safe

Size of Group: 2 to about 20 participants

Props: Towel (for groups of 2 to 4) or tarp for larger groups. Use smaller tarps for smaller groups and larger tarps for larger groups.

Objectives

Activity Goals: Use team strategy to reach a goal or goals, build trust and communication skills

Main FVC Connections: Be Safe, Speak Your Truth, Hear the Truth

Keys to Success Connections: Emotional awareness, behavioral control, establishing positive relationships

Facilitator Guidelines

Setup

When facilitating this activity, it is important to emphasize safety. I usually don't allow people to sit on each other's shoulders, but riding piggyback or standing on each other's feet is usually OK. Spot them as necessary.

Introduction/Metaphor

This activity is one of the most universal in its application and metaphorical possibilities. My introductions are always tailored specifically to my group but usually involve the concept of changing a behavior or improving an aspect of one's life.

For example, if you are working with students who struggle academically, the side of the tarp they are standing on could represent their current grades, while the underside could represent the grades they hope to achieve. The side they are standing on could represent old, bad habits, while the other side could be new, healthier habits. For a depression group, the side they stand on could be unhappiness and underneath, happiness.

Whatever the metaphor is, I like to have the students tell me exactly where they stand now and where they want to be. Often, I will have them write each answer on a piece of masking tape. The one representing the present gets taped to the side they stand on and the one representing their future improvement goes on the underside of the tarp. Additionally, I ask them to tell me one skill or trait they possess that will help them reach their goal.

---

*This adventure classic is an extremely adaptable activity. Another early version called Magic Carpet appears in *Teamwork and Teamplay* (Cain & Jolliff, 1998).

The Action

The basic idea is to have a group of people stand on top of a tarp, towel, or blanket and work to flip it over completely without anyone stepping onto the ground surrounding the tarp.

Any errors result in a restart.

Variation

The group is to fold the tarp in half. With this variation, I am purposely vague about what "half" means. Have the group see how many times they can successfully fold the tarp in half without anyone stepping off.

Debriefing

The debriefing for this activity will depend upon how you've introduced it.

Question for When the Focus Is on Emotional Awareness

- How comfortable were you with the close physical proximity and touching that this activity called for?

Questions for When the Focus Is on Behavioral Control

- How did your group come up with a strategy? Did you modify it as you went along? What are other situations in your life when you've had to modify your original plan to be successful?

- What skills did you use to succeed in this activity? Would those same skills be useful in attaining the goal you wrote on the tape?

- What made this activity difficult? What roadblocks have come up when you are pursuing your goals in life?

Questions for When the Focus Is on Positive Relationships

- Did you reach out to others for support during the activity? How do you seek support toward reaching your goals in your real life?

- Did you support anyone else? Why? How did it help the group reach their goal?

Web of Life*

This is another incredibly versatile activity that focuses on how we're all connected.

Target Group: Any group

Size of Group: 6 to 10 participants

Props: Buddy ropes (optional)

Objectives

Activity Goals: Experience human connectedness, group communication and problem solving, examining individual roles in a group problem-solving situation

Main FVC Connections: Be Safe, Speak Your Truth, Hear the Truth

Keys to Success Connections: Emotional awareness, behavioral control, establishing positive relationships

Facilitator Guidelines

Introduction/Metaphor

To introduce this activity, I like to read "The Web of Life" by Chief Seattle (p. 447). This reading highlights the notion that we are all connected. Whatever we do in life impacts the web of life and, in turn, each other. If you don't use the reading, you can still begin by asking the group what it means when people say, "We're all connected." Another way to frame this activity is to have a discussion about how individual choices impact other people. A final framing option I have used is connecting the activity to the concept of "enmeshment." There are times when our own emotions and lives become too intertwined with the emotions and lives of others.

The Action

The activity begins with a group of people standing in a circle.

Participants close their eyes while reaching both hands into the center and grabbing someone else's hand. This will create quite a tangle of hands.

Without letting go, the group must untangle itself.

(I prefer to use "buddy ropes" for this activity. These are short pieces of rope, about 2 feet long. Each member holds the end of one rope and reaches it into the middle of the circle. With his or her free hand, each group member grabs the end of someone else's rope. This variation allows members to avoid holding hands and provides a bit more personal space. It also makes it easier to see what's going on.)

---

*The first written version of this activity I can find is called Knots in the *The New Games Book* (Fluegelman, 1976). There is also a version called Human Knot in *The Cooperative Sports and Games Book* by Terry Orlick (1978).

There may come a moment in the detangling process when it looks like it won't be possible for the group to fully detangle. This opens up options for the group to decide how to proceed (i.e., give up, allow one member to let go, etc.). Use this situation as an opportunity to connect the activity with the introduction you chose.

Debriefing

While the debriefing for this activity will depend upon how you've introduced it, there are some themes that arise naturally through the activity itself.

Questions for When the Focus Is on Emotional Awareness

- What were some of the emotions you experienced during this activity? What are some life situations in which you've experienced these types of emotions?

Questions for When the Focus Is on Behavioral Control

- How did your choices impact the others in the group during this activity? How do your choices impact those who are close to you in your life?

- How did you detangle the knot? What kind of "knots" do you have in your life to detangle?

Questions for When the Focus Is on Positive Relationships

- Did anyone emerge as a leader in this activity? Why that person?

- When you have "knots" to detangle in your life, do you reach out to others to help you? Whom do you seek out?

Traffic Jam*

This is a classic adventure activity.

Target Group: Middle school age and older

Size of Group: 6 to 10 participants

Props: Gym spots (one more than there are participants)

Objectives

Activity Goals: Group communication and problem solving, coping with frustration

Main FVC Connections: Speak Your Truth, Hear the Truth

Keys to Success Connections: Emotional awareness, behavioral control, establishing positive relationships

Facilitator Guidelines

Introduction/Metaphor

Warning! This initiative can cause stress (just like a real traffic jam). This activity is a kinesthetic puzzle that requires the exchange of ideas and communication. What makes the communication somewhat more difficult is that participants will be standing in a linear pattern (i.e., a straight line), rather than in a circle where everyone can see each other (that's why we "circle up," isn't it?). "What's it like to be in a traffic jam? What are the 'traffic jams' in your life? How do you get out of them?"

The Action

Lay out the gym spots in a straight line with one more spot than there are participants (i.e., seven spots for six participants). Ideally, you will have an even number of participants.

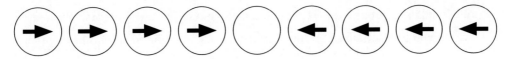

Arrows represent direction of movement.

Divide the group into two subgroups.

Have the participants stand on the spots so that each subgroup member is facing a member from the other subgroup. Leave the middle spot open.

The goal is for the two teams to switch places so that each subgroup finishes on the opposite side of where it began.

---

*A version of this activity also appears in *Silver Bullets* (Rohnke, 1984).

The rules for movement are as follows:

Participants can only move one spot at a time.

No participant can go around anyone on his or her own subgroup (those facing the same way). Participants can go around those facing them (from the other subgroup), provided there is an open spot immediately behind the person they are facing.

Only one person may move at a time.

Two people can never occupy the same spot.

Participants cannot move backward.

The group must determine the pattern of movement that will lead to the successful solution. Each time they end up at a "dead end," participants must return to their original spots and start over.

Variation

Create a tabletop version of this for smaller spaces. Lay out pieces of paper on the table as you would the gym spots, as described above. Participants can use something to represent themselves, placing those items on the paper as they would line up in the original version. If possible, it's best to use items of one color for participants moving in one direction and a different color for those moving in the opposite direction.

Debriefing

Questions for When the Focus Is on Emotional Awareness

- What were some emotions you experienced during this activity? How did you handle these emotions? Did these emotions lead to you performing better or worse?
- How did you feel when you hit a dead end and had to restart? Tell about a time in your life when you hit a "dead end" and felt like you were starting over.

Question for When the Focus Is on Behavioral Control

- What did you do to contribute to the group's success?

Questions for When the Focus Is on Positive Relationships

- How did using group support allow you to be successful in this activity?
- When you have a "traffic jam" in your life, do you get support from others?

Everyone Up*

Sometimes our friends have to help us stand up!

Target Group: Upper elementary age and older

Size of Group: 2 to 24 participants

Props: None

Objectives

Activity Goals: Group problem solving, adapting to changing goals, building trust, highlighting the need for balance in relationships

Main FVC Connections: Be Safe, Speak Your Truth, Hear the Truth

Keys to Success Connections: Emotional awareness, behavioral control, establishing positive relationships

Facilitator Guidelines

Setup

Emphasize safety in this activity. Make it clear that if a particular movement hurts, participants should speak up and stop doing it.

Introduction/Metaphor

"How do we support each other in life? Who are the people who support you? Who do you give support to? How do you support them?"

The Action

Divide your group into pairs. Have group members sit back-to-back with their partner and link arms at the elbows.

On the count of three, while keeping their arms interlocked, participants should try to stand up.

Once the pairs have mastered this task, try it in threes or fours.

Add on until you have the whole group trying to stand up together.

Variation

Have each pair begin by facing each other and, grasping each other's wrists, pull each other into a standing position. Again, you can add on with this variation.

---

*The earliest incarnation of this activity I was able to find is called Stand Up in *The New Games Book* (Fluegelman, 1976).

Debriefing

Questions for When the Focus Is on Emotional Awareness

- Did you believe you were going to succeed? How did this impact the outcome?

Questions for When the Focus Is on Behavioral Control

- What was more important to you and your partner, the goal or keeping each other safe? Were you able to accomplish both?

Questions for When the Focus Is on Positive Relationships

- Did you and your partner (or partners) both (all) believe you were going to succeed? How did this affect the outcome?

- If you believed you would succeed but your partner didn't, did you say or do anything to convince them? What did you do?

- Did you have to make up for differences in size or strength? How did you do that?

- Did you communicate what you needed to each other? How did your partner respond?

Circle the Circle*

Target Group: Any

Size of Group: 6 to 18

Props: Two Hula-Hoops, buddy ropes if desired

Objectives

Activity Goals: Teamwork, group problem solving and communication

Main FVC Connections: Be Here, Speak Your Truth, Hear the Truth

Keys to Success Connections: Emotional awareness, behavioral control, establishing positive relationships

Facilitator Guidelines

Introduction/Metaphor

"This hoop represents the solution to all of life's problems! In order to have access to the solution, the group must unlock the secrets of the hoop." While remaining connected in a circle, the group must move the hoop 360 degrees around the circle. If the connection is lost, the message will remain encrypted until the group completes the 360-degree rotation while remaining connected.

The Action

Have your entire group join hands. You can use buddy ropes (pieces of rope 1 to 2 feet long), if needed.

At the connection point of two people in the group, place a Hula-Hoop. The goal is for the group to pass the Hula-Hoop all the way around the circle without letting go of each other's hands.

If anyone lets go of their neighbor's hand, the hoop must restart and make a complete circle.

Variation 1

Don't allow the hoop to touch the ground.

Variation 2

Use two hoops, one slightly smaller than the other, and have them moving around the circle in opposite directions. Obviously, the hoops will meet at some point and some poor unsuspecting group member will need to figure out how to keep them both going. The hoops must move only in the direction they began.

---

*A version of this activity appears in *Silver Bullets* (Rohnke, 1984).

Variation 3

Use objects other than hoops, such as ropes or raccoon circles.

Debriefing

Questions for When the Focus Is on Emotional Awareness

- How did it feel to have the two hoops converging on you? Would you rather they had converged on someone else?

Questions for When the Focus Is on Behavioral Control

- How did you keep the hoop moving?
- How did you pass the hoops by each other?

Questions for When the Focus Is on Positive Relationships

- Did you help the people next to you? How?
- Did you help anyone who was not next to you? How?
- How did you react when someone else was struggling?

Try Angle Lineup

Target Group: Middle school age and older

Size of Group: 8 to 15 participants

Props: Three boards, planks measuring 1 inch thick x 6 inches across x 8 feet long (or longer if you have more people)

Objectives

Activity Goals: Demonstrate that various strengths in a group can lead to a successful outcome, group communication, group problem solving, building trust

Main FVC Connections: Be Safe, Speak Your Truth, Hear the Truth

Keys to Success Connections: Emotional awareness, behavioral control, establishing positive relationships

Facilitator Guidelines

Introduction/Metaphor

"This activity calls for participants to create and execute a plan of action. It requires creativity, balance, organization, and support. Assessing yourself, which of these areas represents a strength for you that will benefit the group in achieving its goal?"

The Action

Arrange the three boards in a triangular pattern with the ends touching but not overlapping.

Ask the group to stand on the boards and spread out so that there are approximately equal numbers of people on each board.

Inform the participants that they are to order themselves according to specific criteria. The criteria could be birth date, birth month, shortest to tallest, shoe size...whatever you decide.

During the activity, no one may step off the boards.

The following conditions can be applied to make the challenge easier or more difficult:

Only one person at a time may move from his or her spot.

Members must not cross the inside of the triangle but move along the boards.

Movement can only be in a clockwise direction.

Members must pass through at least two corners before getting to the correct spot.

Blindfold half the group.

If you don't have boards, you can use gym spots or even paper plates and follow the same rules.

Debriefing

Your debriefing will depend in part on which rules and variations you choose to use.

Questions for When the Focus Is on Emotional Awareness

- What was the mood of the group at the beginning of the activity? Did it change? How?

Questions for When the Focus Is on Behavioral Control

- How did you use your personal strengths to help the group succeed?
- Did you have any areas of weakness that made this activity difficult for you?

Questions for When the Focus Is on Positive Relationships

- Did anyone seem to step into a leadership role? Why?
- Were there different leaders at different points during the activity? For example, was there a leader during the planning and a different leader during the execution?
- What was your role during this activity?
- Did everyone feel like they were heard during the planning time?
- Did anyone help you during this activity?
- Did you help anyone else during this activity?

Playing Card Lineup*

Target Group: Any

Size of Group: 6 to 52

Props: Deck of cards

Objectives

Activity Goals: Group communication, nonverbal communication, and problem solving

Main FVC Connection: Be Here

Keys to Success Connections: Behavioral control, establishing positive relationships

Facilitator Guidelines

Setup

If you have a group of 6 to 13, you can use the cards from a single suit (all spades, for example). For groups between 14 and 26, you can use the cards from two suits, using the same numbers for each suit. For groups larger than 26, I suggest using all the cards in the deck. Whatever the group size, you can also use the number of randomly chosen cards, resulting in mixed suits.

Introduction/Metaphor

This is a flexible activity that can be used as a low-level or more advanced challenge, depending upon what conditions you put in place. I generally just launch into the activity without much introduction.

The Action

Have each participant pick a card and hold it face down without looking.

On your cue, participants should look at their card and, without any speaking, line up in correct order as quickly as possible. Correct order generally means ascending order (2 through ace) of the same suit. Time the group's trial. After the first attempt, collect the cards and allow the participants some time to plan before a second attempt for an improved time.

Variation 1

To make it easier, allow the group to speak during the activity.

---

*Michelle Cummings, M.S., of Training Wheels (www.training-wheels.com) created the original version of this activity. It is copyrighted in her book *Playing with a Full Deck* (2007).

Variation 2

To make it more challenging, don't allow members to show each other their cards.

Variation 3

Make it even more challenging by not allowing participants to see their own cards. To accomplish this, when instructed, group members should hold cards up to their foreheads, facing out. Of course, there should be no speaking during this variation.

Debriefing

Success in this activity depends on communication. Depending on the variation you use, you may focus on verbal communication, nonverbal communication, or both.

Questions for When the Focus Is on Behavioral Control

- Which variation was the most difficult? Why?
- Did you change your strategy from the first attempt through the last? How?

Questions for When the Focus Is on Positive Relationships

- When you couldn't speak, how did you communicate important information to the others?
- Did any group members seem to take on leadership roles? Who and why?

Who Dropped the Ball?*

Target Group: Any age

Size of Group: 6 to 12 participants

Props: Balloons, markers

Objectives

Activity Goals: Highlight the difficulties in balancing life's responsibilities, especially when alone; group communication and problem solving; asking for and giving help

Main FVC Connections: Be Safe, Speak Your Truth, Hear the Truth

Keys to Success Connections: Emotional awareness, behavioral control, establishing positive relationships

Facilitator Guidelines

Introduction/Metaphor

"Sometimes, life feels like a juggling act. There are so many things to do and take care of; we can easily become overwhelmed by life. What happens when you become overwhelmed? Are there people in your life who help you?"

The Action

Ask members to list the responsibilities they are "juggling" in their lives. School? Work? Social life?

Ask them to blow up balloons and write these responsibilities on their balloons.

The goal is to keep their balloons off the ground without holding them. Easy, right?

While they are doing this, blow up other balloons and write potential roadblocks or distracters on each balloon. TV, cell phones, computers, a concert, alcohol, debt – whatever might be something that gets in the way of people taking care of their responsibilities. It might even be other responsibilities!

One by one, toss these balloons into the fray. This will require group members to work together to keep the balloons aloft or they will fall.

If any balloons hit the ground, yell, "dropped ball!" The balloon must be back into play within 5 seconds or the round is over.

Continue adding balloons until the group becomes overwhelmed. You can offer them some planning time to go for a second try to see if they can handle more balloons (responsibilities).

---

*An early version of this activity called Balloon Frantic appeared in *Silver Bullets* (Rohnke, 1984).

Variation 1

Write each responsibility on a separate balloon and don't include distracters. By doing this, each group member will have multiple balloons representing their multiple responsibilities. You can ask them to figure out how to keep as many aloft as possible.

Variation 2

Have group members list and write goals instead of responsibilities.

Debriefing

Questions for When the Focus Is on Emotional Awareness

- Did you feel overwhelmed at any point? How did you deal with that? How does that compare with the way you deal with that feeling in real life?

Questions for When the Focus Is on Behavioral Control

- What are the distracters in your life? What things get in the way of you taking care of your responsibilities? How do you deal with these?
- What happened when there were so many responsibilities and distracters in the game that the group became overwhelmed? Does this happen in your life?
- Do you usually try to take care of your responsibilities on your own or do you ask for help?

Questions for When the Focus Is on Positive Relationships

- Did you reach out to help others during the activity? Why?
- Did anyone reach out to help you during the activity? What was the outcome?
- Who are the people in your life you can turn to when you feel overwhelmed?
- Are there times when you feel you are doing more than your share to keep things moving forward?

Path to Success*

Target Group: Middle school age and older

Size of Group: Maximum of 12 participants

Props: Gym spots or other markers (or a tarp with a 5-by-5 grid of tape on it)

Objectives

Activity Goals: Developing self-control, using nonverbal communication for group problem solving, asking for help

Main FVC Connections: Be Here, Speak Your Truth (nonverbal), Hear the Truth (nonverbal)

Keys to Success Connections: Emotional awareness, behavioral control, establishing positive relationships

Facilitator Guidelines

Introduction/Metaphor

"As we go through life, sometimes we choose the right path, sometimes the wrong one. The most important thing is to be able to tell the difference before it's too late! If we're on the wrong path, we can find a way to get back on track but this is not always easy! Today, you will seek the right path—the path to success! What does success mean to you?"

You can tailor the path to any type of group (such as Path to Peace for anger management groups or Path to Happiness for depression support groups).

The Action

Arrange gym spots (or other markers) in a 5-by-5 square on the ground. The spots should be about a half-foot from each other.

Draw a picture of your 5-by-5 square on paper and plan a pathway though the maze. (See p. 443 or create your own.) The goal is for your group to successfully navigate the correct path through the maze.

Explain that the following rules are in place:

Only one player may be in the maze at a time.

The group members must go in a predetermined order (set by the group) for each attempt at finding the path. No one may make a second attempt (or third, fourth, etc.) to find the path until everyone else has tried.

The activity must be done in silence.

If a player makes a correct step, they will hear nothing from you.

---

*An early version of this activity called Gridlock was written up by Jim Cain and Barry Jolliff in *Teamwork and Teamplay* (1998).

If an incorrect step is made, they will receive feedback. (I usually buzz or have a kazoo handy for this.)

Give your group some planning time before starting.

When the group is ready to begin, the first participant may step into the maze.

If the first step is correct, say nothing and allow the person to continue until they make an incorrect step (which you will buzz). At this point, the person leaves the maze and the next person takes their turn, hopefully learning from the efforts of the first person!

Continue until all players successfully navigate the maze without any mistakes. If someone does talk, you can give some sort of penalty. I like to give several warnings then blindfold the offending member.

Variation

If this seems too difficult for your group, you can allow them to talk. If you do, you may want to try a second round in silence!

Debriefing

This activity requires visual-spatial memory and skills. If any participants have weak visual-spatial abilities, they will most likely need to rely on nonverbal cues provided by their teammates. Lower functioning groups may have difficulties realizing this, and you may have some participants making several unsuccessful attempts. As a facilitator, you may want to prompt these types of groups to come up with a way of helping each other get through.

To be successful, players must not only tune into their own actions but the actions of others. If they don't, it will take the group much longer to discover the correct pattern.

Questions for When the Focus Is on Emotional Awareness

- Did you utilize any particular strengths that helped you and your team be successful during this activity?

- Was there anything that made this activity particularly difficult for you? How did you overcome this?

- Was focus important for this activity? If you didn't watch your teammates, what happened?

Questions for When the Focus Is on Behavioral Control

- Was it difficult not to talk? How did you communicate?

- How did not being able to talk affect the group? How did it affect each member personally?

- In your life, have you ever felt like you were on the "wrong" path? Looking at the skills we used for this activity, what can you do when you are in that position?

Questions for When the Focus Is on Positive Relationships

- If you saw this activity as a solo venture and focused only on yourself, what impact would that have on the group?

- Did you help anyone? How?
- Did anyone help you? How?
- How did you know if someone needed help when they couldn't tell you with their words?
- Who are the people in your life that can help you make sure you are on the "right" path?
- Were there times when your relationships with others put you on the "wrong" path?

All Aboard*

I enjoy using a fantasy-based introduction for this activity

Target Group: Middle school and older

Size of Group: 6 to 15

Props: All Aboard platform (2-foot by 2-foot wooden platform) or a small towel, pillow-case, or tarp. You could also mark off the desired area with tape.

Objectives

Activity Goals: Build group cohesion and trust, group communication and problem solving, pushing beyond personal and perceived group limits

Main FVC Connection: Be Safe

Keys to Success Connections: Emotional awareness, behavioral control, establishing positive relationships

Facilitator Guidelines

Setup

I generally talk about safety while introducing this activity. My rules include: Don't sit on anyone else's shoulders, don't touch anyone in places they don't want to be touched, and respect each other's needs regarding personal space. This one calls for high levels of group closeness!

Introduction/Metaphor

"Suddenly, your boat capsizes! As you are flailing in the water, hoping that you haven't gasped your last breath, you see it . . . the life raft! As you swim toward it, you realize that the rest of your boat-mates are also on their way to the single raft. You start to wonder, how are we all going to fit on this raft?"

The Action

Explain that the goal of this activity is for your entire group to stand on the platform, without any body part touching the ground, for a certain amount of time without falling off. A 2-by-2 platform can probably hold a group of 16 enterprising teens and maybe more with a group of younger kids.

Once participants are "all aboard," have them sing a song such as "Row Row Row Your Boat" or simply count down the goal time.

---

*A version of this activity is in *Silver Bullets* (Rohnke, 1984).

Variation 1

Begin this activity with a relatively large platform (say a 4 × 4 tarp) that would be easy for the group to fit on. Suddenly, it springs a leak and decreases in size (which means folding it in half or using a smaller platform).

Variation 2

The group is happily swimming along (walking with their tarp) when a shark is spotted. When you yell, "shark!" group members must immediately stop, put the tarp down, and all get on as quickly as possible. I like to use this with the diminishing dimensions version introduced in Variation 1.

Variation 3

Set up several platforms of diminishing size. Create a metaphor based on the changing dimensions. For example, set up four platforms and use the following introduction: "Your group is stranded on a small island, and the rescue boat will arrive in 4 hours. Each hour, the tide moves in a bit more, leaving you with less room to stand on." Each hour is represented by having to move to a smaller platform. After the last is used, the rescue boat arrives to pick up the survivors!

Debriefing

My debriefing generally focuses on planning, balance, and support.

Questions for When the Focus Is on Emotional Awareness

- How comfortable were you being in such close proximity to your group-mates?
- Did you get frustrated at any point during the activity? How did you handle that?

Questions for When the Focus Is on Behavioral Control

- How did you keep yourself and others safe?
- Did the group's strategy change during the activity?
- What strategies worked and what didn't? In life, have you ever had to change your strategy when trying to solve a problem?

Questions for When the Focus Is on Positive Relationships

- How was communication important during this activity?
- Did the group come up with a plan to achieve success? Did it work? Did it need modification?
- How did you support others?
- How did others support you?
- As a group, did you make use of personal strengths and attributes? How?

Helium Hoop

I was introduced to this activity by Bart Crawford at a multiday training program at Project Adventure. Our group had been cruising through every challenge given to us—until Helium Hoop. It propelled our group into a level of chaos expected when entering the Storming phase of group development. We did not achieve the task, but that failure taught us more than had we succeeded!

Target Group: Middle school age and older

Size of Group: 4 to 10 participants

Props: One Hula-Hoop

Objectives

Activity Goals: Push the group's limits of frustration tolerance, increase group focus and communication

Main FVC Connections: Be Here, Speak Your Truth, Hear the Truth

Keys to Success Connections: Emotional awareness, behavioral control, establishing positive relationships

Facilitator Guidelines

Introduction/Metaphor

This activity is one of the most difficult and frustrating activities I have ever attempted. I often use it to intentionally cause frustration within a group. The activity also tends to trigger the "blame response."

I like to use the following introduction: "This Hula-Hoop may look like a normal Hula-Hoop; however, it's not. Just prior to the start of group, I filled it with deactivated helium. It can rest on the ground, and I can hold it with two hands with no problem. However, touched the right way, the helium becomes activated. To activate the helium, the hoop should be touched on only one side, by many single fingers."

The Action

Have your group gather in a circle, shoulder to shoulder, with hands extended in front of them toward the center of the circle.

Have group members point their index fingers toward the center of the circle. Their pointer finger should be on top, pinky finger on bottom, all other fingers folded in, including thumbs. Explain that you will rest the hoop on top of their pointed fingers.

Once placed, the helium is activated. Their job is to lower the hoop to the ground without anyone ever losing contact with it. Sounds easy, right? Give it a try!

Debriefing

Questions for When the Focus Is on Emotional Awareness

- How did you feel when the hoop was first placed on your fingers and it started to rise (because this will happen!).
- How did you feel after several attempts?
- How did your own mood impact the group's mood? How about the group's behavior?

Question for When the Focus Is on Behavioral Control

- How did you respond to the frustration you felt?

Questions for When the Focus Is on Positive Relationships

- How did you respond to others' frustration?
- Why did people start to blame each other as soon as the hoop started to rise? What impact did this have on the group? Have you been in situations in which people begin blaming each other? What is the impact? What is a better approach?

Chair Lift

I use this as an activity for focus and enhancing team cohesion and emotional intelligence.

Target Group: Middle school age and older

Size of Group: Five are needed for the activity; people can rotate in

Props: A chair, relatively soft ground surface (such as a rug, rubber mat, or grass)

Objectives

Activity Goals: Enhance team focus and cohesion, highlight the importance of focus in accomplishing difficult goals

Main FVC Connections: Be Here, Be Safe

Keys to Success Connections: Emotional awareness, behavioral control, establishing positive relationships

Facilitator Guidelines

Setup

Be aware that this activity, done incorrectly, can be very risky physically. Only do this activity with a group that you know well and trust to follow the directions very carefully.

Introduction/Metaphor

"How important is focus for accomplishing a task? Sometimes, focus is so important, it can help you do the impossible!"

I sometimes use this activity when my group is struggling to maintain focus. This activity is more of an in vivo demonstration of how important focus is for accomplishing a task, rather than an activity in the traditional adventure sense.

The Action

Have a volunteer sit in the chair. Make sure they are OK with being touched by you and other group members.

Invite three other volunteers to come up and make sure they are OK with touching the group member on the chair.

Tell them that they will be lifting the seated member up off the chair. Depending on that person's size, you may have reactions of disbelief.

Have each of the three standing volunteers and you place their two hands together and interlock all fingers except the index fingers, which should be pointing straight out with thumbs folded across the top.

Have all four of you place yourselves around the seated person as follows: By right knee, left knee, and behind the seated member by the left or right arm.

Tell them to lift the seated volunteer using only the combined energy of each person's two index fingers. If they do lift the person, they must follow your directions to lower the participant slowly and carefully, not moving away until the person is back in the chair.

Have the members at the knees place their fingers under the knees. From behind, you and the fourth volunteer place your fingers under the armpit area of the seated member.

On your three count, the group should attempt to lift the person off the chair about a foot or two and return them to a seated position.

Your group will either not be able to lift the person or if they do, lifting will be somewhat challenging. Again, this is dependent, in part, on the size ratios of lifters to the seated person.

For phase two, instruct the members that the four lifters will now get focused and make the lift much easier.

From the original starting position, place your right hand at about face height over the legs of the seated person.

Instruct the person lifting under the other arm to place their right hand a few inches above yours. The person by the same knee will place their hand above the other "arm" person and finally, the person at the knee on your side will place their right hand above all three hands.

Follow the same pattern with the left hands. (See picture below for final arrangement.)

Now, instruct them to take their hands away slowly, one at a time in reverse order.

Once this is done, attempt the lift again. Magically, the person, no matter how big they are, will seem light as a feather!

Debriefing

This activity tends to debrief itself! I generally start by saying, "So, what happened?" The conversation goes from there.

Questions for When the Focus Is on Emotional Awareness

- How did you feel when you were about to be lifted?
- How did the lifters feel when they were about to lift the volunteer the first time? How about before the second attempt?

Questions for When the Focus Is on Behavioral Control

- How did it feel being lifted the first time? How about the second time? What were the differences?
- How did it feel the first time we tried lifting? How about the second time? What were the differences?
- Why did it work the way it did?

Questions for When the Focus Is on Positive Relationships

- When is it necessary to be a very focused group? How can you create that focus in a group?

Find Your Family

This activity lends itself well to exploring diversity as well as dealing with social conflicts and cliques. I was originally introduced to it by Dr. Jim Cain.

Target Group: Middle school age and older

Size of Group: 8 or more people

Props: Wooden craft cutouts of animals and other objects.

Objectives

Activity Goals: Promote acceptance of diversity, explore inclusion versus exclusion in groups and cliques

Main FVC Connections: Be Safe, Speak Your Truth, Hear the Truth

Keys to Success Connections: Emotional awareness, behavioral control, establishing positive relationships

Facilitator Guidelines

Setup

Wooden craft cutouts are cheap and available at most craft stores. All objects must be in pairs, with the exception of one shape of which there is only one. For one, I use a star shape. I buy plain wooden objects then color them myself making sure that each object has a color match that is different from its shape match. For example, I may paint one dog yellow and another green that match a yellow cat and green duck. I also make one item spotted (do not use your single object for this).

To prepare for this activity, place the same number of objects in a bag that you have members participating, no more, no less. Make sure that the single object (star in this case) and spotted object (camel in this case) are included and all objects have at least one matching-shaped object (except the star). I like to have several broader categories represented as well. For example, I will include pairs of seagulls and geese, which are both birds.

Introduction/Metaphor

Depending upon which topic fits best with my group, I will start off with a conversation about what "family" means or what cliques are.

The Action

Have participants choose one object from the bag without looking. Instruct them to hold it in their hands behind their back so that they can't see it. Encourage other group members not to look at anyone else's object.

Once everyone has an object, ask participants to "find their family." This means that, without looking at the objects, they should try to find others in the group who are holding a matching object. Most likely, they will interpret this as meaning they should find others whose piece is the same shape.

When everyone has found their partner, allow them to look at the objects to see if they were correct. Of course, the poor star will be all alone.

Open up a discussion about the fact that the star is alone. How did he or she feel while searching for a "family" and not finding one? Did anyone try to help out?

For the next round, instruct the group to find a way to include the star. Often, the group will break into groups by color, which will now leave the spotted object out.

Discuss the criteria by which they chose to group. You can do this several times if you choose to.

For the final round, instruct the group to make one big "family." What criteria would include all the objects (other than that they are all made of wood)?

Debriefing

This is one of those activities in which the discussion almost leads itself. It truly strikes at the heart of many issues that kids and teens deal with about inclusion and exclusion from social groups.

Questions for When the Focus Is on Emotional Awareness

- How did it feel when you realized that you were all alone?
- How did people react when you tried to join their group but didn't "fit in?"
- How did it feel watching other participants trying to find their group?
- How did it feel when you found a match to your own piece?

Question for When the Focus Is on Behavioral Control

- How did you respond to people when they tried to join your group and didn't "fit in?"

Questions for When the Focus Is on Positive Relationships

- Did anyone reach out to include you even though you didn't exactly "fit in?"
- How did you decide what criteria you would use for inclusion in and exclusion from your group?

Electric Fence*

Target Group: Upper elementary age and older

Size of Group: 4 to 12 participants

Props: Rope or string, and two stationary objects to tie it to (such as poles or trees)

Objectives

Activity Goals: Group communication and problem solving, enhancing trust, support and group cohesion

Main FVC Connection: Be Safe

Keys to Success Connections: Behavioral control, establishing positive relationships

Facilitator Guidelines

Setup

Make sure you discuss safe lifting and spotting first!

Introduction/Metaphor

During this activity, your group will attempt to move from one place to another while remaining connected. Metaphorically, where are the individuals in your group trying to move? How will they get the support they need to reach their destinies? For example, in facilitating this activity with a depression support group, I might ask them how they would feel if the depression was gone. Happy? Energized? Ecstatic? The other side of the fence represents those emotional targets. How will they get there? By using the support of their peers!

The Action

Tie a rope about waist height between two trees or, if you are inside, between two poles or other parts of the room that would hold the rope (or string).

The goal is for your group to get over the rope fence while maintaining a chain of contact with all other group members at all times. If the chain is broken, the group must start over.

Every group member will be in contact with two people except for the first and last, who will only be in contact with one person each. The group is not allowed to go around the rope or under the rope.

You can start low and give the group several attempts, raising the height of the rope each time.

---

*Although I can't find the original Electric Fence, Karl Rohnke wrote about a variation called Nuclear Fence in *Quicksilver* (1995).

Variation 1

Have the group form a connected circle so that everyone remains in contact with the person to their left and their right.

Variation 2

Blindfold half (or more) of the members of the group.

Debriefing

As a whole, did the group achieve its goal? Using the metaphor set up from the beginning, did the group reaching its goal allow the individual members to reach theirs (or at least move toward them)?

Questions for When the Focus Is on Behavioral Control

- What did you do to contribute to the safety of the group?
- What did you do that helped the group reach its goal?
- What did others do to help you move toward your own goals?

Questions for When the Focus Is on Positive Relationships

- How did the group members support each other? Was it difficult? How so?
- Did you feel a sense of responsibility to those on either side of you?

Initiatives Designed for Larger Spaces

Don't Break the Ice

I learned this activity when co-facilitating with colleague and friend Jim Gayeski. It has become one of my absolute favorites!

Target Group: Upper elementary and older

Size of Group: 10 to 24

Props: Rope (about 60 to 70 feet) for a boundary and one gym spot per person

Objectives

Activity Goals: As a group, adapting to an increasingly challenging task, building trust and group cohesion, group communication

Main FVC Connections: Be Safe, Speak Your Truth, Hear the Truth

Keys to Success Connections: Emotional awareness, behavioral control, establishing positive relationships

Facilitator Guidelines

Introduction/Metaphor

I provide the following introduction once the rope boundary is set up and members have tossed the gym spots into the playing area as described in The Action section (below): "Growing up in the northeast, I couldn't wait to skate on the ponds and lakes in the winter! It was always so much more fun than the ice rinks. It was also a bit scary because sometimes you weren't quite sure how solid the ice was. There was always that period of time between Thanksgiving and New Year's when the ponds would start to freeze but the ice was not quite solid enough to skate on. Today, you and your group will be taking a trek out onto some thin ice and must return safely to shore without falling through! Luckily, this particular pond has some rocks sticking out of the ice for you to step on."

For a less fantasy-based introduction, you can begin with a discussion about what it means to be on "thin ice."

The Action

Create a circular boundary about 20 feet across. Give each member a gym spot and ask them to place the spot somewhere within the circle and return to the outside of the circle.

Introduce the activity as described above.

The first goal is for all participants to be standing safely on one of the gym spots (which represent the "rocks" in the frozen pond) within the boundary. It does not have to be the one they placed. Group members may not touch the "ice," represented by the area within the rope circle between the rocks. They must only step on the rocks.

Once the group has safely made their way onto the rocks, they must exit the pond, again without breaking the ice. If any participant steps on the ice, the entire group must exit and restart.

For the next phase, the group must unanimously decide on one spot to move. It can be any spot and it can be moved anywhere within the boundary.

Once they have moved the spot, the group must unanimously decide on another spot to remove from the pond. This will leave the group with one fewer spot than people.

The processes of move and remove will continue after each successful round of entering and exiting the pond without breaking the ice.

After the second round, I ask the group to set a goal for the lowest number of spots they believe the entire group can successfully stand on safely and return to shore without touching the ice. If the group meets their goal, have them decide whether they would like to attempt to exceed the goal!

Debriefing

Questions for When the Focus Is on Emotional Awareness

- Did the feel or emotion of the group change as the activity progressed? How so?
- Did you doubt the group's ability to accomplish any tasks as you went along?

Questions for When the Focus Is on Behavioral Control

- How did you adapt to the changing aspects of the activity? How do you adapt to change in your life?
- When you find yourself on "thin ice" in your life, how do you handle it?

Questions for When the Focus Is on Positive Relationships

- How did your group account for individual strengths and weaknesses?
- How did you support each other?
- How did you decide in each round which spot to move and which to remove?
- Did you meet or exceed your goal? Do you usually set goals that are too lofty or not high enough?
- When you are on "thin ice" in your life, are there people you can turn to for help and support?

Liberty Golf/Longest Catch*

Target Group: Upper elementary age and older

Size of Group: 4 to 24 participants

Props: Foam hoops, bucket. Frisbees can be used as an alternative to hoops. If this is the case, participants can actually catch the Frisbees as opposed to the way they "catch" the hoops.

Objectives

Activity Goals: Weigh pros and cons and use strengths and weaknesses to arrive at a joint decision, friendly competition

Main FVC Connection: Be Here

Keys to Success Connections: Emotional awareness, behavioral control, establishing positive relationships

Facilitator Guidelines

Introduction/Metaphor

Gather your group in a circle. "In America, land of the free, we love to play golf! Since we have no clubs today, we will play a different variety of golf called Liberty Golf!"

The Action

Identify a starting point and an end point. Place the bucket at the end point.

Have your participants do their best Statue of Liberty imitation, with one hand raised high in the air as if holding that torch of freedom. This will be the catching position. (Working in pairs, throwing partners will toss the hoop while the other will "catch" it by putting their hands in the Statue of Liberty position and allowing the hoop to go over their hands and slide onto their arms.)

Divide your group into pairs. Give each pair one hoop.

Tell the group that the goal is to get the hoop into the bucket using as few tosses as possible.

Rules for tossing are:

When you have the hoop, you must stay put (no walking with the hoop).

You must toss the hoop to your partner.

If your partner "catches" the hoop, you can move ahead of your partner for the next throw. It is up to you and your partner to decide how far to go.

---

*The original version of this activity was written up as Italian Golf in *Cowstails and Cobras II* (Rohnke, 1989).

If your partner does not catch the hoop, you must remain in place, and your partner will return the hoop to you for another throw.

You must keep track of how many throws you and your partner make (and be honest!).

The final throw is into the bucket.

Remind your group members that this is not a race. Finishing first is irrelevant. The object is to get the hoop in the bucket in as few throws as possible.

Variation 1

Have participants attempt to make the longest throw/catch they can. Have all pairs start at the same starting line and, one at a time, toss it to their partners. Use a predetermined number of rounds.

Variation 2

Instead of the small hoops, have participants use Hula-Hoops. For this variation, the "catching" partner will stand straight with hands together overhead. The throwing partner tosses the hoop, which must land around the catching partner.

Variation 3

Create two teams. Set start (A) and end (B) points. See how many times the team can relay one hoop from point A to point B and back within a certain time limit.

Debriefing

Questions for When the Focus Is on Emotional Awareness

- For those who did not win, how did it feel as you watched others getting ahead? How did it impact your actions toward each other? Did it impact the way you approached the task?

Questions for When the Focus Is on Behavioral Control

- How did you decide how far each throw should be?
- Did you change your strategy as the game went on? Why?

Question for When the Focus Is on Positive Relationships

- Did you take into consideration your and your partner's strengths and weaknesses?

Tumble 'n' Toss*

I originally learned this when facilitating with William "Sully" Sullivan at the Riverfront Recapture Ropes Course in Hartford, Connecticut. It provides a great sequence of increasingly difficult challenges.

Target Group: Middle school age and older

Size of Group: At least 8 participants

Props: One small tarp (6 × 8 feet works well) for every 4 people, toss-able objects

Objectives

Activity Goals: Adapt to a changing challenge, reach a solution using group communication and strategy within and between groups

Main FVC Connections: Be Safe, Speak Your Truth, Hear the Truth

Keys to Success Connections: Behavioral control, establishing positive relationships

Facilitator Guidelines

Introduction/Metaphor

This is a progressive activity. It begins in small groups with each group attempting to reach its own goal. Eventually, all of the small groups will unite toward a larger goal. There are many possible ways to frame this activity given this sequence. For example, if I was working with an anger management group, I might use the first part of the activity as a metaphor for dealing with our own anger. Once multiple groups are involved, I might address the reality that it's simply not enough for us to deal with our own feelings of anger; we have to learn to cope with others' anger.

The Action

Divide your group into smaller groups of four (five or six is OK if needed). Each group is given a small tarp and a single toss-able item.

For each variation presented below, the group members must keep their hands on the tarp at all times and are not allowed to touch the toss-able unless it falls and they need to pick it up.

The groups can be presented with any of the following challenges, listed in order of least to most challenging. You can use one or more of them sequentially.

Have the group launch the toss-able into the air and catch it in the tarp. Got it once? Try for two or three in a row. See how high they can toss and catch.

---

*Early versions have been written up as Collective Blanket Ball (*Cooperative Sports and Games Book*, Orlick, 1978) and Big Pig Air in the 2001 Winter volume of Project Adventure's journal *Zip Lines: The Voice for Adventure Education*. It was submitted by Amy Kohut.

Have the group turn the tarp over without dropping the toss-able. In the end, the toss-able item will end up on what was originally the underside of the tarp.

Using one toss-able item for two small groups, have the groups launch the item from one tarp to the other without allowing it to hit the ground. How about twice in a row? How about doubling the distance?

If you have more than two groups, have the toss-able make its way from tarp to tarp until it is back where it started. Got it? How quickly can you do it?

Have two groups each start with their own toss-able. Simultaneously, each group will launch their toss-able toward the other group and catch the one coming to them.

Have all of your groups launch their toss-ables and catch another group's toss-able simultaneously.

Variation

Have groups see who can launch their toss-able the farthest. I enforce the rule that all hands beginning on the tarp must remain on the tarp until the object is launched.

Debriefing

Questions for When the Focus Is on Behavioral Control

- How did your strategy change from one round to the next? What are some situations in life in which you must change your strategy based on changes in the situation?

Questions for When the Focus Is on Positive Relationships

- How did your group come up with solutions to this challenge?
- How did you communicate with other groups?
- Did you see this activity as competitive or cooperative? Did that change during the activity with the different phases?

Water Relay

This activity was created out of necessity one scorching summer day in Windsor, Connecticut, when I was working with a group of elementary school kids. Not only did it prove to be a great challenge but it also kept us cool!

Target Group: Any age

Size of Group: 10 to 30 participants

Props: Two buckets per team, water, Styrofoam cups. (Other kinds of cups work as well, but there is a difference, as you will see. If you are environmentally conscious and choose to avoid Styrofoam, you can use wax-coated paper cups.)

Objectives

Activity Goal: Learn to use resources wisely to accomplish a goal

Main FVC Connections: Speak Your Truth, Hear the Truth

Keys to Success Connections: Behavioral control, establishing positive relationships

Facilitator Guidelines

Introduction/Metaphor

This activity is well suited for "traditional" adventure activity introductions that involve transporting some sort of potion from one place to another. I tend to tailor it to the theme of the group. If it's an anger management group, we might be attempting to transport an anti-anger serum. For a leadership group, it may be cups of Vitamin L (where L stands for Leadership, of course!).

The Action

Divide your group into two or more equal (or nearly equal) teams of at least five participants.

Have the teams line up between two buckets. The distance between buckets should be equal to about three times as many feet as people. For example, if you have five people per team, place your buckets about 15 feet apart.

One bucket for each team should be filled with water. The second bucket for each team is empty with a line marking the point each team needs to fill the bucket to.

The person closest to the full bucket is given two Styrofoam cups.

On your "go," the race begins! The first person dips their cup into the full bucket of water and passes the full cup down the line. The last person in line must empty the cup into the empty bucket.

Once the empty bucket is filled to a marked point, the race is over and a winner declared.

If the first cup starts to fall apart, replace it with a second cup. What you are likely to find is that the cups will begin to fall apart, thus encouraging the team to use this "resource" more carefully.

Debriefing

I have only done this with Styrofoam cups. This gave us a new unexpected challenge as we tried transporting water in crumbling cups!

Questions for When the Focus Is on Behavioral Control

- Were there any strategies you tried that didn't work?
- Did you have to change your strategy as the game progressed?
- How did you handle the cup falling apart?
- Are there times in life when you did not take care of your resources? What were the results?

Questions for When the Focus Is on Positive Relationships

- How did you decide where in the line each person should stand?
- How did you (or your team) handle it when teammates messed up? Did your responses help or hurt the team?

School of Fish

Being around other facilitators at conferences can be very inspirational. It gets the creative juices flowing. A few years ago, while at the NCCPS, I was standing by a pond after lunch. A school of small fish was idling a few feet offshore. All of the fish were facing my direction, and it seemed as though they were waiting for me to do something! I began to think about what an activity called "School of Fish" might entail. Although I didn't share my ideas with those particular fish, this activity was the result of that moment of creativity!

Target Group: Any age

Size of Group: 8 to 20 participants

Props: None

Objectives

Activity Goals: Enhance focus and observation skills, improve group cohesion, understand the attributes of leading and following

Main FVC Connection: Be Here

Keys to Success Connections: Behavioral control, establishing positive relationships

Facilitator Guidelines

Introduction/Metaphor

"Have you ever watched the Discovery or National Geographic channels when they have shows about fish? Isn't it cool to watch how a whole school of fish moves together, especially when there's a predator in the water? It seems like they all move at once, and you can never really tell which fish moved first. It's like they all share a brain and don't have a leader! But, there has to be one fish that starts the move, right? Today, we are going to try to find the leader in our own school of fish!"

The Action

Select one group member as the "Fish Researcher." The rest of the group members will comprise the "School" of fish. Have the Fish Researcher step out of the room while the group decides which member will be the "Head Fish" (or "fish head") who leads the school. Have the School of fish gather in a tight group and begin moving slowly around the room or area. Invite the Fish Researcher back into the room. The Researcher's job is to determine who is the Head Fish. As the group moves, the Head Fish will slowly change directions and all the other fish should follow. Encourage fish to make it more difficult by not staring directly at the leader. If they watch any single fish in the School, they will still be able to follow the movement. The Researcher has up to three guesses or 1 minute to figure out who the Head Fish is.

Variation

Have larger groups spread out over a larger area. Then choose the Head Fish and the Fish Researcher. Members should wander about until the leader stops moving, then stop as well. When the Head Fish moves, the others move. The Researcher has the same three tries and 1 minute to decide who the Head Fish is.

Debriefing

Questions for When the Focus Is on Behavioral Control

- As the Head Fish, how did you try to keep your identity secret? Are there times when you want to be a "silent leader?"

- As a fish in the School, did you try to help keep your leader's identity secret? Are there times when you have to put someone else's needs ahead of your own?

Questions for When the Focus Is on Positive Relationships

- In this activity, when you were a fish, you followed the School. When is it good to "follow the school" and when is it good to break away and follow your own lead?

Medicine Movers

This activity was inspired by Monarch Migration, an activity created through Project Adventure, in which rubber butterflies are knocked off the back of participants' hands by folks throwing toss-ables.

Target Group: Upper elementary school age and older

Size of Group: 6 to 24 participants

Props: Plastic cups, water (optional), ropes for boundaries, toss-ables (without hard parts), gym spots (optional)

Objectives

Activity Goals: Role differentiation on teams, overcome challenges to accomplish a group goal

Main FVC Connection: Be Safe

Keys to Success Connections: Emotional awareness, behavioral control, establishing positive relationships

Facilitator Guidelines

Setup

Create a rectangular playing area with two long side boundaries and shorter starting and ending points. (See diagram for measurements.)

Place the cups and bucket of water (if you are using water) at the starting line along one of the shorter sides. If you are using water, place a small, empty bucket on the opposite side.

Introduction/Metaphor

"The pharmaceutical company Cure-All has created a new medicine that actually cures (insert ailment of your choice based on the theme of your group). Your group has been entrusted to transport this medicine to a group of scientists who will be able to create enough of it to cure this ailment worldwide and at affordable prices. Unfortunately, other companies have heard about this and are quite upset. Some have created their own version and are trying to profit from it. The other medicines treat this ailment but don't cure it. They want to keep your group from succeeding and have hired special Snipers to destroy the medicine."

The Action

Divide your group in two. One group will be the medicine movers and the other group, the snipers.

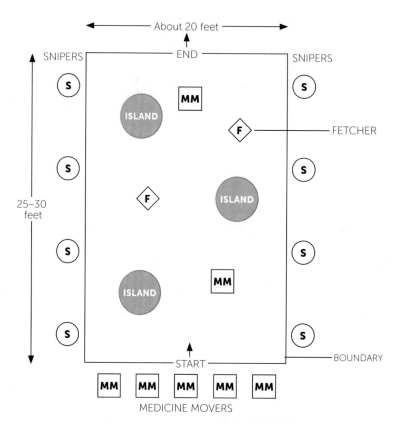

Position of boundaries and participants in Medicine Movers

The goal is for the medicine movers to transport as much "medicine" to the finish line as possible while the snipers attempt to prevent their success.

Medicine movers will carry cups on the back side of their outstretched hands. They can not use any part of their body (especially hands) to protect their cups from being hit. They can, however, turn their bodies in different directions.

The snipers will try to hit the cups off the hands of the medicine movers by throwing the toss-ables. The snipers must stay outside the longer sideline boundaries. They may designate as many players as they choose to be fetchers of the toss-ables. However, the fetchers can only throw the toss-ables back to their teammates, never at the medicine movers.

If you want to make the game easier for the medicine movers, put several gym spots in the playing area that represent islands of safety. Movers cannot be hit with toss-ables when on the islands. If they are hit while on an island, the player who hit them is out of the game.

If you are using the water, the medicine movers are to deposit the medicine in the empty bucket on the far side. You can give a time limit to get the most medicine possible in the bucket, see how long it takes to fill the bucket, or designate a certain number of cups that need to cross and time the effort.

If you are not using water, you can give a time limit to see how many cups can be safely transported across or see how long it takes to transport a designated number of cups.

Whether using water or not, when a medicine mover's cup is knocked down, they must restart their journey.

Variation 1

Don't use cups. Instead of the medicine metaphor, the people moving from one end to another are "frogs" on a freeway. "If you don't keep up on the Freeway of Life, you'll get squashed! But, keeping up is not always so easy. Each of us has some "traffic" on our freeway that gets in the way of us reaching our destination. What is the traffic on your freeway of life? What prevents you from reaching your destinations? What skills do you need to cope with the traffic on your freeway?" Those trying to hit the frogs with fleece balls are the "traffic." Those fetching the fleece balls are "tow trucks."

The variations below can be used with either presentation.

Variation 2

Frogs who are hit by fleece balls are out. Count the number of frogs that make it successfully to the other end.

Variation 3

Start with many spots, making it fairly easy for the frogs or medicine movers. Each round, remove a spot. You can have the frog/movers team choose which spot to remove. You can also have the traffic/sniper team choose one to remove. You can continue until there are no spots left. This variation allows the challenge to be changed with each round.

Debriefing

Questions for When the Focus Is on Emotional Awareness

- Have you ever been counted on by others to do something successfully? How did it feel? How did it feel to succeed (or not succeed)? How does it feel to either meet, exceed, or not meet someone's expectations?

- What things in life do you feel you need to protect?

- Have you ever been responsible for stopping someone else from being successful? How did that feel?

Questions for When the Focus Is on Behavioral Control

- How did you try to keep your medicine safe? Did your strategy change as you went along?

- What was your strategy as a sniper? How do you protect what's important to you?

Questions for When the Focus Is on Positive Relationships

- As medicine movers, did you attempt this activity solo or as a team? How about as snipers?

- How did you try to help others? Did anyone help you?

Knot My Issue*

This activity highlights ways in which we tend to make life harder for ourselves when we don't make good choices. Problems left for others usually fall into our own laps in the end.

Target Group: Middle school age and older

Size of Group: 12 or more participants

Props: Ropes (6 to 15 feet long) or raccoon circles

Objectives

Activity Goals: Highlight how our choices often have a larger impact on ourselves than on others; demonstrate that when we don't deal with our own problems, they tend to get worse

Main FVC Connections: Be Here, Be Safe

Keys to Success Connections: Emotional awareness, behavioral control, establishing positive relationships

Facilitator Guidelines

Setup

Lay out the ropes or raccoon circles in star patterns of three or four (or more) ropes.

You must have at least two arrangements that include the same number of ropes. The number of ropes in the arrangement should be half the number of participants (meaning you need an even number of participants). For example, you will use three ropes for six participants or four ropes for eight and so on. Each arrangement should be several feet away from the other arrangements.

Introduction/Metaphor

Since this activity has several phases, the introduction is incorporated into the activity.

The Action

Divide the participants into subgroups and ask them to gather around their group's rope arrangement.

Each person will pick up and hold one rope end with their right hand, forming a natural circle. The group's task is to use their ropes to make a knot without letting go of their ropes. This usually involves members walking back and forth and over, under, and across the circle.

Give the groups 1 minute to make their knots.

---

*A similar activity is written up as KNOT Our Problem in *The Revised and Expanded Book of Raccoon Circles* (2002) by Jim Cain and Tom Smith.

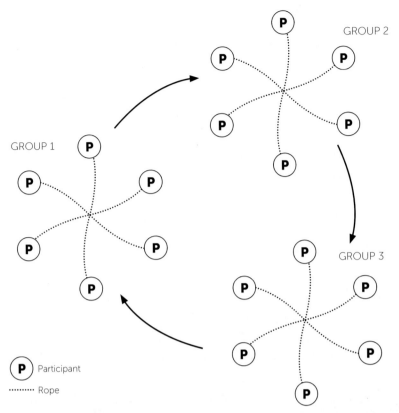

GROUP 1

GROUP 2

GROUP 3

P Participant

.... Rope

At the end of the first phase of Knot My Issue, groups rotate. Group 1 moves to Group 2's spot.
Group 2 to Group 3's, and Group 3 moves to Group 1's location.

At the end of the minute, instruct the groups to place their ropes on the ground and examine their knot creations.

Next, ask them to move away from their creation and go clockwise to the creation to their right, or switch knots if you only have two groups. (See diagram.) At this point, you may want to inform your group that they made a mess and are leaving that mess for others to clean up.

Have them pick up the ends of the knot they just moved to and, without letting go of the ropes, untangle their knots. (You can engage in some debriefing at this point.)

Next, instruct the groups that they will have another minute to make another knot. Most groups work very hard to make a difficult knot this second time because they assume they will be leaving their mess for another group.

When they are done, have them place their ropes on the ground again to admire their newest creations.

Point out that when we create problems for other people, they often end up being our own problems in the end. Instruct the members to pick up their own ropes and untangle the knots they just made.

Debriefing

Questions for When the Focus Is on Emotional Awareness

- How did you feel when you got to leave your knot behind? Have you ever left a problem for someone else to deal with?

- How did it feel to have to untie someone else's knot? Have you ever inherited a problem from someone else?

- How did you feel when you had the chance to tie the second knot? Did you try to make it more difficult for the other group? Why?

- How did you feel when you realized you'd be untying the second knot you made? Have you ever made a problem worse for yourself without realizing it?

Question for When the Focus Is on Behavioral Control

- How did you respond when you had the opportunity to tie the second knot and assumed another group would have to deal with it?

Questions for When the Focus Is on Positive Relationships

- How did you and your group approach the task of creating the first knot? How about the second?

- How did your group approach the task of untying the knots?

- Did you feel as though you were in competition with other groups? Why? How did that impact your group's choices?

- During a conflict, do you usually consider how someone else is feeling or experiencing the conflict?

- How many times in life have you created problems that others had to fix? How many times have you felt like you had to fix other people's problems?

Clean Your Mess*

Target Group: Upper elementary age and older

Size of Group: 12 to 24 participants

Props: 20 to 40 tennis balls (or other small balls, stuffed animals, fleece balls, etc.), 5 Hula-Hoops, 8 gym spots

Objectives

Activity Goals: Group planning and decision-making to reach a common goal, adapting to changing situations, inhibiting impulses in favor of planning

Main FVC Connections: Be Here, Be Safe

Keys to Success Connections: Emotional awareness, behavioral control, establishing positive relationships

Facilitator Guidelines

Setup

Set up a square playing area by placing a Hula-Hoop on each corner about 20 feet apart from each other.

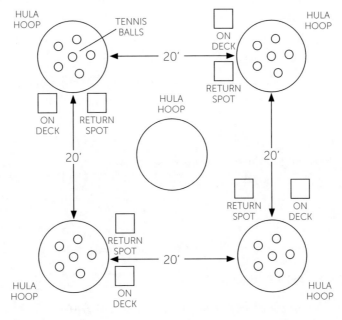

A bird's eye view of the activity

Place a fifth hoop in the center of the area. Place two gym spots next to each hoop. In each of the corner hoops, place five to 10 tennis balls (an equal number in each hoop).

---

*I learned the original version of this activity from colleague Joanne Tedford many years ago.

Introduction/Metaphor

"How many times in life do we have a mess to clean up? Sometimes it is our own mess. Sometimes it's someone else's mess. Sometimes it's a real mess with clothes and dishes and sometimes it's a metaphorical mess like broken relationships and unwanted consequences for poor choices. Most of us have some sort of 'mess' in our lives and sometimes it's not so easy to clean up. What are some messes in your lives? How do you try to clean them up? This challenge is about cleaning up our messes."

The Action

Divide your group into four teams. Each team will claim one corner of the setup square. The tennis balls in the team's hoop represent the group's "mess." The team must work together to completely clean up their mess. The rules are:

Only one player from each team can be in the playing area at a time. Players must establish an order within their team so that no player goes twice before everyone goes once. The order must be maintained.

Tennis balls cannot be tossed, thrown, or rolled and must be placed in hoops.

The player whose turn it is can remove one tennis ball from his or her team's hoop and place it in the hoop of any other team or in the middle hoop. Balls placed in the middle hoop are out of play for the remainder of the round. Balls placed in an opposing team's hoop are now part of that team's mess and can be moved on that team's successive turns.

If a ball rolls out of a hoop, it is the responsibility of the player who placed it there to put it back into the hoop. If he or she fails to do this, that ball is not counted against the team whose hoop it was intended for until a player from that team or another team places it directly in the hoop.

The team that completely gets rid of its mess first, wins.

Emphasize that everyone is to play fair (don't interfere with other players) and play safe, as there is a lot of fast-paced movement with players focused on their targets rather than each other.

One gym spot should be used by players getting ready to take their turn and the other for the player returning to the team from his or her turn. When that player steps on the spot, the next player can go.

Debriefing

Question for When the Focus Is on Emotional Awareness

• How did the competition impact you?

Question for When the Focus Is on Behavioral Control

• How did you protect your own safety as well as the safety of others?

Questions for When the Focus Is on Positive Relationships

• Did your team have a strategy? Did it change over successive rounds?

- Were you a good teammate?
- Were you a good sport in response to other teams?
- When you are in a "messy" situation, do you seek the support of others?
- Do you ever feel as though others are trying to bring you down? How did you deal with that today? How do you deal with that in life?

Cross the Great Divide*

This adventure classic can be adapted to virtually any group. It is deceptively more difficult than it appears once "group panic" begins to set in!

Target Group: Upper elementary-school age and older

Size of Group: 6 to 20 participants

Props: Gym spots (one per participant); starting-point and endpoint markers, such as rope; assorted random items, if desired

Objectives

Activity Goals: Group communication and problem solving, performing under pressure, coping with diminishing resources

Main FVC Connections: Be Safe, Speak Your Truth, Hear the Truth

Keys to Success Connections: Emotional awareness, behavioral control, establishing positive relationships

Facilitator Guidelines

Setup

Create an area with a starting point and endpoint that are both clearly marked with a rope or other boundary marker. The area in between the boundary markers should be about 10 yards long (more or less, depending on group size and functioning level).

Introduction/Metaphor

This classic challenge initiative has a plethora of variations and metaphorical applications. The "divide" to be crossed can represent any obstacle typically encountered by the members of your group. For example, if you are working with a depression support group, you can have them cross the Canyon of Despair. If it's an anger management group, it can be Rage Ravine. Ask group members what skills they possess to help the group cross the divide. As each member states their contribution, hand them a gym spot. A typical introduction might go as follows:

"Today, you will be crossing the Canyon of Despair, the area between this line and that one. Often, you have found yourself in this dark canyon alone, struggling to survive and climb out to safety. Today, you come with others. Together, you will cross from this side of the canyon to the other side, which is the Land of Hope."

The Action

Explain that participants cannot touch the canyon area with any part of their body otherwise they fall to the bottom and the group must restart.

---

*A version of this activity, called Stepping Stones, appears in *Quicksilver* (Rohnke & Butler, 1995).

Each group member is given a gym spot, or "magic step," that can float on air above the canyon. The steps must remain in contact with some part of a participant at all times. If a magic step is not in contact with someone, it disappears into the abyss (you take it), leaving the group with one less step.

The goal is for the entire group to cross the area between the start and endpoints.

With these rules in place, the group is given a definitive amount of time to plan, then asked to begin. Some typical questions members may ask:

Can more than one person stand on a step at a time? (Yes.)

Can we slide or throw steps? (No.)

Can we help each other? (Yes.)

Many groups struggle early on and lose several magic steps. If a group loses too many steps to be successful, you as the facilitator may decide to return some to the group. In order to get the magic step back, I often ask the group a question such as, "Which skill stated in the beginning can you use more of?"

Variation 1

Blindfold half the group.

Variation 2

Allow verbal communication only from select members (such as the quietest ones, which nudges them into leadership positions).

Variation 3

Place obstacles in front of the group that they must go around.

Variation 4

Have two groups moving at one time from opposite cliffs. You can place a floating island in the middle to allow them to rest and chat, or even switch steps with a predetermined partner from the other group.

Variation 5

Make the path across crooked.

Debriefing

The debriefing for this activity will depend greatly on the introduction. However, there are some general themes you can address with any group.

Questions for When the Focus Is on Emotional Awareness

- How did it feel to give support to your fellow participants?
- How did it feel to receive support from others?

Questions for When the Focus Is on Behavioral Control

- This activity required balance. How do you find "balance" in your lives? Do you get help from others to find that balance?

- Did you ask for help during this activity? Was it easy or difficult for you? How about in your real life?

- Did you help anyone else during this activity? Was it easier for you to help others or to receive help from others?

Questions for When the Focus Is on Positive Relationships

- Could you have conquered this challenge alone? How was it essential to work together to overcome the obstacles?

Key Punch*

Target Group: Middle school age and older

Size of Group: 6 to 30 participants

Props: Gym spots numbered 1 to 30, two ropes to mark off boundary areas, one of them at least 30 feet long.

Objectives

Activity Goals: Group communication and problem solving, adapting a solution based on experience, finding the balance between speed and accuracy

Main FVC Connections: Speak Your Truth, Hear the Truth

Keys to Success Connections: Behavioral control, establishing positive relationships

Facilitator Guidelines

Setup

Create a circular area with a rope roughly 10 to 20 feet across. Place the numbered gym spots within this rope circle in a somewhat random order but make sure that successive numbers are not too close to each other. This will serve as the "keypad" as described below. About 30 feet away, lay the other rope in a straight line. This will be the group's starting point. (See diagram.)

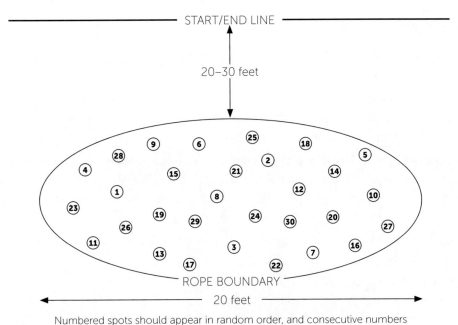

Numbered spots should appear in random order, and consecutive numbers should not be placed near one another.

---

*The original version of this classic initiative is found in *Quicksilver* (Rohnke & Butler, 1995).

Introduction/Metaphor

"Input the code and unlock the greatest secrets!" If I am working with a leadership group, it is the Big Book of Leadership that needs to be unlocked. If it's a social skills group, I might have the Secrets of Friendship locked in a box. A great general introduction is to begin a discussion about what it means to have "potential," as in "How do we unlock potential?"

As they are about to try out the activity, I will often refer to my group members as "PICOUPs." This stands for Person in Charge of Unlocking Potential, a phrase created by my late colleague and friend Michael Gessford. As a side note, each year at the Association for Experiential Education Northeast Regional Conference, there is an annual PICOUP award given to an experiential educator who selflessly tries to help others unlock their potential.

The Action

For the first round, give the introduction and instructions, but do not afford the group any planning time.

Once they understand the directions, have them make their first attempt to establish a baseline time. You can inform the group that they need to perform the task within a certain time limit in order to unlock the "potential."

Alternatively, you can challenge the group to improve upon their time on each of three (or however many you choose) successive attempts. Before their second and other successive attempts, give the group planning time. I generally allow three or four attempts. Groups tend to lose focus and motivation after that.

The goal of the group is to step on the numbers in order (1 through 30) with the following rules in effect:

Only one person may be on the "keypad" at any given time. Any violations of this will result in a 5-second penalty (5 seconds added to the final time). When you say, "go," all participants can cross the starting line and stand around the keypad; they just have to enter one at a time.

The group must go in an established order in which no one takes another turn until all others have taken a turn.

Numbers may be touched with any part of the body.

The challenge begins when the facilitator says, "go," and ends when the entire group has crossed back over the start/finish line.

If a number is touched out of order or more than one person is in the circle at a given time, a 5-second penalty is added to the final time.

Variation 1

Use letters instead of numbers. Participants must tap out the alphabet in order.

Variation 2

Create a tabletop version by either using small, numbered circles that are touched by hand or by printing out the numbers 1 through 30 (or 60) in a random order on a piece of paper. You can print several copies and have participants try it solo first.

Debriefing

The debriefing will depend greatly on how the activity is framed.

Questions for When the Focus Is on Behavioral Control

- How did you keep yourself from jumping into the circle at the wrong time?
- Did the group meet the goal of improving their time at each attempt?
- What behaviors did the participants show that helped the group be successful? How are these connected to unlocking potential?

Questions for When the Focus Is on Positive Relationships

- Have you been in positions where other people were counting on you? How did it feel?
- Did anyone demonstrate positive leadership during this activity? How so?
- As a group, were you successful? How did working together help you "unlock potential?" How do people in your life help you unlock your potential?

Frisbee Relay

One day, I had planned to do the activity Liberty Golf (p. 339) with a group but forgot to bring the necessary rings. Because I had Frisbees, we decided to try a similar activity with the Frisbees. We had a wide-open field and decided that a relay would be a lot of fun. We were right!

Target Group: Any age

Size of Group: 4 to 24 participants

Props: Frisbees, markers for starting and ending points

Objectives

Activity Goals: Group communication and problem solving

Main FVC Connections: Speak Your Truth, Hear the Truth

Keys to Success Connection: Establishing positive relationships

Facilitator Guidelines

Setup

Set up start and endpoints at least a few hundred feet apart. If you don't have that much room, you can make the playing area shorter but have the group members play to one end and come back.

Introduction/Metaphor

"The decisions we make determine the outcomes we experience. Sometimes, the right choices are not so obvious. Can you think of any times when the obvious choice turned out not to be the right one? In this game, you and your teammates will have to make decisions as to what will be the best strategy."

The Action

Divide your group into smaller groups of two to six. Give each group one Frisbee.

The goal is for the group to get the Frisbee from the starting point to the end point as quickly as possible by throwing it person to person. To determine a winner, you can use criteria such as least amount of throws or shortest amount of time.

You can also use a group goal such as combined times or total number of tosses. Teams must abide by the following rules:

The Frisbee must go from one team member to the next in a predetermined order.

Members can only move one foot when holding the Frisbee (for pivoting).

Players cannot interfere with other groups.

If the Frisbee hits the ground, that group must start over (or, alternatively and easier, they must redo that throw from the same point).

Debriefing

Questions for When the Focus Is on Positive Relationships

- Did you and your teammates create a strategy before you began?
- Did you each have input into the strategy?
- Did your strategy take into account your group's individual strengths and weaknesses?
- Did your team's strategy change as the activity unfolded? What factors led to these changes?

Never Ending Funball*

Target Group: Upper elementary school participants and older

Size of Group: 6 to 30

Props: Beach ball (or several) or balloons for small spaces or younger groups, roll of masking tape, and marker or pen

Objectives

Activity Goals: Group communication and problem solving

Main FVC Connections: Be Here, Be Safe

Keys to Success Connections: Behavioral control, establishing positive relationships

Facilitator Guidelines

Introduction/Metaphor

"Let the good times roll! When something is good in life, we want to keep it going as long as possible. What are some good things that you never wanted to see end? A family vacation? Summer? School? Write each response on a piece of masking tape and tape the responses to the beach ball. Let's try to keep all of these things going for as long as we can!"

The Action

The object is to keep the beach ball aloft for as long as possible (or, as a group, score as many hits as possible).

Have the group spread out in the playing area. No player may hit the ball twice in succession.

Count the number of hits made without the ball hitting the ground or time how long the ball stays aloft. If the ball does hit the ground, have the group restart and try to beat their best time or score.

Variation 1

No one can hit the ball until all other group members have hit the ball. This is significantly more difficult and should only be used with groups who can handle it.

---

*According to Terry Orlick, an early version of this game originated with the Caribou people in the 1800s. The first written version I can find is in *The New Games Book* (Fluegelman, 1976). Several similar activities appear in *Cooperative Sports and Games Book* (Orlick, 1978) in the section Collective-Score Games. In *Silver Bullets* (1984), Karl Rohnke wrote up Moonball, which has had dozens of variations since.

Variation 2

Using Hula-Hoops, have the group divide into smaller groups of three to five members. Each group is assigned a hoop and each member must keep one foot in the hoop at all times. The number of hoops and distance from each other will change the level of challenge. You can increase the challenge further by ruling that the ball must be sent to each group before it returns to any particular group.

Debriefing

Question for When the Focus Is on Behavioral Control

- When it wasn't your turn to hit the ball, how did you help your team?

Questions for When the Focus Is on Positive Relationships

- Was there any point at which you felt as if you were in a competition?
- In relationships, there is "give and take." How did you have to give and take during this activity? What about in your life?

Balloon Volleyball

This activity takes the competitive sport of volleyball and creates a challenging team initiative!

Target Group: Upper elementary-school age and older

Size of Group: 4 to 10 people

Props: Balloons, volleyball net or rope strung across the room

Objectives

Activity Goals: Differentiate between cooperation and competition, enhance group communication and problem-solving skills

Main FVC Connections: Be Safe, Speak Your Truth, Hear the Truth

Keys to Success Connections: Behavioral control, establishing positive relationships

Facilitator Guidelines

Introduction/Metaphor

"If there are two teams, does it mean you are competing with each other?" This depends on the goal. If both teams have the same goal (such as a total number of points) instead of opposing goals (each team wanting to win a contest), it's not a competition! This is one of those activities that can appear to be a competition when, in fact, it's not.

The Action

Divide your group in two. Have each group stand on one side of the net or rope.

The goal is to get the balloon from one side of the net to the other following some basic rules:

The balloon cannot hit the ground.

No group member can hit the balloon twice in succession.

The balloon must go over the net (as opposed to under or around).

Players cannot touch the net.

Have the group see how many times they can get the balloon back and forth over the net successfully.

Variation 1

Each time a member hits the balloon over, he or she goes under the net to the other side. The group has achieved their goal when each player is on the opposite side they started on. You can also see how many people swaps they can successfully complete.

Variation 2

Hang a tarp or blanket over the net or rope so members cannot see what's happening on the other side. This can be used with either the regular version or Variation 1.

Variation 3

Have each group member connected to his or her teammates by holding buddy ropes (pieces of rope 1 to 2 feet long). Count the number of successful hits over the net without the balloon hitting the ground or buddy ropes coming out of players' hands.

Debriefing

Questions for When the Focus Is on Behavioral Control

- Was it easier or more difficult using a balloon rather than a regular volleyball? Why?
- Before the activity, did you think it would be easier to volley a balloon or a ball? Were you right or wrong?
- What other things in your life seemed easy at first but later proved to be difficult?

Questions for When the Focus Is on Positive Relationships

- Did you work with the other group or compete with them? Why do we automatically assume something is a competition as soon as a group is divided into two smaller groups?
- What strategies did your group use to accomplish the task?

Bull Ring*

Target Group: Middle school and older

Size of Group: 4 to12 per group; multiple groups possible

Props: Golf ball, bull ring (the bull ring consists of a metal ring 1 ½ inches in diameter attached to brightly colored mason lines or twine)

Objectives

Activity Goals: Group communication and problem solving, inhibiting impulses, differentiating between leading and following and recognizing the need for both

Main FVC Connections: Be Safe, Speak Your Truth, Hear the Truth

Keys to Success Connections: Emotional awareness, behavioral control, establishing positive relationships

Facilitator Guidelines

Introduction/Metaphor

This is truly one of the most versatile activities in terms of metaphorical possibilities. The activity can represent a journey in which the group is transporting a volatile material that will self-destruct upon contact with the ground if not returned to the ring in 5 seconds. What that material is can be related to the theme of the group. For example, in a leadership group, it can be a potion that will help people become great leaders. What are the ingredients of that potion? Confidence? Communication skills? Success depends upon your group's ability to work together!

The Action

Set up the bull ring so that it is lying on the ground, strings separated from each other and extended outward from the ring (like the rays of the sun).

Depending on how many members you have per group, each member should grab at least one string, possibly two or three.

The goal is to transport the golf ball from point A to point B without dropping it. This is accomplished by the group members lifting the ring by the attached strings and walking from point A to point B.

Members may not touch the ball (unless it falls and they need to reset it). They also must hold the far end of the strings, no more than 3 inches from the end farthest from the ring.

---

*Bull Ring was written up originally by Jim Cain and Tom Smith in *Teamwork and Teamplay* (1998). Since then, Jim has created numerous types of bull rings with all sorts of twists.

Variation 1

Make sure that point A and point B have obstacles between them, such as trees if outside or desks if inside.

Variation 2

Blindfold half the group.

Variation 3

Blindfold all but one member.

Variation 4

Using Variation 1, 2 or 3, limit who can speak (e.g., only those with blindfolds can speak, only those without blindfolds can speak, only one member may speak and the group has to decide who it will be, etc.).

Variation 5

Have more than one group going at a time with endpoints that are very close to each other. You may also have it that the groups must cross paths in tight quarters.

Variation 6

Have more than one group going at a time. At a predetermined midpoint, group members must switch groups until all members have transitioned to the other bull ring.

Debriefing

Questions for When the Focus Is on Emotional Awareness

- Did you become frustrated at any point? How did you handle it?

Questions for When the Focus Is on Behavioral Control

- What skills did you use to successfully complete this activity?
- What made this activity difficult?

Questions for When the Focus Is on Positive Relationships

- Did any members step into leadership roles? Why?
- Did your group use a strategy? Did it change as you went along?

15 Trust Activities

While many of the initiatives in the previous chapter help enhance trust, the following activities are specifically designed to get to the heart of trust within the group. Generally speaking, they will be used at the same points in a group's development as the more challenging initiatives, that is, once the group has solidly established its norms and is generally abiding by the FVC. These activities should not be used with groups that are not demonstrating the ability to maintain physical and emotional safety. The choice to use a trust activity as opposed to another challenge usually relates to the goals you have for the group and what makes the most sense to you as a facilitator at that time.

Field of Distraction*

This activity is one of my favorites. It carries with it so many possible lessons!

Target Group: Middle school and older

Size of Group: 6 to 16

Props: Blindfolds, numbered gym spots, assorted stuffed animals and other "clutter" objects

Objectives

Activity Goals: Developing trust within the group, coping with external distractions from our goals, identifying and using resources, goal-setting, coping with frustration and stress

Main FVC Connections: Be Safe, Speak Your Truth, Hear The Truth

Keys to Success Connections: Emotional awareness, behavioral control, establishing positive relationships

Facilitator Guidelines

Setup

Create a boundary to the play area by placing numbered gym spots (one for every two people in the group) in a circle. The circle should be at least 20 feet in diameter but could be larger. The larger the circle, the more difficult the activity will be. Within the play area, randomly scatter objects such as other stuffed animals, tennis balls, coiled ropes, and other assorted adventure equipment. These are "distracters."

Introduction/Metaphor

For this activity, group members will be seeking a specific object. The object should represent a goal. If it's a theme group, the goal should be something related to that theme. For example, in an anger management group, the goal could be something the participant hopes to achieve due to improved anger management skills such as a better relationship with parents. Have the group members state their goals. As they do, give each one a stuffed animal.

The Action

Have your group divide into pairs and assign each pair a numbered spot. Give each pair a blindfold.

Once on their spot, partners should decide who will be the first one into the field. That person puts on the blindfold.

---

*Original versions of this activity were called Minefield in Karl Rohnke's *Silver Bullets* (1984) and 3D Minefield in *Quicksilver* (Rohnke & Butler, 1995).

When one member from each pair is blindfolded, take the blindfolded partner's "critter" (the one that represents his or her goal) and place it amidst the distracters. To make it more difficult, place each pair's critter toward the opposite end of the circle.

While remaining on the numbered spot, the sighted partner must verbally guide the blindfolded partner into the field to retrieve the critter. If the blindfolded partner touches any distracters or other participants, the facilitator guides him or her back to the numbered spot to restart.

Once all the pairs finish, have them discuss the results, plan for the next round, and switch roles.

Make sure that blindfolded participants walk with "bumpers up," meaning that their hands are out in front of them, palms out, bent at the elbow.

Debriefing

Questions for When the Focus Is on Emotional Awareness

- How did you feel during this activity?
- How did you feel when you had to restart?
- What was it like to be the one giving the verbal directions?
- What was it like to be the one receiving the directions?

Questions for When the Focus Is on Behavioral Control

- How did you deal with the "distracters" in the field? How do you deal with distractions in life?
- (To the blindfolded partners) How did you keep yourself and others safe?
- (To the non-blindfolded partners) How did you deal with the distraction of other voices?

Questions for When the Focus Is on Positive Relationships

- How were you and your partner successful? What skills did you use to accomplish your goal?
- How did you communicate with each other?
- Did anyone communicate with other group members besides their partner? Why or why not?
- Did anyone view this activity as a competition? Why or why not?

Come Together*

Target Group: Middle school age and older

Size of Group: 6 to 24 participants

Props: Long rope

Objectives

Activity Goals: Group communication and problem solving, communicating without visual input, trust

Main FVC Connections: Be Safe, Speak Your Truth, Hear the Truth

Keys to Success Connections: Emotional awareness, behavioral control, establishing positive relationships

Facilitator Guidelines

Introduction/Metaphor

You might begin this activity by discussing what it means for people to "come together" and how that is best accomplished.

The Action

Lay the rope out and have your group spread out evenly along the length of it.

Once everyone has found a spot, ask participants to put on blindfolds and pick up the rope. Group members must not let go of the rope once they pick it up.

Instruct the group to "come together" in various shapes. Begin with simpler shapes like a square or circle. If the group does well with the simpler shapes, move to more difficult ones like triangle or letters of the alphabet.

Between each round, participants can lift the blindfold from their eyes to admire their success!

Variation 1

Allow only one person or several people to speak.

Variation 2

Do not allow anyone to speak. This is extremely difficult and requires the group to carefully plan ahead.

---

*The origin of this activity is from Blind Polygon (Square) described in *Cowstails and Cobras II* (Rohnke, 1989).

Variation 3

Allow one person to be sighted. This person cannot touch the rope or other participants but can speak. No one else may speak.

Variation 4

Don't allow the sighted person to speak but allow this person to touch the participants.

Debriefing

Questions for When the Focus Is on Emotional Awareness

- How did you feel during this experience?
- What was it like to not be able to see?

Questions for When the Focus Is on Behavioral Control

- Did anyone step up into a leadership role? What did this person do to lead? Was it effective? How does this translate into effective leadership skills outside of this group?
- Did you try any strategies that didn't work? Why didn't it work? What did you do about that?

Questions for When the Focus Is on Positive Relationships

- As a group, how did you communicate? How was communication important? What was difficult about communicating during the activity?
- How were you successful in coming together in the shape of a square (or whatever shape the group formed)? Are these skills that can be used to bring people together outside of group?

Sherpa Walk*

This adventure classic provides participants an opportunity to experience life without sight. It places the participants in a position to rely on others and allows them to focus on senses we usually consider secondary to sight.

Target Group: Upper elementary age and older

Size of Group: 3 to 18 people

Props: Enough blindfolds for all but one (or a few) member(s)

Objectives

Activity Goals: Build trust, develop leadership, experience life without sight, and bring a heightened awareness to our other senses

Main FVC Connections: Be Here, Be Safe

Keys to Success Connections: Emotional awareness, behavioral control, establishing positive relationships

Facilitator Guidelines

Introduction/Metaphor

I begin this activity by asking the group if they know what a Sherpa is. "Sherpas are people of Tibetan descent living in the region of the Himalayas. They are renowned hiking guides that lead travelers up the tallest mountains in the world, most notably, Mt. Everest. What skills do the Sherpas possess that make them amazing guides? Today's trek will take the group through a blinding mountain blizzard. The only ones able to see are the Sherpas because they grew up with this type of weather and their eyes have adapted to their environment."

The Action

For this activity, at least one group member will serve as the "Sherpa" or guide. The other members will be the "Adventurers." For larger groups, I prefer a ratio of about one Sherpa to six Adventurers.

Have your group stand in a straight line with one Sherpa at the front and, if there are more than six participants, one at the back. If you have more Sherpas, they should be spaced evenly throughout the center of the group.

Ask the Adventurers to put on their blindfolds and connect by placing their hands on the shoulders of the person in front of them. Alternatively, you can use a rope for all of them to hold onto.

*The original version of this activity appears in *Silver Bullets* (Rohnke, 1984).

Because the Adventurers will be without their sight, encourage them to tune in to their other senses. Remaining silent throughout the activity will help. Members should only speak to give or receive safety-related information.

Encourage the Sherpas not to tell the rest of the group where they are.

When the group is ready, have the lead Sherpa follow you as you walk slowly toward your destination. If possible, lead the group on a path that includes changes in terrain, elevation and levels of sunlight (such as field that leads into woods). Even slight inclines or declines will be perceived as steep hills by blindfolded members.

Debriefing

Questions for When the Focus Is on Emotional Awareness

- As an Adventurer, how did it feel to be without your sight?
- What did you notice with your other senses?
- As a Sherpa, how did it feel to be responsible for the group's safety?

Questions for When the Focus Is on Behavioral Control

- As a Sherpa, what did you do to make sure your group arrived safely at their destination?
- As an Adventurer, what did you do to make sure you were safe?

Questions for When the Focus Is on Positive Relationships

- Did you trust your Sherpas to get you to your destination safely? What actions did they take that made you feel this way?
- As a blindfolded participant, did you speak up when you needed something from the group or the Sherpa? Were you heard?

Pairs Walk*

While similar to a Sherpa Walk (p. 376), Pairs Walk has a different dynamic as participants work in pairs.

Target Group: Upper elementary age and older

Size of Group: 2 to 24 people (about three or four pairs per facilitator for safety reasons)

Props: One blindfold for each pair

Objectives

Activity Goals: Build trust, explore life without sight and what it means to rely on someone else, develop leadership

Main FVC Connections: Be Here, Be Safe

Keys to Success Connections: Emotional awareness, behavioral control, establishing positive relationships

Facilitator Guidelines

Introduction/Metaphor

The introduction to this activity depends upon what aspect of the activity you choose to focus on. If you focus on being deprived of sight, you might ask group members what they think life would be like without one of their senses. You could ask which sense they would choose to give up if they had to and which they would be least likely to give up. Encourage participants to pay attention to their other senses when blindfolded.

If you focus on the trust aspect, you can ask what characteristics someone must demonstrate in order to be considered trustworthy. Then, once in pairs, ask if the guides are willing to demonstrate those characteristics.

The Action

Divide your group into pairs. Depending upon how advanced they are, you may want to allow them to choose partners. (Be careful of emotional safety as this can leave some group members out.)

Once your group is divided, give each pair one bandanna. One partner will use the bandanna as a blindfold while the other partner remains sighted.

Require the pairs to maintain contact any time the blindfold is on. This can take the form of a hand on a shoulder, hooking elbows, etc.

Take the group on a guided walk in which each sighted partner must follow you. Create a path that changes elevation and terrain and has obstacles in the way. If you have a final destination, have partners switch roles halfway through.

---

*This activity was originally written up in *Quicksilver* (Rohnke & Butler, 1995).

Variation 1

Have sighted partners lead their blindfolded partners to a specific place or give a specified amount of time to take their partners on a journey of their choosing. Make sure that partners have a chance to switch roles.

Variation 2

Have guides offer only verbal directions with no physical contact between blindfolded and sighted partners (the exception being if safety cannot be maintained with verbal directions only).

Debriefing

I generally open the debriefing by asking participants what they noticed while blindfolded. Which senses were heightened? Would they have noticed the same things had they been sighted?

Questions for When the Focus Is on Emotional Awareness

- How did it feel to lose your sense of sight?
- How did it feel to have someone rely on you for their safety? When does this happen in life?
- Did you notice anything using your other senses that you might miss if you were able to see? What did you hear? What did you feel? Smell?

Questions for When the Focus Is on Behavioral Control

- Did you feel unsafe at any time? What did you do about that?
- Was it difficult to remain quiet? Why?

Questions for When the Focus Is on Positive Relationships

- How did it feel to put your trust in the hands of a peer?
- What did your partner do that allowed you to trust him or her?
- In your life, are there times when you have to put your trust in others? Are there times when others need to trust you? How do you handle these situations?

Hog Call 2.0*

Target Group: Any age

Size of Group: 2 to 30 people

Props: One blindfold for each member, word pairs cut up, word pairs list

Objectives

Activity Goals: Communication, cope with challenges to accomplishing our goals, trust, connect with others

Main FVC Connections: Be Safe, Speak Your Truth, Hear the Truth

Keys to Success Connections: Emotional awareness, behavioral control, establishing positive relationships

Facilitator Guidelines

Introduction/Metaphor

"Sometimes it's tough to find someone to connect with in this crazy life. Today, amidst life's confusion, you will find a friend. How do you go about finding people to connect with in this world?"

The Action

The original Hog Call version calls for the group to be broken down into pairs. Each pair is given words that go together (such as *peanut butter* and *jelly*).

Each partner is given a blindfold. They should put on the blindfolds after moving to opposite sides of the playing area.

Participants then shuffle about on their side of the playing area so they are not directly across from their partner. Remind them to keep their "bumpers up" (hands out with palms facing outward, arms bent at elbows).

The partners then call each other's word while moving toward each other until they eventually meet up somewhere in the middle of the field.

For the Hog Call 2.0 version, have a list of word pairs such as *peanut butter* and *jelly* or *cats* and *dogs*. If you have a theme for your group, the word pairs can be related to the theme. For example, in an anger management group, I might pair words such as *breathe* and *calm*.

On a duplicate list, cut up the word pairs into single words and place them in a bag. There should be one word for each participant—no more, no less. Have participants pick a word from the bag without showing anyone what word they have.

---

*The original version of this activity is called Hog Call in Karl Rohnke's *Silver Bullets* (1984).

Read the word pairs from your list so that each person knows what word matches the one they picked.

Give each member a blindfold and have them move to the edges of the playing area (which should be at least the size of a gym and no bigger than half a football field). Once each member has found a spot, they should put on their blindfold.

On your "go," with bumpers up, the group members should start calling out the word they picked while listening for their matching word to be called. Once partners find each other, have them discuss what skills it took to find "friends" in all the chaos.

Debriefing

Question for When the Focus Is on Emotional Awareness

- What did it feel like to be blindfolded as you tried to find each other during this activity?
- How did you feel about not knowing who your partner would be before we began?

Question for When the Focus Is on Behavioral Control

- What skills did you need to locate each other?

Questions for When the Focus Is on Positive Relationships

- Are there times in life when it's tough to find a friend? How did you find the people you are closest to?
- What gets in the way of forming relationships?

Field Wild Woozey

This activity is about giving and receiving support. It is a ground version of a popular low-ropes course element called the Wild Woozey.

Target Group: Upper elementary-school age and older

Size of Group: 2 to 24 people

Props: None

Objectives

Activity Goals: Explore the concepts of give and take and support as they pertain to relationships, develop trust, explore the concept of balance

Main FVC Connections: Be Safe, Speak Your Truth, Hear the Truth

Keys to Success Connections: Emotional awareness, behavioral control, establishing positive relationships

Facilitator Guidelines

Introduction/Metaphor

"What does it mean to support someone in a relationship? How do you get support? How do you give support?"

The Action

This activity should be done on a level surface that is not too hard (such as grass or carpeting).

Have the group pair off and spread out so they are not too close to anyone else.

Standing a few feet apart, have the partners face each other, get in "bumpers up" position, and go palm-to-palm with their partner. Make sure no one has fingers intertwined.

Ask group members to explore pressure and balance with their partner by leaning toward each other to get used to the feeling of physically supporting another person while simultaneously being supported by them.

Once they have done this for a few minutes, ask the partners to raise their hands just above head level while keeping their palms flat against their partner's palms.

When they are ready, partners should lean into each other. Little by little, they should move their feet backward, leaning forward more and more. Encourage pairs to go as far as they can go while still safely supporting each other. This means they need to keep communicating!

Variation 1

Try this in reverse! Have partners hold hands (again, fingers not entwined) and lean backward, with their toes touching in the middle. Again, encourage partners to communicate throughout the activity and let each other know what they need from their partner. This can be done with more than two people holding hands.

Variation 2

Have participants work in groups of three or four or more!

Debriefing

Questions for When the Focus Is on Emotional Awareness

- How did it feel to support another person? In your daily life, who do you support? How do you do that?
- How did it feel to be supported? In your daily life, who supports you? How do they support you?

Question for When the Focus Is on Behavioral Control

- How did you keep each other safe?

Questions for When the Focus Is on Positive Relationships

- How did you communicate with your partner?
- How did you and your partner do this successfully? How do those skills/behaviors translate to having positive relationships?
- How did you find a balance point of providing enough support while still being supported? How do you find that point in your relationships?

Blindly Follow the Leader

This activity came out of a workshop I conducted at NCCPS in Boulder, Colorado. The workshop was called "The Name of the Game Is...." In the workshop, participants in small groups chose an activity name from a list I had created. Their task was to create an activity based on the name. The original name of this was Pinwheel, but with one sighted leader and the rest of the group blindfolded, the new name seemed to better capture the potential metaphorical connections of the activity.

Target Group: Middle school age and older

Size of Group: 6 to 15 participants

Props: Blindfolds for all but one participant

Objectives

Activity Goals: Build trust, develop leadership, explore concepts of leading and following, communicate without visual cues

Main FVC Connection: Be Safe

Keys to Success Connections: Emotional awareness, behavioral control, establishing positive relationships

Facilitator Guidelines

Introduction/Metaphor

"Are there any situations in which people just blindly follow a leader, doing whatever the leader tells them to do? Is it ever good to blindly follow a leader? Is it ever not a good thing?"

The Action

For this activity, all group members but one will be blindfolded. Have the blindfolded members join hands and form a circle, facing the sighted group member (the leader) who stands in the center of the circle.

Designate an endpoint for the group to reach and show the sighted leader where it is. The group must get from the starting point to the end point without touching any objects or the leader.

The leader will give verbal commands to the blindfolded members to accomplish the task.

If there are any violations, you can either have the group restart (possibly with a new leader) or count the number of violations and make a second attempt to see if the group can accomplish the task with fewer violations.

Variation 1

Vary the difficulty level by having the group move past obstacles, through narrow passages, or up and down hills (versus on a flat, clear path).

Variation 2

Don't allow the blindfolded members to speak. This significantly increases the difficulty level.

Variation 3

The most difficult scenario is to not allow the leader to speak.

Debriefing

Questions for When the Focus Is on Emotional Awareness

- How did it feel to be the only sighted one? Do you ever have situations in life where you feel like you are the only one who can really see what is going on?
- How did it feel to be blindfolded and relying on someone else to keep you safe? Have you ever been in a position of relying on another to keep you safe? How does it feel? How would you feel if they didn't keep you safe?
- As the sighted member, how did it feel to be responsible for everyone's safety?

Questions for When the Focus Is on Behavioral Control

- For those who were blindfolded, how did you stay calm?
- What did the leader do to make you trust that they would keep you safe?

Questions for When the Focus Is on Positive Relationships

- How did you, as a blindfolded member, communicate effectively with the sighted leader?
- How did you, as the leader, communicate with the blindfolded members?
- Did anyone feel unsafe at any point during the activity?

Wavy Lines*

Target Group: Upper elementary-school age and older

Size of Group: 10 to 24 participants

Props: None

Objectives

Activity Goals: Enhance focus, build trust, develop support within the group

Main FVC Connections: Be Here, Be Safe

Keys to Success Connections: Emotional awareness, behavioral control, establishing positive relationships

Facilitator Guidelines

Introduction/Metaphor

This activity involves trust and journeying. If I am working with an anger management group, participants will travel from the Land of Rage to the Island of Peace. For depression support, they may journey from Sadness Mountain to Pleasant Valley. In order to successfully travel from one place to another, they will need protection from a sometimes harsh environment. This protection comes from "protective factors." One protective factor might be family support, another might be friendship, and another, listening to music. The protective factors are what help a person cope with their problems. The more protective factors one has, the higher the level of protection from the environment. Have members state what protective factors they have in their lives just before they take their turn moving through the Wavy Lines.

The Action

Arrange your group so that you have two equal lines of people facing each other.

Members of each line should be standing nearly shoulder to shoulder with arms extended in front of them. Their arms should interweave in zipper fashion with the arms reaching out from the other side. Fingertips should extend to about the elbow of the person across.

Have a volunteer stand at one end of the lines. On your "go," the volunteer begins walking nonstop between the two lines of people. As they go, participants in line raise their arms overhead.

Once the walker passes, the people in the lines lower their arms and put their hands straight out again. When the walker reaches the end, have him or her switch places with someone in line who will then walk the Wavy Lines.

For the second round, have participants walk through quicker, choosing the speed.

---

*A similar activity called Trust Wave appears in *Quicksilver* (Rohnke & Butler, 1995).

Variation 1

The people in the lines can extend pool noodles (instead of their arms).

Variation 2

Have the walker wear a blindfold.

Debriefing

Questions for When the Focus Is on Emotional Awareness

- How did it feel to walk between the lines?
- How did it feel to be part of the wave lines?
- How did if feel when someone decided to move very quickly through the lines?
- Did you trust yourself to keep the walker safe? Were there any points when you doubted yourself?

Questions for When the Focus Is on Behavioral Control

- Did you stay focused and move your arms at the correct time?
- What factors did you weigh into your choice about how fast to go when walking down the aisle?

Questions for When the Focus Is on Positive Relationships

- Are there other situations in your life in which you have to trust others with your safety?
- Is it easy for you to trust others?
- To do this activity, you must put your trust in others. Did the group prove themselves worthy of your trust?

Carpool

This activity came out of a workshop I conducted at NCCPS in Boulder, Colorado. The workshop was called "The Name of the Game Is...." In the workshop, participants in small groups chose an activity name from a list I had created. Their task was to create a new activity based on the name. Carpool provides yet another twist on the trust-building activities.

Target Group: Middle school age and older

Size of Group: 6 to 24 participants

Props: Enough blindfolds for almost all members, gym spots and ropes to mark starting and ending points

Objectives

Activity Goals: Enhance trust within the group, learn to give up control, develop leadership skills

Main FVC Connection: Be Safe

Keys to Success Connections: Emotional awareness, behavioral control, establishing positive relationships

Facilitator Guidelines

Setup

Designate a starting point by laying a rope on the ground. Beyond the rope, in the playing area, lay out the gym spots at least 10 feet apart.

Introduction/Metaphor

"If I am in a car, I like to be the driver so I am in control. Of course sometimes I'm not the driver and that can be nerve-wracking for me. But it's just reality, and I have to deal with not being in control when someone else is driving. Today you are going to take a ride and trust the driver to get you home safely. Of course, there may be some ways you can help your driver do this."

The Action

If you have a large group, break the group into smaller groups of six to eight members. Lay out two fewer gym spots than group members. For example, if you have eight group members, you will need six gym spots. If you have two groups of eight, you will need 12 spots.

Each smaller group will choose a "Car" and a "Steering Wheel." The rest of the participants will be "Passengers."

Have the Car and Steering Wheel stand behind the starting line. Cars will put on a blindfold.

Have each Passenger stand on a gym spot and put on a blindfold. Passengers remain on the spots until the Car comes to pick them up.

To play, the Steering Wheel must verbally guide the Car to each Passenger while remaining behind the starting line throughout the activity.

Once the Car arrives, he or she should pick up the Passenger (linking arms or hands on shoulders) and continue toward the next Passenger. The Car has completed the journey when all Passengers are safely delivered to the finish line.

Variation 1

Don't allow the Car to verbally communicate with the Steering Wheel.

Variation 2

Add obstacles that, if touched, will cause the Car to lose a Passenger or go back to the starting point.

Variation 3

To make it more competitive, don't break into smaller groups. Simply designate more than one Car and Steering Wheel team and see who can safely pick up the most Passengers.

Debriefing

Questions for When the Focus Is on Emotional Awareness

- How did it feel to be the Steering Wheel in this activity?
- How did it feel to be the Car in this activity?
- How did it feel to be a Passenger in this activity?

Question for When the Focus Is on Behavioral Control

- How did each of the three roles contribute to keeping everyone safe?

Questions for When the Focus Is on Positive Relationships

- As the Car, was it difficult for you to understand the Steering Wheel's directions? Are there ever times in your life when you have to follow directions that are not easy to understand? What do you do about it?
- Did the Steering Wheel's ability to give directions improve as the activity progressed?
- As a Passenger, did you help the Car find you? Did you help once you were picked up? How?
- Were you more concerned with either your own safety or that of the others in the group?

Trust Leans*

I often use this activity with groups preparing to start on low- or high-ropes course elements as a way to get used to spotting. You can also use it as the first step in a longer trust sequence that includes the next several activities.

Target Group: Any, preadolescent or older, that can handle this level of trust and responsibility

Size of Group: No higher than a 12:1 participant-to-staff ratio for supervision purposes.

Props: None

Objectives

Activity Goals: Enhance trust, develop spotting skills, explore concept of support

Main FVC Connections: Be Here, Be Safe

Keys to Success Connections: Emotional awareness, behavioral control, establishing positive relationships

Facilitator Guidelines

Setup

All group members must demonstrate proper spotting position: Participants will keep their bodies squared, facing forward. One foot should be forward, the other behind, about shoulder width (or slightly more) apart. The front foot should face forward and the rear foot should be at a 90-degree angle to the front foot, creating an "L" shape with the two feet. The knees are slightly bent and ready to act as shock absorbers. Participants should place their hands in front of their chest with elbows bent, palms in front as if pushing something (see picture). I like to test the stance by going around the group and pushing on participants' palms, helping them make necessary adjustments as I go. Ideally, Spotters should absorb the energy of the push with their knees (not arms) by bending with the weight, like shock absorbers.

The second position the group must learn is the falling position. This is achieved by standing straight up, body stiff, feet together, and hands folded across the chest.

Finally, there is a brief series of questions and responses that each member must know:

    Faller: Spotter ready?

  Spotter: (Only when truly ready.) Spotter ready!

    Faller: Ready to fall.

  Spotter: Fall away!

Once you have made sure that everyone understands the spotting and falling techniques and the commands, you can proceed with the activity.

---

*Trust Leans is written up as Two-Person Trust Fall in *Cowstails and Cobras II* (Rohnke, 1989), though I suspect the activity was first tried long before the book!

Introduction/Metaphor

Two-person trust leans are akin to the game you played as a kid in which you extend your arms out to your sides and fall backward into someone's waiting arms just before you hit the floor. If you notice, younger kids do this with ease, whereas older kids and adults are not often seen playing this game. The innocence of childhood allows us to trust without question. Inevitably, life teaches us that trust should not always be easily given and must be earned. This activity begins to bring us back to the place where we can let go of our inhibitions and trust again.

The way I introduce this activity depends on my goal for using it, as well as the age and "personality" of the group itself. If I am using it as an activity to teach spotting techniques, I may start by asking the group to demonstrate their best "ninja" pose in order to work toward correct technique. A ninja pose can be different things to different people. When all group members are showing their best ninja poses, I choose one that seems close to the correct spotting pose and give them instructions to adapt their pose into the proper spotting technique. I ask the group if they know what "spotting" means. I emphasize that the purpose of spotting someone is to help break their fall and protecting the head and neck, as opposed to catching the person.

If I am using this activity as the first in a sequence of trust exercises, I generally start by having the group members pair up. If they can handle it, I will have them pair with someone they haven't worked with much or at all. To me, the tone that needs to be set as a group moves into a trust sequence is serious. The level of both emotional and physical risk and responsibility will increase dramatically in the course of a relatively short period of time. I will often state this at the onset and reinforce the FVC and Challenge by Choice philosophies. See Chapter 3.

The Action

In pairs, the groups will practice the falling and spotting positions and commands: The Spotter should be behind the Faller with his or her hands only a few inches from the Faller's shoulders. (Sometimes, it's helpful for the Spotter to place his or her hands on the Faller's shoulders to reassure them once they are in straight standing position.)

A three-person trust lean

Fallers, after going through the series of commands, should fall straight backward toward their Spotters, keeping their bodies stiff and feet in place. The Spotters should absorb the Fallers' weight and gently push them back to standing position.

You can allow the group members to experiment with increasingly larger falls as you see fit. Move in small increments and watch for unsafe behavior.

Three-person trust leans are the logical next step. With your group divided into triads, have one Spotter stand in front of the Faller and the other Spotter behind. The Faller can fall either forward or backward and will be gently pushed to the other Spotter, eventually being stood straight up in the middle with a reassuring grasp on the shoulders at the end.

Debriefing

As a facilitator, you can easily spot the participants who have a difficult time trusting others as they will struggle to keep their bodies stiff when falling.

Questions for When the Focus Is on Emotional Awareness

- How did you feel as the Faller the first time you tried it? How about the second time?
- How did you feel as the Spotter, knowing you were responsible for someone else's safety?
- How did it feel to be trusted?

Questions for When the Focus Is on Behavioral Control

- What did you do as the Faller to ensure both your and your partner's safety?
- What did you do as the Spotter to ensure both your and your partner's safety?
- Were there any safety violations?

Questions for When the Focus Is on Positive Relationships

- How were you able to trust the person you worked with? What behaviors did they show to allow you to trust them?

Wind in the Willows*

Target Group: Middle school age or older participants who have already demonstrated trustworthiness and understand spotting techniques and commands. I never use this activity until the group has successfully done a series of Trust Leans as described on page 390.

Size of Group: 8 to 12 participants (per facilitator)

Props: None

Objectives

Activity Goals: Enhance trust within the group, explore the concept of letting go

Main FVC Connections: Be Here, Be Safe

Keys to Success Connections: Emotional awareness, behavioral control, establishing positive relationships

Facilitator Guidelines

Setup

Falling and spotting techniques and the command series are described in the Trust Leans activity on page 390.

Introduction/Metaphor

"Have you ever seen a willow tree on a breezy day? It's truly beautiful to watch the leaves swaying, gently in the breeze. I have often wondered what it's like to be one of those wispy branches of leaves, letting the wind guide my movements." This activity is about trusting and "letting go."

The Action

Have your participants form a tight circle, shoulder to shoulder.

Ask for a volunteer to enter the middle of the circle and assume the falling position while the participants standing in the circle around them get into proper spotting position with hands several inches from the Faller. (I offer Fallers the option of closing their eyes.)

When the Faller is ready, he or she should initiate the command series. The Faller may fall in any direction.

Spotters should absorb the Faller's weight and gently push the Faller back toward the center of the circle, allowing the Faller to fall toward another group member.

---

*The oldest versions of this activity I have found are in *Cowstails and Cobras* (Rohnke, 1977) and in the *Cooperative Sports and Games Book* (Orlick, 1978) as the activity Circle of Friends. It appears as Willow in the Winds in *Cowstails and Cobras II* (Rohnke, 1989)

When using this activity, make sure that Spotters organize themselves in such a way as to have a balance of size and strength around the circle (rather than all the largest or strongest participants on one side).

After a few falls, stand the Faller up in the center of the circle with a reassuring pat on the shoulders to close out his or her turn.

Variation

Organize the group as described above. Have the Faller look around the group to see that everyone is ready. The Faller should then close his or her eyes and begin a count aloud to "20 Mississippi." While the Faller is counting, the rest of the group should quietly leave and hide nearby. When the count is complete, the Faller should open his or her eyes and briefly look around. Ideally, the Faller will not see or hear any of the other participants. The Faller will then close his or her eyes and repeat the count to 20 Mississippi. While the Faller is counting, the group should quietly return to the circle and assume their spotting positions. At the end of this count, the Faller should just fall (no further commands). If you see that the group was not able to reassemble themselves in proper spotting position, don't allow the Faller to fall!

Debriefing

Questions for When the Focus Is on Emotional Awareness

- How did this feel compared with the Trust Leans?
- What was it like to let go and let others take control? Are there times in life when "letting go" is important?

Questions for When the Focus Is on Behavioral Control

- What did you do as the Faller to ensure your safety as well as the safety of others?
- What did you do as the Spotter to ensure your safety as well as the safety of others?

Questions for When the Focus Is on Positive Relationships

- Was it easy for you to trust the group? Why or why not?

Levitation*

I never use this activity until the group has successfully done a series of Trust Leans and Wind in the Willows activities as described on pages 390 and 393, respectively.

Target Group: Middle school age or older participants who have already demonstrated trustworthiness and understand spotting techniques and commands

Size of Group: 8 to 12 participants per facilitator

Props: None

Objectives

Activity Goals: Enhance trust within the group, explore the concept of letting go

Main FVC Connections: Be Here, Be Safe

Keys to Success Connections: Emotional awareness, behavioral control, establishing positive relationships

Facilitator Guidelines

Introduction/Metaphor

I generally use this activity as the third, culminating activity in a series (Trust Leans and Wind in the Willows preceding it) and therefore don't generally provide any metaphorical introductions. There are, however, opportunities to introduce the activity by connecting it to trust, support and "letting go."

The Action

Have your participants form a circle. Briefly discuss safe and appropriate touching. Ask for a volunteer to enter the middle of the circle and assume the falling position.

Have the rest of your participants gather around as Spotters and place their hands behind the Faller. Make sure that one participant is solely responsible for the Faller's head. (I offer Fallers the option of closing their eyes.)

Once the group is in place, the Faller can go through the command sequence and slowly fall backward into the waiting hands of the rest of the group.

The Spotters should place their hands along the Faller's back and backside of their legs. Spotters should allow the Faller to slowly fall backward while lifting the feet and legs until the Faller is lying down parallel to the ground, supported by the hands of the group-mates.

---

*This activity is written up in *Cowstails and Cobras II* (Rohnke, 1989).

Advanced groups can try the full-lift variation
of the Levitation activity.

The Spotters can gently rock the Faller back and forth for a few seconds before slowly lowering him or her to the ground.

All Spotters should remain in place until the Faller is flat on the ground.

Variation

Begin with the Faller laying flat on his or her back. Emphasize to the Spotters that lifting with the knees, and not the back, is important. Have the group reach under and lift the Faller from the ground—first to knee level, then waist level and, if the group is very strong and trustworthy, to chest level.

Debriefing

Question for When the Focus Is on Emotional Awareness

- How did this feel compared with the Trust Leans and Wind in the Willows activities?

Questions for When the Focus Is on Behavioral Control

- What did you do as the Faller to ensure your safety as well as the safety of others?
- What did you do as the Spotter to ensure your safety as well as the safety of others?

Questions for When the Focus Is on Positive Relationships

- Was it easy for you to trust the group? Why or why not?

Eyes, Mouth, Body

This activity combines elements of the trust activities with the challenges posed by higher-level initiatives. It is a great challenge for high-functioning groups.

Target Group: Teenage and older participants who are fairly highly functioning

Size of Group: 4 to 40 people, possibly more

Props: Bandanna and an item to find; other props will vary based on the version of the activity you present

Objectives

Activity Goals: Develop group communication and trust, group problem solving, explore the concept of role diversification, practice inhibiting impulses

Main FVC Connections: Be Safe, Speak Your Truth, Hear the Truth

Keys to Success Connections: Emotional awareness, behavioral control, establishing positive relationships

Facilitator Guidelines

Introduction/Metaphor

There are several approaches I have used to introduce this initiative. You can focus on the sensory deprivation the activity calls for, communication, or trust. For sensory deprivation, you can begin by asking the group how life would be different if they lost their sense of sight or their ability to talk. Which would be worse?

If you focus on communication in your introduction, you can check in with group members as to how they typically communicate, drawing attention to the differences between verbal and nonverbal communication. After some discussion, follow up with questions about how deprivation of senses or abilities might compromise the way they give and receive information.

By the time you use this activity, the group should have a fairly high level of trust among members. Ask them if they trust other members with their personal safety. Do they trust themselves to keep others safe?

The Action

This initiative involves four roles: Eyes, Mouth, Body, and Bodyguard.

The Eyes can see but cannot move or talk. This role can be filled by one person, or by many people.

The Mouth can talk but cannot move or see (one person only).

The Body can move and talk as well as grab objects but cannot see (one person only).

The Bodyguard can see and move but cannot pick up objects or talk, unless safety is a concern (one person only). This job is solely to help maintain the safety of the Body.

Depending on the size of your group, you may have more than one team doing this activity. You need a minimum of four players per group or team—one for each role. If you have more, you can have multiple Eyes, but no other role can be filled by more than one person on a team.

The group will have a target item placed in a central playing area. If there is more than one team, one item per team will be placed in the playing area. You can arrange the teams however you would like: next to each other, opposite from each other, etc. The Eyes are facing the play area and can see where the item is placed but cannot say anything. The Mouth will not see where it is placed as this player is facing away from the play area and looking at the Eyes. So, the person in the Mouth role can only see those who are the Eyes. The Body is blindfolded. The Eyes will try to communicate nonverbally to the Mouth where the Body should go to retrieve their team's item. The Bodyguard will walk with the Body solely for safety reasons and should not help in any other way.

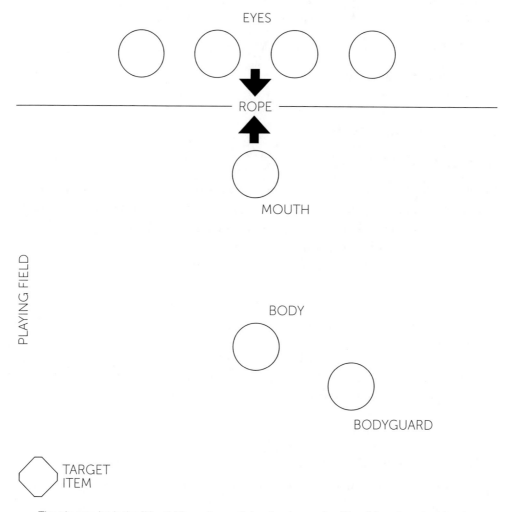

The player who is the "Mouth" faces the participants who are the "Eyes." Eyes face the Mouth.

There are several variations for this initiative that I use regularly. Each can also impact how you present the activity during the brief.

Variation 1

A stuffed animal or toss-able as the target item can represent a goal in their lives.

Variation 2

Using keyed locks, place a color-coordinated lock in one spot and its key in another. You can use multiple locks and keys if you have several teams but make sure that they are able to identify their lock and key by the color coding. This can represent what type of future they wish to "unlock" for themselves. Have the Body find both the lock and its key and unlock the lock.

Variation 3

A higher-level lock-and-key variation involves two teams working together. The Body from one team finds the key, and the Body from the other team finds the lock. They must then find each other and open the lock. This can metaphorically represent bringing two disparate groups together (i.e., gangs, racially divided groups, etc.).

Variation 4

This activity can be combined with Field of Distraction (p. 372). When teams are in the process of retrieving an item, other items can be in the play area, which if they accidentally come in contact with the Body, will send the players back to their starting position. These can be metaphorical distracters from goals or "bumps in the road" on the way to a future you hope to unlock!

Variation 5

Using a simple puzzle such as a toddler's three-piece shape puzzle, each team is assigned a shape to find. The puzzle can be placed in a location somewhere in the middle of the playing area. The Body from each team retrieves their assigned piece and places it in the puzzle. Metaphorically, this can represent cliques (e.g., the Squares, the Circles, the Triangles, etc.).

When there are multiple teams, communication issues increase as there are many voices yelling different directions. Spreading the initiative over a larger area further complicates communication. If members view the initiative as a competition, they will not be likely to help other groups. Occasionally, someone becomes aware that the groups can help each other. For example, if Team A's Body is closer to Team B's Mouth and Team B's Body is closer to Team A's Mouth, they can switch roles temporarily. If teams don't do this (and they typically won't), you can ask during the debriefing if people felt the activity was a competition. If they say that they didn't, why didn't they think to help each other?

Debriefing

This activity can trigger a range of emotions that may be difficult to handle and each role within the activity may trigger different feelings. I sometimes front-load the activity by noting that participants may experience emotions such as confusion, fear, and frustration.

Questions for When the Focus Is on Emotional Awareness

- How did it feel to be the Eyes?
- How did it feel to be the Mouth?
- How did it feel to be the Body?
- How did it feel to be the Bodyguard?

Questions for When the Focus Is on Behavioral Control

- What did each of you do to work around the limitations placed on your role? Do you place limitations on yourself? How do you push past your perceived limitations?

Questions for When the Focus Is on Positive Relationships

- When you couldn't see, did you trust that those responsible for you would keep you safe? Why? What behaviors did they demonstrate that made you feel safe?
- As the Eyes, how did you communicate what you saw? What were the challenges? How did you overcome them?
- As the Mouth, how did you understand the Eyes? How did you respond when you didn't understand? What did the Eyes do that helped you understand and what did they do that didn't help?

I Got You

I learned the original version of this fun but intense trust activity from my friend and colleague Frankie Piela.

Target Group: Middle school age and older

Size of Group: 10 to 30 participants

Props: None

Objectives

Activity Goals: Building trust and support within the group, taking initiative, and helping others

Main FVC Connections: Be Safe, Speak Your Truth, Hear the Truth

Keys to Success Connections: Emotional awareness, behavioral control, establishing positive relationships

Facilitator Guidelines

Introduction/Metaphor

"When we are stumbling in life, it's always good to know someone is there to catch us. Who catches you when you stumble? Whom do you catch?"

The Action

Have your group gather in a fairly large circle (so that if they reach out their hands, fingertips would touch). Ask for a volunteer (or volunteer yourself) to stand in the middle of the circle.

When the volunteer is ready, that person will say aloud, "Do you have me?" The group will respond, "We got you!"

At this point, the person in the center closes his or her eyes, folds both arms and puts them out in a do-si-do position and begins running in any direction.

It will quickly become apparent to one or more folks in the circle that the person is running toward them. As the runner draws closer, one person will step in toward the runner with her arms in do-si-do position and say loudly, "I got you!" The person from the circle must make sure that she hooks one arm to the arm of the runner, spins the runner around, and sends the runner back into the center where he or she runs in a new direction toward another member of the circle. A new person will step in and do the same.

I generally allow people in the center to determine how many connections to make and ask them to stop running and open their eyes when ready. Make sure you have time to give everyone in the group a chance to run.

Debriefing

Questions for When the Focus Is on Emotional Awareness

- What was it like to run with your eyes closed? Do you ever feel like you are moving forward in your life so blindly?

- What was it like to be in such a position and hear that someone was going to keep you safe?

Questions for When the Focus Is on Behavioral Control

- What did you do to keep yourself safe when you were the runner?

- What did you do as a player in the circle to make sure the person in the middle was safe? Were there times when you weren't sure you should step forward? Are there times when you are not sure it's your place to reach out and offer help?

Questions for When the Focus Is on Positive Relationships

- How did it feel to know that someone was going to help you when you needed it? Who is there to help you in your life?

- How did it feel to reach out and help someone who needed it? Who can rely on you in your life?

Yurt Circle*

I often use this activity as a closing to demonstrate how the group has developed and grown.

Target Group: Middle school age and older

Size of Group: 6 to 20 participants

Props: Raccoon circles, climbing rope or a rope rated to hold several thousand pounds. The rope should be tied in a secure knot that tightens when pressure is applied.

Objectives

Activity Goals: Recognize the growth of the group toward a solid, supportive unit; enhance trust

Main FVC Connections: Be Safe, Speak Your Truth, Hear the Truth

Keys to Success Connections: Emotional awareness, behavioral control, establishing positive relationships

Facilitator Guidelines

Introduction/Metaphor

I like to introduce the activity by discussing the properties of a yurt: "Yurts are round structures initially used as portable shelters by nomadic peoples of central Asia. While very lightweight and constructed of basic materials, the circular shape of the yurt gives it amazing strength. Like the yurt, our group circle has become an amazing source of strength."

The Action

Lay out the knotted rope on the ground as a circle. Ask your group to stand around the outside of the circle.

Discuss the amazing yurt as described above.

Ask the group members to hold the rope in their hands without pulling it. What does it feel like? Usually, people will state that it feels limp, flexible, or loose. Discuss how this relates to the group at the onset of the adventure they are completing.

Ask that everyone hold the rope with both hands. On your count, participants should slowly lean back while maintaining their grip on the rope. Ask that no one make any sudden movements and that they try to find their balance point.

Once everyone is leaning back and being supported by the rope, ask the group to describe how the rope feels. Often I hear that it now feels stiff or solid. What gave the rope

---

*This classic trust activity appears in *Cowstails and Cobras II* (Rohnke, 1989). Rohnke's version does not use the rope or raccoon circle.

its solid properties? The group of course. Metaphorically speaking, a group of loose, flexible people came together and created something solid that can support everyone.

When the group is ready, have everyone slowly come back to a standing position, allowing the rope to become limp again.

Variation 1

On your count, have the group slowly lean back into sitting position. You can also have them go from sitting to standing.

Variation 2

Do any of the above versions with eyes closed.

Debriefing

As stated above, I often use this as a closing activity for the day or time the group is together. In this way, the activity is often used as a debriefing. Much of the debriefing occurs during the activity.

Question for When the Focus Is on Emotional Awareness

- How does it feel to be supported by others?

Question for When the Focus Is on Behavioral Control

- What behaviors have we shown that allowed us to do this activity?

Questions for When the Focus Is on Positive Relationships

- In this activity, we took a rope that felt limp and loose and made it something that felt very strong and solid. How does this represent our group? How did our interactions with each other lead us to the point where we trusted each other enough to get to this place?

APPENDIX

A

Tips for Working with Emotionally or Behaviorally Challenged Kids and Teens

Most of my group work is with teens who have significant emotional and behavioral challenges. Because of their issues, these kids pose challenges to facilitators. They often have more difficulties focusing, demonstrate inappropriate boundaries, and can often behave in ways that violate the tenets of the FVC. Over the years, I have found some tools and tactics that have helped me work with these challenging participants. Below you'll find some advice that may help you.

Focusing Attention

When beginning a group with kids who have difficulties with self-control, it's usually best to start in a smaller space. This type of group often has difficulties containing themselves in more open spaces.

- When working with kids who struggle to remain focused, a highly entertaining first activity will often do the trick to get them to buy in, such as Listen Up, Gotcha, or Trigger Finger. It's also important to avoid down time. Keep the group moving, flowing from activity to activity. Especially early on, it may be best to keep debriefing to a minimum.

- "If you can hear me, clap once." I will say this along with clapping once when I need the attention of an off-task group of any size. Usually, a few people will hear me and clap once. I then say, "If you can hear me, clap twice." By that point, I usually have approximately half the group clapping twice. Continue this way until you have the entire group's attention. I rarely need to go more than three or four claps, but I sometimes do just to keep them focused and even entertained for a few more seconds.

- Other methods of getting the attention of the group include holding your hand up in a traditional, two-fingered peace sign and asking that when folks see it, they should follow suit. A colleague of mine uses a musical triangle that has a nice, mellow ring to it. A call-and-response system works well. For mine, I say "Hey!" and the group responds with "Yo!"

- If you have ever tried to get a group of highly distractible kids or teens to "circle up," try this: lay out gym spots in a circle before the group arrives. When the kids arrive, I simply ask them to stand on any spot. If you have numbered spots or colored

405

spots, you'll see them going to specific numbers or colors. This can be an interesting jumping off point for getting to know each other. For example, have them look at the number or color on the spot and when they go around say their name, add something interesting about themselves that relates to that color or number. Another benefit to using numbered spots is that you will know exactly how many participants you have without counting if you put the numbers out in order. For example, I place the numbers 1 through 20 in a circle and when my group arrives, two spots are empty. I know I have 18 members without even counting!

Encouraging New and Positive Behavior

- "In a moment but not yet, I'm going to ask you to…" This phrase works really well for all groups but is especially useful when you are giving instructions to groups of kids who are impulsive. It prevents them from doing what you are instructing them to do right at the moment you are saying it. (Thanks to Tom Leahy from Leahy and Associates for this one).

- After name games, ask for a volunteer to name each person in the group. Not only does this request promote stepping out of one's comfort zone but it's fun and helps reinforce the names for the rest of the group.

- "Pair and share." Many of your clients may feel too intimidated to speak in front of a group of people. You can always pair participants up to debrief with each other and ask for volunteers to share out to the group about the discussion they had with partners.

- Use props to help them express themselves. For example, having participants choose a stuffed animal that represents how they feel or how they cope with depression, anger, etc. Often, explaining their thoughts through the prop is easier. Chiji Cards, facial expression cards, or word cards like those in the appendices of this book or other pictures or picture cards also work well.

Keeping the Session On Track

- Over-plan! Make sure you have various activities that you can use and be ready to shift away from your original plan if the group's needs dictate it. It helps to have a lot of no-prop or minimal prop activities memorized for use at any moment. It helps me to have a typed list of the activities I use with any frequency, broken down by category. If I don't have my list, I often forget what I know!

- Don't ignore inappropriate behaviors, especially early in a group's time together. The tone set at the onset of a group will be difficult to change later on. Make it crystal clear that you are not going to accept violations of the FVC. If you don't, your group may not progress very far.

- Co-facilitate whenever possible. Your partner will see what you miss and vice versa. Co-facilitation also allows you to create a better flow. For example, while one partner is wrapping up an activity, the other can be setting up the next one. Also, when there are issues in the group, one partner can deal with the issue while the other continues working with the group.

- "Peace Out!" When I have processed through a significant issue with a group, and it seems that all that needs to be said has been said, I will ask everyone to circle up (if they aren't already in a circle) and put the two-finger, peace sign into the middle of the circle. I will then ask if there is anything left to say about the topic. Once everyone who feels the need says their last words (or everyone agrees that all has been said), we do a three count and say "Peace Out!" while pulling our peace signs out of the circle. This officially closes the topic and indicates that it's time to "let go and move on" (Thanks to Project Adventure Staff for this one).

Working with Anger Management Groups

As the *Keys to Success* philosophy maintains, the basic ingredients for successful relationships are emotional awareness and an ability to control one's behaviors in response to one's emotions. When people who struggle with these skills must work with others to accomplish a common goal, as they do in adventured-based counseling groups, problem behaviors are likely to surface. This can have its benefits. When using traditional individual or group counseling methods, rarely do I witness the anger-related behaviors I am trying to help my client control. I find I'm dealing with a "second hand" or vaguely defined problem. Many of these clients have participated in traditional groups that utilize a highly structured curriculum that focuses on specific behavioral skills. When I speak to these clients about anger management, quite often they know many anger management techniques and know what they should do when they are angry, but this awareness doesn't always translate into actual behavior change. In traditional counseling settings, it is very easy for clients to avoid dealing with their anger issues (or even deny their existence).

The interactions and relationships among group members is a central component of experiential group work. Conflict and emotional problems can surface. This can be intimidating to counselors whose first reaction may be to redirect the group away from the conflict. This reaction is rarely beneficial. My first experience with adventure-based counseling at Project Adventure taught me that conflict is a natural and necessary part of group development and when handled well by a facilitator, can be an unparalleled catalyst for personal and group growth. Experiential activities expose emotional and behavioral control issues within a controlled environment and provide an opportunity for skilled facilitators to guide group members towards personal growth.

Of course, there are potential pitfalls in facilitating experiential groups with those who have anger-management problems. Tempers can flare very quickly, and there is an increased risk of serious safety violations. However, there are steps facilitators can take to minimize the potential for these violations to arise. Facilitators of these groups must make careful preparations to ensure that the group experience stays safe and positive.

Interview Participants

If you have the luxury, I recommend interviewing each member individually before the start of any experiential group, but particularly before anger management groups. Interviewing participants allows you to informally assess the person's basic anger management abilities and get an idea of the potential for anger-related behaviors. Do they have an understanding of anger cycles? Can they tell you some techniques they are trying to use to cope with anger? Most importantly, are they dedicated to working on improving their anger management abilities?

Set Expectations

During the interview, you should be very clear about what behavior you expect with an emphasis on the safety of all participants. If potential members cannot verbalize their agreement with basic safety and behavioral expectations, they are not ready for this type of group.

Determine Consequences and Notify Potential Group Members of Them

During the interview, notify potential group members of what will happen if there are serious safety violations during the group. Will they be kicked out of the group? Will they be referred to their administrator or probation officer? These consequences are up to you to determine based on your particular situation. Whatever you decide, be clear about what consequences are for specific behaviors before the group starts and be ready to follow through if someone violates the safety agreements.

Consider Co-Facilitation

If possible, don't facilitate an experiential anger-management group alone. If you feel that you need a second facilitator to keep it safe, make sure that happens. You must also make sure that external supports are in place. For example, if you are working in a school environment, do you have an administrative team that will back you up if you are in a crisis or need to remove a member of the group? If you are in a hospital setting, is there a protocol for handling physical aggression in a group?

At the onset of an anger management group, the facilitator will likely need to be more authoritative than with other types of experiential groups. Safety violations cannot be ignored and must be addressed immediately and directly by the facilitator. By doing this, a facilitator communicates the message that ultimately, the facilitator is in charge and will be looking out for safety of each member. If you have the luxury of handpicking your group, it's often beneficial to include members in the group who are more advanced in their anger management abilities, particularly if they possess basic leadership skills.

If a safe environment is created, the facilitator can look forward to using the clients' frustration and conflict as an opportunity to help members move forward in their development. Through the briefs and debriefs, facilitators can help members draw connections between their emotions and behaviors as well as between their behaviors and relationships with others. They will begin to understand how their anger impacts those around them through the immediate feedback they receive from peers and the facilitator during group time.

The following is a sample of an eight-session sequence of activities that you can use when facilitating an anger management group.

Sample Plan for an Eight-Session Anger Management Group

Session 1

Goals

- Learn names
- Begin to develop FVC
- Begin to explore anger as it relates to the group members. This connects to Key to Success 1. Emotional Awareness.

Activities

Step 1. Basic introduction. Offer an overview of the next eight sessions. Emphasize to group members that this group is not only about learning anger management skills but it's also about using these skills. Not only will group members learn about emotional coping, behavioral management, and relationships, they will also be using the group to practice these skills. They will actually have to cope with difficult emotions and deal with controlling their own behavior and responses to others' behaviors. Finally, as part of this group, they will be developing positive, trusting relationships. Remind group members what they have already agreed to in the interviews as far as expectations for behavior and participation.

Step 2. Brief the activity Name Whip (p. 86) and follow-up name games (See Chapter 9).

Step 3. Have group members partner up to discuss what behaviors they hope to diminish or eliminate as well as the behaviors they hope to increase and why. For example, one may want to eliminate "swearing at parents" when angry and increase "leaving the situation."

Step 3. Debriefing. Regroup and create a list based on what each pair reports. This list will become the basis of the FVC in that the behaviors members seek to increase will be kept "inside" the group and those they are hoping to decrease will be kept "outside" the group.

Step 4. Assign homework. Discuss using a 1 to 10 scale to summarize levels of anger. For example, a 1 would be totally calm and happy. A 10 would be completely irate and possibly out of control. Ask members to write down the number of the highest level of anger they experience each day until the next session. This will be their anger management journal. This homework assignment helps members begin to be aware of how often they become angry as well as to what level of intensity their anger escalates on a regular basis.

Session 2

Goals

- Complete FVC

- Develop increased trust and connection with group members
- Understand the connection between anger, behavior, and relationships with others.

Activities

Step 1. Introduce and facilitate the activity Listen Up (p. 59). Debrief the activity by discussing the importance of focusing during the group in order to get the most out of the experience. How difficult is it to listen when you are angry? Do people listen to you when you are angry?

Step 2. Introduce and facilitate the activity Anger Line Up. Use the basic rules for Line Up By Number 1.0 (p. 65). Have group members stand in a line from 1 to 10, each number delineating the level of anger they experienced for each day since the last group. (One represents the lowest level to 10 the highest.) Create lineups for each day they've kept their journals, taking note of those who are at the extremes each day or are repeatedly at the higher end. Discuss what events occurred to trigger the anger they experienced and ask group members to provide feedback to each other about their observations during this activity.

Step 3. Review and refine the list from Session One of behaviors to increase in group members' lives and those to eliminate.

Step 4. Introduce and facilitate the activity The Body (p. 73). Create The Body using the list of behaviors you have created. This will serve as the group's FVC.

Step 5. Assign homework. Ask members to take a copy of the FVC (as created in The Body activity) home with them. Ask them to use their anger management journals to document their angry emotions and behaviors during the time between group sessions. Indicate that members should try to use the principles of the FVC to react behaviorally to their anger in more productive ways. This assignment focuses on anger awareness and begins to draw the connection between how the emotion drives behaviors.

Session 3

Goals

- Enhance emotional vocabulary and understanding of anger
- Begin to challenge frustration-tolerance levels
- Further understand how one's anger, behavior, and relationships connect
- Increase trust and bonding with the group

Activities

Step 1. Introduce and facilitate Transformer Tag (p. 115). Briefing: Using the anger management journals, check in with the group members about the predominant way that they dealt with their anger during the past week. Ask them to summarize their week by choosing one of the three signs for Transformer Tag: heads, butts, or guts.

Step 2. Introduce and facilitate Line Up by Number. From the Emotions List (p. 465, Appendix G), write each emotion under the Anger category on a separate index card. Give each member one card. Using the cards, have group members line up in order from least intense to most intense emotion. The entire group must be in agreement. You can shuffle and try it again as there will be more cards than participants. You can also play a game of having group members do a group shuffle and get back in the same order of cards as the previous round.

Step 3. Introduce and facilitate Traffic Jam (p. 309). Using the order members finish in during Line Up by Number, have them each stand on a step as instructed in the activity Traffic Jam. One possible introduction for this during an anger management group might be, "When we are angry, sometimes we get all jammed up; we can't think right, we can't talk right and we don't act in ways we should. We get stuck in bad situations. When this happens, what are some skills that you can use to help you get unjammed?"

Debrief Traffic Jam with particular attention to what techniques they used to get themselves out of the "jam" they were in. Question the members as to the level of frustration they were feeling (reflecting back to the words used during Line Up by Number) and how they dealt with it during the activity. As the facilitator, help them make the connection between what happened during the activity and their daily lives.

Step 4. Assign homework. Keep the anger management journal as stated in the second session. This time, they should include any anger triggers they notice. Have each member set a specific behavioral goal for the week that relates to a behavior they are trying to increase or decrease. For example, "I will not swear at my parents. If I do, I will do a 'random act of kindness' for them afterwards."

Session 4

Goals

- Continue developing trust and bonding within the group
- Increase frustration tolerance when facing challenges
- Develop empathy for others

Activities

Step 1. Introduce and facilitate Concentric Circles (p. 210), Variation 1. Have each pair choose an incident from their journals to discuss. In the first pairing, have each group member relate to the person he or she is facing what happened during the incident chosen. Paired group members should include the trigger and how they responded. For the second pairing, have members talk about how the incident impacted other people in their lives. For the third pairing, have members of the pairs recap the incident, their reactions, and the impact on others. Have each member offer feedback as to how to better handle similar situations in the future.

Step 2. Introduce and facilitate Hi Lo Yo (p. 155). This activity sets the stage to increase group members' empathy as they focus on applauding peers as they make mistakes. Afterwards discuss how it felt to be applauded for mistakes. Are mistakes good or bad? Can they be useful? Question the group about times that they came down on others for messing up. What about times when others came down on them for messing up? What was the impact? What would have been different if they had supported that person instead or if they had been supported by others when making mistakes? Discuss how this relates to empathy and how this is an important component of developing relationships as well as controlling anger.

Step 3. Introduce and facilitate Cross the Great Divide (p. 356). A possible introduction for this activity for an anger management group might be,

> In front of you lies the Valley of Rage. It's a very dangerous place. If you step into it, you will plummet to the bottom and have to crawl your way out to the place you began. You goal is to have the entire group cross this valley safely. While navigating the Valley of Rage sometimes may be a solo venture, today you will have each other as resources and supports. Use the empathy you discovered in the last activity to help you. Another resource you have is yourself! You have skills! What is one way that you try to deal with rage that works?

As each member responds to the question, hand them a step. During the debriefing, find out if members used the anger management skills they noted at the beginning of the activity. How did the group deal with frustration and obstacles to their success? How can they apply the skills they used during the activity to their lives? Did they reach out to support others? Does supporting others help us to better handle our own difficulties and reach our own goals?

Step 4. Assign homework. Emphasize once again that the members will be expected to use the FVC in their personal lives. They will be expected to use the skills they demonstrated during the session's activities to meet the FVC. In addition to keeping their journals, members should write about three instances during the week in which they were able to empathize with another person's feelings.

Session 5

Goals

- Continue to enhance trust and bonding
- Continue to increase the challenge to participants' frustration tolerance
- Begin developing improved communication skills to effectively resolve conflicts

Activities

Step 1. Dump out a bag of stuffed animals. Ask members to each pick one stuffed animal that represents how they fared for the last week in their attempts to control their anger and live the FVC outside of the group. Have each member share his or her experience.

Step 2. Introduce and facilitate Group Juggle 2 (p. 89). Based on their performance of the past week, ask members to each state one skill that they will be working to improve during the session and week ahead. Their stuffed animals should represent that skill for

Group Juggle 2. During the debriefing, check to see if members used that skill during the activity. Debrief the communication skills the group needed to successfully complete this activity. What communication skills are needed to effectively negotiate a peaceful resolution to a conflict?

Step 3. Introduce and facilitate the activity Take a Stand (p. 200). This is a great activity to help your group learn how to disagree verbally without becoming abusive. It begins to teach negotiation skills that teens will need to resolve conflicts.

Step 4. Debriefing. After the activity, have group members share instances from the past week of times when they empathized with the emotions of another person. What impact could empathy have on negotiating peaceful resolutions to conflicts? If you empathize with someone, how would it impact the way you communicate with that person when upset? Are there skills from the activities used in this session that would help?

Step 5. Assign homework. In addition to maintaining the anger management journal, group members should focus on the physiological aspects of anger. What do they notice happens to their own bodies when they get angry? What are the first signs of serious anger they can tune into? They should write a summary of their observations prior to the next group session. Additionally, ask members to tune into nonverbal cues about people's moods, such as body language and facial expressions. What do they notice about the nonverbal communication of the people close to them? They should also summarize this for at least one person in their lives.

Session 6

Goals

- Continue enhancing bonding and trust within the group
- Enhance awareness of verbal and nonverbal communication of emotions
- Enhance verbal communication skills

Activities

Step 1. Introduce and facilitate the activity Culture Shock (p. 295). This activity highlights the fact that communication is a two-way street and not everyone communicates in the same way. For example, teens and parents may communicate differently. What nonverbal cues were people sending? Did they override the verbal? When you are angry, does your nonverbal communication match your verbal communication? When they don't match, what is the impact? You can also ask about what factors contribute to how we learned to communicate as children. How can we best work with others who communicate differently? What role does empathy play in this process?

Step 2. Introduce and facilitate Transmitter and Receptor (p. 283). Taking what was learned from the debriefing in the first activity, participants should focus on effective verbal communication skills. This activity eliminates the nonverbal aspect.

Step 3. Conduct the debriefing. How did the session's activities fit in with what they recorded from last week's assignment about physiological aspects of anger and verbal versus nonverbal communication of emotions?

Step 4. Assign homework. In addition to keeping the anger management journal, members should write a paragraph about trust. Who do they trust? How can trusting relationships help foster their goals of coping better with anger and conflict? Also, have members write down three things about themselves or their lives that others in the group would not yet know. Challenge them to make these things others would be surprised to know. Along with these three statements, they should create one lie. They should *not* tell anyone what these are.

Session 7

Goals

- Focus on using previously learned skills from weeks one through six
- Deepen the trust within the group
- Increase the challenge to members' frustration tolerance levels
- Move members towards demonstrating improved skills

Activities

Step 1. Introduce and facilitate Three Truths and a Lie (p. 229). Using the truths and lies they wrote as part of their homework, group members take a risk in trusting others with their personal information.

Step 2. Introduce and facilitate Eyes Mouth Body (p. 397). This activity ups the ante in terms of trust and pushes the group to use the communication and frustration-tolerance skills they have been working on. During the debriefing, focus on how well they did this.

Step 3. Introduce and facilitate Helium Hoop (p. 326). Often, even in high-functioning groups, blame comes quickly during this activity. Debrief on how extremely difficult situations can undermine all they have learned and worked towards. What situations in their lives might undermine all they have accomplished in the group?

Step 4. Lead debriefing discussion. Review the anger management journal including the information about trusting relationships. Tie this in with the activities of the session and how the Helium Hoop impacted the group.

Step 5. Assign homework. In addition to keeping their anger management journals, members should determine what roadblocks, present and future, could undermine their paths to successfully coping with their anger.

Session 8

Goals

- Deepen the trust level in the group

- Review learned skills and progress during the group and how this will impact their lives moving forward
- Celebrate success and bring closure to the group

Activities

Step 1. Review the journals from the past week with particular emphasis on the potential roadblocks to group members' success. This will lead into the activities:

Step 2. Introduce and facilitate Field of Distraction (p. 372). This activity will significantly test group members' communication skills, ability to trust one another, and ability to support another person towards meeting a common goal while overcoming roadblocks.

Step 3. Introduce and facilitate Trust Leans/ Wind in the Willows/Levitation (pp. 390–396). The group members will metaphorically rise above their problems with the support of those around them. During the debriefing, ask if this activity would have been possible to carry out in the first session. What allowed the group to do it successfully during the last session? What does this say about where they started and where they are ending? What skills have they improved and what still needs work? Who will be their support system in their continuous growth once the group ends?

Step 4. Introduce and facilitate Bracelet Share. Close out with this activity that uses pipe cleaners and colored beads (purchased in bulk from an arts and crafts store). Give each person a pipe cleaner and only as many beads as there are people in the group. Each group member should give each of the other members a bead. With the bead should go a wish or affirmation based on what the person learned about the recipient during the group. The pipe cleaners can be closed into a bracelet or simple decoration for each member to take home.

APPENDIX

Working with Depression Support Groups

There are many challenges and rewards in using experiential counseling to work with depressed teens and young adults. With adolescents, particularly boys, depression may be expressed as irritability, characterized by outwardly negative behaviors. To complicate the issue further, several types of depression may stem from a wide range of etiologies. In short, your depression support group may have a great deal of variation within it. At first, it may seem that the common symptoms of depression (listed below) would work against the methods of experiential groups. In fact, the activities of experiential counseling can provide some of the emotional intelligence and interpersonal skills this population of teens may need.

Depressed individuals may experience

Low energy levels

A lack of motivation

Sense of hopelessness and pessimism

Poor self-confidence

Low self-esteem

Feelings of loneliness

A preference for being alone

Difficulties focusing

Difficulties trusting others

Aversion to physical touch

Experiential group work may, in fact, be of benefit to depressed individuals and help these participants manage or lessen some of the symptoms mentioned.

- Experiential activities increase the likelihood that members will remain focused and participate. The activities are multimodal and may invite more personal engagement than more traditional therapeutic techniques that are based only on talking.

- Experiential activities often raise energy and motivation levels. Early activities are aimed at creating an energetic and fun atmosphere.

- When facilitated well, experiential groups have the ability to be therapeutic in the areas of trusting others, allowing for safe physical touch, and enhancing both self-con-

419

fidence and self-esteem. The group may be *the one place* where group members can receive nonjudgmental support from others who share a similar emotional experience.

- The main goal of the *Keys to Success* is to increase emotional intelligence. According to Daniel Goleman (1994), depression and other psychological problems are often intertwined with deficits in emotional intelligence. This position has been supported by recent research. In a study conducted by a team of psychiatrists from Swinburne University of Technology, people who scored low on tests of emotional intelligence were found to be at a higher risk of developing clinical depression (Downey, Johnston, Hansen, Schembri, Stough, Tuckwell, and Schweitzer, 2008). Another study indicated that higher emotional intelligence may help protect at-risk individuals from developing depression by promoting healthier interpersonal relationships (Amitay and Mongrain, 2007).

Several ingredients of experiential counseling help depression-support group members enhance emotional intelligence, which, in turn, helps set the stage for therapeutic change

The Full Value Commitment

The tenets of the FVC provide an environment where safety, acceptance, and acknowledgment in being heard are the expectation and norm. For individuals with depression who often feel emotionally vulnerable, this is incredibly important. Strict adherence to the FVC sets the stage for positive therapeutic change and personal growth.

The Challenge by Choice Philosophy

In experiential counseling, the facilitator invites group members to stretch their personal limits by participating in activities. Each group member has the final determination as to how they will participate and what challenges they will accept. Often times, your participants may feel a sense of powerlessness in controlling their own destiny or coping with the demands of their environments. Choosing one's own level of challenge can be both empowering and therapeutic, boosting confidence and esteem.

Facilitators running experiential-counseling activities for depression support groups should pay attention to particular elements of the program. They will also find a sample eight-session support-group plan in the following pages.

Activity Sequencing

While it is very important for a facilitator to carefully sequence activities for any group, this is particularly true when working with depressed or otherwise emotionally compromised individuals. Low levels of confidence and trust may make movement through the activity sequence quite slow. Facilitators need to tune into the needs of the group and be ready to modify activities or change direction at any time, being careful not to push too quickly through the sequence of activities.

Strong Debriefings

In my experience, once individuals with depression feel comfortable in the group, they often enjoy going deeper into the debriefing. Keep in mind that, in this case, the actual experiential activities serve as the vehicle to access the deeper emotions that group members experience. The debriefing can easily be considered the most important part of the Adventure Wave for this type of group. Drawing the connections between what has occurred during the group with their lives outside the group are the keys to success.

Sample Plan for Eight-Session Depression Support Group (Ten Members)

Session 1

Goals

- Introduce the group with eight-week overview of the sessions
- Get to know names of group members
- Have group members get to know one another
- Introduce the FVC and Challenge by Choice concept

Activities

Step 1. Provide introduction and overview. Offer an overview of what group members can expect during their eight weekly sessions. Emphasize that the group is not simply a place where members will learn skills to cope with depression. The group experience is about building up "depression defense systems" through creating real, trusting relationships with the facilitators and peers, sharing meaningful experiences, and transferring the benefits of these in-group experiences to life outside the group. The support systems created within the group can continue when the group is over.

Step 2. Introduce and facilitate Elevator Air (p. 172). This activity highlights the beneficial influence of a positive attitude on the "feel" of the group.

Step 3. Introduce and facilitate Name Gesture Replay (p. 100). Group members get to learn a little bit about each other while learning each other's names.

Step 4. Introduce and facilitate Learning Style FVC (p. 69). Discuss the importance of the FVC and let the group know that you will periodically review how well the group is meeting this commitment. Discuss Challenge by Choice.

Step 5. Introduce and facilitate Group Handshake (p. 53). This activity, which will continue throughout the eight weeks, helps the group begin to create an identity and foster the personal connections that will be so important for the members.

Step 6. Introduce and facilitate Seeds of Change (p. 55). What aspects of their lives would group members like to see change during the course of the group? What do they need to do to "grow" in their Depression Defense System?

Step 7. Assign homework. Group members should begin depression-tracking journals. A simple journal may involve rating their depression on a 1-to-10 scale at different points during the day. A more in-depth journal may consist of writing about their feelings on a daily basis.

Session 2

Goals

- Increase emotional awareness
- Help group members get to know each other on a deeper level
- Enhance trust within the group
- Have group members begin to show support for each other

Activities

Step 1. Introduce and facilitate Whamp 'Em (p. 98), a fun way to refresh participants' memories of group members' names.

Step 2. Introduce and facilitate Full Value Towel Toss (p. 264). This is a simple transition from Whamp 'Em to reviewing the FVC. It's also a nice transition to the upcoming review and discussion.

Step 3. Review and discuss. Have the group add one step to the Group Handshake and practice with each other. Check in on the newly planted seeds. Check in on the journals. Ask if anyone would like to share what he or she had written.

Step 4. Introduce and facilitate Comfort Zone (p. 218). This is an excellent opportunity as a facilitator to help participants expand their emotional vocabulary through framing or reframing their experiences in new terms. This activity will also help group members begin to understand each other's personal limits and preferences as well as develop trust.

Step 5. Introduce and facilitate Human Treasure Hunt (p. 223). For this activity, use a sheet created specifically for this type of group with statements about experiences, particularly ones that are connected to strong emotions that may be common to those suffering from depression. For example, "Find someone who has felt lonely in the past month." Discuss the activity as a group afterwards. For groups this size, you may have to modify the requirement that each person's name appear only once on a sheet.

Step 6. Assign homework. Have the group members continue writing in the depression-tracking journal.

Session 3

Goals

- Help group members begin connecting their emotions with behaviors (past and present)
- Increase trust and unity within the group to foster support

Activities

Step 1. Introduce and facilitate Transformer Tag (p. 115). Use this activity to help participants begin connecting how they have reacted behaviorally to difficult emotional times in their lives. For example, ask them to think about a time they felt "confused and lost." Did they react by "stopping," which can be shown by a hand up, palm out (like you might do if you were singing "Stop in the Name of Love")? Did they "run"? This can be shown by swinging a bent arm back and forth as if running. Or did they "seek more information," which they can demonstrate by pointing to their head. After the first round, change the emotion (and the signs if you wish). Debrief about these experiences between rounds.

Step 2. Facilitate discussion. Review the depression journal. How well are participants able to accurately assess their own emotions? Discuss how the plants are progressing, drawing parallels to their own progress so far.

Step 3. Facilitate Group Handshake (p. 53). Based on the discussion, have the group add the next piece to the handshake. Have them create a step that parallels where they think the group is in terms of the support system they've created so far. Debrief this, paying attention to where the group still needs to improve as well as where participants need to improve as individuals. Write this information on pieces of masking tape.

Step 4. Introduce and facilitate Turn Over a New Leaf (p. 305). Place on the tarp the masking tape that the group wrote on during the debriefing of Group Handshake. Lay the tarp on the ground so that the words are on the underside of the tarp. The group must come together in support of each other in order to be successful in this activity. Debrief with and place emphasis on mutual trust and support.

Step 5. Assign homework. Continue the depression-tracking journal. Have members identify and write about people they consider their support system outside the group. What behaviors do these people show to support them? What is lacking in their support systems in terms of people or behaviors that are missing?

Session 4

Goals

- Help members begin creating more adaptive behaviors when experiencing difficult emotions
- Increase trust and support amongst the group members

Activities

Step 1. Introduce and facilitate Clap-Stomp-Snap! (p. 153). Introduce this activity by briefly discussing times when group members have had to change their behavior. When did their actions cause them more problems than they solved? Debrief by discussing how difficult it was to change behaviors during the activity and relate this to their real lives.

Step 2. Introduce and facilitate Unity Tag 'n' Jelly Roll (p. 110). After this activity, debrief by describing how the activity connects to emotional support from others.

Step 3. Introduce and facilitate Don't Break the Ice (p. 337). This activity nicely ties in both of the session's goals. Each round, members must approach a similar problem differently. Additionally, they must "lean" on each other for support.

Step 4. Lead discussion. Discuss the homework and relate it to the support given and received during the session's activities. Check in with the progress of the plants. Add a step to the handshake that sums up what group members have learned during the session.

Step 5. Assign homework. Continue the depression-tracking journal. Have members identify behaviors that they can change and actions they can take to enhance their support system. This may include what they need to say to others who are already part of the system.

Session 5

Goals

- Help group members identify adaptive behaviors that work for them
- Increase assertiveness and communication skills
- Increase trust and support within the group

Activities

Step 1. Introduce and facilitate Evolution (p. 167). Create signs that align with the idea of changing maladaptive behaviors to adaptive ones. A good idea might be to read "The Egg, the Carrot, and the Coffee Bean" (p. 446). Create signs for these three: the egg being the lowest, followed by the carrot, and finally the coffee bean. All three represent different ways of dealing with difficult issues.

Step 2. Introduce and facilitate Transmitter and Receiver (p. 283). For the first round, don't allow the drawers to speak. For the second round, remove this limitation. How was the experience different? In the second, you were allowed to ask for help and get clarification. How does this help in real life? Why don't we do that more often?

Step 3. Lead discussion and review homework. How did members work to enhance their support systems? Check on the plants and have the group add a step to the group handshake that embodies the assertiveness needed to ask for help.

Step 4. Introduce and facilitate Sherpa Walk (p. 376). This activity creates a situation in which one participant is totally reliant on the other. It also puts the second person in a position of control where they must make decisions that impact other people. During the debriefing, be sure to include how it felt to be in each position and what leadership characteristics were shown during the activity.

Step 5. Assign homework. Continue the depression-tracking journal. Encourage participants to think "outside themselves." How can they support others? What do they need to change to be more assertive?

Session 6

Goals

- Helping participants define ways to support others and overcome obstacles in being a support for someone else

---

- Have participants begin to assess the changes they have made so far during the group

Activities

Step 1. Who Dropped the Ball? (p. 319). On a piece of masking tape, have participants write one way others can support them as well as one way they can support others. Put each person's piece of tape on a balloon. During the activity, add in balloons showing potential roadblocks to support, with words such as *symptoms of depression* and *lack of assertiveness* written on masking tape and taped to the balloons. During the debriefing, connect how the members completed the activity with how they can overcome the barriers to giving and receiving support.

Step 2. Debrief using pictures, such as Chiji cards or the Facial Expressions appearing on p. 464. Have group members choose pictures that describe their depression. This can be followed by pictures that represent the past, present, and future. Discuss the differences between the pictures chosen by each participant. Focus on the differences between the past, present and future pictures.

Step 3. Lead discussion. Review the journals connecting the previous sessions' homework assignments with the current sessions' activities.

Step 4. Assign homework. Continue the depression-tracking journal. Ask participants to reflect on changes they have made or noticed in themselves and others during the group.

Session 7

Goals

Help participants understand the nature of trust in supportive relationships

Activities

Step 1. Have group members pair up and discuss their homework assignments. Review goals and check on plants. Have the pairs share with the full group.

Step 2. Introduce and facilitate Everyone Up (p. 311). Beginning with the pairs from the Pair and Share, eventually working your way to the full group. Discuss how the group has developed a higher level of trust and increased ability to support each other. How do you develop trust with others in your life? How can you become a trustworthy person?

Step 3. Introduce and facilitate Field Wild Woozey (p. 382). Have group members return to the original pairings and discuss how to stretch one's own personal limits. Engage in the activity. Have participants experiment with other ways of striking a balance through mutual support.

Step 4. Assign homework. Have group members reflect on the group and how the group has moved to becoming a support system.

Session 8

Goals

- Participants continue to develop trust
- Sum up learning from the group and help participants to transfer it to their lives outside the group
- Close the group and allow participants to say "good-bye"

Activities

Step 1. Introduce and facilitate Trust Leans (p. 390). Begin with two-person trust leans. This should be followed by three-person trust leans.

Step 2. Introduce and facilitate Wind in the Willows and Levitation (p. 393, 395). Transition from the trust leans to these intensive trust activities.

Step 3. Lead discussion. Review each person's progress during the course of the group.

Step 4. Introduce and facilitate Yurt Circle (p. 403). Focus on how each of them contributed to creating a solid group that supported itself.

Step 5. Introduce and facilitate What I Like about You (p. 227). Use this activity to bring closure to the group. Allow members to take home the sheets of paper from this activity as well as the plants. Encourage members to transplant their plants to larger pots and keep their goal sheets found at the bottom of the pot.

APPENDIX

D Working with Leadership Groups

You can observe emerging leadership qualities quite clearly in some children from an early age. As a facilitator, if you are fortunate enough to be helping natural-born leaders develop their innate abilities, consider yourself lucky! In many cases, if you are conducting a leadership development group, you will have a mix of participants, some who are more oriented towards leadership and some who are not. In offering leadership programs to middle school age kids through a community-based program, I have found most often that the participants are in fact children who lack basic leadership characteristics such as self-confidence and positive social and communication skills. Often, these are children with high intellectual skills but lesser emotional intelligence. This makes adventure groups an ideal setting for the development of basic leadership characteristics and skills. Participants can learn and practice these skills in a safe environment within an atmosphere of fun.

When I facilitate leadership groups, I realize that not every participant will become a "leader" in the typical sense of the word. In response, I often broaden my definition of leadership to include the ability to assert oneself in the face of challenging situations, such as making the right decisions under pressure from peer cultures to make the easy decision. I also focus on developing self-confidence, assertiveness and communication skills, the skills that are essential to healthy development and success in all aspects of life.

While I have my own view of what characteristics and skills are essential for positive leadership, I try to remain experiential rather than didactic in my facilitation of leadership groups. I allow the group to determine what leadership characteristics and skills are rather than provide them. I find that this struggle to define leadership provides an excellent framework for developing those very characteristics and skills.

The following is a sample sequence of activities that you can use in an experiential group on leadership.

Sample Plan for an Eight-Session Leadership Group

Session 1

Goals

- Introduce program
- Learn names
- Begin to answer the question, "What is a leader?"

Activities

Step 1. Introduce program and facilitators.

Step 2. Introduce and facilitate a variation of Cross Town Connection (p. 160). The activity setup will include greetings representative of the following different leaders: a king greeting, presidential greeting, four-star general greeting, band director greeting, or make up your own leader greeting. Emphasize that partners should share names upon greeting each other.

Step 3. Have participants pair up for 1-minute intervals (changing partners after each discussion) and share the following information with each other:

a. Tell about a time when you were in a leadership position.

b. Tell about a leader that you admire.

c. If you were the leader of our country, what would you do differently than the present leader?

d. What are characteristics of good leaders?

e. What are characteristics of poor leaders?

Have volunteers share what they have heard from each other between each question. Make a master list of the characteristics of both good and poor leaders.

Session 2

Goals

- Develop the FVC
- Have participants begin to examine their own leadership abilities and styles

Activities

Step 1. Introduce the Full Value Commitment (FVC). Divide the group into smaller subgroups. Using the lists of positive and negative leadership characteristics, have group members discuss what types of behaviors would be acceptable and unacceptable in group. Combine similar ones. Entrust the group to use the information to create five statements that will serve as the FVC.

Step 2. Introduce and facilitate Transformer Tag (p. 115). Explain "heads" versus "hearts." Front load what each is and choose quick and play. Debrief by looking at pros and cons of deciding with one's heart or one's head. (Use flip chart.)

Step 3. Introduce and facilitate Rock-Paper-Scissors Olympics Trials (p. 174). If you win a round, you continue on as a leader. If you lose, you must become a follower. Discuss (and use flip chart) what is good about being a leader? What is challenging about it? Is it ever good to be a follower? When is that not desirable?

Step 4. Introduce and facilitate Bears, Salmon, and Mosquitoes (p. 106). Use the debriefing on team decision-making, as described in the activity.

Session 3

Goal

Examine leadership skills and styles. Find some great leadership quotes. Print out the quotes and cut the printout so that one quote appears on one piece of paper

Activities

Step 1. Introduce Simon Says. (Michelle Cummings and Scott Gurst have a video online that offers great tips for leading a non-elimination version of this game: http://www.youtube.com/user/TrainingWheelsLLC) Conduct the debriefing: What were my goals as leader? What were their goals as participants? What skills or character traits were needed to do well in each position? Write answers to these questions on large pieces of paper. Tape them around the room.

Step 2. Give out the leadership quotes you have printed out. Have the group divide into pairs. Ask partners to discuss the quotes and see which skill or characteristic the quote most closely aligns with. Have each pair go to the place in the room where that skill appears on the taped-up piece of paper. Have participants tell why they think the quote reflects this particular skill or characteristic.

Step 3. Introduce and facilitate Spectrum (p. 208). Have participants place themselves where they believe they belong on a spectrum for each of the character traits and skills taped to the walls.

Session 4

Goals

- Help define the leadership role as being part of a group, not separate from the group
- Provide challenges in which participants must utilize leadership characteristics when making decisions that impact the whole group

Activities

Step 1. Introduce and facilitate Do As I Say (p. 261). This leadership activity focuses on following a leader and aligning words and actions.

Step 2. Introduce and facilitate a version of FVC Team Memory (p. 77). Using the leadership characteristics from Session 1, create Team Memory cards. Frontload by comparing the clear leader/follower role of Do As I Say with the "all in this together" way this game will be played out. Discuss personal strengths to be focused on as part of helping the team.

Step 3. Organize the debriefing. Using the cards from Team Memory, have the group come to a consensus about what are the most important five.

Session 5

Goals

- Put leadership characteristics into action
- Practice communication and leadership skills
- Build consensus through communication and adaptability

Activities

Step 1. Introduce and facilitate Bull Ring (p. 368). The five most important leadership characteristics developed during Session 4 serve as the basis for the information being transported in this activity. Have the group transport five balls, each attempt using new routes and obstacles. How do you maintain those characteristics in the face of all the obstacles?

Step 2. Introduce and facilitate Take a Stand (p. 200). Use the variation that involves debating. In this activity, have participants do several rounds without debate. Once you get deeper into the topics, have members of opposite sides pair up and discuss/debate their position and try to convince the other about why their choice is best.

Session 6

Goal

Use consensus building, adaptability, and communication.

Activity

Step 1. Introduce and facilitate Don't Break the Ice (p. 337).

Step 2. Lead the debriefing. This activity focuses on shared responsibility for choices, consensus, adaptability and the ability to support each other. Elements of goal setting and trust can also be debriefed.

Session 7

Goals

Introduce the concept of taking responsibility for the outcomes of your leadership

Activities

Step 1. Introduce and facilitate Clean Your Mess (p. 353). This activity focuses on team decision-making, quick thinking, and taking responsibility for your choices.

Step 2. Introduce and facilitate Eyes, Mouth, Body (p. 397). Use the variation with keys and locks. Introduce the activity by discussing how to unlock the leadership potential that each member has. The debriefing can focus on the elements of trust, communication, and responsibility for ourselves and others as leaders.

Session 8

Goal

Take responsibility for the outcomes of your leadership

Activities

Step 1. Introduce and facilitate Pairs Walk (p. 378). During Sherpa Walk, leaders are taking full responsibility for the safety of their partner. Leaders are expected to take responsibility for all outcomes of those they are guiding.

Step 2. Introduce and facilitate What I Like About You (p. 227). When writing messages to each other, ask group members to focus on how they've seen their peers develop as leaders during the time the group was together. This will guide your final, closing debriefing.

E Activity Tools

1. How do you react behaviorally to anger?
2. Do you believe in a Higher Power?
3. What do you believe happens after we die?
4. What is your number one goal for the next year?
5. What is one place you would like to travel to?
6. Who is your hero?
7. Should pot be legalized?
8. Is it ever OK to kill someone?
9. What is something that you would never ever do?
10. What are you afraid of?
11. What would be your ideal career?
12. What are your strengths?
13. What are your weaknesses?
14. When was a time you needed help?
15. What makes a good teacher?
16. What makes a bad teacher?
17. What will your life be like five years from now?
18. If you could receive one gift, what would it be?
19. If you could give anyone one gift, what would it be and who would you give it to?
20. If you were going to be an animal, what kind would it be and why?
21. What is different about your generation from older generations?
22. What is something you believed as a kid that you don't now?
23. Finish this sentence: I wish my mother…
24. Finish this sentence: I wish my father…
25. What does it mean to be smart?
26. Have you ever been bullied? Tell about it.
27. Have you ever bullied others? Tell about it.
28. Tell about a time you were sad.
29. Has anyone close to you passed away? Tell about it.
30. Why are you here on this Earth? What is your purpose?
31. What do you think of the current political environment?
32. What are you thankful for in life?
33. What is your ethnic background?
34. What is one of your family traditions?

35. Tell a story from your family ancestry.

36. What's the easiest thing about school for you?

37. What's the hardest thing about school for you?

38. How do you deal with stress?

39. What characteristics make a good leader?

40. Are you a leader or follower? Give evidence.

41. What do you like to do in your free time?

42. What are your worst habits?

43. Do you have any pets? Tell about them.

44. What does community mean to you?

45. Tell about a time when you did something to help someone else.

46. What kind of music do you like and why?

47. What makes you happy?

48. Tell about a time that you did something you are proud of.

49. Tell about a time you did something you are embarrassed or ashamed of.

50. If you won the lottery, what would you do with the money?

51. When is it OK to lie?

52. Do you think most about the past, present, or future?

53. How do you think you will die and at what age?

54. What is something in life that is unfair?

Hot Categories

Round Things	Girls Names
Boys Names	Magazines
TV Shows	Movies
Stores	Restaurants
Vegetables	Fruits
Colors	Drinks
Animals	Types of Dogs
Names Starting with the Letter…	Sports
Music Groups	States
Countries	Towns in Your State
Presidents	Famous People
Feelings	Jobs
Board Games	Musical Instruments
Athletes	Sports Teams
Car Types	Birds
Clothing Brands	Shoe Brands
Snack Foods	Objects Found in School
Farm Animals	Things Found in Nature
Modes of Transportation	Plants and Trees
Basketball Teams	Baseball Teams
Song Titles	Football Teams
Nouns	Verbs
Words Ending in "ly"	Adjectives

Human Treasure Hunt

Name   **Description**

_____   lives closest to me.

_____   lives closest to the mall.

_____   has lived in another town. (What town? _____)

_____   has the same number of siblings as I do. (How many?_____)

_____   has met a famous person. (Who? _____)

_____   is a lefty.

_____   has played on a sports team. (What team? _____)

_____   plays a musical instrument. (What instrument?_____)

_____   has a dog. (What kind of dog and what's its name? _____)

_____   has a cat. (What kind of cat and what's its name? _____)

_____   has been to another country. (What country? _____)

_____   has lived in another state. (What state? _____)

_____   has been told they look like a famous person. (Who? _____)

_____   has the same favorite color that I do. (What color? _____)

_____   has the same favorite food that I have. (What food? _____)

_____   has traveled farther than any of us. (Where? _____)

_____   has the next birthday. (When is it? _____)

_____   is the same astrological sign that I am. (What sign? _____)

_____   is the same religion as I am. (What religion?_____)

From *Experiential Activities for Enhancing Emotional Intelligence: A Group Counseling Guide to the Keys to Success,*
© 2014 by S. I. Goldsmith, Champaign, IL: Research Press (www.researchpress.com, 800-519-2707).

Three Read

Passage 1

The relationship between teens and their parents can be tough. Part of the problem is that teens want more freedom than parents want to give. Teens usually want the freedom quickly. Parents give it slowly. It's natural for teens to want more freedom. But more freedom means more responsibility. Parents want to see their teens showing responsible behavior in order to earn more freedom. Because of this, parents give freedom more slowly than teens would like. Priorities are also a potential problem. Often teens' priorities are not the same as their parents'. Parents want teens to focus on school and their future. Many teens are more focused on their social life, technology, and what is happening now without thinking much about the future. Most teens will get more serious as they get older and are better able to make decisions using logic. Life will also teach them lessons. Many teens get along better with their parents once they are old enough to move out on their own.

Passage 2

In today's world, teens are constantly flooded with messages about who they should be, how they should act, and what they should wear. These messages come from many sources. One source is parents. Unfortunately, the influence of parents seems to decrease as kids become teens. Peers become more influential as teens try to figure out who they are and how they fit in. Teens may make poor choices because they feel pressured by their friends. Friends can also be positive influences and pressure each other to do the right thing. Technology and media have also become major sources of influence over today's teens. Everything from movies to music and commercials to video games can influence how teens think and act. These things can influence their beliefs, priorities, and goals for the future. With all these different influences, it's sometimes difficult for teens to know what is best for them. It's up to parents and other adults, such as teachers, to help guide today's teens to making the best decisions they can.

Passage 3

When most people think of intelligence, they think about being school or book smart. There is another kind of intelligence: emotional intelligence. Many people believe that this type of intelligence may be even more important in determining how successful someone will be in many aspects of life. While being smart and getting good grades are important, being able to understand and manage your emotions is a key to your success. Imagine the well-educated, smart businessman who cannot manage his anger. He may end up yelling at his boss after she got him upset. In the end, she may fire him for his actions. People with high emotional intelligence not only understand and control their own emotions but they also understand other peoples' emotions and have the ability to "put themselves into someone else's shoes." People with high emotional intelligence are generally able to form and maintain positive relationships with others. This is difficult for someone who cannot control his or her emotions or behaviors.

From *Experiential Activities for Enhancing Emotional Intelligence: A Group Counseling Guide to the Keys to Success,* © 2014 by S. I. Goldsmith, Champaign, IL: Research Press (www.researchpress.com, 800-519-2707).

Culture Shock Instruction Lists

You only like to communicate when you are standing directly in front of and less than 1 yard (3 feet) away from the person you are talking to.

You only like to communicate when you are standing at least 2 yards (6 feet) away from the person you are talking to.

You only like to communicate when you are not looking at the person you are talking to.

From *Experiential Activities for Enhancing Emotional Intelligence: A Group Counseling Guide to the Keys to Success,* © 2014 by S. I. Goldsmith, Champaign, IL: Research Press (www.researchpress.com, 800-519-2707).

Path to Success Pattern

	↓			
	1	2		
		4	3	
	6	5		
7	8			
	9	10	11 ↓	

Transmitter and Receiver Designs

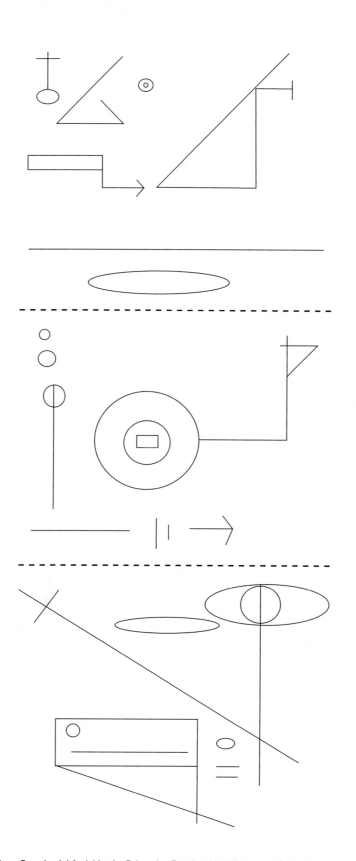

APPENDIX

F Readings

The Egg, the Carrot, and the Coffee Bean

A young woman went to her mother and told her about her life and how things were so hard for her. She didn't know how she was going to make it and wanted to give up. She was tired of fighting and struggling. It seemed that when one problem was solved, a new one arose.

Her mother took her to the kitchen. She filled three pots with water and placed each on a stove burner. Soon the pots came to boil. In the first she placed a carrot, in the second she placed an egg and in the last she placed ground coffee beans. She let them sit and boil, without saying a word.

In about 20 minutes the mother turned off the burners. She fished the carrots out and placed them in a bowl. She pulled the eggs out and placed them in a bowl. Then she ladled the coffee out and placed it in a bowl. Turning to her daughter, she asked, "Tell me what you see."

"Carrots, eggs, and coffee," she replied.

Her mother brought her closer and asked her to feel the carrots. She did and noted that they were soft. The mother then asked the daughter to take an egg and break it. After pulling off the shell, she observed the hard-boiled egg. Finally, the mother asked the daughter to sip the coffee. The daughter smiled, as she tasted its rich aroma and asked her mother, "What does this all mean?"

Her mother explained that each of these objects had faced the same adversity: boiling water. Each reacted differently.

- The carrot went in strong, hard, and unrelenting. However, after being subjected to the boiling water, it softened and became weak.

- The egg had been fragile. Its thin outer shell had protected its liquid interior, but after sitting through the boiling water, its insides became hardened.

- The ground coffee beans were unique, however. After they were in the boiling water, they changed the water.

"Which are you?" she asked her daughter. "When adversity knocks on your door, how do you respond? Are you a carrot, an egg, or a coffee bean?"

—Author Unknown

From *Experiential Activities for Enhancing Emotional Intelligence: A Group Counseling Guide to the Keys to Success,* © 2014 by S. I. Goldsmith, Champaign, IL: Research Press (www.researchpress.com, 800-519-2707).

The Web of Life

This we know...

The earth does not belong to man,

man belongs to the earth.

All things are connected

like the blood that unites us all.

Man did not weave the web of life,

he is merely a strand in it.

Whatever he does to the web, he does to himself.

—*attributed to Chief Seattle*

Debriefing Questions and Facilitator Tips on Using the Keys to Success

Helping Clients Develop Emotional Awareness and Understanding (Key to Success 1)

In addition to the questions below, there are several tools and activities aimed at helping clients process what they are feeling. These include the Emotion Cards and Emotions List and Favorite Check-Ins. You can find these tools in Appendix H (p. 457). The Emotion Cards and Emotions List can be used to help clients respond to the questions below.

- What one word describes how you are feeling at this moment?

- Your response to my question about how you feel was that you want to "run away" from this group. That tells me what you want to do but not how you feel. What is the emotion that you are feeling that makes you want to "run away"?

- What does your body feel like right now? Are you tense? Is your heart racing? What does this tell you about how you feel emotionally?

- How do you think John is feeling right now? What makes you think that?

- If someone said that to you, how would you feel? Do you think that's how she feels? Why do you thinks he might feel differently than you would if someone said that to you?

- Jane said that she is feeling hurt by what you did. Can you understand how your actions caused her to feel this way? What do you think you can say or do to help her to feel better?

- Since we are not in control of what others do, what can you do to help yourself feel better since it doesn't seem like Johnny is going to help you feel better?

- How did it feel to have other people support you (or not support you)?

- How did it feel to have other people trust you (or not trust you)?

- How did it feel to have other people listen to your ideas (or not listen to your ideas)?

- How did it feel to take a leadership role?

- How did it feel to conquer a task you told me couldn't be accomplished?

- How do members feel knowing that we did not reach our goal?

- How did other members of this group help you get through your fear (or anger, or sadness)?

Processing Questions That Can Help Participants Examine Their Behavioral Reactions to Their Emotions (Key to Success 2)

- What happens when you get angry (or sad, or happy, or scared, or confused...)?

- What behaviors do you typically show when you are angry (or sad, or happy, or scared, or confused...)?

- What happens automatically inside your body when you get angry (or sad, or happy, or scared, or confused...)?

- What thoughts do you have when you are angry (or sad, or happy, or scared, or confused...)?

- With what emotions do you have the hardest time coping? When are you most likely to show your worst behaviors?

- The behavior you just showed was not appropriate. It violated the commitment we made to each other. Think about what you were feeling that triggered that reaction. Are there other behaviors you could have chosen that would have helped the situation rather worsen it?

- I am guessing from your behavior that you are angry. Am I correct? How did I know? Is that a positive way to show that emotion? What other ways could you have let us know you were angry?

- Why did you do that? Did it work for you?

- How come you react that way when you are feeling angry (or sad, or happy, or scared, or confused...)? Are there experiences in your life that led to this?

- If you had chosen to say, "I was hurt," rather than walking away from the group, how do you think we would have responded?

- If you told John you were angry with him in a calm way rather than yelling, how do you think he would have reacted? How do you think the rest of the group would have reacted?

- What are you trying to tell me through your behavior right now? If you are feeling that way again, what might you do differently?

Questions and Tips To Help Improve Skills Related to Establishing and Maintaining Positive Relationships (Key to Success 3)

Questions for Enhancing Attention Skills

- Did you notice…
- What happened?
- Were you focused during that activity?
- How did your level of focus impact the outcome of this activity?
- How did the focus of the group impact the outcome of this activity?

Tips to Help with Attention Skills

- Be aware of and, as much as possible, minimize environmental distractions. Occasionally, you will find the group's attention taken up by an unavoidable environmental distraction. Rather than fight it, you may be able to incorporate the distraction into the program. For example, at a recent outdoor program, the group became distracted by a pair of low-flying hawks. We stopped what we were doing and observed them. This was followed by a hearty discussion about what we observed and how important it was to notice the world around us.
- Many kids (and adults) have more difficulties focusing in early morning, just before lunchtime, and at the end of a long day. Acknowledge this and plan accordingly. Invite the group to problem-solve if this is an issue.
- Make sure to give the group breaks if participants' attention seems to be wandering. These activities can be quite draining and sometimes a break will help. Make sure the breaks have a specific ending point. Often, after returning from longer breaks (such as lunch), I like to use an icebreaker to regain the group members' attention.

Questions to Help with Listening Skills

- What did you hear me say?
- Did anyone hear what Johnny just said? No? Johnny, please say it again.
- Tell me in your own words, how this activity is going to work.
- Can someone summarize for the group what we just discussed?

Questions while a group is planning an activity, particularly if they are struggling

- As I watch you guys creating your plan, I hear a lot of talking. What are you hearing from each other?

- It seems like there's a whole lot of conversations going on at once. How can you get together and plan this as a group?
- Might I suggest getting in a circle to facilitate your communication?
- Does your whole group know what is expected of them right now?

Tip to Help with Listening Skills

Make sure that you get the group's attention before giving directions or other relevant verbal information. This can be accomplished by techniques from the tips on focusing attention found in Appendix A, such as If You Can Hear Me Clap Once, Peace Sign, and Call and Response.

Questions to Help in Understanding Nonverbal Communication

- Tell me about Johnny's tone of voice when he just said that. What did that tone mean to you?
- Johnny, your voice is getting louder and has an angry tone. Are you feeling angry?
- Look around the group. What is the group's body language telling us? What are the group's facial expressions telling us? What is the group's behavior telling us?
- I see Johnny standing off to the side. What's going on?
- Do you think that what was just said was said respectfully? Why?
- Well, I heard what he said. It seems that you heard those words too but don't feel that he's being straight with you. What is it that makes you think this?
- I hear what you are saying with your words. But what do you think your tone of voice is telling me?

Tips to Help Groups' Understand Nonverbal Communication

- Be aware of cultural differences regarding body language. For example, in some Native American and Asian cultures, direct eye contact with authority figures is considered disrespectful.
- Be aware of your own body language. Are you conveying openness, confidence, and sincerity?
- Help the group differentiate between safe and non-safe touching. Be aware that some cultures discourage physical contact, especially between males and females. Also, be aware of and respect different group member's sensitivity to physical contact.

Questions that Help Cultivate Open-Mindedness

- Even though you see it this way, can you respect the way Johnny sees it?
- While you may not agree with what Johnny said to you, I hope you can think about it since he seems to be speaking his truth.
- I encourage you to listen respectfully to what Johnny has to tell you, consider what he says, and then decide what you want to do with his feedback.

- Did everyone get to share their ideas as to how to approach this challenge? Why not?
- Did the group consider all the possible solutions that were suggested?

Questions that Help Cultivate Integrity and Trust

- Did you accomplish this task following all the guidelines that I set out in the beginning? Were there any exceptions? If so, did anyone notice? What made you decide not to talk about these violations?
- If Johnny had been honest, the entire group would have had to start over. How would you all have handled that? Johnny, is that what you would have expected?
- I noticed that you did not quite follow all of the instructions I laid out for accomplishing this task. What did you leave out? Why?
- Were there any violations of each other's trust during that activity? Were there any violations of my trust in you?
- What happens when you violate someone's trust? What happened here?

Check-Ins and Debriefing Tools

Favorite Check-Ins

At the beginning of a group session, I often like to check in with my participants to see how they are doing. In traditional group counseling, the therapist might ask a straightforward question such as, "How is everyone doing today?" While a talkative group (or a few talkative members) might give you high-quality answers to general questions, often you will be met by one-word responses and not much real information.

With adventure groups, I try to use creative check-ins that elicit more insightful responses from my participants. Many of these check-ins can also be used as debriefing tools to help group members express their feelings about how a particular activity went. Some activities in this book such as Spectrum (p. 208) and Take a Stand (p. 200) can also be used as check-ins or debriefings. Here are some of my favorite check-ins.

Critter Check-In

Over the years, I have acquired quite a collection of stuffed animals. For this check-in, I dump 30 or so stuffed animals on the floor at the center of my group. I ask group members to each choose an animal that represents how they are feeling today. This check-in can be varied many ways. For example, I might ask them to choose an animal that represents how they deal with conflict or anger or one that reflects a goal they have in life.

Thumb-ometer

This is a simple check-in that allows you to gauge the overall status of the group as well as the state of individual members. Simply ask participants to show you with their thumbs how they are doing today. Thumbs up is great; thumbs down is terrible; and of course, there are many stops between. You can further check in as to why a participant has a thumbs up, down, or somewhere in the middle.

Color Check-In

Ask your group members to pick a color that represents how they are feeling right now. Once they tell you the color, you can ask why they chose that color. High 5 Adventure Learning Center has printable color swatches with and without associated words on its website: http://high5adventure.org/community-blog/print-and-play/.

One Word

Have participants each pick one word that describes how they feel at the moment. You can make it a bit more specific and challenging by limiting their response to a verb, adjective, or place, etc.

Expression Check-In

Have each participant choose one of the expressions on cards created from the Facial Expressions chart in Appendix H.

Emotion Check-In

Using cards made from the Emotion Cards in Appendix H, have each participant choose one that helps them express how they are feeling.

Cards

There are many different and effective check-in and debriefing tools available on the market. You can also create your own using the same concepts. The Emotion Cards or the Character and Debriefing Words that appear in Appendix H towards the end of this book are useful for check-in and debriefing. Some of the other ones I have used are:

- Chiji cards and Pocket Processors (http://www.chiji.com)
- Postcard Processing Kit and many other check-in, icebreaker, and debriefing tools are available on Michelle Cummings' website (http://store.training-wheels.com/)

Emotion Cards

Happy	Satisfied	Delighted	Thankful
Important	Ecstatic	Optimistic	Thrilled
Calm	Peaceful	Comfortable	Confident
Energetic	Excited	Inspired	Hopeful

Angry	Irritated	Annoyed	Upset
Offended	Resentful	Irate	Enraged
Violent	Bitter	Insulted	Mad
Hateful	Revengeful	Furious	Aggravated

Sad	Guilty	Desperate	Alienated
Depressed	Lost	Rejected	Hopeless
Disappointed	Pained	Tormented	Miserable
Ashamed	Lonely	Heartbroken	Unhappy

Facial Expressions

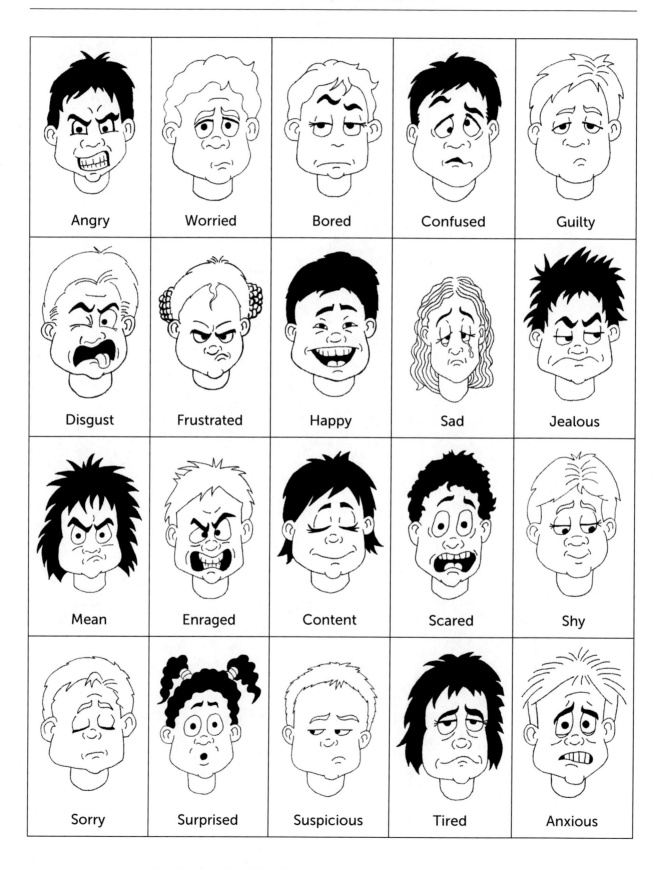

Angry	Worried	Bored	Confused	Guilty
Disgust	Frustrated	Happy	Sad	Jealous
Mean	Enraged	Content	Scared	Shy
Sorry	Surprised	Suspicious	Tired	Anxious

From *Experiential Activities for Enhancing Emotional Intelligence: A Group Counseling Guide to the Keys to Success,*
© 2014 by S. I. Goldsmith, Champaign, IL: Research Press (www.researchpress.com, 800-519-2707).

Emotions List

Happy	Sad	Angry	Afraid
Satisfied	Depressed	Irritated	Scared
Delighted	Disappointed	Annoyed	Worried
Thankful	Ashamed	Upset	Shy
Important	Guilty	Offended	Shaky
Ecstatic	In Despair	Resentful	Doubtful
Cheerful	Sulky	Irate	Wary
Optimistic	Lost	Enraged	Terrified
Thrilled	Tearful	Violent	Horrified
Calm	Pained	Bitter	Paranoid
Peaceful	Lonely	Fuming	Anxious
Comfortable	Desperate	Insulted	Jittery
Confident	Pessimistic	Mad	Confused
Energetic	Tormented	Boiling	Uneasy
Excited	Rejected	Hateful	Tense
Inspired	Heartbroken		Uncertain
Eager	Alienated		
Hopeful	In Agony		
Content	Hopeless		

From *Experiential Activities for Enhancing Emotional Intelligence: A Group Counseling Guide to the Keys to Success,*
© 2014 by S. I. Goldsmith, Champaign, IL: Research Press (www.researchpress.com, 800-519-2707).

Five Question Processing Model
and Keys to Success Cards*

5 Question Processing Model	5 Question Processing Model	5 Question Processing Model
1. Did you notice…? or What did you notice during…?	1. Did you notice…? or What did you notice during…?	1. Did you notice…? or What did you notice during…?
2. Why does that happen?	2. Why does that happen?	2. Why does that happen?
3. Does that happen in life? Or Does it happen in school?	3. Does that happen in life? Or Does it happen in school?	3. Does that happen in life? Or Does it happen in school?
4. Why does it happen?	4. Why does it happen?	4. Why does it happen?
5. How can you use this information?	5. How can you use this information?	5. How can you use this information?
From the book *Open to Outcome*	From the book *Open to Outcome*	From the book *Open to Outcome*

The Three Keys to Success!	The Three Keys to Success!	The Three Keys to Success!
1. Emotional Awareness *Understand and manage your emotions.*	1. Emotional Awareness *Understand and manage your emotions.*	1. Emotional Awareness *Understand and manage your emotions.*
2. Behavioral Control *Control your behavior in response to your emotions.*	2. Behavioral Control *Control your behavior in response to your emotions.*	2. Behavioral Control *Control your behavior in response to your emotions.*
3. Positive Relationships *Establish and maintain positive relationships with other people*	3. Positive Relationships *Establish and maintain positive relationships with other people*	3. Positive Relationships *Establish and maintain positive relationships with other people*

*The 5 Question Processing Model used with permission of publisher. Jacobon, M., & Ruddy, M. (2004). *Open to Outcome: A Practical Guide for Facilitating & Teaching Experiential Reflection*, p. 42, Wood 'n' Barnes Publishing.

Character and Debriefing Words

Enthusiasm	Patience	Faith	Loyalty
Honesty	Flexibility	Responsible	Respectful
Forgiving	Accepting	Cautious	Grateful
Self-Control	Sensitive	Sincerity	Creativity
Cooperative	Dependable	Wisdom	Courageous
Commitment	Focus	Adaptable	Resilient
Humor	Kind	Energetic	Open-Minded
Understanding	Perseverance	Self-Discipline	Fairness

From *Experiential Activities for Enhancing Emotional Intelligence: A Group Counseling Guide to the Keys to Success,*
© 2014 by S. I. Goldsmith, Champaign, IL: Research Press (www.researchpress.com, 800-519-2707).

Guiding Participants on Speaking in Group Activities

When working with clients who have social and emotional difficulties, you are likely to encounter extremes of verbal communication: group participants who don't speak or ones who can't seem to stop talking. Here are some tips for helping kids deal with these issues.

Those Who Don't Speak Enough

- Make sure the environment is emotionally safe.

- Ask more concrete questions of these students. Yes-or-no questions allow them to begin speaking by using single words. This is much less "threatening" to these kids than is attempting to answer open-ended questions.

- Use props such as the Emotion Cards (see p. 461) to allow those who are less verbal to express their feelings. This will lead them to becoming increasingly comfortable speaking up.

- Have group members process activities in smaller groups or pairs and nominate one person as a spokesperson.

- Use physical check-ins such as Thumb-ometer and Critter Check-In (p. 459) with silent participants.

- Brief the person before group about what will be going on during group.

- In some situations, you can modify activities so that the quieter members are placed in positions where they are the only ones allowed speak. This should only be done if the person has been making progress and is ready for this type of pressure.

Those Who Speak Too Much

- Give time limits for members to speak. You might convey these time limits by saying, for example, "Tell me in 30 seconds or less...".

- Encourage these members to think out what they want to say before they start speaking. You can remind them of this right before they are about to speak.

- Tell them that even though what they have to say is important, you must hear from others in the group as well.

- At the beginning of a group session, give all members tickets representing a certain amount of time or number of opportunities they will be given to speak when processing an activity. For example, each ticket represents up to 1 minute and each member gets five for the session.

- Create a rule that whoever is holding the rubber chicken during processing can speak. If there is no rubber chicken in your hand, you cannot speak. This also enhances listening for the whole group. Of course, you can use any item that suits your fancy... I just like rubber chickens!

References

Amitay, O., & Mongrain, M. (2007). From emotional intelligence to intelligent partner choice. *Journal of Social Psychology.* 147(4): 325–43.

Bandura, A. (1977). *Social Learning Theory.* Englewood Cliffs, NJ: Prentice Hall.

Cain, J., Hannon, C., & Knobbe, D. (2009). *Essential Staff Training Activities.* Dubuque, IA: Kendall Hunt Publishing.

Cain, J., & Jolliff, B. (1998). *Teamwork and Teamplay.* Dubuque, IA: Kendall Hunt.

Cain, J., & Smith, T. (2007). *The Revised and Expanded Book of Raccoon Circles: A Facilitator's Guide to Building Unity, Community, Connection and Teamwork through Active Learning.* Dubuque, IA: Kendall Hunt.

Cavert, C., & Sikes, S. (2002). *50 More Ways to Use Your Noodle.* Oklahoma City, OK: Wood 'n' Barnes.

Cavert, C., & Sikes, S. (1997). *50 Ways to Use Your Noodle.* Oklahoma City, OK: Wood 'n' Barnes.

Cherniss, C., & Goleman, D. (Eds.). (2001). *The Emotionally Intelligent Workplace: How To Select for, Measure, and Improve Emotional Intelligence in Individuals, Groups, and Organizations.* San Francisco: Jossey-Bass.

Chuck, E. (2013, April 23). Innovative science teacher honored as national teacher of the year. NBC News. *NBC News.* Retrieved from http://usnews.nbcnews.com

Collard, M. (2008). *Count Me In: Large Group Activities That Work.* Beverley, MA: Project Adventure Inc.

Collard, M. (2005). *No Props: Great Games with No Equipment.* Beverley, MA: Project Adventure Inc.

Covey, S. (2004). *7 Habits of Highly Effective People: Restoring the Character Ethic.* Rev. ed. New York: Free Press.

Crawford, B. (1995). This is a what? It's a what? This is life *Zip Lines.* Summer(36), 33.

Cummings, M. (2007). *Playing With a Full Deck.* Dubuque, IA: Kendall Hunt Publishing.

Downey, L., Johnston, P., Hansen K., Schembri, R., Stough, C., Tuckwell, V., & Schweitzer, I. (2008). The relationship between emotional intelligence and depression in a clinical sample. *European Journal of Psychiatry*, 22(2), 93–98.

Empathy. (2013). In Merriam-Webster. retrieved from http://www.merriam-webster.com.

Erikson, E. (1950). *Childhood and Society.* New York, NY: Norton.

Fark, J. (1994). *Team Challenge: Introduction to Low Initiatives Training.* Columbus OH: Ohio State University Leadership Center.

Fluegelman, A. (Ed.). (1976). *The New Games Book.* Garden City, NY: Doubleday & Company, Inc.

Gardner, H. (1983). *Frames of Mind: The Theory of Multiple Intelligences.* New York, NY: Basic Books.

Goldstein, K. (1995). *The Organism: A Holistic Approach to Biology Derived from Pathological Data in Man.* New York, NY: Zone Books.

Goleman, D. (1994). *Emotional Intelligence.* New York, NY: Bantam Books.

Goleman, D. (1998). *Working with Emotional Intelligence.* New York, NY: Bantam Books.

Inhibit. (1980). *American Dictionary of the English Language.* New York, NY: Houghton Mifflin.

"It is the height of absurdity...." (2004). In Toliver, W. (Ed.) *Little Encyclopedia of Inspirational Quotes.* New York, NY: Sterling Publishing Co.

Jacobson, M., & Ruddy, M. (2004). *Open To Outcome: A Practical Guide For Facilitating & Teaching Experiential Reflection.* Oklahoma City, OK: Wood 'n' Barnes.

Kohut, A. (2001). Big pig air. *Zip Lines: The Voice for Adventure Education.* Winter(2): 12–13.

Lampton, B. How to make a strong first impression: Seven tips that really work. *Business Know-How.* Retrieved from http://www.businessknowhow.com/marketing/seventips.htm

LeFevre, D. (1988). *New Games for the Whole Family.* New York, NY: Putnam.

Lynn, A. B. (2008). *The EQ Interview: Finding Employees With High Emotional Intelligence.* New York, NY: AMACOM.

Maslow, A. H. (1943). A theory of human motivation. *Psychological Review,* 50(4), 370–396.

Mayer, J. D., & Salovey, P. (1997). What is emotional intelligence? In P. Salovey & D. Sluyter (Eds.) *Emotional Development and Emotional Intelligence: Implications for Educators* (pp. 3–31). New York, NY: Basic Books.

Mehrabian, A. (1971). *Silent Messages.* Belmont, CA: Wadsworth.

Orlick, T. (1978). *The Cooperative Sports and Games Book.* New York, NY: Pantheon Books.

Peck, S. (1990). From group to community. In J. Schoel & M. Stratton (Eds.) *Gold Nuggets: Readings for Experiential Education* (p. 26). Beverly, MA: Project Adventure, Inc.

Ramsey, L. (2008). *Manners that Sell: Adding the Polish that Adds Profits*. Gretna, LA: Pelican Publishing.

Resmovits, J. (2013, April 23). Teacher of the Year 2012 Finalists Honored by Jill Biden in Washington D.C. *Huffington Post*. Retrieved from http://huffingtonpost.com

Rohnke, K. (1991). *The Bottomless Bag Again*. Dubuque, IA: Kendall Hunt Publishing Company.

Rohnke, K. (1989). *Cowstails and Cobras II: A Guide to Games, Initiatives, Ropes Courses, & Adventure Curriculum*. Dubuque, IA: Project Adventure, Inc., Kendall Hunt Publishing Company.

Rohnke, K. (1995). *Funn Stuff* (Vol. 1). Dubuque, IA: Kendall Hunt Publishing Company.

Rohnke, K. (1996). *Funn Stuff* (Vol. 2). Dubuque, IA: Kendall Hunt Publishing Company.

Rohnke, K. (2000). *Funn Stuff* (Vol. 4). Dubuque, IA: Kendall Hunt Publishing Company.

Rohnke, K. (1984). *Silver Bullets*. Covington, GA: Project Adventure.

Rohnke, K., & Butler, S. (1995). *Quicksilver*. Dubuque, IA: Kendall Hunt Publishing.

Rohnke, K., & Grout, J. (1998). *Back Pocket Adventure*. Beverly, MA: Project Adventure Inc.

Salovey, P., & Mayer, J. (1990). Emotional intelligence. *Journal of Imagination, Cognition, and Personality*. 9, 185–211.

Shapiro, L. (1998). *How to Raise a Child with a High EQ: A Parents' Guide to Emotional Intelligence*. New York, NY: HarperCollins.

Schoel, J., & Maizell R. S. (2002). *Exploring Islands of Healing: New Perspectives on Adventure Based Counseling*. Beverly, MA: Project Adventure Inc.

Schoel, J., Prouty, D, & Radcliffe, P. (1988). *Islands of Healing: A Guide to Adventure Based Counseling*. Hamilton, MA: Project Adventure, Inc.

Schoel, J., & Stratton, M. (1990). *Gold Nuggets: Reading for Experiential Education*. Beverly, MA: Project Adventure Inc.

Stanchfield, J. (2007). *Tips & Tools: The Art of Group Facilitation*. Oklahoma City, OK: Wood 'n' Barnes Publishing.

Sterling, M. First impressions. *Student to Career*. Retrieved from http://www.cobstudentsuccess.com/resources/first-impressions-0

Thorndike, E. L. (1920, January). Intelligence and its use. *Harper's*. 140, 227–235.

Tuckman, B. (1965). Developmental sequence in small groups. *Psychological Bulletin*, 63 (6): 384–399.

Tuckman, B. W., & Jensen, M. A. C. (1977). Stages of small group development revisited. *Group and Organizational Studies*. 2, 419–427.

Wechsler, D. (2008). *Wechsler Adult Intelligence Scale*. 4th edition. San Antonio, TX: Pearson.

Recommended Resources

Websites

Chiji Institute for Experiential Learning
http://www.chiji.com

HelpGuide.org
http://www.helpguide.org

High 5 Adventure Learning Center
http://high5adventure.org

Project Adventure
http://pa.org

Teamwork & Teamplay
http://www.teamworkandteamplay.com

Training Wheels
http://training-wheels.com

Resources for Experiential Activities for Enhancing Emotional Intelligence

Worksheets from the appendices
http://www.researchpress.com/downloads

Additional photos of the activities
http://www.researchpress.com/downloads

About the Author

Scott Goldsmith, M.S., LPC, is the school psychologist at Manchester Regional Academy, an alternative school for students with emotional and behavioral difficulties. He is also a licensed counselor, owner of the team-building and experiential training group Outside the Box Experiential, LLC (www.outsidetheboxexperiential.com), and the co-coordinator of the Manchester Ropes Challenge Course. Scott has created and facilitated adventure programs, trainings, and workshops for diverse groups of corporate, community, mental health, and educational organizations. Known for his passion, charisma, humor, and creativity, Scott's ability to quickly and effectively create community and help others elevate to a higher self has been experienced in numerous workshops at local, state, regional, and national conferences. A professional musician and a black belt in tae kwon do, Scott constantly seeks out physical and mental challenges that foster personal and professional growth for himself and others around him. This book is part of Scott's ongoing effort to bring the gift of experiential counseling to more counseling professionals and youth workers. Scott lives in Connecticut with his wife and three daughters.

To inquire about staff training and development or team-building workshops, you can contact Scott at outsidetheboxexperiential@gmail.com.